Digital Twins for Simulation-Based Decision-Making

Vinay Kulkarni
Tony Clark
Balbir S. Barn
Editors

Digital Twins for Simulation-Based Decision-Making

Springer

Editors
Vinay Kulkarni
Tata Consultancy Services
Pune, Maharashtra, India

Tony Clark
School of Engineering and Applied Science
Aston University
Birmingham, UK

Balbir S. Barn
Faculty of Science and Technology
Middlesex University
London, UK

ISBN 978-3-031-89653-8 ISBN 978-3-031-89654-5 (eBook)
https://doi.org/10.1007/978-3-031-89654-5

This Springer imprint is published by the registered company Springer Nature Switzerland AG
The registered company address is: Gewerbestrasse 11, 6330 Cham, Switzerland

Preface

We live in a world replete with a complex system of systems that need to operate in a dynamic and uncertain environment, thus necessitating continuous adaptation for delivering required goals that may also change over time. These systems, characterized by scale, non-determinism, and non-linear interactions, are spread across spaces such as information-only, cyber-physical, societal, and biological. They raise several new concerns such as *Why are things the way they are?*, *What are the right interventions to bring the system back to the desired state?*, *How to ascertain effectiveness of these interventions a priori?*, *Are better states possible and what are they?*, *How to transform the system from as-is to to-be state?* and so on. Large size of the system, complex non-linear interactions, partial information, and rapid dynamics make addressing these concerns difficult.

Current practice takes a three-pronged approach to address these concerns: (1) a mathematics-based approach wherein system behaviour is specified in precise analytic terms such that the decision-making problem is formulated as a multi-variable optimization for which several techniques such as linear programming, integer programming, etc. are available to arrive at a globally optimal solution; (2) relying solely on past data to learn a model of system behaviour using statistical means and using this model for predictive analysis; and (3) relying on human expertise and experience. While a mathematics-based approach can deliver a globally optimal solution, it demands system behaviour to be known a priori. However, the large size, complex non-linear interactions, and partial information make it impossible. Similarly, while deep penetration of digitalization in a domain enables approaches relying on past data, it suffers from two shortcomings. First, the data represents behaviour the system has exhibited so far but is mute on behaviours the system is capable of exhibiting. As a result, the model learnt solely from past data is likely to be a subset of a true model, and analysis derivable from this subset model is likely to be sub-optimal and even inaccurate. Second, this approach works only when future is in a ballpark similar to the past. Unpredictability of the future cannot ensure that it will always be so. Human experts typically do come up with a solution, but this approach does not scale and is vulnerable to the law of bounded rationality.

Thus, it can be said that the current practice of addressing the key concerns of a complex system of systems is found wanting.

Digital twin is emerging as a promising technology to overcome the above limitations through a confluence of fields such as modelling and simulation, artificial intelligence, control theory, knowledge engineering, and software engineering. In essence, digital twin is a purposive high-fidelity simulatable model of the complex system of systems. Digital twins enable a data-driven simulation-based and justification-backed approach wherein it is possible to (1) hold a mirror to the system, thus explaining an as-is state; (2) perform decision-space navigation through what-if simulation to identify the right interventions through in silico experimentation; (3) perform design space exploration to identify a possible better state; and (4) devise a transformative path from as-is to to-be state through in silico experimentation.

Digital twins are not a new concept. Till very recently, digital twins of only the systems governed by physical laws were in use. Their main focus was on improving product and process quality. Now we see the concept of digital twin getting wider acceptance, e.g. for systems not governed by physical laws, systems where humans are key participants, systems dealing with information/data/knowledge, and any combination of these systems. With ever-increasing digitalization, the pervasiveness of digital twins is likely to continue to increase.

This book introduces the concept of digital twin, technology infrastructure for construction and use of purposive digital twins and the method support necessary. The landscape of digital twins is illustrated through a range of use cases spread across different domains.

Pune, Maharashtra, India — Vinay Kulkarni
Birmingham, UK — Tony Clark
London, UK — Balbir S. Barn

Contents

About the Editors

Vinay Kulkarni is a TCS Fellow at TCS Research where he heads Software Systems & Services research. His research interests include enterprise digital twins, learning-native software systems, multi agent systems, model-driven software engineering, and enterprise modelling. At present, he is exploring the feasibility of imparting learning-aided adaptation to enterprises at strategy, process, and systems level through the use of modelling, simulation, and analytics. The vision is to integrate modelling, AI, and control theory to support dynamic adaptation of complex systems of systems using digital twins. Further information can be found at https://in.linkedin.com/in/vinay-vkulkarni. Contact him at vinay.vkulkarni@tcs.com and https://www.linkedin.com/in/vinayvkulkarni/.

Tony Clark is Associate Pro-Vice Chancellor and Professor of Computer Science in the College of Engineering and Physical Sciences at Aston University. He has experience of working in both academia and industry on a range of software projects and consultancies. His current interests are using adaptation and model-based techniques to create digital twins. Further information can be found at https://research.aston.ac.uk/en/persons/tony-clark. Contact him at tony.clark@aston.ac.uk.

Balbir S. Barn is Professor of Software Engineering and Dean of the Faculty of Science and Technology at Middlesex University. His current research interests are methodologies and software tools for defining digital twins and socio-technical digital twins, languages and modelling for agent-based adaptive systems, and conceptual modelling as research method for inter-disciplinary domains such as surveillance, cyber-crime, and theory building. Further information can be found at https: https://www.mdx.ac.uk/about-us/our-people/staff-directory/prof-balbir-barn/. Contact him at b.barn@mdx.ac.uk.

Chapter 1
An Introduction to Digital Twins

Tony Clark, Vinay Kulkarni, and Balbir S. Barn

Abstract The idea of digital twin is not new. NASA used it first in the 1960s for its space program. It got revived in the early 2000s mainly in manufacturing and automotive industry. The idea was to create a digital replica of the product and the process that was synchronised with real world as per the need. The key characteristics of the real system being twinned were well-defined, well-bounded, and controlled by physical laws. The principal objective of creating digital twin was to ensure product and process quality. Since the past 10 years, adoption of digital twins has spread even to socio-techno systems characterised by emergent behaviour, and so has the spread of use cases. Today, technology is available, though with wide variance of effectiveness, to address digital twin life cycle. Recent advance in AI and especially Gen AI has helped reduce the cognitive burden too. However, many challenges remain, e.g. robust method, effective repurposing of digital twin to a different context, or transferring the learning courtesy domain-specific purposive digital twins to other domains for the same or similar purpose. All in all, these are exciting times to be working in digital twin space.

T. Clark
School of Engineering and Applied Science, Aston University, Birmingham, UK
e-mail: tony.clark@aston.ac.uk

V. Kulkarni (✉)
TCS Research, Tata Consultancy Services, Pune, Maharashtra, India
e-mail: vinay.vkulkarni@tcs.com

B. S. Barn
Faculty of Science and Technology, Middlesex University, London, UK
e-mail: b.barn@mdx.ac.uk

V. Kulkarni et al. (eds.), *Digital Twins for Simulation-Based Decision-Making*,
https://doi.org/10.1007/978-3-031-89654-5_1

Background

The idea of a digital twin originates with NASA in the 1960s, motivated by the need to simulate mission scenarios for astronaut training and safety checking. During the Apollo 13 mission, an explosion caused damage to the spacecraft; NASA used a digital twin in real time to diagnose the problem and to remotely develop a solution. Once the astronauts returned, the twin supported forensic analysis of the explosion, leading to improved safety and reliability of future missions.

Subsequently, the idea of simulation became more sophisticated. It continued to be used by the aerospace industry for safety and performance but also broadened out into other industries including manufacturing, healthcare, and infrastructure projects. The development of sensor networking technology greatly enhanced the idea of simulations linked to real-world data.

The term *digital twin* was coined by Dr. Michael Grieves in 2002 when he defined it to be a virtual representation serving as a *real-time digital counterpart of a physical object or process*. Grieves used digital twins to create models of products prior to their physical construction, thereby allowing then to be analysed for problems and increasing their efficiency in terms of construction and operation.

Following Grieves' seminal work in outlining digital twins, the field has grown significantly. Early adopters included the aerospace and automotive industries. The growth in sensor technologies supported adoption in other areas where systems could be monitored in real time. The growth in AI and machine learning allowed digital twins to expand further by supporting both monitoring and prediction.

The market size for digital twins was estimated at $16.75 billion in 2023 and projected to grow at 37% annually. We are seeing digital twin technologies being embedded in most industries with strong growth in the civic realm, for example, with the aim of achieving smart cities.

This chapter provides an overview of digital twins, what they are, their applications, capability levels, and the technologies that are typically used to implement them. Design methods for digital twins is an under-developed area, which is addressed in this chapter by providing a conceptual view of twins from a computational perspective and an associated lightweight method for capturing and structuring design requirements. The method is illustrated using a simple example. The chapter concludes with an overview of the challenges related to digital twin adoption.

What Is a Digital Twin?

There are many different definitions of a digital twin. If we take the broadest possible view, then a digital twin consists of the following components as shown in Fig. 1.1:

- A real system that we are seeking to design, monitor, or control via the twin.
- Sensors that instrument the real system. The sensor data is usually provided to the twin in real time, but for some digital twins, the sensor data may be historic or even synthetic.

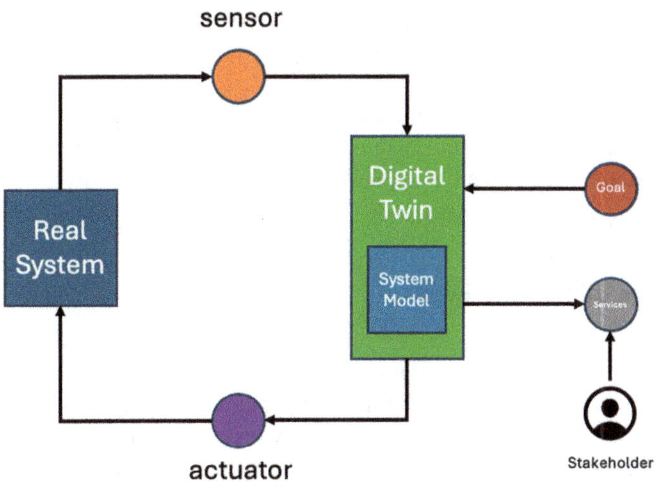

Fig. 1.1 Digital twin

- The digital twin itself is a software system that maintains a model of some aspect of the real system that is relevant to its task. The system model maintained by the twin aims to be in some correspondence to an aspect of interest in the real system. In addition, the digital twin may use a collection of models that supports its functions. These may be:
  - Data models that define features of information managed by the twin
  - Structural models that represent aspects of the real system that typically do not change, for example, road layouts or anatomical structure
  - Predictive models that are used to derive some properties of the system based on its current state, for example, detecting that a bridge may need repair
  - Simulation models that are used to construct possible future states, for example, when selecting the best action to perform in the current situation
- A digital twin has a goal, which is the task it is trying to achieve. Typically, a twin is used in one of the following ways:
  - To understand some property of the real system or the system that is to be constructed
  - To detect situations that occur in the real system, perhaps to ensure that they are repaired
  - To predict an action to perform on the real system, perhaps an action that will ensure that the real system behaves optimally or that the real system takes action to avoid undesirable situations or that it takes action to maximise the likelihood of desirable situations occurring in the future
  - To offer up support to a human operator in the form of suggestions or alerts
- A digital twin offers services to its stakeholders. These are often presented in terms of a user interface. A particular type of digital twin is used to understand

the current state of the real system in the form of dashboards showing properties or in the form of representations of the real world, for example, on maps, layouts, or 3D representations.
- Some digital twins may control the real system using actuators. By using controls sent to the real world, a twin may close the loop and, in principle, autonomously adapt a real system to achieve the goal.

Categories of Digital Twin

A digital twin may be categorised into several types depending on their scope: *component* twins relate to individual atomic components of the real system; *asset* twins represent coherent parts of a system; *system* twins correspond to co-ordinated collections of assets. In contrast, a *process* twin addresses a process or workflow in a system and helps understand, monitor, or optimise a process.

A twin may be categorised in terms of the data connectivity to the real system and whether the twin relates to a component or a process. A twin is termed a digital *model* when the data connection is not real time and is often offline or manual. The model may be *dynamic* or *static*, depending on whether the data is provided from the live system or not.

A twin is termed a digital *shadow* when data is provided to the twin from the real system, but not the other way round. A digital *thread* is a twin of a process as opposed to a system or one of its components. The term *digital twin* tends to mean there is bidirectional flow of information in real time; however, it is also used as a term to cover all the different types.

Digital Twin Capabilities

The different types of digital twin can be arranged in a capability hierarchy as shown in Fig. 1.2. Each capability level subsumes the levels below and broadly represents the abilities of any type of digital twin.

Digital twins represent a technology advance in several areas of system development and operation. They can support product design since a new system can be designed and optimised in silico prior to expensive development. They can improve the lifetime of systems and reduce their downtime by monitoring their properties and identifying maintenance activities before the situation becomes critical.

System operation can be optimised by real-time modification of system parameters. In some cases, digital twins can replace more traditional methods, for example, by running alongside supply chains and logistics systems to dynamically adapt them compared to undertaking time-consuming planning prior to deployment. Digital twins can be used to enhance safety and reduce risk by monitoring system states in real time.

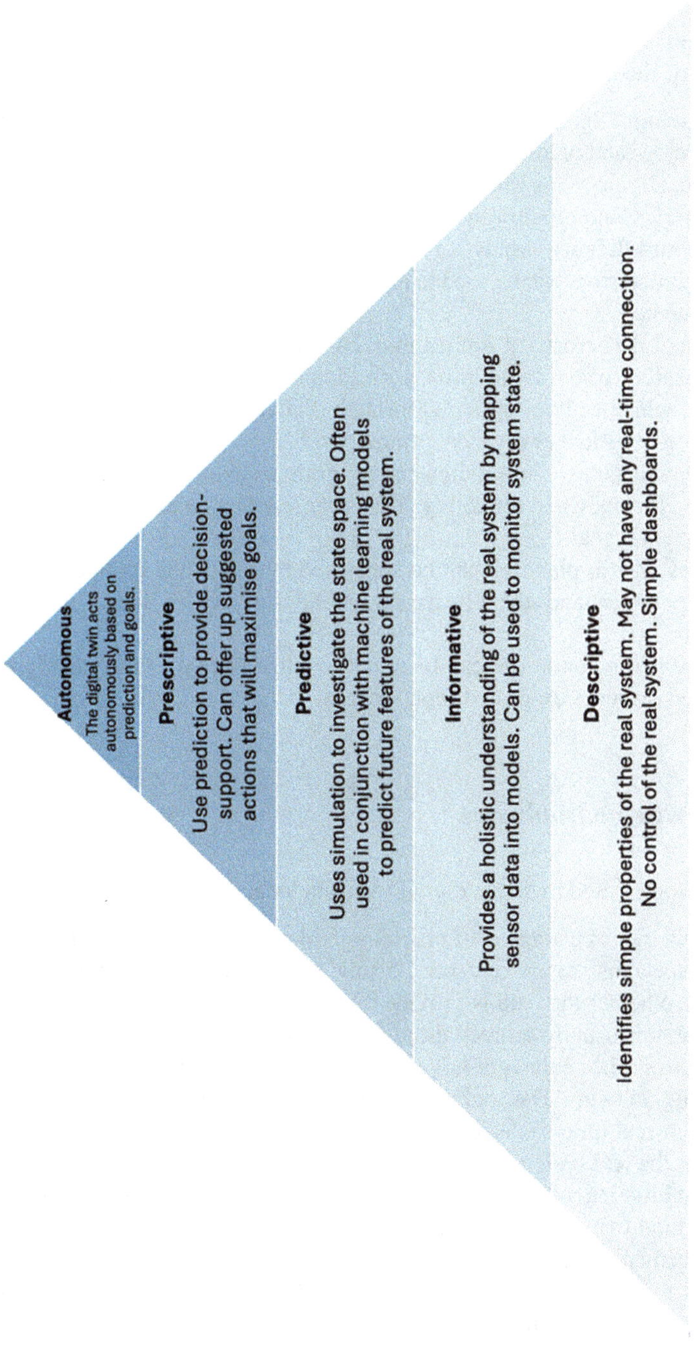

Fig. 1.2 Digital twin capability hierarchy

Digital Twin Applications

Digital twins are applied in an increasingly diverse range of application areas. Traditionally, the main areas of application are:

Manufacturing: Digital threads can be used to monitor and optimise manufacturing processes and predict maintenance needs.

Healthcare: Digital twins can be used to create personalised treatment plans, simulate surgeries, and monitor medical devices.

Aerospace and defence: Many aerospace systems are very expensive to build and test. Digital mirrors can be used to explore the design space and test the safety of such systems.

Automotive: Like aerospace applications, car manufacturing is expensive and must achieve safety goals. In addition, cars should be designed to achieve fuel efficiencies, which can be supported through digital twin monitoring and dynamic adaptation of virtual or physical prototypes.

Energy: Digital twins can monitor energy grids to optimise the use of power to improve efficiency and reliability. Twins can use adaptation to achieve net-zero environmental goals.

Smart cities: Urban planning can be supported by twins that monitor traffic flow and help understand the effects on public services of individual planning decisions.

Agriculture: Crop conditions can be monitored to ensure the best yield leading to optimised resource usage and food security.

Digital Twin Technologies

The technologies used to create digital twins include:

IoT: The Internet of Things is of crucial importance to many digital twin applications since most twins rely on consolidating data from multiple real-world sources. Whether the data is provided from historic information or provided in real-time, it is usually sourced through sensor-based instrumentation.

Data analytics: The analysis of large amounts of data is critical for the implementation of digital twins. The analysis may be historic to create a predictive model or may be in real time to detect patterns and anomalies and to create an accurate model of the real system.

AI and **machine learning**: Historic labelled data can be used to train models that allow digital twins to predict properties or future situations for the real system. Reinforcement learning can be used to gradually optimise a predictive model and to adapt the behaviour of a digital twin, which is controlling the real system. Typically, a digital twin will use some form of deep neural network to implement a model produced by machine learning.

Modelling: Models are used in several different ways to create and deploy digital twins. Static models of assets such as buildings, energy grids, or 3D models are used to support twin functionality, including the creation of realistic displays showing information. Physical models of the real system, such as finite element analysis and fluid dynamics, can be used to predict and simulate operational behaviour. Models may be used to design a digital twin by capturing requirements and specifying behaviour.

Simulation: There are many different technology platforms that can support simulation for digital twin operation. The choice depends on the application domain of the digital twin. For example, SIMULIA supports physics-based simulations, Siemens NX integrates CAD/CAM with simulation, and Simulink provides supports for a variety of dynamic system modelling and simulation. Different types of system simulation may be employed depending on the application: discrete event, agent based, Monte Carlo, stock and flow.

Cloud computing: Digital twins often require scalable computing due to the scale of real-time data and associated computing power required. Cloud computing platforms such as Azure offer a flexible way of dealing with these issues and a way of integrating with a wide range of supporting technologies.

Edge computing: Edge computing supports the processing of data close to the source, which reduces latency and improves performance. This is relevant to digital twins because of the large number of sensors producing vast amounts of data required by some applications. The use of edge computing means that much of the data processing can happen prior to the central integration phase within the core of the twin application.

Blockchain: The use of blockchain addresses issues of data security, integrity, and traceability within digital twins. Given the scale of twin applications and the need to often construct them as complex systems of systems, blockchain addresses the need for decentralised data management and enhanced collaboration.

Digital Twin Design Concepts

When developing a digital twin, there are many aspects that must be addressed including both the computational and commercial. The commercial aspect will vary depending on the context, but the computational aspects are common to many twin applications.

The concepts that are key to digital twin designs are shown in Fig. 1.3. The twin has the following concepts:

- **Measurements** are time-stamped sequences of *data* typically provided in real time by sensors. These may also be synthetic or historical measurements. Usually, a twin is driven by its streams of measurements.

- A twin has a current *world state*, which is modified in relation to user operations and updates from measurements. The initial world state may be subject to *levers*, which are used to select between a range of optional starting values.
- As the twin executes, it generates a sequence of world states, which is its *history*. The history of a twin must satisfy the *goal*, which determines the desired behaviour of the twin. For example, the goal may say that values in the world state must increase, decrease, or be maintained. In addition, the goal may define conditions that should be avoided.
- The twin has a collection of *stakeholders* who will benefit from, or use, the twin. Stakeholder benefits are expressed by the goal, and the use of the twin is defined by its *operations*. When an operation is performed by a stakeholder, the twin uses the current state and a collection of static *models* to service the operation.
- When a change is performed on the world state, either through a measurement update or through an operation, the state will produce *projections*. A projection is communicated to stakeholders via a user interface. It corresponds to the result of a query on the world state.
- In addition to the projections, changes to the world state may produce *controls*. A control is an event that should be handled by some external agent. For example, the twin may be required to detect certain undesirable situations, in which case an event is signalled to the operator. Another type of control is used to send events to the real system to adapt it in some way.

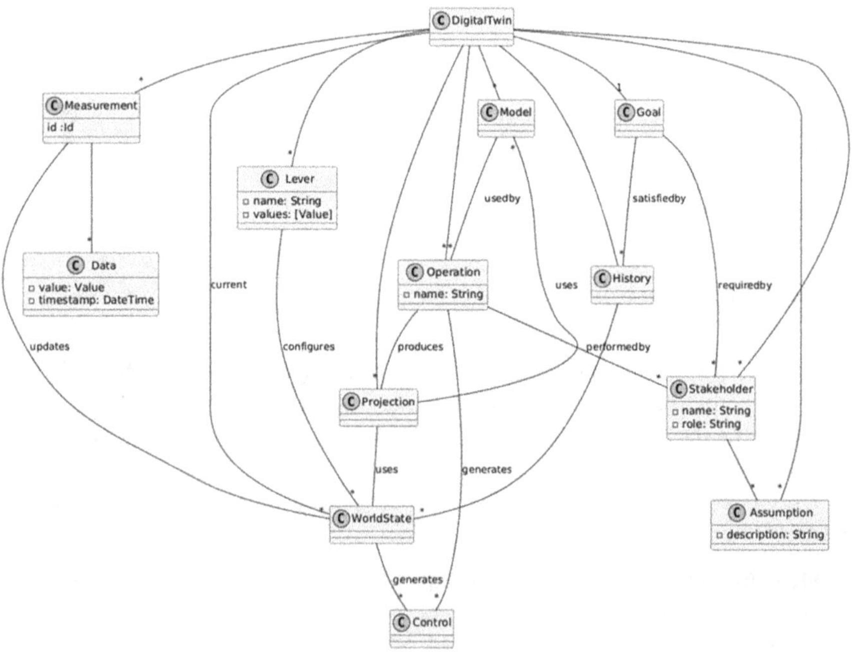

Fig. 1.3 Digital twin computational concepts

Digital Twin Design Method: Magic Spell

The concepts described in the previous section are all required to produce a digital twin design. The mnemonic MAGIC SPELL can be used to help remember the concepts:

Measures	**S**takeholders
Assumptions	**P**rojections
Goal	Mod**E**ls
Interface	**L**evers
Control	Wor**L**d State

The method is implemented by completing a form through a workshop with the stakeholders. The form has the following structure:

Measures	Assumptions	Goal	Interface	Control
Stakeholders	Projection	ModEls	Levers	WorLd State

The workshops should start with the definition of the goal of the digital twin. Once defined, the goal can lead to a definition of the interface of operations required by the stakeholders that will be required to ensure the goal is achieved. This leads to a design of the world state and associated models (static, predictive, simulation, etc.), which will be required to support the operations and to check whether the goal is achieved. The world state is created from the measures that are linked to data that is available from the real system. Finally, a discussion about optionality will lead to the definition of levers. Throughout, the stakeholders should be asked to document any assumptions they are making.

When following the method, the workshop organiser can be guided by the following questions:

Goal: What is the digital twin intended to do or achieve?

Stakeholders and interface: Who will use or benefit from the digital twin? How will they interact with the digital twin?

World state: How will you tell that the goal has been achieved? Thinking of the goal as a condition to be met: write down the condition, and make note of the properties and relationships that must be checked.

Measures and models: If you are going to build the world state (to check the goal), what information must be available? Which bits of the information are available now (static models), and which information will be supplied during system execution (measures)?

Projection: How will the stakeholders get information from the digital twin? What format will be used for the information (e.g. 3D models, maps, dashboards)?

Control: Are there any situations where the digital twin needs to interact with an external system or stakeholder? Does the digital twin control the real system in any way?

Assumptions: When answering any of the questions, make a note of any assumptions that are made.

Once the information has been documented on the form, it can be handed to design engineers who can formalise the information. The interface of operations is structured using use-case models. The world state and associated models are documented using class models. Measures are also documented using class models together with information about the timing of the updates. The goal can be formalised (e.g. using OCL) as a predicate over sequences of the world states.

Requirements for executable models such as predictive or simulation models can be specified as functions using conditions on their inputs and outputs. The behaviour of the twin provided by the operations can be specified using a state machine that is driven by operation events and measurement updates. The actions of the state machine are control events and updates to the user interface as described by the projection. The levers can be expressed through product-line-style markup of the models.

Together, the models described above provide the basis for digital twin implementation. This could take the form of further elaboration of the models until they become executable via an engine that uses model-based engineering technologies. Alternatively, they can be elaborated and translated into code by hand. Such models have the benefit that they are also a basis for designing test cases for the digital twin implementation.

Example

A racing car is connected to a twin that measures various properties of the car as it drives around the track. As it drives, the car uses fuel. The overall aim of the car is to perform a given number of laps within a given time without crashing or running out of fuel. Problems with fuel can be avoided by making a pit stop where unlimited amounts of fuel are available. However, pit stops delay the car and should only be used when essential. The car will crash if it accelerates while on a bend; otherwise, the car can accelerate at will, although doing so increases fuel consumption and tyre wear.

MAGIC SPELL can be applied to the racing car scenario to produce a populated form as shown below:

Measures	**Assumptions**	**Goal**	**Interface**	**Control**
The Digital Twin receives regular updates: • The position of the vehicle. • The speed of the Vehicle. • The amount of fuel in the Vehicle.	Position measures are received sufficiently frequently and are accurate.	• Don't crash on the curves. • Don't run out of fuel. • Finish within M minutes.	• The Digital Twin is entirely under human control. • The operator uses the projection (display) to select a control.	Used to control the behaviour of the vehicle: • Speed Up • Slow Down • Refuel
Stakeholders	**Projection**	**ModEls**	**Levers**	**WorLd State**
There are two stakeholders: • The Driver of the vehicle who receives control messages via a HUD. • The Operator who manages the Digital Twin.	Use the current world state and the model of the track to draw a diagram showing the complete track and the position of the vehicle.	• A map of the track showing curves and straights. • Allows a vehicle position to be mapped onto a track position. • Can be used to determine whether a vehicle is currently on the straight or a curve. • Can be used to determine whether a vehicle is at the start or at the finish line.	Things that can vary at the start of the Digital Twin operation are: • The amount of fuel. • The number of laps. • The value of M.	• Current position. • Current speed. • Current fuel level.

The information in the form is the starting point for more detailed conversations with the stakeholders, after which it is supplied to the development engineers.

Challenges

Implementing a digital twin is a challenging task. Firstly, although we have given a definition of key features of a digital twin, there is no consensus amongst practitioners regarding a precise categorisation and definition of the key technologies and approaches. Furthermore, there are very few design methods for twins that are developed to any level of detail. The approach provided here seems to be both representative and provides a structured basis that goes beyond those available to date. There are many practical technical challenges; these include:

Data integration: where the twin uses real-time data; this must be integrated to build the world state and generate events. The scale, frequency, and quality of the data are a technical challenge.

Cost: Development of a digital twin is a significant cost for an organisation. Given that some twins add value to existing systems and processes, such additional discretionary cost may be seen as delivering insufficient value.

Expertise: The field of digital twins is relatively new, and although knowledge about individual aspects of a twin is readily available, the expertise relating to the holistic development of a twin may be difficult to obtain.

Security: Implementing a digital twin involves integration with other systems through monitoring their data and, in some cases, introducing adaptive controls. Attaching a twin to existing systems introduces the threat of cyberattacks and may compromise data security.

Regulation: Often, a twin will be based around the use of AI and machine learning, which introduces inherently unpredictable behaviour. This makes it difficult to verify such systems in terms of their regulatory compliance.

Standards: There are currently no standards for twin design and implementation. Given that twins are heavily reliant on data and are often implemented as systems of systems, it is important that data standards are addressed to ensure that multiple twins can work together or that twins can be redeployed in new environments.

The research community can contribute to addressing these challenges by helping clarify the definition of digital twins through the creation of mathematical and computational models, through the creation of standards related to data and systems architectures, approaches to data security, the use of quantum computing to help support the application of digital twins to very complex systems at scale, and by improving the efficient use of advanced technologies such as machine learning in order to reduce the impact on the environment.

Conclusion

In conclusion, while implementing digital twins has challenges such as data integration, high costs, technical expertise, and cybersecurity concerns, the potential benefits far outweigh these hurdles. The benefits include operational efficiency, reduction of costs including predictive maintenance and resource usage, and increased decision support, leading to business competitive advantages. The successful adoption of digital twins by industry giants like TCS, Siemens, General Electric, IBM, Microsoft, Bosch, Oracle, and Cisco demonstrates the transformative power of this technology. As digital twins continue to evolve, integrating advanced technologies like AI, machine learning, and quantum computing, their applications will expand, offering unprecedented opportunities for efficiency and sustainability.

The future of digital twins is very encouraging, promising a world where physical and digital systems are seamlessly interconnected, leading to smarter, more efficient, and more resilient and adaptable systems. Embracing this technology will be crucial for organisations aiming to stay competitive and innovative in the rapidly changing landscape of the digital age.

Chapter 2
Control and Optimization Using Digital Twins: Principles and Case Studies

Aditya A. Paranjape

Abstract Digital twins are fast becoming an essential technology for decision-making at every level in the industry in the face of uncertainty, competition, and rapid developments in technology. The increasing modeling complexity can hinder rapid, verifiable decision-making, which we seek to address using what we refer to as control-oriented digital twins. Control-oriented digital twins are created by applying model order reduction techniques and multi-modeling approaches to full-scale models. The purpose of this chapter is to review the principles underlying model order reduction and multi-modeling. These techniques are illustrated through two case studies, one based on a chemical industrial plant and one based on a social system.

Introduction

Digital twins (DTs) have fast evolved into a must-have technology for industries. The growing use and complexity of DTs has been enabled by a parallel growth in computing power and distributed sensors together with increasingly faster and more robust automated decision-making algorithms. Digital twins are seen as an enabling technology for automated decision-making in complex real-world systems, including business decisions, risk assessment, and (adverse) event prediction.

One key question of interest to designers and end users seeking to minimize the complexity of DTs is as follows: How much information does a DT need to contain in order to qualify as a faithful representation of the "twinned" real-world system? In this chapter, we make an attempt to answer this question using tools from control theory, providing in the process formal mechanisms to construct digital twins. Our starting point is the proposition that the complexity of a DT can be capped at the

A. A. Paranjape (✉)
Monash University, Melbourne, Australia
e-mail: aditya.paranjape@monash.edu

V. Kulkarni et al. (eds.), *Digital Twins for Simulation-Based Decision-Making*, https://doi.org/10.1007/978-3-031-89654-5_2

point where it is just good enough for the purpose for which it is designed. We present case studies that illustrate the design principles.

We view the DT fundamentally as *a specialized instance of a general parametric model*. The "model" in question might capture the behaviour of all possible objects in its class (e.g. all aircraft of a certain family), while a DT would capture the behaviour and the history of one specific individual (in this example, one specific aircraft together with its systems and engines). A DT is then a software representation of a real-world system (RWS) whose outputs are *sufficiently similar* to that of the RWS of interest. In general, the more *similarity metrics* one prescribes, the greater the fidelity of the DT and its "resemblance" to the RWS. While a close resemblance between a DT and its parent RWS might appear desirable, a compact and minimal task-specific DT often suffices for control and optimization.

An interesting by-product of using "limited" similarity metrics to construct control-oriented DTs is that a resulting DT might capture, accurately, the behaviour of a completely different albeit related real-world system, presenting the possibility of transferring know-how between the two. For instance, in the world of flight physics, the concept of *dynamic similarity* (going beyond the familiar geometric similarity) is used to design scaled aircraft for exploratory flight testing and research, e.g. the NASA AirSTAR program [1]. The dynamic characteristics of the scaled aircraft, such as the natural frequency of pitch oscillations measured with respect to an appropriately scaled time, are identical to those of the original, full-sized aircraft. Thus, the DTs of the two aircraft, when designed for the purpose of designing and verifying flight control laws and handling qualities, would be identical up to a suitably scaled time although the aircraft are vastly different in size and fly at vastly different speeds and altitudes. This similarity allows for a partial validation of flight control laws designed for functions such as envelope protection and upset recovery before they are implemented on a manned, full-scale test aircraft.

The purpose of this chapter is to review and illustrate the technical foundations of control-oriented digital twins, drawing upon well-known concepts in control theory. We use mathematical notation for describing the foundations in a concise and unambiguous manner. After reviewing some preliminary concepts in the Section "Preliminaries," we present key results from control theory in the Section "Principles and Ideas from Control Theory," which can be used to construct control-oriented digital twins. We illustrate the key concepts and results with examples where possible. Next, we present two case studies in the Section "Case Studies" to illustrate the manner in which control theoretic ideas apply to the construction of control-oriented digital twins. We wrap up the chapter with a concluding discussion in the Section "Concluding Discussion."

Preliminaries

Mathematically, a digital twin D is conceptualized as a tuple $D = (M, q_0)$, where M is a simulatable model of the RWS, while $q_0 \in Q$ denotes parameter values that are specific to a given instance of the RWS. These may be time-varying or may be set once and for all at the start of operation. The inclusion of q_0 distinguishes D from the arbitrary simulatable model M, as we explain later. At the same time, it follows that any given D can be viewed as an instance of M for a particular q_0. The simulatable model M is usually described mathematically using differential or difference equations:

$$x^{+}[k] = f(x[0:k], u[0:k], p[k]), x[0] = x_0$$
$$(y[k], z[k]) = h(x[k], u[k]),$$

where $x \in X$ is the state, X is called the *state space*, $p \in P$ denotes the system parameters (including q from the definition above), u is the control input, y denotes the outputs of interest (KPIs), and z denotes the supporting measurements (i.e. measurements in addition to y). We use the notation $x[k]$ to denote the value of x at time instant k and $x[0{:}k]$ to denote the collection (memory) of values from time 0 to k. The function $f()$ is the state transition law (also referred to often as *the model* or *the dynamics*). For continuous time systems, x^+ is the time derivative, while for discrete time systems, $x^+[k] = x[k + 1]$. The control input is computed using a *control law* or a decision-making algorithm, which is supplied by the operator of the RWS. It may be fixed or *tuned* periodically using the DT. The human operators may take the place of an automated control law in human-in-the-loop systems.

The core simulation model is augmented with two following components to form the DT:

- A *similarity metric* $S(y - y_{\text{ref}}, z - z_{\text{ref}})$, which compares the outputs and the measurements of the DT with those of the real word $(y_{\text{ref}}, z_{\text{ref}})$. It reflects the purpose of the DT and plays a key role in tuning the model M. In the case of Covid-19, for instance, a DT tuned to minimize the error in the predicted number of critical cases did not always minimize the error in the number of active infections and vice versa, because of the assumptions made in M to determine the number of people that experienced a critical illness as a fraction of the total infected individuals in a given cohort.
- An online *parameter estimator* for $(p[k], x_0)$ aligns the function $f()$ with the real-world dynamics by minimizing the similarity metric $S()$. Notice that the initial value x_0 of the state may also be a parameter, as illustrated for the example of Covid-19 in the Section "Case Studies."

The schematic of a typical DT-driven control system is shown in Fig. 2.1. Notice that the control law gets inputs from the real world and the DT. This follows the philosophy of model reference adaptive control (MRAC), wherein feedback from

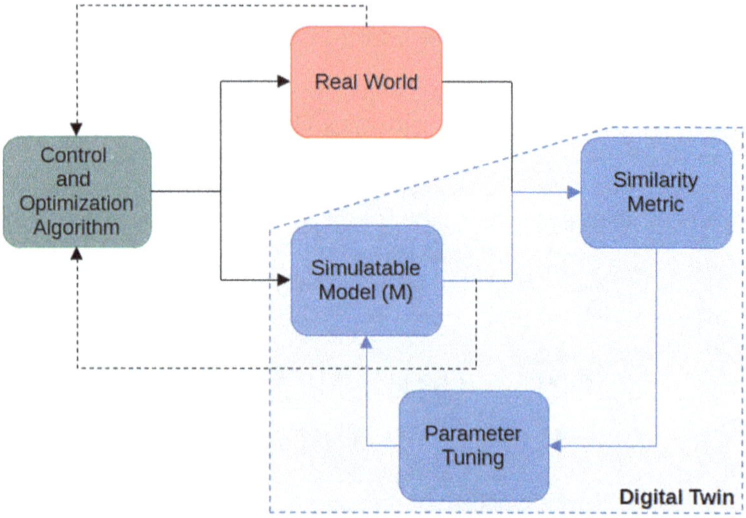

Fig. 2.1 Schematic of a control system equipped with a digital twin

the model is used to tune the parameters of the control law (often in conjunction with real-world feedback), while the real-world feedback is used to compute the actual control input to be sent to the two systems.

In Fig. 2.1, we have shown the similarity metric and the parameter tuning logic as part of the DT. While this does not tally with our tuple-based Definition 1, it is useful in practice because the choice of the similarity metric and the parameter tuning logic are dependent on the choice of the simulatable model. In this chapter, we will not dwell upon the similarity metric and the parameter tuning logic, except in the Section "Case Studies."

The architecture shown in Fig. 2.1 can be used to devise a scheme for using a DT for training a learning-based control law. The control law is first tuned using the simulatable model in its nominal form, i.e. wherein its parameters are not perfectly tuned to minimize the similarity metric. Thereafter, once the DT and the control law are deployed in the real world, either or both of them can be tuned online to ensure that the KPIs meet the targets. However, the online tuning of the control law is usually "local" in a neighbourhood of the nominal control law and is referred to as "adaptation." To achieve a larger improvement in performance ("transformation"), the control law can be periodically retrained offline by disconnecting the RWS once the DT has been tuned to a satisfactory degree. This makes the system "adaptive" to non-local, long-term changes in the RWS.

The specifications for designing a DT, particularly the state space X and the similarity metric S, depend on the uniqueness of the RWS and the composition of its life cycle. We identify four canonical classes of RWS in Table 2.1.

For systems with non-recurrent behaviour, the initial condition x_0 is, in theory, never revisited. As a result, the consequences of a given action (control as well as

Table 2.1 Taxonomy of dynamical systems based on uniqueness and recurrence

Recurrence (→) Uniqueness	Non-recurrent behaviour	Recurrent behaviour
Unique instance	Biological ageing of an individual	Bespoke assembly line or chemical plant
One of multiple instances	An epidemic	Individual aircraft from a mass-produced lot

parameter tuning) are irreversible. The control design challenge is exacerbated if the model M has parameters that need to be tuned using real-time data or if it has a large number of states that need to be estimated using the measured data for the purpose of control. In either case, the model takes a finite amount of time to "match" the RWS. When there are multiple asynchronous instances of the RWS, it might be possible in some cases to transfer the learned parameters from one DT to another. This possibility is obviously lost when there is a single instance of the RWS.

Example 1 Consider a digital twin of Earth's climate that may be employed to predict global warming and design mitigation strategies. While several climatic trends do recur on an annual (the seasons) or quasi-periodic basis (e.g. the El Niño effect), the long-term warming and the resulting phenomena are non-recurrent on reasonable human timescales. There is no other known planet whose climate can be modeled for the purpose of tuning the parameters of Earth's climatic model. The resulting variability in predicting long-term outcomes with certainty has been one of the factors that has hindered the implementation of remedial policies designed using existing models.

Example 2 Trajectories of epidemics such as SARS and Covid-19 are inherently non-recurrent. However, they have proven to be predictable (probabilistically) over short timescales due to social interaction models that are independent of the pathogen and which can thus be learned partially from data recorded during previous epidemics. The social mixing models can be combined with the virulence of the specific strain of the pathogen to estimate the growth in the number of cases.

While it is generally helpful to ensure that the state space X as well as the set of parameters P is minimal, this is particularly so in non-recurrent systems due to the limited opportunity to tune the parameters and explore the state space. In contrast, models of systems with recurrent dynamics can be tuned accurately online, provided several operational cycles can be allowed to elapse *sub-optimally* but safely. This is the basis of control methods based on safe reinforcement learning and model-based adaptive control. Such models are typically first created offline using the known governing equations, refined using offline learning methods or historical data, and then *adapted* in real time using parameter update laws. At each step, safety is guaranteed by imposing constraints on the (state-dependent) envelope of control actions. The control envelope is also tuned as part of the training. Recurring trajectories help establish and verify rigorous guarantees on parameter convergence and optimality in runtime.

Principles and Ideas from Control Theory

In this section, we review key principles and methods from control theory that can be employed fruitfully to construct control-oriented digital twins (CODTs). First, we formally define a CODT.

Definition 1 Definition: a CODT is a tuple (M, x_0), where M is a simulatable model, equipped with a similarity metric $S(y - y_{\text{ref}})$, which is minimized for a class of control inputs $u \in U$ and $y_{\text{ref}} \in Y$.

We notice two major differences between a CODT and a more general DT defined earlier. First, the similarity metric is a function of only the outputs of interest, i.e. the KPIs. It follows not only that the other measured variables (z) may not match between the CODT and the actual system but also that the state space X of the CODT may not contain z. Second, the similarity metric has to match correctly for only a class U of control signals and Y of outputs. This captures the intuitive notion that the DT needs to have just about enough information to assess the effect of the control actions correctly within a well-defined operating envelope.

The concept of a CODT is rooted in two well-known constructs from control theory: the *internal model principle* (IMP) and a *state observer*. We refer to the generic block diagram of a control system in Fig. 2.2a, wherein the plant G is driven by a controller C, which seeks to match the outputs of the plant P and an exogenous system E. The IMP says that the controller must incorporate a model of E in order to ensure that the output of G tracks the reference produced by E. The *state observer* is a replica dynamical model of G, with a matching state space, whose states are used by the controller to stabilize and control G. We refer the reader to [2] for a detailed description of these constructs. An observer-based controller is depicted in Fig. 2.2b, which should be viewed as a special case of Fig. 2.2a.

It is clear how a CODT can play the role of a state observer for the control law: this becomes apparent when one compares the architecture of Fig. 2.2b with the block diagram shown in Fig. 2.1 albeit without a parameter tuning logic. Likewise, one can view E as a replica of G and the target signal generated by E (i.e. by G) as some ideal behaviour for an unknown reference input, which is assumed to exist and lie within the realizable set of C. In this case, it follows from IMP that the controller must have a model (i.e. a CODT) for the plant G.

The next idea that we consider is that of model order reduction. Consider the input-output map $G : u \mapsto y$, i.e. $y = G(u)$. For linear systems, the map G is called the transfer function of the system. The poles (eigenvalues) of the transfer function G can be ordered, and poles with negative real parts less than (i.e. more negative than) some threshold can be ignored without affecting the input-output response significantly. Formally, for an induced norm $||G||$ and some tolerance e, one constructs a reduced order system G' formally by solving $G' = \arg\ \min O(G')$ such that $||G - G'|| < \epsilon$, where $O()$ denotes the model order. It turns out minimizing $||G - G'||$ is equivalent to minimizing the similarity metric $||y - y_{\text{ref}}||$, where y_{ref} and y are the outputs of the maps G and G', respectively.

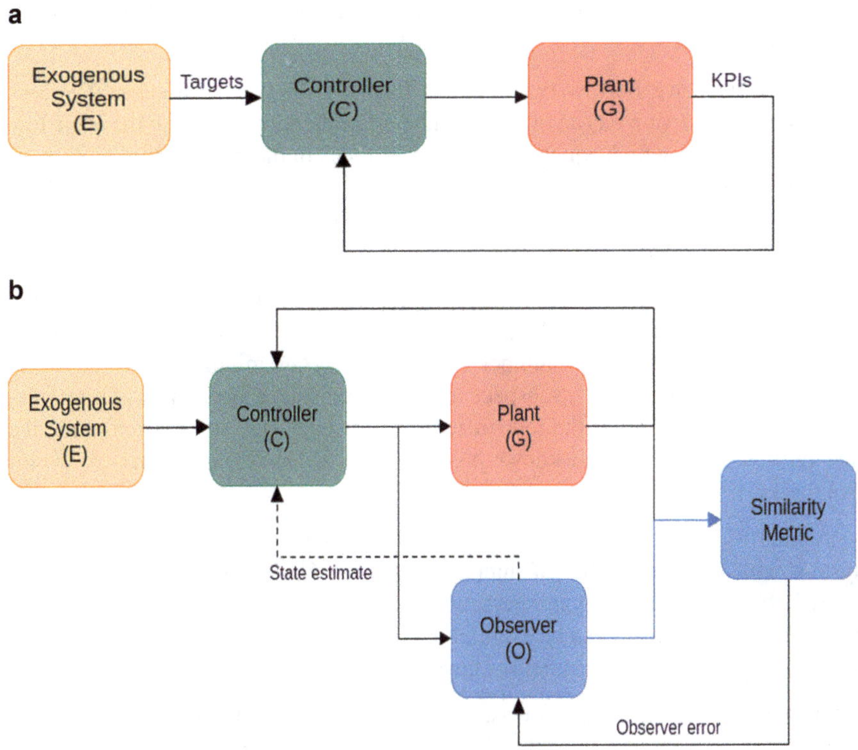

Fig. 2.2 (**a**) A generic control system. (**b**) Observer-based control system

The model order reduction technique described above can be generalized naturally to realize the principle of *time scale separation* when the ordered eigenvalues can be clustered such that each group is sufficiently far from the other groups. The corresponding *eigenvectors* are grouped together into a collection of states that form a *subsystem*. Thus, the parent system is decomposed into a collection of subsystems such that the dynamics of each subsystem is decoupled from that of the other subsystems. Only those subsystems that "contain" the outputs Y and the control inputs U are retained to construct the CODT. When the eigenvectors are not perfectly aligned with the principal (physically meaningful) states, the principle of time scale separation needs to be applied cautiously, as illustrated in the next example.

Example 3 A rigid aircraft has three degrees of freedom in the vertical plane: two translational (forward and up/down) and one rotation (pitch). The time scale of the translational motion (referred to as the phugoid mode) is slower than pitch (called the short period mode) by a full order of magnitude, although neither the phugoid eigenvectors nor the short period eigenvectors are aligned entirely with their respective principal states. The translational variables (flight speed and flight path angle) can be ignored altogether for the purpose of designing pitch control laws. However, pitch rate cannot be ignored entirely for controlling phugoid since phugoid oscillations trigger slow oscillations in the pitch rate and these need to be fed back into a phugoid controller.

Another idea we borrow from control theory is that of minimal realizations: every transfer function has an infinite number of realizations, all with the same lowest possible order, which equals the number of poles in the transfer function. In our context, this means that there is an infinite number of candidate state spaces X for the CODT and there is no requirement that the chosen space X contain physically or intuitively relevant variables.

Example 4 The admissibility of non-unique realizations is stretched to its extreme when M is represented as a hidden Markov model, such as using a recursive neural network (RNN). Unless the number of hidden states is minimal, an input-output model would be trained on a subspace of the hidden state space. Unless the training guarantees the stability of the hidden states, the model may suffer from numerical instabilities. This is the well-known problem of unstable zero dynamics [3] in control theory.

A final tool for constructing digital twins relies on *mean field* behaviour in a system with a large number of interacting agents. Under the hypothesis that the overall effect of the inter-agent interaction is dominated by the average behaviour of the agents, the dynamics can be examined by modeling the mean field in detail, usually leading to differential equations governing the number of agents in each state.

Example 5 Consider a flock consisting of a large number of birds, and suppose we were trying to ascertain how the flock would move given a known behavioural model of individual birds. Such DTs have been employed for designing strategies for herding flocks of birds away from airports. It is clear that the trajectory of individual birds is largely irrelevant; the position of the flock and its dimensions are all that matter in practical settings. In such cases, instead of modeling and tracking the motion of individual birds, one can convert the underlying differential equations into a compact Focker-Planck differential equation, which tracks the motion of the centre of mass of the flock and its geometry (more precisely, the distribution of the birds around the centre of mass) as shown in Fig. 2.3.

The next example illustrates the risks of intuition-driven model simplification when the DT is required to capture complex non-equilibrium behaviour.

Example 6 A mitogen-activated protein kinase (MAPK) cascade regulates cellular activities such as gene expression, differentiation, and apoptosis in eukaryotic (e.g. mammals) cells. Each tier of a MAPK cascade consists of interacting proteins as shown in Fig. 2.4(i). The dynamics of the interaction between N, Np, and Npp are similar to a hysteretic loop (Fig. 2.4(iv)), while an integrator action through the kinase "kin" induces relay-relaxation oscillations as shown in Fig. 2.4(v). The concentration of Np is small and almost constant when compared to the oscillations seen in the other proteins. A reduced order model resulting from the assumption that Np is constant lacks a hysteretic loop, and the addition of an integrator feedback no longer results in oscillatory behaviour, as shown in Fig. 2.4(vi).

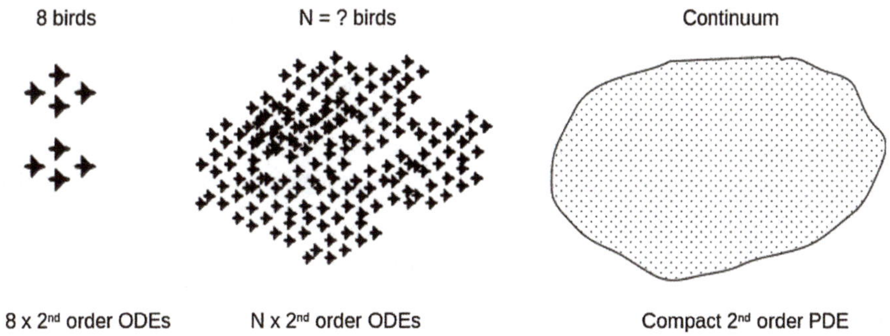

Fig. 2.3 Individual (agent)—based v/s a continuum view of swarms

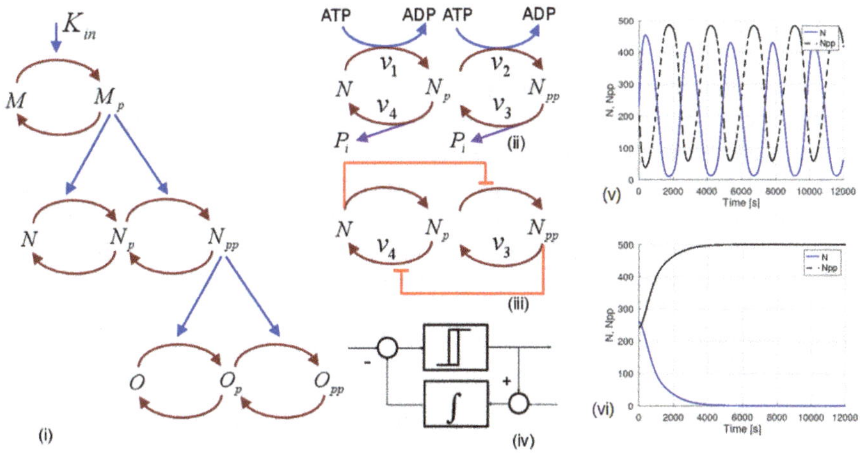

Fig. 2.4 MAPK cascade and trajectories

In the subsequent sections, we will present case studies to illustrate the aforementioned tools for constructing purposive CODTs. The reader should note that each tool attempts to reduce the complexity of the DT by ignoring or simplifying a part of the governing dynamics. Thus, it is essential to identify the limitations of each tool and, as a corollary, when it can be used safely for control design.

Case Studies

In this section, we will look at two case studies drawn from the author's prior work, which will serve to illustrate the concepts and the principles discussed above. One key element that we omit in this section is that of parameter tuning to match the real-world system and the DT.

The first example deals with scheduling the transfer of crude between two parts of an oil refinery. This problem serves to illustrate the principles of time scale separation and the manner in which multiple CODTs can be employed to solve the control problem by viewing it as a composition of timescale separated problems. It also shows how DTs can be used to train a learning-based control law. The second example illustrates the principle of mean-field aggregation applied to a Covid-19 epidemiological model.

Case Study 1 Scheduling Crude Transfer to an Oil Refinery: Control Using Multiple Hierarchical DTs and Learning

Context and Problem Formulation

The setting for this particular case study came from an actual European refinery, which is located a few kilometres inland from the nearest port at which crude is offloaded and stored. The crude is transferred to the refinery for processing through a high-capacity pipeline, which we call PRL (pipe to refinery line). Figure 2.5 shows a schematic of the port and the refinery. The coloured blocks (except grey) in Fig. 2.5 are the storage tanks, where each colour is specific to one of four types of crude (L, M, N, and O) processed at the refinery. The portside tank "ARL" is a virtual tank and represents a single "packet" of N-type crude drawn from another upstream storage facility. The two CDUs in the refinery, CDU1 and CDU2, operate continuously. The maximum amount of crude that can be transferred through the PRL in 38 h is equal to the amount of crude processed by the CDUs during that time. There are additional production constraints: for instance, the L type crude

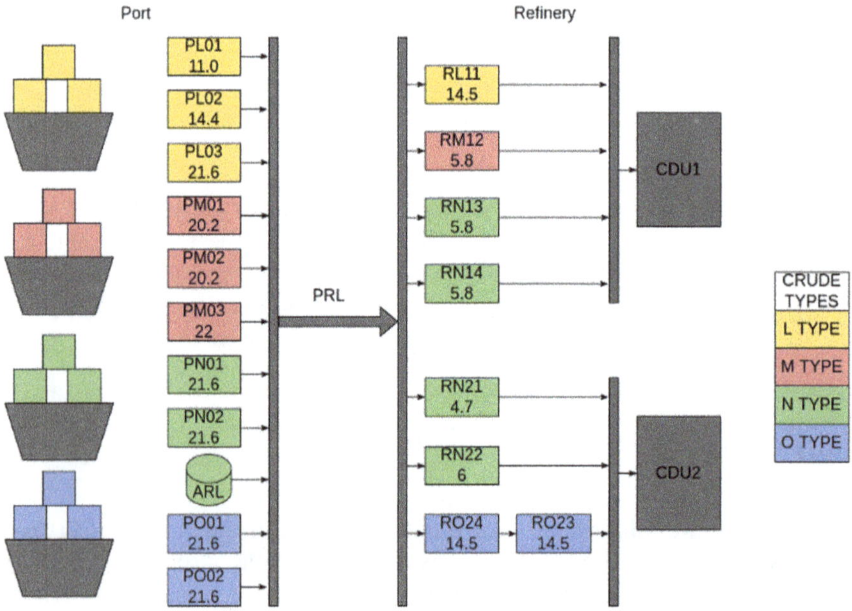

Fig. 2.5 Schematic of the port and refinery showing the tanks and the flow channels

(low sulphur and low metal) needs to be processed in contiguous blocks of 2 days for maximum value, while N-type crude needs to be processed every day by exactly one of the two CDUs.

The arrival schedule of the oil tankers at the port is known ahead of time, and the nominal arrival schedule is used to generate production targets for the refinery. The control objective considered here is that of deriving a monthly schedule for the transfer of crude through the PRL that satisfies the production requirements and the aforementioned storage constraints while being robust to uncertainties in the delivery of crude. Since the transfer capacity of the PRL over a 38-h window is equal to the amount of crude processed by the refinery in the same time period, the problem is one of guaranteeing a feasible solution rather than optimizing over a non-trivial set of feasible solutions.

Control Using Multiple CODTs: Time Scale Separation, Aggregation, and Learning

The scheduling problem can be solved using mixed-integer linear programming as explained in [4]. While the time taken by contemporary solvers to solve the MILP problem may be acceptable in an operational setting, MILP requires that the dynamical system be known perfectly. In our case, this implies that the crude arrival schedule has to be known with complete certainty. An alternative approach involves breaking down the scheduling problem into two sub-problems: determining the volume of crude of each type to be transferred during a given 19.8-h window and then distributing the resulting crude volumes into packets of 15 min. The problem of ensuring robustness to uncertainties in crude delivery is absorbed into the first sub-problem. One may also include (although not done here) robustness to unplanned interruptions in the PRL as a consideration in the same subproblem. We use reinforcement learning (RL) to solve the first sub-problem. Once the RL agent determines the amount of crude to be transferred over a 19.8-h window, any of a number of methods can be used (including MILP) to solve the second subproblem, i.e. distribute the crude optimally into 15 min packets.

We designed four different CODTs for the refinery by aggregating over space and time, as listed in Table 2.2. When feasible, tanks holding the same grade of crude were aggregated into "zones." In some cases, the tanks are ignored altogether, as explained presently. Temporal aggregation refers to the use of a 38-h time step for determining the volume of crude to be transferred during a 19.8-h window.

Table 2.2 Abstractions of the port and refinery system

Model name	Port tanks	Refinery tanks	Time step	Utility
Sim0	–	Zones	38 h	State space for feature space of RL agent
Sim1	–	Zones	15 min	Heuristics-based optimizer (not discussed here)
Sim2	Zones	Tanks	15 min	Policy evaluation for RL
Sim3	Tanks	Tanks	15 min	MILP

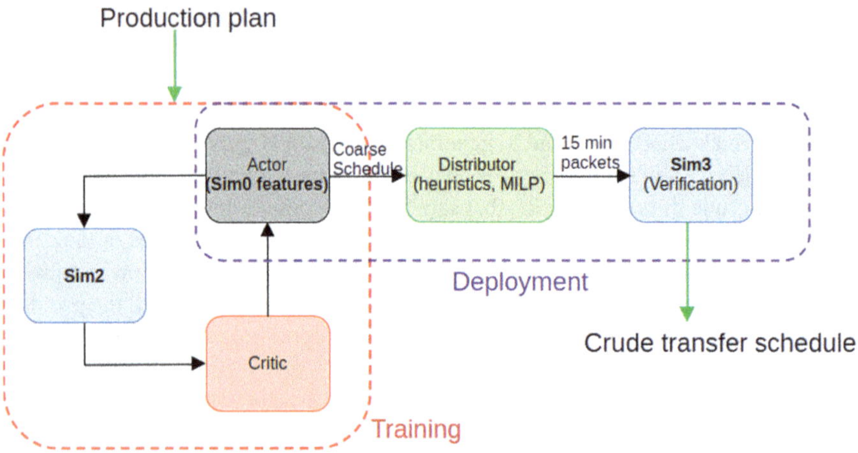

Fig. 2.6 Digital twins in refinery control

Table 2.2 also lists the utility of each model (recall that the fidelity of a digital twin is matched to its purpose). Sim3 is the most detailed model of the refinery for the purpose of scheduling and is used only for solving the scheduling problem in its entirety using MILP. In Sim0 and Sim1, the port-side tanks are ignored altogether under the assumption that there is enough crude in those tanks. Sim2 bridges the fidelity gap between Sim1 and Sim3.

The compact (and, arguably, minimal) model Sim0 is used for training a reinforcement learning agent, which uses an actor-critic architecture. The state space of Sim0 and the crude delivery schedule are used to define the input features for a reinforcement learning agent. Since Sim0 groups refinery-side tanks feeding each CDU into zones, it is unable to capture the logic for allocating crude between the tanks and for deciding which tank supplies the CDU at any given time. Since this logic needs the fidelity of Sim2 at the very least, Sim2 with a heuristic allocation logic is used to compute the value function (the reward or the penalty) while training the RL agent.

Figure 2.6 shows the final scheme for training and deploying the scheduler, together with the roles played by Sim0, Sim2, and Sim3, as explained earlier. The controller is referred to as the *actor*, since it is trained using the well-known actor-critic architecture and a deep deterministic policy gradients (DDPG) algorithm. Notice that the critic and Sim2 are not needed by the actor in the deployment phase: the actor is said to be trained *offline*. The actor can be tuned *online* by including the critic in the deployment block with the connection from Sim2 replaced by a connection from Sim3.

Case Study 2 The Covid-19 Epidemic in Pune, India—Multi-fidelity DTs
India went into a nationwide lockdown in March 2020 in response to the growing threat of the Covid-19 pandemic. The immediate priorities for epidemiological modeling were those of assessing the viability of the healthcare system and

determining a timeline for "unlocking" the country and resuming economic activity that got underway in June 2020. These efforts, while largely successful, ran into a major hurdle in early 2021 when the then-unknown delta variant triggered a massive unexpected surge in the number of infections as well as deaths, leading to effectively a second nationwide lockdown. The author was part of a group of modelers and epidemiologists that advised the local administration in the city of Pune, India, during the initial lockdown in 2020 as well as in the lead-up to the lockdown in 2021. A detailed account of the group's work and experience is presented in Chap. 9. In this section, we review the group's work on multi-modeling and a retrospective perspective on how it could have been better employed to manage the second lockdown.

Epidemiological DTs

Epidemiological models come in a variety of scales and fidelity. Agent-based models, which model the movement and the health of each individual in detail, provide the highest level of granularity and fidelity. At the other end, compartmental models aggregate entire sub-populations into a small number of "compartments," and the model keeps track of only the fraction of the population in each compartment over time.

Once correctly tuned and initialized, the fine-grained ABMs offer a detailed picture of the evolution of the epidemic and allow for the design of low-level non-pharmaceutical interventions (NPIs). However, they are difficult to tune and initialize, particularly in the early stages of an epidemic, due to the large number of modeling parameters in a typical ABM. Second, the resemblance between ABMs and the real world (in the sense of agents resembling actual individuals and places) means that modelers and users are highly susceptible to confirmatory bias once the model has been tuned successfully and may be slow to react to any divergence that may occur due to unmodeled real world dynamics (e.g. a mutated pathogen).

We propose a multi-modeling approach, based on compartmental models, to mitigate the limitations of ABMs. Coarse-grained compartmental models, also called SIR (susceptible-infected-recovered) models, are implemented in the form of a limited number of differential equations. A simulation covering a period of several months can be run in a matter of seconds on a typical personal computer.

SIR models cannot be used to capture or resolve the effect of individual NPIs in as much detail as ABMs. Instead, they can be used to rapidly derive high-level design objectives for NPIs and for triggering a recalibration of ABMs when there is a mismatch between ABMs and the ground truth. One such *multi-model* architecture is shown in Fig. 2.7. It resembles the general DT-based control and optimization architecture of Fig. 2.1, with the compartmental model playing the role of the parameter tuning logic. It should be noted here that parameter tuning is not always automated and, in fact, significant human expertise is needed for initial parameter tuning and in the event of a significant change in the conditions on the ground.

Lessons from the Covid-19: Multi-modeling

The Covid-19 case study in Chap. 9 provides a detailed account of the ABM developed to predict the course of the epidemic in the city of Pune in India. The predictions made by the ABM were found to be reliable until mid-February 2021,

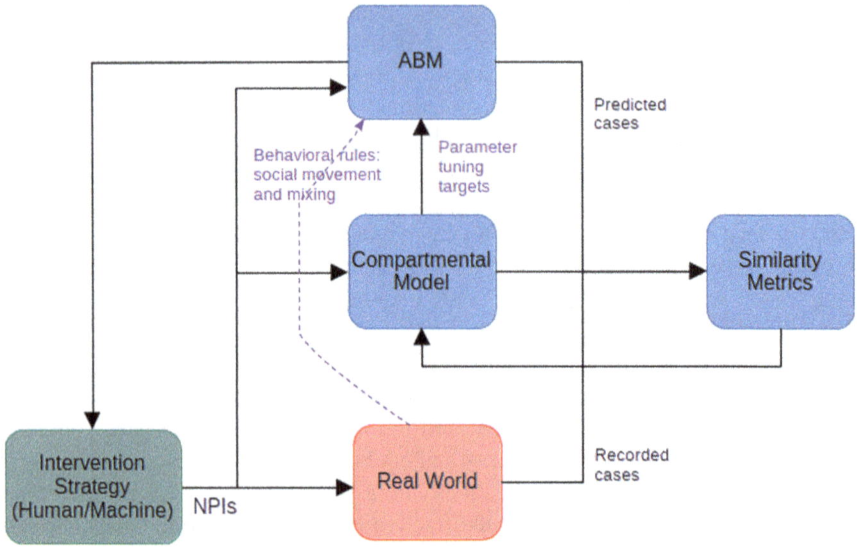

Fig. 2.7 Multi-modeling approach for epidemics

following which, there were early signs of a gradual divergence, which was initially ascribed to greater-than-anticipated social mixing. In the absence of an official notification about a more infectious or virulent variant in circulation, it was deemed inappropriate to modify the properties of the pathogen in the ABM. It was observed in the following weeks that the rate of divergence was greater than that with even the most liberal social mixing models in the ABM. The ABM could no longer track the number of cases correctly for the purpose of informing policy interventions. At that point, an opportunity was lost to flag a new and potentially more infectious variant, which was eventually notified officially only in mid-May 2021 as the delta variant.

In retrospect, a multi-model approach, such as the one in Fig. 2.7, could have provided an early indication of the new variant. The key enabling feature of the highly aggregated SIR model in this regard is that it does not discriminate between the effects of mixing and infectiousness. Instead, it provides bounds on the *product* of the two. Figure 2.8 shows the expected trajectory of the epidemic for three different values of the product in addition to the ABM baseline for a 3-month period starting Feb 1, 2021. The three values of the product chosen here provided a close match with the early surge in cases in February and March 2021. The SIR model was able to identify correctly, based on data available up to mid-March, that the peak of the imminent wave would be substantially higher than the ABM baseline. By maximizing the mixing in the ABM and calculating the resulting lower bound on the infectiousness of the circulating variant using the smallest likely value of the product, it would have been apparent that a new variant, with an infectiousness between two and four times that of the original alpha variant, was very likely in circulation. The updated ABM could have provided better estimates for the peak

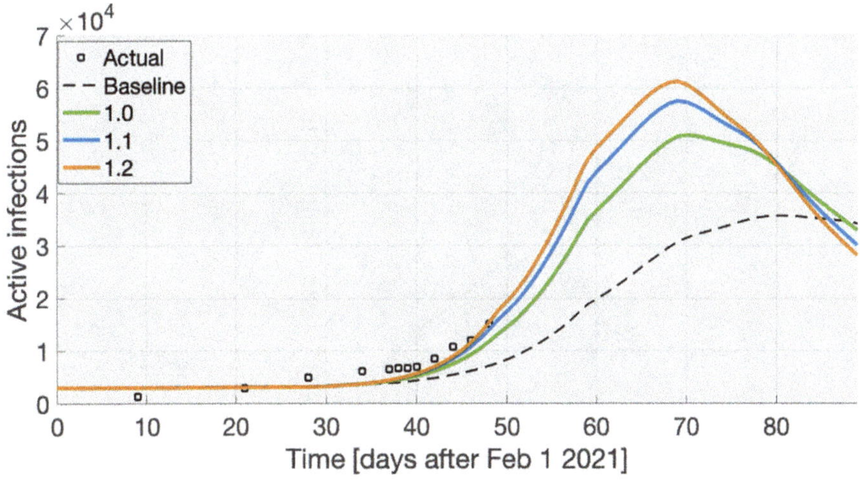

Fig. 2.8 Near-term trajectory of Covid-19 in Pune: actual and predictions

load on the healthcare system as well as ways to minimize the severity of the lockdown that followed.

Lessons from Covid-19: Similarity Metrics

The similarity metrics used for tuning epidemiological DTs are expected to be mutually consistent, in the sense that optimizing either metric should yield qualitatively identical conclusions. However, differences in the accuracy of measuring the metrics can lead to qualitative inconsistencies in the DT. In the specific case of Covid-19, the number of critical cases could be measured accurately because critical patients were usually hospitalized. On the other hand, a large number of active but mild or asymptomatic cases went unreported.

For the SIR model considered here, the primary set of parameters that had to be tuned consisted of the piecewise-constant-in-time values of the product of mixing and infectiousness. The trajectory of the epidemic predicted by models tuned to minimize the error in the number of *active infections* is shown in Fig. 2.9. We considered two sets of scenarios, one corresponding to no reinfection (i.e. lasting immunity following an initial infection, orange curve in the figure) and one corresponding to 10% reinfection (yellow and green curves in the figure). The blue curves in Fig. 2.9 show the officially reported statistics.

We note that the models tuned to minimize the error in the number of active cases overestimated the number of critical cases at the peak and mostly underestimated the cumulative number of deaths. This suggests a number of possibilities that need to be validated using an ABM. In this particular case, the most plausible such scenario (see Fig. 2.10) is that a fewer number of active cases turned critical due to immunity gained from previous infections, while a higher number of critical patients died due to the increased virulence of the variant.

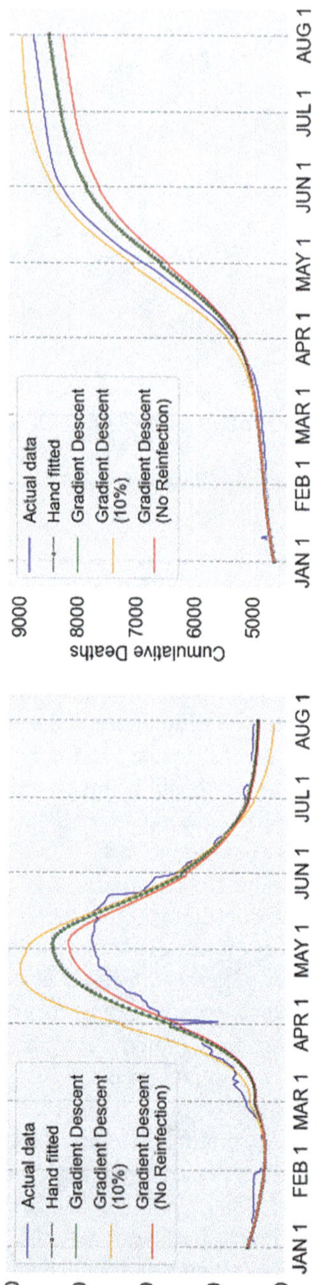

Fig. 2.9 Critical cases and cumulative deaths

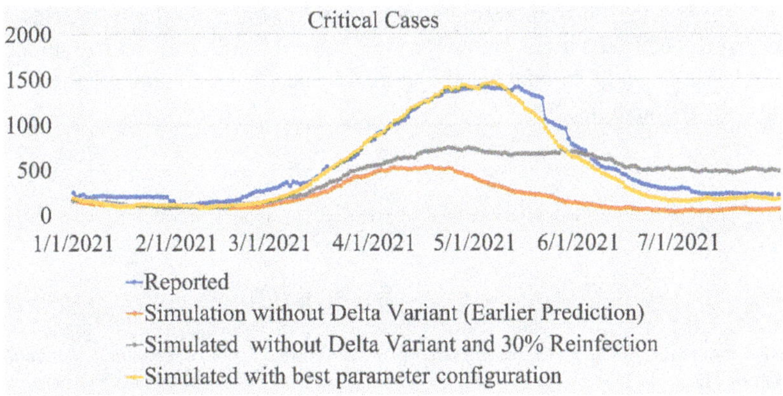

Fig. 2.10 Post hoc analysis of the trend in the number of critical cases

Concluding Discussion

Digital twins are a powerful tool to visualize, assess, and even transform real-world systems. In their stereotypical form, digital twins achieve a high degree of visual as well as behavioural fidelity by composing component-level twins. The resulting models may be too complex for the purpose of designing control and optimization algorithms, especially algorithms that rely on parameter search or learning-based methods. We reviewed formal model order reduction tools that can be employed in such cases to construct control-oriented digital twins (CODTs), which retain a faithful input-output representation for the purpose of designing control and optimization algorithms. Although CODTs are adequate for control *design*, the traditional high-fidelity twins are still necessary for verification of the control algorithms as well as the hypotheses obtained using the CODTs. This multi-model approach was demonstrated in this chapter via two case studies. The first case study featured an oil and gas refinery, as an example of systems governed by deterministic engineering principles. The second case study, based on an epidemiological model for Covid-19, illustrated similar working principles for a system governed by local, non-deterministic rules, wherein a low-fidelity model was used as an aid to parameter tuning in the high-fidelity DT.

A key challenge in operationalizing DTs is that of simultaneous state estimation and parameter and control law tuning. This is because state estimation relies on an accurate knowledge of the underlying dynamical system, including the tunable parameters, while parameter tuning requires a knowledge of the system state. While the problem of simultaneous state and parameter estimation has been solved in only the simplest of cases involving a class of linear systems (e.g. [5]), it remains an open problem for general systems. A partial, albeit practically useful, solution to this problem involves creating a library of models wherein the parameters are fixed at some prescribed value for each model in the library. Thereafter, a supervisory logic is used to select the most appropriate model based on the similarity metrics. This approach has been used traditionally for fault detection and isolation in engineering systems [6] and can be extended using more advanced classification methods [7] to digital twin applications.

References

1. Jordan, T., Langford, W., Belcastro, C., Foster, J., Shah, G., Howland, G., & Kidd, R. (2004). Development of a dynamically scaled generic transport model testbed for flight research experiments. In *AUVSI's unmanned systems North America 2004 symposium and exhibition*.
2. Astrom, K. J., & Murray, R. F. (2009). *Feedback systems: An introduction for scientists and engineers*. Princeton University Press.
3. Isidori, A. (2013). The zero dynamics of a nonlinear system: From the origin to the latest progresses of a long successful story. *European Journal of Control, 19*, 369–378.
4. Baranwal, M., Selukar, M., Lotti, R., Paranjape, A. A., Majumder, S., & Rocher, J. (2023). A scalable optimization framework for refinery operation and management. *Computers and Chemical Engineering, 174*, 108242.
5. Astrom, K. J., & Wittenmark, B. (2013). *Adaptive control* (2nd ed.). Dover Publications.
6. Blom, H. A. P., & Bar-Shalom, Y. (1988). The interacting multiple model algorithm for systems with Markovian switching coefficients. *IEEE Transactions on Automatic Control, 33*(8), 780–783.
7. Kapteyn, M. G., Pretorius, J. V. R., & Willcox, K. E. (2021). A probabilistic graphical model foundation for enabling predictive digital twins at scale. *Nature Computational Science, 1*(5), 337–347.

Chapter 3
Role of Enterprise Digital Twin in Enhancing Business Agility

Dushyanthi Mulpuru, Kaustav Bhattacharya, and Souvik Barat

Abstract In today's rapidly evolving business landscape, enterprises are increasingly confronted with a multitude of uncertainties arising from technological advancements, shifting customer preferences, competitive pressures, and global disruptions, such as pandemics and economic fluctuations. Navigating these uncertainties has become a critical determinant of organizational success and sustainability. Enterprises must not only respond to external challenges but also proactively optimize their internal capabilities to maintain a competitive edge. This necessitates enterprise to be agile to efficiently manage disruptions, seizing opportunities and sustaining performance under changing business conditions. This chapter introduces the concept of the enterprise digital twin (EDT) as an aid for risk-free business experimentation. By supporting simulation of enterprise and its environment including the entire ecosystem, the EDT empowers organizations to explore complex decision spaces, evaluate strategic options, and make evidence-based decisions. The chapter presents an overview of EDT and demonstrates its potential to enhance business agility.

D. Mulpuru (✉)
TCS Research, Tata Consultancy Services, Hyderabad, Telangana, India
e-mail: dushyanthi.mulpuru@tcs.com

K. Bhattacharya
Tata Consultancy Services, Chennai, Tamil Nadu, India
e-mail: kaustav.bhattacharya@tcs.com

S. Barat
TCS Research, Tata Consultancy Services, Pune, Maharashtra, India
e-mail: souvik.barat@tcs.com

V. Kulkarni et al. (eds.), *Digital Twins for Simulation-Based Decision-Making*,
https://doi.org/10.1007/978-3-031-89654-5_3

Introduction

Enterprises today operate in an environment characterized by unprecedented levels of volatility, uncertainty, complexity, and ambiguity (VUCA) [1]. They face disruptions across multiple dimensions including rapid technological advancements, volatile market dynamics, regulatory transformations, and global uncertainties [2]. These challenges are compounded by evolving customer expectations and the growing complexity of interconnected ecosystems. Modern enterprises are no longer isolated entities; they are part of a large dynamic ecosystem comprising customers, regulators, competitors, suppliers, etc.—where decisions in one entity such as supply chain disruptions or regulatory changes, etc. often have cascading effects across the entire ecosystem, significantly impacting enterprise resilience and performance. The ability to not just survive but thrive in such an environment has become a critical organizational imperative.

Enterprise agility is the ability of an enterprise to sense and respond rapidly to changes in its sociotechnical environment by dynamically orchestrating and changing strategic, tactical, and operational capabilities [3]. It involves adapting to evolving business contexts while maximizing productivity, enhancing customer satisfaction, and achieving enterprise goals. This requires enterprises to sense evolving context; understand their implication across interconnected systems; identify bottlenecks, threats, and opportunities; and take decisive action to mitigate potential disruptions.

However, decision-making in a volatile and uncertain environment is non-trivial. The complexity of enterprise decision-making arises from several factors, which include the need for balancing multiple, often conflicting, perspectives—such as strategic objectives, operational efficiency, financial constraints, customer satisfaction, technological capabilities, and so on. Decisions that optimize one perspective often have unintended consequences on others, revealing interdependencies that are not immediately apparent. This interconnected nature implies the local optimizations don't necessarily lead to global improvements. Additionally, enterprises must address varying forms of uncertainty: from well-understood processes (known-knowns) to recognized uncertainties with estimable probabilities (known-unknowns), hidden patterns in organizational data (unknown-knowns), and completely unforeseen disruptions (unknown-unknowns) at both enterprise and ecosystem level. Also, enterprise knowledge exists in diverse forms—from structured processes and operational data to expert knowledge, each requiring different approaches for representation and analysis.

Traditional approaches to enterprise decision-making prove inadequate in this context. Intuition-based decisions often fail to grasp complex system-wide implications. Pure data analytics, while valuable, struggle to capture emergent behaviors and non-linear relationships. Real-world experimentation carries prohibitive risks and costs, necessitating the ability to conduct risk-free business experimentation. This calls for sophisticated mechanisms capable of capturing the multifaceted nature of enterprises and enabling virtual experimentation to evaluate potential strategies, optimize decisions, and ensure sustained effectiveness across multiple time horizons before implementation in the real world.

Digital twin technology, having demonstrated significant value in physical and manufacturing systems, is well suited for addressing such challenges. By creating high-fidelity virtual representations of enterprise operations, processes, and behaviors, digital twins enable organizations to experiment with different scenarios and evaluate their impacts without real-world risks. This capability opens new business opportunities: from optimizing current operations and testing new business strategies to identifying potential vulnerabilities and developing preventive strategies. Enterprises can explore strategic alternatives and understand their implications across multiple dimensions before implementation.

However, applying digital twin technology to enterprises presents unique challenges. Unlike physical systems governed by natural laws, enterprises are complex socio-technical systems characterized by human behaviors, emergent behaviors, and evolving boundaries. Enterprise digital twins must capture this complexity while remaining practical for business decision-making. As discussed earlier, they need to handle multiple forms of uncertainty, integrate diverse data sources, and support analysis across different organizational perspectives and time horizons.

Our framework addresses these challenges through a comprehensive approach that combines an abstraction of actor/agent, metamodelling technique, and simulation capability. EDT uses actor abstraction to accurately mimic system of systems characteristic of enterprise. It uses a set of metamodels to capture the strategic and operational aspects of the enterprise in a structured and machine-processable form. Two metamodels are considered, namely, goal-measure-lever (GML) metamodel and actor metamodels. The GML metamodel provides a structured way to connect strategic objectives to operational decisions, while the Actor metamodel enables detailed modeling of relevant enterprise components and their interactions. This dual modeling approach ensures that EDT can effectively capture both "what" and "how" of enterprise operations, which would then be implemented in a simulatable specification. These models drive simulation-based analysis, enabling detailed what-if analyses and systematic evaluation of interventions across different time horizons. Through simulation-based experimentation, organizations can explore complex scenarios and understand their implications before implementation. The framework enables evidence-backed decision-making by integrating multiple forms of enterprise knowledge—from structured processes and historical data to expert knowledge and emerging patterns. It supports analysis across different organizational perspectives while handling various forms of uncertainty. Through real-world application in telecom industry, we demonstrate how EDTs enhance organizational resilience by enabling systematic exploration of strategic options and their implications.

The next section provides a brief background on enterprise agility and enterprise decision-making and explores the evolution of digital twin technology. We then discuss the characteristics and complexity of enterprises that necessitate specialized approaches. We then present our EDT framework, detailing its technical foundations, implementation methodology, and validation approaches. We then demonstrate the practical application of EDT on a real-life case. We conclude by discussing future directions.

Background

Enterprise Agility

Enterprise agility has become essential for sustaining competitiveness and achieving resilience in an environment characterized by uncertainty and dynamism. This requirement is becoming critical for modern enterprises due to intense competition, shifting market demands, and emerging sociotechnical disruptions. Agility within an enterprise can be visualized from two distinct but interconnected perspectives: strategic and operational.

From a strategic perspective, enterprises must rapidly adapt their strategies to capture emerging opportunities and mitigate potential threats. Such strategic agility empowers enterprises to design and reconfigure their products, services, and value propositions to ensure alignment with long-term goals while responding to a constantly evolving external environment. In contrast, operational agility focuses on the efficient execution of business-as-usual activities and processes. This involves optimizing workflows, aligning resources, and ensuring responsiveness to immediate threats without compromising overall performance. Achieving enterprise agility requires synergy between these strategic and operational dimensions.

Complexity in Achieving Enterprise Agility

Attaining enterprise agility is inherently complex due to the multifaceted nature of contemporary enterprises where complexity arises from several factors:

System of systems: Large enterprises are not monolithic business units; rather, they are complex system of systems. They comprise a large number of interconnected units or departments with diverse objectives, processes, people, and infrastructure. These units work together, yet their distinct goals and interdependencies create dynamic behaviors making the enterprise highly intricate and adaptive.

Nonlinearity: Relationships between different components of an enterprise are nonlinear, i.e., small changes in one area can lead to disproportionate effects elsewhere. This characteristic makes predicting outcomes and managing changes highly challenging.

Emergent behavior: The interconnected subsystems within an enterprise often exhibit emergent behaviors, where the system as a whole behaves in ways that cannot be directly inferred from its individual components. This unpredictability complicates decision-making for both strategic and operational changes.

Uncertainty: Enterprises operate in environments characterized by high levels of uncertainty, including technological disruptions, regulatory shifts, and economic volatility. This uncertainty necessitates continuous monitoring and the capacity for rapid responses, which are both knowledge- and effort-intensive activities.

Dynamism: Rapidly changing internal and external conditions require enterprises to continuously adapt their processes and strategies. Managing such dynamism without creating inefficiencies poses a significant challenge.

Capabilities Required to Achieve Enterprise Agility

To address these complexities and achieve the desired level of agility, enterprises must develop two critical capabilities that allow them to navigate challenges effectively.

Sense and predict: Enterprises must explore mechanisms for sensing and predicting the state of the enterprise. Sensing and prediction should include identification of bottlenecks, understanding their root causes, and predicting potential future states if operations continue unchanged. This involves the ability to interpret environmental events, recognize emerging trends, and assess disruptions or opportunities systematically.

Analyze and act: Enterprises need to enhance their ability to evaluate and act through risk-free exploration and evidence-based decision-making. This shift from intuition-based to evidence-driven approaches requires actionable insights derived from rigorous analysis. State-of-the-art exploration, often involving trial-and-error experimentation, is inherently resource-intensive; moreover, they are vulnerable to risk. Therefore, enterprises must develop a system that can facilitate a controlled and risk-mitigated evaluations of new initiatives.

Enterprise Decision-Making

Modern enterprises must make effective strategic and operational decisions to achieve their goals while operating in highly dynamic environments. This requires a systematic approach to precisely understand the enterprise and dynamism of the environment, evaluating possible interventions and implementing changes. We represent enterprise decision-making process using a conceptual model shown in Fig. 3.1. As shown in the figure, enterprise decision-making process typically triggers from an intension to achieve a set of goals or target state. These goals are measured by introspecting key performance indicators (KPIs), which we term as measures. Measures are evaluated through state variables representing current state and historical states (termed as trace in the figure). Decision-making process considers changes or interventions either when goals are not achieved (often termed as reactive decision-making) or there is a possibility to miss the target in future (termed

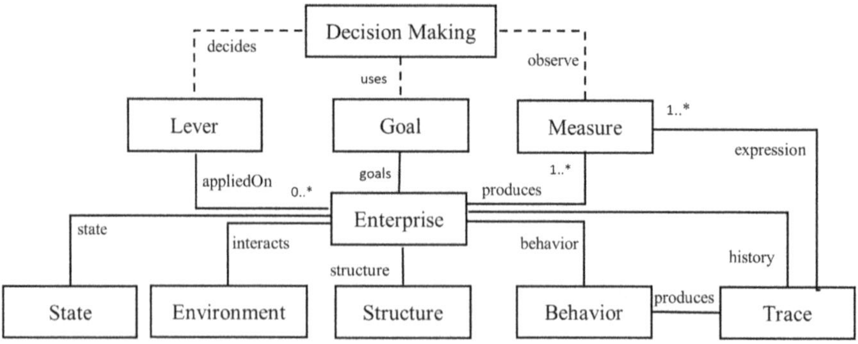

Fig. 3.1 Metamodel of enterprise decision-making

as proactive decision-making). We call these changes in enterprise structure or interventions in behavior of enterprise units or people as levers. The key question of a decision-making process is to identify the potential levers and understand their efficacies toward achieving the desired target or goals.

In this conceptual decision-making framework, goals drive organizational direction and help identify the appropriate measures. Measures track the enterprise state and progress toward goals. Levers represent the actionable interventions available to decision-makers to influence enterprise behavior and drive desired outcomes. As changes are implemented through these levers, they influence the enterprise structure and behavior, creating observable state changes that are captured by measures. The enterprise maintains trace of actions and their outcomes (i.e., corporate memory) that can influence future decisions. The dynamic interplay between these elements creates feedback mechanisms. For instance, when a lever is applied to specific units or people, it creates cascading changes across different enterprise units. These changes manifest in measure values, which in turn influence the future decision choices. The feedback mechanism between lever configuration and its measured outcomes is complex because multiple interconnected measures respond at different times and scales.

For instance, consider a telecom enterprise seeking to optimize revenue through customer plan upgrades: Primary goal of revenue optimization decomposes into sub-goals like increasing plan upgrades and improving customer retention. Measures might include tracking average revenue per user (ARPU), plan conversion rates, usage patterns, etc. Levers include changes in pricing, introduction of a new plan, plan feature adjustments, and so on. The interactions between these elements create complex dynamics. For instance, implementing a price change lever might immediately affect customer behavior, leading to gradual or sudden shift in usage patterns, resulting in additional load on customer care with long-term impacts on customer satisfaction and churn—all providing feedback on that single lever configuration. These changes could trigger both positive outcomes like increased ARPU and potential risks like decreased satisfaction and higher churn, which influence goal achievement. This interrelated set of measures makes it challenging to isolate cause-and-effect relationships and optimize lever settings. This multidimensional feedback nature combined with the autonomous behavior of enterprise components makes it challenging to predict efficacy of levers through traditional analytical approaches. The enterprise must monitor these measure changes to validate lever effectiveness and potentially adjust its intervention strategy.

In enterprise digital twin, we consider this decision-making model as a purpose for constructing a digital twin. The section "Enterprise Digital Twin" builds upon this foundation to create digital twins that enable systematic in silico exploration of strategic and operational levers prior to their implementation.

Digital Twin

While the term "digital twin" traces its origins to 2002 when Michael Grieves at the University of Michigan introduced the "Mirrored Spaces Model" while working on product life cycle management [4], the concept exists since the late 1990s. This canonical model of digital twin establishes three core components that continue to define digital twins today: the physical space (real system), virtual space (digital model), and the connecting data flow between them. By 2006, this evolved into the "information mirroring model" emphasizing the importance of bidirectional information flow and the ability to maintain multiple virtual representations of a single physical entity [5].

The term "digital twin" also appeared in NASA's 2010 technology roadmap [6], where it was defined as an integrated multi-physics, multi-scale simulation that could mirror physical systems. This period established technology's practical value for complex system management in the aerospace sector, with NASA utilizing digital twin concepts for space vehicle development and US Air Force adopting the technology for aircraft design and maintenance.

Technology progressed through distinct levels of sophistication as shown in Fig. 3.2—from basic digital models with manual data exchange between physical and virtual objects to digital shadows with automated one-way data flow from physical to the digital object and finally to true digital twins featuring complete bidirectional automation. The Center for Digital Built Britain describes digital shadow as "Static Digital Model" and digital twin as "Dynamic Digital Model," as the data in

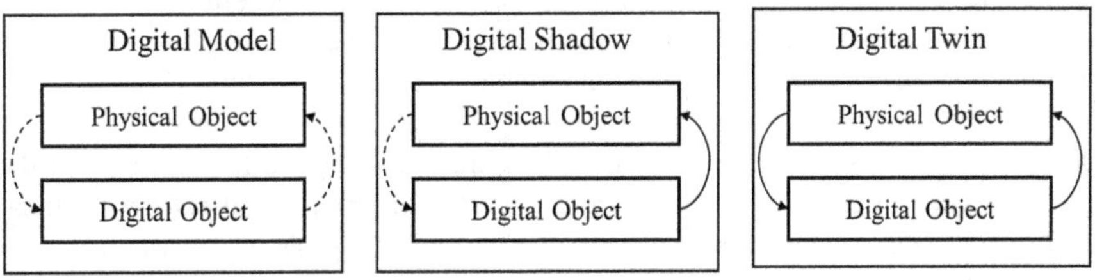

Fig. 3.2 Types of DT based on data exchange

the dynamic one are fed live, which can be used for a real-time control mechanism, whereas in the static model, data are added with time, making it more suitable for strategic planning.

This progression, coupled with advances in computing power, has opened new possibilities of leveraging digital twin across various domains. Domains, such as manufacturing, automotive, and aerospace, which are well studied and chiefly governed by scientific laws, have experienced high adoption rates. In 2018, Gartner [7] highlighted digital twin technology as an emerging technology and predicted its hype cycle. Since this report, many organizations have started exploring various possibilities of digital twin for a wide range of business domains for defining strategies and optimizing operational aspects.

Applying Digital Twin for Enterprise

Digital twin technology, while proven effective for physical systems, presents unique challenges for application to enterprise systems. The fundamental difference lies in the nature of the systems being modeled. Physical systems operate under well-defined scientific laws with clearly defined behaviors and a relatively static environment. In contrast, modern enterprises represent complex socio-technical systems characterized by high degrees of uncertainty, emergent behaviors, and less clearly defined boundaries as discussed in the earlier section. Unlike physical systems, which are often conceptualized as monolithic unit and modelled using a set of mathematical equations, an enterprise is a combination of a large number of units, subunits, and people, each having their individual objectives. These units and people act based on their localized objectives with incomplete information and shifting priorities, all of which significantly affect the system's behavior. The collective effect of these elements results in emergent patterns that can either amplify or dampen organizational objectives in ways that couldn't be predicted from individual behavior alone. Therefore, modelling an enterprise using traditional modelling techniques, such as mathematical equation, is not a pragmatic approach.

From systems theory perspective, enterprise complexity emerges from the intricate interplay between structural elements (organizational units, processes, resources), behavioral dynamics (localized decisions, interactions), and environmental factors (e.g., micro- and macro-uncertainties in market forces, technological change, regulatory requirement). Within this context, cause-and-effect relationships are rarely linear, and system boundaries continually evolve as enterprises respond to internal and external changes. These interactions generate dynamic behaviors that manifest across both spatial and temporal perspectives. For instance, a strategic decision like introducing a new product line creates a ripple effect throughout the organization—affecting everything from operational process and resource allocation to customer relationships and market positioning. These effects aren't merely additive; they create emergent behaviors that arise from the collective interactions between various organizational components and cannot be predicted by analyzing components in isolation.

Moreover, enterprises must deal with varying levels of uncertainty in modeling the behaviors. The nature of enterprise operations requires varying approaches to represent how different units and people behave and interact—from well-understood processes that can be explicitly specified to situations requiring probabilistic handling due to uncertainty to behaviors involving multiple interacting criteria to patterns that can be learned from historical data. These factors necessitate a paradigm shift in how digital twins are constructed and implemented for enterprise contexts. The system must support multiple forms of knowledge representation and uncertainty handling while capturing both structured processes and emergent behaviors. The system must support decision-making across different time horizons and multi-perspective analysis while maintaining practical usability for business stakeholders.

Enterprise Digital Twin

Building on the enterprise decision-making framework discussed earlier, enterprise digital twin (EDT) serves as aid for evaluating levers toward achieving goals in an enterprise with its socio-technical characteristics. Fundamentally, EDT is implemented using an actor-based framework [8] that enables modeling and analysis of complex enterprise through bottom-up model construction and simulation. This approach is particularly effective for capturing inherent complexities of socio-technical system of systems, where behaviors emerge from interactions of autonomous entities. It represents enterprise entities as computational actors that maintain state and interact with other actors through events, naturally mapping to real-world enterprise structures where different organizational units operate with varying degrees of independence while remaining interconnected through well-defined interactions.

Modeling Abstraction

Figure 3.3 provides a conceptual mapping between enterprise and enterprise decision-making concepts to actor-based realization. As shown in the figure, decision-making concepts like goal, measure, and lever and enterprise-specific concepts, such as state, structure, and behavior of the entities, are mapped to an extended form of actor and its properties. In abstract, entities are represented using an extended form of conventional actors [8] where these extended actors encapsulate the required state, behavioral specification, and interaction capabilities of enterprise entities. These actors can contain other actors, creating natural hierarchical structures that mirror enterprise structure and system of system nature.

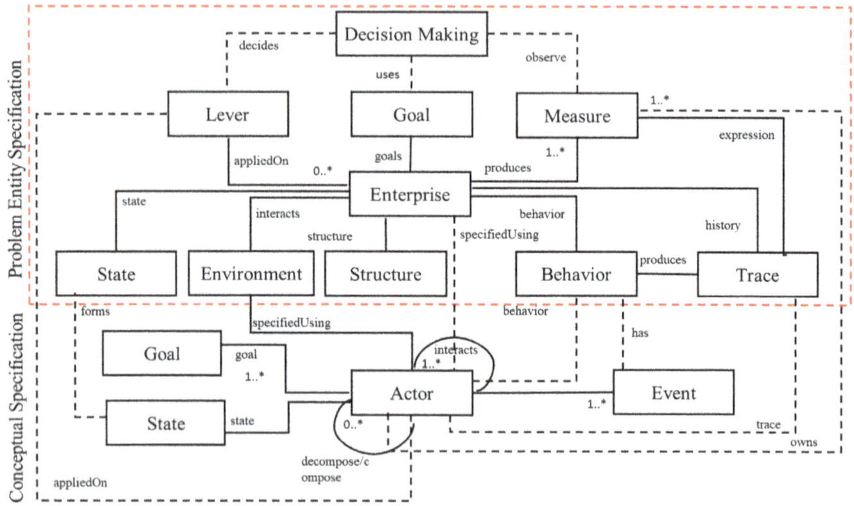

Fig. 3.3 Mapping from enterprise concepts to implementation

To represent enterprise entities in a faithful manner, these actors encapsulate two types of attributes, state variables and characteristic variables, as illustrated in Fig. 3.4. State variables (shown using $SV_1 \ldots SV_m$ in Fig. 3.4) represent dynamic properties of the actor that change over time, while characteristic variables (i.e., $CV_1 \ldots CV_n$) represent fixed properties or affinities of enterprise entities. Abstraction also supports a sophisticated event-handling mechanism to mimic entity behavior and interaction patterns. Events can be either time based or interaction based. Time-based events are triggered by temporal or state conditions, comprising periodic events, such as daily reports and monthly bill generation, as well as state-dependent events such as capacity thresholds being reached or performance triggers being activated. Interaction-based events enable actor to actor communication, which is implemented through a messaging mechanism within the framework. System-wide events can affect multiple actors simultaneously. They are crucial for modeling ecosystem phenomenon like regulatory changes or market disruptions. The behavior of actors can be specified using events (i.e., $E_1 \ldots E_k$) and actions ($A_1 \ldots A_z$) sets as shown in Fig. 3.4. The framework supports multi-modelling technique to specify actor behaviors for different situations:

(a) For well-understood known-known behaviors, it supports a deterministic rule-based event-condition-action (ECA) paradigm. In this type of specification, event triggers evaluation of conditions over actor attributes to determine appropriate actions.
(b) Where behavior involves uncertainty (i.e., known-unknown behavior), ECA rules are augmented with probabilistic affinities to introduce stochasticity while performing actions.

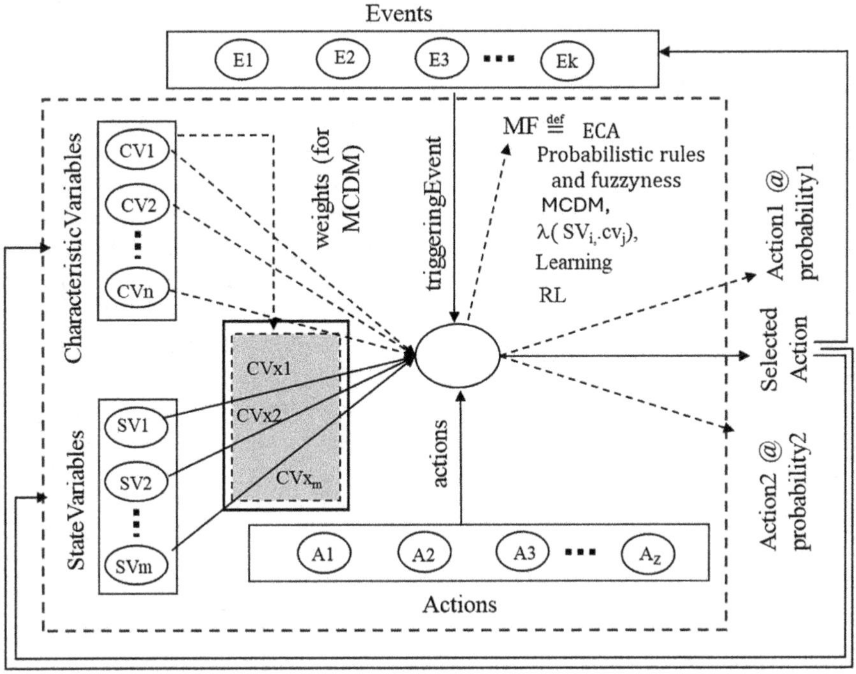

Fig. 3.4 Multi-modelling abstraction

(c) For unknown-known situations, i.e., behavior is not known explicitly but data describing historical contexts exist, the perceptron or neural network–based specification is considered, where weighted sum of characteristic variables and threshold value is used to trigger actions.
(d) For complex decisions involving multiple criteria, such as matching products to customer preferences, MCDM formulas help rank and select actions based on weighted attributes and utility functions.

The difference between the perception and utility MCDM–based approaches is how the characteristics variables (weights for input values and resistance function) are derived. For perception, these characteristics variables are trained based on historical data, whereas these values are specified by domain experts from their experience MCDM. In cases where behavior patterns must be learned from historical data, machine learning models can be integrated. This fine-grained modeling approach enables representation of enterprise complexities including autonomy in actor behavior, uncertainty through probabilistic specifications, and emergent behavior through bottom-up composition of actor behaviors.

Specifications

As illustrated in Fig. 3.5, two complimentary metamodels that provide a structured framework for capturing intent and behavioral aspects are considered: goal-measures-levers (GML) metamodel and actor metamodel. GML metamodel serves as the primary lens for capturing intent of decision-making through goal decomposition structure, key performance indicators (KPIs), and levers. In this formalism, the goals are hierarchically decomposed into finer goals, and leaf-level goals are linked to measures. These measures track achievements of leaf-level goals. Levers influence system structure and behavior—an aid for constructing what-if and if-what analyses. The actor metamodel, in contrast, provides a structured way of representing enterprise units and their interactions. These include actors as a means to decompose system into autonomous units representing the system-of-system nature of the enterprise. These actors encapsulate their states, characteristics, and behaviors using attributes, events, and actions. These actors use events to specify interaction patterns.

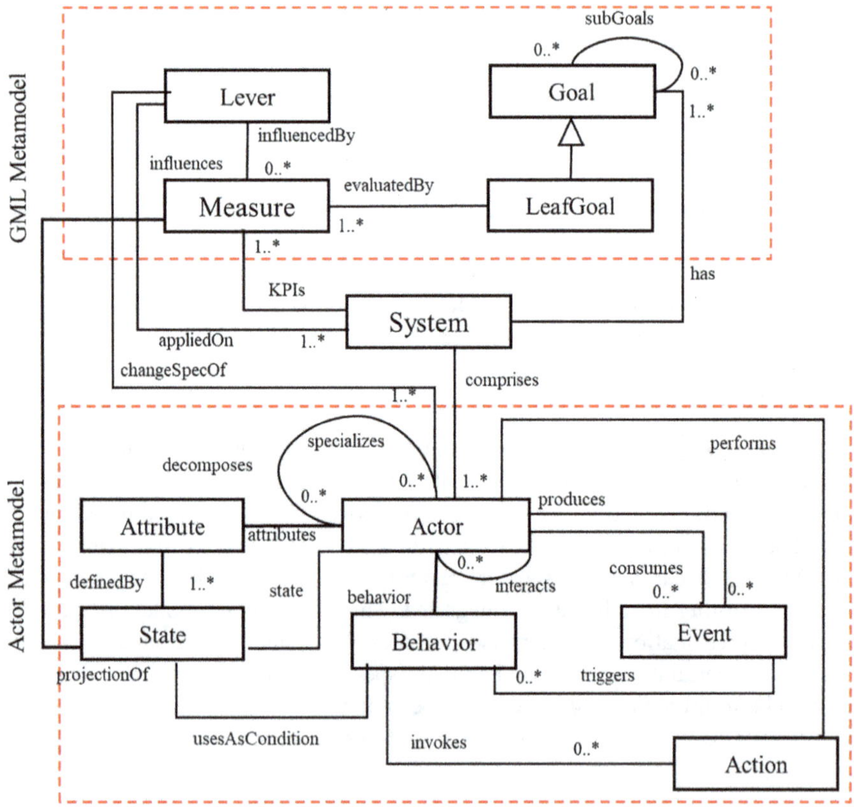

Fig. 3.5 Digital twin metamodels

Together, these metamodels constitute the requirement space. The GML metamodel guides the identification of actors and their behaviors by establishing the goals to be achieved, measures to track progress, and the levers available for intervention, while the actor metamodel drives the implementation specification by capturing the requirements that need to be incorporated into simulatable EDT specification. This structured approach ensures traceability between organizational goals and their implementation in the digital twin. The metamodel-based specifications are implemented in ESL (enterprise simulation language) [9], a textual actor–based modeling language extended to support EDT's modeling abstractions and simulation requirements. ESL provides the implementation framework for actor specifications and the runtime environment for simulation.

Construction Methodology

EDT construction methodology has evolved from a traditional effort- and time-intensive domain expert–led approach to LLM-led semi-automated process that maintains model fidelity while improving accessibility and efficiency.

Traditional Domain Expert–Led Construction

Knowledge Elicitation

The traditional approach relies heavily on direct interactions between modelers and subject matter experts (SMEs) or domain experts. Figure 3.6 depicts the SME-led conceptual model construction method. Modelers conduct systematic interviews with SMEs, often involving multiple SMEs across several sessions. These interactions take the form of iterative question-answer sessions where modelers formulate

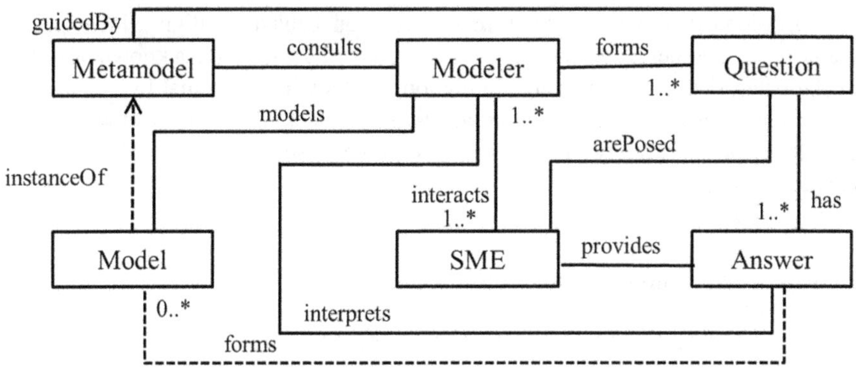

Fig. 3.6 SME-led conceptual model construction

specific questions guided by metamodels and SMEs provide detailed answers based on their domain expertise.

Questions based on the GML metamodel explore the following aspects: "What are the goals of the enterprise?" "Can these goals be broken down into smaller goals?", "What indicators help understand the achievability of these goals?", and "What interventions/levers can improve these measures?" Similarly, the types of questions derived from actor metamodels include the following: "Who are the relevant business stakeholders, actors, and agents that form the system?", "What are their attributes or variables?", and "What is their behavior?" This question-answer process continues until modelers complete navigation of all concepts defined in the metamodel and SMEs confirm that all relevant aspects have been captured in a comprehensive manner in a conceptual model form.

Model Construction

The elicited knowledge in conceptual model is first transformed into a conceptual model as instances of actor metamodel. In this step, modelers interpret SME responses and convert them into model instances following actor metamodel structures. Subsequently, this conceptual model is translated into simulatable specification, where we use ESL as simulatable specification. This transformation needs to ensure that domain knowledge is accurately reflected into the final specification while maintaining actor-based semantics required for simulation.

Validation

As shown in Fig. 3.7, validation operates throughout the construction process across multiple dimensions. It begins with conceptual validation to ensure accurate representation of real-world system. As models are translated to computational form, computerized model verification ensures faithful implementation. Data validity ensures the data flowing from real system to the simulation model is accurate.

Operational validation verifies that simulation behaviors align with expected real-world outcomes. It is done by calibrating the model to match a known past state of the enterprise and comparing simulation results with the actual historical data. This comprehensive validation approach with feedback loops ensures the resulting digital twin accurately represents the enterprise system's behavior and characteristics.

LLM-Assisted Semi-automated Construction

The approach has evolved to leverage metamodels more systematically through integration with LLMs, which serve as virtual SMEs while maintaining SME oversight. Figure 3.8 depicts the LLM-led conceptual model construction method. The approach has two core components: prompt generator and model creator.

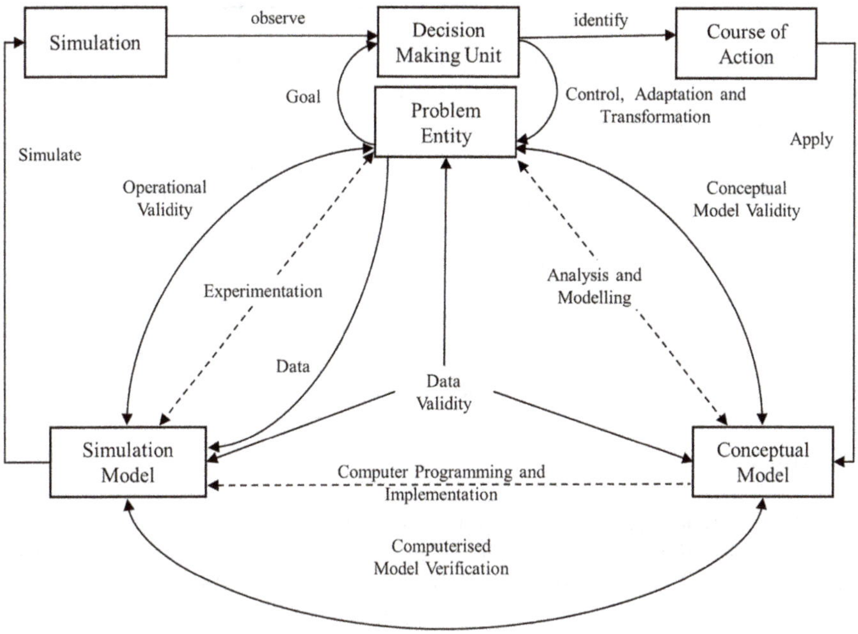

Fig. 3.7 Construction, validation, and experimentation method

Prompt Generation System

Prompt generator generates a sequence of well-formed prompts. It considers inputs from three components: objective, context, and org knowledge. Objective component navigates metamodel entities and associations to produce sequence of prompts. Context component stores previously extracted model instances in an orderly manner and sequentially supply them as context. Org knowledge contains organization-specific information to augment the prompt generator for supplementing the prompt with suitable example and/or additional information. The prompts are further augmented with certain guardrails and formatting instructions and then prompted to LLM for response as shown in the below textbox.

Explore Sub-Goal(s)
Goal (Improve revenue).
Provide response strictly as a string separated by commas. Strictly no bullet points, quotes or any other formatting
Provide the names of Actors
System (Telecom)

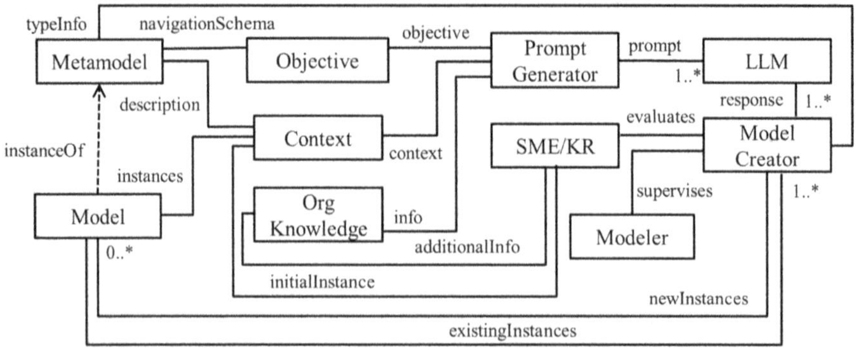

Fig. 3.8 LLM-led conceptual model construction

Model Generation Pipeline

The model creator processes LLM responses to automatically generate model instances maintaining consistency. Each response is processed to extract relevant information and transformed into formal model elements while ensuring consistency with metamodel constraints. The resulting model instances are then automatically translated into ESL specifications through well-defined transformation rules, maintaining traceability between conceptual and computational representations.

Construction Modes and Validation

LLM-assisted approach supports two distinct modes of model construction and validation: automated and user-assisted mode. In automated mode, the prompt generator generates prompts, and the model generator processes LLM responses and creates model instances. Complete model construction occurs in an automated manner without user intervention. However, users can subsequently refine the generated model by overwriting LLM responses. The system allows for multiple executions of the same prompt—since LLMs are stochastic, meaning the same prompt may produce different responses. These responses are aggregated to create a more comprehensive model. The prompt execution count is configurable but remains fixed across all prompts.

The user-guided mode, in contrast, requires SME evaluation at each step. After each LLM response, SMEs have the option to modify, accept, or reject the LLM response, as well as provide additional context for improvement. User has control over the number of times each prompt is executed. The final response must be approved by the SMEs before moving on to the next prompt. This flexibility of having these two construction modes allows organizations to choose between rapid model creation and fine-grained control.

Expert oversight remains crucial throughout this process, with SMEs reviewing generated elements, validating relationships, and refining organizational context.

The validation layer includes mechanisms for capturing expert feedback and incorporating it into subsequent model refinements. This human-in-the-loop approach combines the efficiency of automation with the accuracy of expert knowledge.

Comparative Analysis of Construction Method

Both traditional SME-led approach and LLM-based SME-in-the-loop approach present distinct advantages and unique challenges. Traditional approaches, while capable of producing high-fidelity models, face limitations including heavy reliance on scarce modeling expertise, the time and effort-intensive nature of capturing domain knowledge, coordination challenges due to SME availability, and the potential for inconsistencies in how knowledge is interpreted by modelers.

The LLM-assisted approach addresses these limitations through accelerated model creation and systematic metamodel coverage providing structured knowledge capture and transformation. The transformation process maintains bidirectional traceability between metamodels, instance models, and their ESL implementation, while model-checking capabilities validate structural consistency and conformance to metamodel. This structured approach ensures comprehensive coverage of both purposive aspects (what needs to be achieved) and computational elements (how it will be implemented). However, the approach may require additional validation cycles to ensure accuracy (chiefly caused by LLM limitations like hallucinations).

Simulation-Led Experimentation

The digital twin enables risk-free experimentation through simulation. As illustrated in Fig. 3.9, a journey of risk-free experimentation begins with the creation of a purposive digital twin with specific GML model and actor model—a high-fidelity

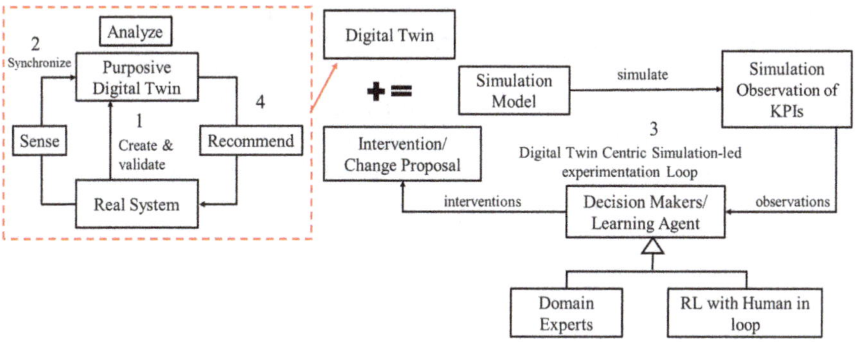

Fig. 3.9 Applying simulation as decision-making aid

virtual representation of the real system constructed to capture specific aspects critical for decision-making scenarios. The systematic processes of creation, validation, and synchronization align the digital twin with the real system.

The experimentation loop allows testing different interventions without risking disruption to the real organization, i.e., digital-twin led what-if and if-what analyses. The experimentation follows a structured approach, where the process of an experiment or what-if analysis for a scenario starts with proposing an intervention or lever—for example, changing resource budget. These levers can be identified through multiple approaches: domain experts leveraging their experience and contextual understanding, reinforcement learning for automated intervention discovery of levers [10], or qualitative methods such as design thinking methodology [11].

The proposed levers are fed into the conceptual model and then introduced into the simulation model performing simulation-led experimentation. The simulation model processes these levers and generates measures for the scenario—indicating how the proposed changes might affect the organization. Domain experts, with their experience and contextual understanding, analyze simulation results to interpret outcomes, or alternatively, a reinforcement learning (RL) system with human in the loop can be employed. Based on analysis of each simulation run, levers can be adjusted using any of the three approaches—domain experts can suggest refinements, RL systems can propose optimized configurations, or design thinking methods can guide systematic modifications. This creates a continuous learning loop where each iteration helps better understand the influence of interventions on the system.

Systematic Scenario Exploration

Scenario exploration follows a structured, iterative process designed to understand organizational behavior under varying conditions:

Initial setup: Actors and their attributes are configured to accurately represent the current state of the enterprise. This setup establishes the baseline for experimentation, allowing interventions to be evaluated against it.

Scenario definition: Scenarios are created by systematically varying lever configurations to influence actor behaviors, attributes, and interactions. This step involves defining the scenario parameters and their possible ranges.

Simulation strategy: Multiple simulation runs are conducted for each scenario to ensure the statistical validity of observed behaviors. For probabilistic scenarios, enough runs are performed to ensure statistical convergence.

Analysis: The impact of levers on organizational objectives is evaluated, identifying patterns that emerge across various scenarios. This analysis provides decision-makers with evidence-based insights to guide strategic decisions.

Case Studies

Over the years, we have applied EDT to a broad range of enterprise-level decision problems, such as enhancing throughput, operational excellence and resource utilization of sorting terminals in the postal industry [12], and addressing supply chain-related issues in the retail space [10]. Additionally, our technology has been used in various societal problems, such as predicting the spread of the Covid-19 epidemic in an Indian city with a population of four million and evaluating the efficacy of non-pharmaceutical interventions to reduce infection spread [13]. During the Covid-19 pandemic, it has also been leveraged to understand the project-level impact of Covid infections on employees and their family members within our organization, which comprises 400,000+ employees [14]. Through these applications, EDT has demonstrated its value as an effective approach for risk-free business experimentation and evidence-backed decision-making. In this section, we illustrate the practical application of EDT framework using one such scenario from a telecom domain, where a leading telecom company used EDT to optimize their customer migration strategy during the Covid-19 pandemic [15].

The Covid-19-pandemic-induced restrictions drove a surge in demand for telecom services as people relied on connectivity for work and entertainment. This presented a leading telecom provider with a complex business challenge of optimizing their customer base migration strategy. Analytics showed Average Revenue per User (ARPU) of metered customers was 40–45% lower than unlimited plan customers. While major telcos offered free extra GBs of data to their metered customers to help citizens adapt to the new normal, the eventual objective was to nudge customers toward unlimited plans. For the telco we worked with, around 16% were metered customers, constituting a significant revenue growth opportunity through conversion to unlimited plan subscribers.

The complexity of this business challenge manifested across multiple dimensions. The organization needed to understand not only how to nudge maximum number of metered customers but also determine the ideal product offerings and optimal timing for each customer segment. More importantly, achieving good "take rates" during the free trial period was insufficient—customers needed to retain the offer post-trial period to contribute to revenue and ARPU uplift. This required nuanced understanding of customer behavior and preferences for unlimited plans while determining the optimal timing for conversion initiatives. This also needs to account for the unprecedented circumstances of the pandemic, which had fundamentally altered typical usage patterns and economic conditions. These challenges were further complicated by the need to manage service delivery during pandemic restrictions all while maintaining revenue growth in an increasingly uncertain economic environment.

To address these challenges, we constructed an EDT featuring a comprehensive model of the telecom ecosystem. Figure 3.10 illustrates the model structure and key relationships: The customer forms the customer base, which contributes to the revenue and ARPU metrics. Each customer subscribes to the Products/Plans offered by

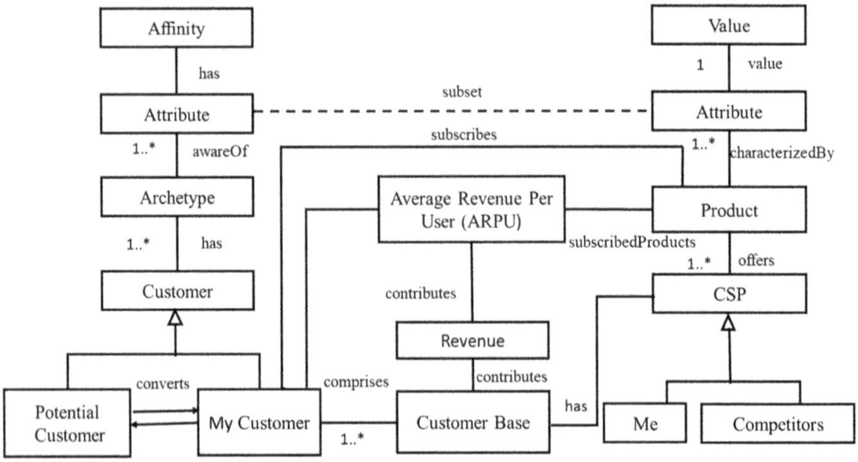

Fig. 3.10 An overview of the telecom model

CSP (Communication Service Provider), which includes the provider in our context (Me) and the competitors. The model captures product-customer relationships—each product in the product portfolio is characterized by product attributes having specific value. It is linked to customer affinities, which are derived from customer archetypes, creating a mapping between the customer characteristics and product features. This mapping enables us to employ MCDM approaches to simulate customer choices, where product selection decisions are based on multiple factors including product attributes, customer affinities, and contextual conditions.

The implementation included 374,000 targeted customers segmented into 109 distinct archetypes, along with the complete product portfolio of existing and proposed service plans, the trial rollout process, and all channels and technology resources involved in supporting and measuring campaign success. It incorporated revenue tracking through detailed ARPU calculations. KPI metrics include CIR, survey and feedback score, active customers per plan, plan-specific revenue, overall revenue trends, post-trail retention rates, conversion rates from metered to unlimited plans, customer care service loads, and service interaction patterns. The digital twin captured both structural and behavioral aspects of this complex business system. Each customer was modeled as an actor with state variables capturing current plan status, usage patterns, response to offers and service interactions, and so on, while characteristic attributes include device specifications, customer profiles and location data, various affinities about preferred channels for offer related communication, usage patterns, and behavioral patterns, such as brand consciousness and other interests. The behavior specifications include probabilistic responses to offers based on customer segment, time-dependent usage patterns reflecting pandemic phases, channel-specific interaction patterns, and so on. Customer segmentation into 109 distinct archetypes enabled precise definition of probability ranges for various behaviors determined through a combination of machine learning models applied to historical customer data and expert adjustment for evolving situations. Various types of events incorporated in the simulation include:

- Time-based events: monthly billing cycles, offer expiration period
- State-dependent events: usage threshold triggers, payment patterns
- Interaction events: customer service interactions, offer responses
- System-wide events: lockdown implementations, policy changes

The simulation was designed to handle multiple time scales, a characteristic of enterprise operations:

- Short term: daily usage patterns and service interactions
- Medium term: trial period behaviors and initial conversions
- Long term: post-trial retention and revenue impacts

Environmental factors formed a crucial component of the implementation, particularly given the unique circumstances of the pandemic. The model incorporated lockdown measures and their phased relaxation as time-bound stochastic behaviors, enabling representation of unprecedented changes in customer behavior and market conditions. This approach allowed the digital twin to capture not just individual customer responses but also the emergent patterns of collective behavior that arose from changing social and economic conditions. Service consumption patterns, for instance, emerged not merely from individual usage decisions but from the complex interplay between work-from-home requirements, economic constraints, and evolving digital needs.

The EDT was validated through multiple approaches:

- Conceptual validation: model elements verified with domain experts.
- Operational validation: DT was contextualized with precise as-is product definitions, and environment situation is simulated from January 2020. The simulation results are compared till April 2020 for validation.

Illustrative KPI values are shown using EDT dashboard in Fig. 3.11 (actual results are not depicted due to confidentiality). The validation process revealed several insights that challenged initial assumptions about customer behavior during the pandemic. While the initial hypothesis suggested mobile data usage would surge exponentially during lockdown, detailed analysis revealed a different pattern—most data traffic was being routed through fiber broadband-based high-speed home Internet. Further examination of data usage revealed that the buying power of target customers had diminished during the pandemic, largely due to business environment uncertainty and week-on-week economic conditions. These insights required adjustments to the digital twin as part of the validation and correction process, ensuring conceptual validity and operational validity for necessary corrections.

The validated EDT enabled systematic exploration of various business scenarios, particularly in product configuration and pricing strategies, few of which are illustrated in Fig. 3.12. Through virtual experimentation, the organization tested different combinations of unlimited plan features, exploring various price points, add-on allowances, and voice minutes conditionality, providing insights into customer

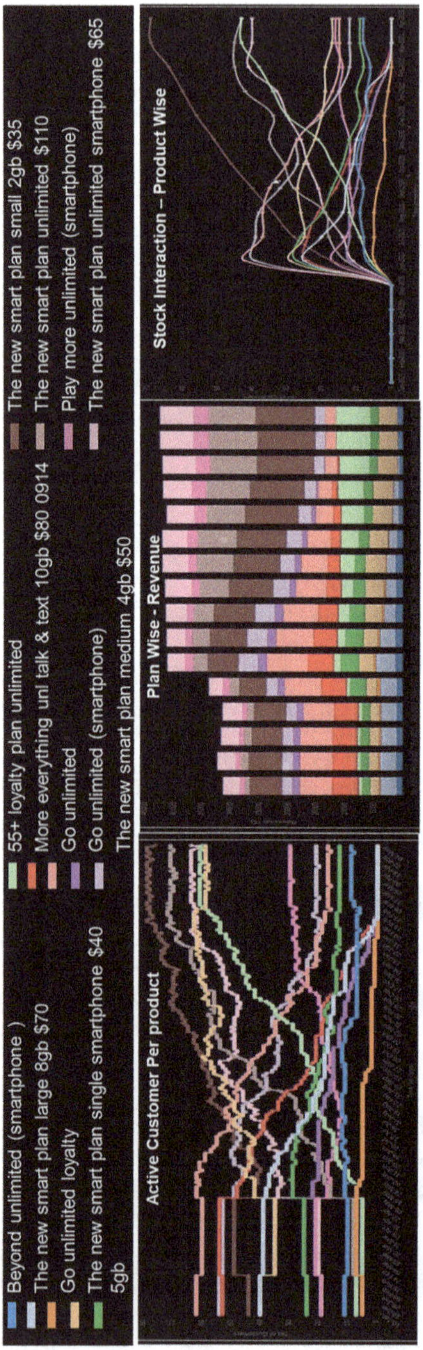

(a) Trends on Active Customer per Product (b) Overall and product specific revenue (c) Load on customer care service

Fig. 3.11 EDT simulation dashboard

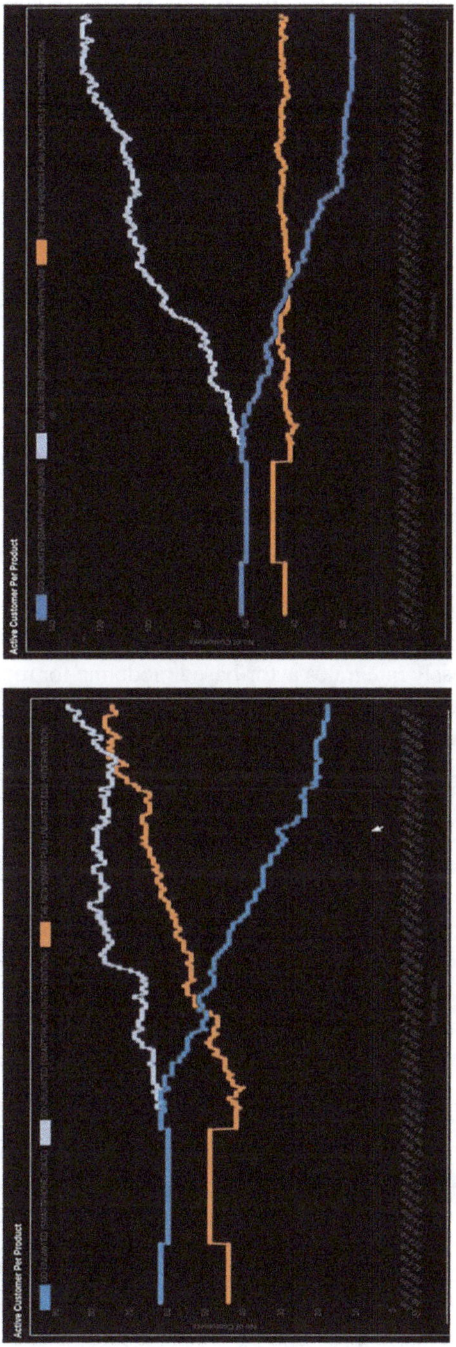

(a) Trend for as-is product vs Configuration 1

(b) Trend for Configuration 2

Fig. 3.12 Comparative analysis and trade-offs

preferences and adoption likelihood across different segments. This systematic experimentation process, replacing traditional A/B testing, provided insights into which features would positively influence specific customer archetypes. Our approach demonstrated significant advantages including risk-free experimentation at scale and the ability to capture complex interactions between product features and customer behaviors while accounting for environmental factors in behavior modelling. The refinement process highlighted the importance of model flexibility to accommodate rapidly changing circumstances and evolving customer behaviors. The iterative experimentation approach provided a robust framework for testing and validating different business strategies before real-world implementation.

Conclusion

The imperative for business agility has driven the need for more sophisticated approaches to business experimentation and evidence-based decision-making. As discussed throughout this chapter, traditional methods—whether intuition-based decision-making or pure data analytics—fall short in capturing the dynamic complexity of modern enterprises. Through sophisticated modeling and simulation capabilities, EDT serves as aid for risk-free experimentation in the face of socio-technical complexities leading to evidence-backed decision-making.

Our approach seamlessly integrates actor-based modeling for representing enterprise components and their interactions, probabilistic specifications for handling uncertainty, machine learning for leveraging available data, and multi-criteria decision-making for managing conflicting objectives, providing a robust foundation for enterprise modeling and simulation. The actor-based framework enables representation of enterprise components at appropriate levels of granularity, while its sophisticated event-handling mechanism supports dynamic behavior simulation—a crucial capability given the system-of-system nature of enterprises.

Application of proposed digital twin for a wide range of case studies validates effectiveness of EDT in practice. For example, by modeling 374,000 customers across 109 distinct archetypes in a telecom case study, EDT enabled precise evaluation of product strategies without costly real-world experiments, proving it valuable in situations where traditional experimentation would be impractical or risky. It revealed unexpected insights, such as shift in data usage patterns toward home broadband and the impact of diminished buying power, which significantly influenced product strategy decisions. Similarly, EDT helped organizations gain insight into complex interdependencies and behavioral patterns that were not apparent through conventional analysis. Our future work includes broader adoption in key sustainability initiatives (such as net-zero strategies and water quality improvement) and smart city transformations (such as enabling smart transportation systems, advancing healthcare delivery, and developing smart infrastructure), addressing complex social challenges at scale.

References

1. Bennett, N., James, G., & Lemoine. (2014). What a difference a word makes: Understanding threats to performance in a VUCA world. *Business Horizons, 57*(3), 311–317.
2. Sanchez, R. (1997). Preparing for an uncertain future: Managing organizations for strategic flexibility. *International Studies of Management & Organization, 27*(2), 71–94.
3. Karvonen, T., Sharp, H., & Barroca, L. (2018). Enterprise agility: Why is transformation so hard? In *International conference on agile software development* (pp. 131–145). Springer.
4. Grieves, M. (2016). *Origins of the digital twin concept*. https://doi.org/10.13140/RG.2.2.26367.6160.
5. Singh, M., et al. (2021). Digital twin: Origin to future. *Applied System Innovation, 4*(2), 36.
6. Shafto, M., et al. (2010). Draft modeling, simulation, information technology & processing roadmap. *Technology area, 11*, 1–32.
7. Cearley, D., Burke, B., Searle, S., Walker, M. J., & Claunch, C. (2018). *Top 10 strategic technology trends for 2018*. Gartner. Retrieved 31 May, 2023, from https://www.gartner.com/smarterwithgartner/gartnerstop-10-technology-trends-2018.
8. Agha, G. A., Mason, I. A., Smith, S. F., & Talcott, C. L. (1997). A foundation for actor computation. *Journal of Functional Programming, 7*(1), 1–72.
9. Clark, T., et al. (2017). ESL: An actor-based platform for developing emergent behaviour organisation simulations. In *Advances in practical applications of cyber-physical multi-agent systems: The PAAMS collection: 15th international conference, PAAMS 2017, Porto, Portugal, June 21–23, 2017, Proceedings 15* (pp. 311–315). Springer.
10. Barat, S., Khadilkar, H., Meisheri, H., Kulkarni, V., Baniwal, V., Kumar, P., & Gajrani, M. (2019). Actor based simulation for closed loop control of supply chain using reinforcement learning. In *Proceedings of the 18th international conference on autonomous agents and multiagent systems* (pp. 1802–1804).
11. Barat, S., et al. Symbiotic use of digital twin, simulation and design thinking approach for resilient enterprise. In *2023 Winter simulation conference (WSC)* (Vol. 2023, pp. 686–697). IEEE.
12. Barat, S., Kulkarni, V., Paranjape, A., Dhandapani, S., Manuelraj, S., & Parameswaran, S. P. (2022). Agent based digital twin of sorting terminal to improve efficiency and resiliency in parcel delivery. In *International conference on practical applications of agents and multi-agent systems* (pp. 24–35). Springer.
13. Barat, S., Paranjape, A., Parchure, R., Darak, S., & Kulkarni, V. (2022). Agent based Simulatable City digital twin to explore dynamics of Covid-19 pandemic. In *2022 winter simulation conference (WSC)* (pp. 557–568). IEEE.
14. Barat, S., Mulpuru, D., Yadav, A., Basu, A., Kulkarni, V., Samudrala, S., Bhide, A., Thomas, P., Krishna, K., Yadav, A., et al. (2022). A digital twin based approach for ensuring business continuity plan and safe return to workplace. In *2022 Annual modeling and simulation conference (ANNSIM)* (pp. 126–139). IEEE.
15. Barat, S., Kulkarni, V., & Bhattacharya, K. (2022). Enterprise digital twins for risk free business experimentations. In *2022 winter simulation conference (WSC)* (pp. 2864–2875). IEEE.

Chapter 4
Improving Operational Efficiency of Sorting Terminals in Logistics Industry

Himabindu Thogaru, Tharun Tammali, Subramaniam Dhandapani, Sai Prasad Parameswaran, and Souvik Barat

Abstract Contemporary logistics companies operate within an increasingly complex and dynamic environment characterized by growing parcel volumes, fluctuating business demands, and evolving customer expectations for faster and more reliable delivery. Sorting terminals, as critical nodes within logistics networks, face significant operational challenges due to the intricate interdependencies between design-time capabilities, operational configurations, and key performance indicators (KPIs) such as sorting time, chute blockages, and resource utilization. These complexities are further amplified by uncertainties in parcel inflow patterns and the non-linear interactions among system components leading to potential inefficiencies that can cascade across the network. This chapter explores the critical role of sorting terminals in modern logistics operations and examines the challenges they face in maintaining operational efficiency. It advocates a digital twin-based approach as a robust decision-making aid to address these challenges. By providing an accurate, agent-based representation of sorting terminal components and their behaviors and interactions, a sorting terminal digital twin enables precise evaluation of operational interventions. Its in silico simulation capabilities offer a means to continuously align operational strategies with business goals, adapt to growing demands, and meet changing customer preferences. Through a detailed discussion of the complexities inherent in sorting terminal operations and effective utilization of digital

H. Thogaru (✉)
TCS Research, Tata Consultancy Services, Hyderabad, Telangana, India
e-mail: himabindu.thogaru@tcs.com

T. Tammali · S. P. Parameswaran
Tata Consultancy Services, Bangalore, Karnataka, India
e-mail: tharun.tammali@tcs.com; p.sai@tcs.com

S. Dhandapani
Tata Consultancy Services, Stockholm, Sweden
e-mail: s.dhandapani@tcs.com

S. Barat
TCS Research, Tata Consultancy Services, Pune, Maharashtra, India
e-mail: souvik.barat@tcs.com

V. Kulkarni et al. (eds.), *Digital Twins for Simulation-Based Decision-Making*,
https://doi.org/10.1007/978-3-031-89654-5_4

twin technology, this chapter highlights the potential of digital twin for evidence-based decision-making to drive resilience, adaptability, and efficiency in the logistics sector.

Introduction

Have you ever dispatched a parcel via any courier firm? Have you ever received parcels in your home or office? I am sure most of you would have had these experiences. However, have you ever wondered how a parcel makes its way through a complex network of transports and operators to finally reach its destination within the expected time? Did you know that for each action, including the coordination between each entity, takes an enormous amount of human intelligence, planning, physical tasks, automated systems, scanners, sorters, various means of transport, network planning, etc.? How is it humanly possible to achieve all this coordination between various entities each day every day and yet they successfully manage to send these parcels on time? Did you also know that sorting of your couriers is done semi-automatically through sorters and that letters and parcels are sorted differently due to their size and volumes?

Logistics companies have been managing these complexities with ease for years. But in recent times, the demand for parcel delivery is increasing, and the logistics industry has emerged as a critical backbone supporting the operations and growth of numerous businesses. It increasingly is becoming a critical enabler to empower e-commerce business and global trades, facilitating the seamless movement of goods from producers to consumers across geographies. A vital subset of supply chain management (SCM), logistics industry focuses on supporting transportation, warehousing, and distribution needs, which directly impact the efficiency and responsiveness of supply chains in a cost-effective manner. While SCM encompasses the entire coordination of activities—from procurement and manufacturing to delivery—logistics specializes in executing these functions within the supply chain framework. This specialized service and globally interconnected network are fundamental to addressing the distinct needs of both B2B and B2C markets, where expectations for speed, reliability, and cost-efficiency continue to rise. Moreover, logistics companies play a pivotal role in facilitating C2C business growth by providing cost-effective services and wide network reachability tailored to the unique needs of C2C transactions. These B2B, B2C, and emerging C2C business opportunities are fueling the growth of the logistics industry, driving a significant surge in parcel delivery volumes worldwide. For instance, US parcel volumes grew by 37% in 2020, reaching 20 billion parcels, up from 15 billion in 2019. Projections suggest this volume will nearly double by 2026, reaching 32–39 billion annually, with an annual growth rate of 10% from 2021 to 2025 [1]. These trends highlight substantial opportunities for logistics providers to expand their capabilities, particularly in B2C and C2C segments fueled by e-commerce. Conversely, B2B logistics emphasizes large-scale, consistent deliveries to support manufacturing and retail operations. All these sectors, however, demand robust and efficient logistics systems to cater to their distinct requirements, ranging from bulk transport in B2B to fragmented, time-sensitive deliveries of different types of items.

Logistics companies capitalize these growing business opportunities by establishing a wide logistics network comprising of interconnected facilities, such as collection centers, distribution centers, and sorting terminals, along with robust transportation systems. Collection centers collect goods or parcels of varying sizes, weights, shapes, and service requirements (e.g., one-day delivery) from individuals or businesses. Sorting terminals are hubs where parcels are classified, regrouped, and routed based on their destinations and characteristics. Distribution centers handle the final stage, preparing and dispatching parcels for delivery to end customers. These facilities are seamlessly connected through a network of transportation systems, including trucks, rail, air, and sea, to enable efficient movement of goods across the network. These companies strategically position collection centers to maximize parcel collection, decide distribution center locations for enabling broader delivery reach, and conveniently position sorting terminals to manage parcel delivery in an effective manner at macro-level. Additionally, they focus on improving the operational efficiency of sorting terminals in a localized context to support seamless and cost-effective logistics operations.

Industry studies highlight that logistics companies failing to achieve operational efficiency of their sorting terminals risk jeopardizing their overall supply chain performance and market competitiveness [2]. Amid these challenges, the focus on sorting terminals—pivotal components of logistics operations—emerges as a strategic priority before targeting a robust and optimized logistic network. Sorting terminals frequently grapple with resource allocation inefficiencies, scalability limitations, and the inability to respond effectively to fluctuating demands. Optimizing the performance of these terminals is, therefore, critical for ensuring the smooth and timely movement of parcels.

To overcome challenges related to sorting terminals, we leverage the concept of digital twin—a virtual replica of sorting terminal to enable risk-free in silico what-if and if-simulation to optimize throughput, allocate resources effectively, and proactively address bottlenecks. This evidence-driven quantitative approach enables managers and other stakeholders to make informed decisions. By utilizing a digital twin technology, here we aim to enhance the operational efficiency of sorting terminals, thereby transforming how logistics companies navigate the complexities of supply chain management, thus enhancing the entire supply chain ecosystem.

The rest of this chapter is organized as follows: The chapter continues with an overview of the logistics network, followed by a discussion on sorting terminal operations. Next, the components of the sorting terminal are explored, followed by an analysis of the operational efficiencies it achieves. Key challenges in sorting terminal operations are then highlighted, before presenting the state of the art in the field. Our approach to addressing these challenges is then outlined, followed by a detailed case study. The chapter concludes with a summary of key findings and recommendations.

Overview of Logistics Network

A logistics network is an intricate system of systems, which is designed to ensure the efficient movement of parcels (i.e., any kind of goods) from origin to destination. Conforming to network principles, it consists of nodes and links, where nodes include collection centers, distribution centers, and sorting terminals, while links are transport systems comprising vehicles of various modalities as illustrated in Fig. 4.1. Collection centers serve as the initial touchpoints to gather parcels from diverse sources in B2B, B2C, or C2C business cases. Distribution centers facilitate the last mile of distribution to end customers. Vehicles enable the seamless transfer of parcels between nodes. Among the nodes, sorting terminals, also known as hubs, are primary processing units where parcels from various nodes are collected, categorized, and dispatched to their respective destinations through dedicated links.

Conceptually, each of these sorting terminals can be visualized as a complex cyber-physical system comprising interconnected mechanical components, algorithms, and people. Mechanical components, such as infeed system, conveyor belt, scanners, and chutes, have predefined tasks and dynamics. For example, infeed systems manage the initial entry of parcels, scanners are responsible for sensing and classifying parcels based on destination and other parcel characteristics, conveyor belts transport parcels throughout the facility of the sorting terminal and redistribute them to designated chutes, and chutes collect parcels for predefined destinations. Algorithms, such as sort plans, are pre-defined rules that guide mechanical components in decision-making, such as determining a parcel's destination chute based on its final delivery point, weight, dimensions, and service level agreements (e.g., one-day delivery).

People, i.e., loader and sorter, play crucial roles in the sorting terminal. They manage ill-defined tasks. Sorters are responsible for moving roller cages to destinations, move parcels from chutes into roller cages, and clear chute blockages. Loaders are often tasked to transfer sorted parcels to outbound vehicles. In order to make a sorting terminal efficient, these components must operate in harmony. Coordinated

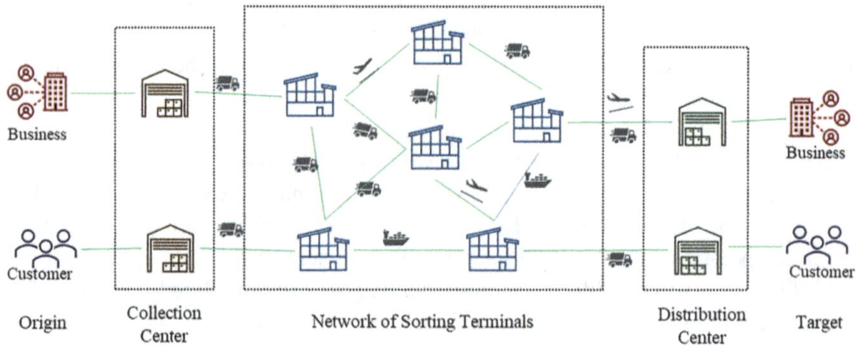

Fig. 4.1 Logistics network

optimization helps manage growing parcel volumes and meet service demands like same-day delivery, whereas inefficiencies can create bottlenecks resulting network-wide delays and increased costs.

The key components that constitute a sorting terminal, including infeed systems, conveyor belts, chutes, sorters, and scanners, are shown in Fig. 4.2. Each of these components play a distinct role ensuring seamless operations, yet their interdependence introduces significant complexities. In this section, we first describe various types of operations within a sorting terminal, identifying key performance indicators (KPIs) and detailing the core components along with their respective functionalities. Subsequently, we discuss the challenges and inherent uncertainties and how inefficiencies in one component can cascade through the terminal, affecting overall performance.

Operation

The operations of a sorting terminal can be understood in four distinct phases: unload, special handling sorting, distribution sorting, and dispatch. Each phase is critical to the smooth functioning of the sorting terminal and introduces its own set of complexities as shown in Fig. 4.3.

Unload: The unload phase begins with parcels arriving at the sorting terminal from inbound transportation systems such as trucks and aircraft. These parcels are transferred to the terminal infrastructure through manual unloading or automated systems like roller conveyors or robotic arms. However, variations in parcel volumes, sizes, and arrival schedules can create complexities resulting in bottlenecks, especially during peak periods. Seasonal surges or delays in transport arrival further complicate this phase, requiring flexible resource allocation and real-time operational adjustments.

Special handling sorting: It is an initial screening and segregation phase, where parcels requiring unique handling are identified and separated from the regular sorting stream. Examples include oversized parcels, fragile items, and hazardous materials. Such parcels are flagged during the scanning process and redirected to dedicated processing areas. Any errors at this stage can disrupt automated sorting flows and increase the need for manual interventions, thus slowing overall operations if not managed effectively.

Distribution sorting: This is the core of the sorting terminal's operations, where parcels are categorized and routed based on their final destinations and delivery requirements. Mostly automated systems, such as cross-belt and tilt-tray sorters (conveyor belt) guided by advanced algorithms (i.e., sorting logic), direct parcels to specific chutes for consolidation. This phase is particularly complex due to the need to handle diverse parcel profiles including varying sizes, weights, and delivery priorities while maintaining high throughput. Equipment malfunctions,

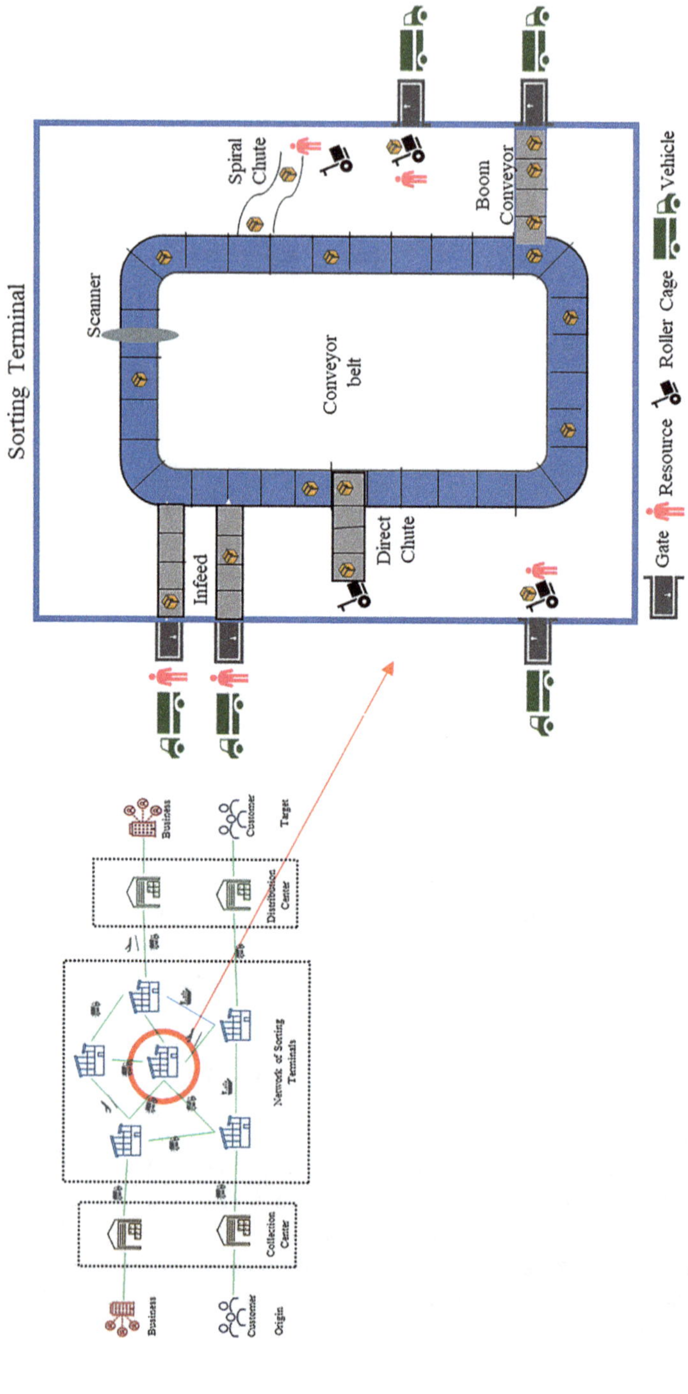

Fig. 4.2 Inside a sorting terminal

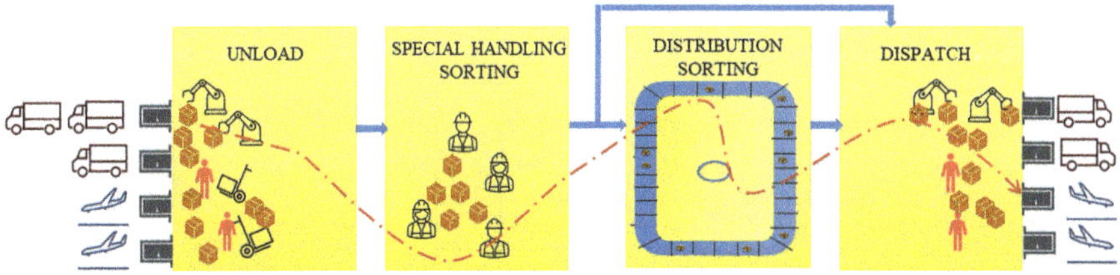

Fig. 4.3 Phases of sorting terminal operations

misreads, or algorithmic errors can cause delays that ripple through the entire terminal.

Dispatch phase: It involves the preparation and transfer of parcels to outbound transportation systems for their next destinations. Sorted parcels are consolidated and systematically loaded onto vehicles such as trucks or aircraft. The complexities in this phase arise from the need to match sorted parcels accurately with the appropriate vehicles, ensure compliance with departure schedules, and avoid congestion at loading docks. Any inefficiencies during dispatch can result in delays that affect delivery timelines and disrupt downstream operations.

These phases collectively define the operational flow of a sorting terminal. Inefficiencies in any one phase can cascade, affecting subsequent processes and potentially disrupting the entire logistics network.

Components

A sorting terminal is a complex cyber-physical system comprising various components that work together to ensure seamless operation as shown using a metamodel in Fig. 4.4. Conceptually, these components can be categorized into physical structures, assets and infrastructure, carriers, algorithms, and resources as follows.

Physical structure: Sorting terminal is a large building or facility with physical structures and specific layout. The key physical structures that significantly contribute to sorting terminal operation are inbound and outbound gates. Inbound gates are designed to receive parcels from other nodes through the vehicle, and outbound gates handle the loading and dispatch of parcels to their next destination. These gates are often strategically positioned to minimize the movement of parcels within the sorting terminal and ensure smooth workflows.

Assets and infrastructure: This includes the machines and mechanical systems that enable the sorting process. Key components are:

Infeed: The infeed is the entry point of parcels to the sorting terminal. This is where parcels are fed into the sorting terminal. This can be done manually or with the help of automated systems like tippers.

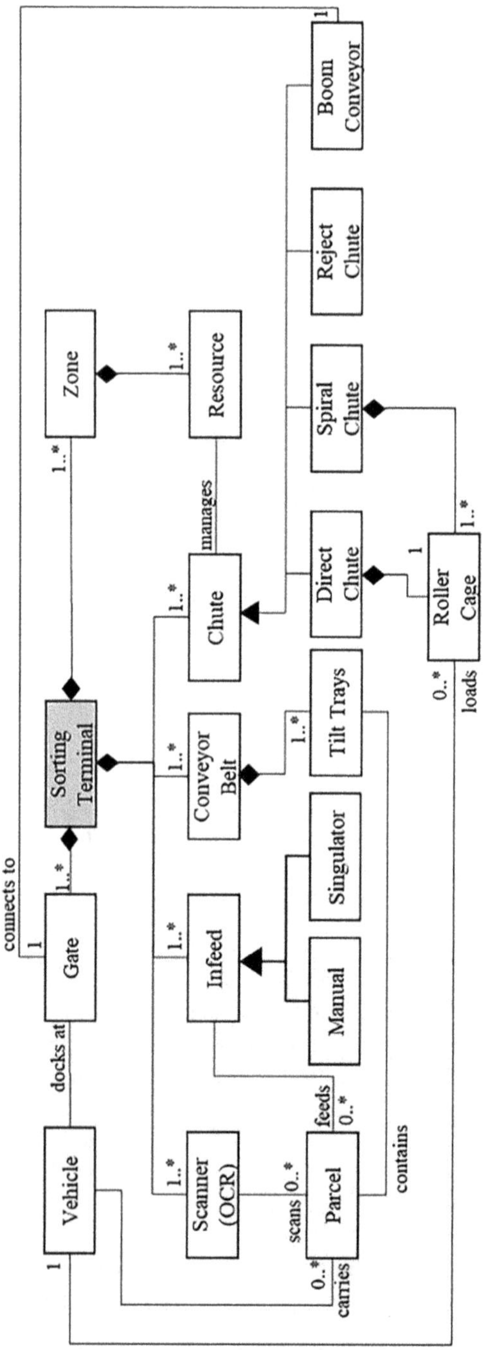

Fig. 4.4 Components of sorting terminal

Conveyor belt: The conveyor belt is a large transport belt for all parcels. A conveyor belt is typically divided into several slots, where one slot can host one parcel. The infeeds introduce parcels to the conveyor belt slots, which then rotate at predefined speed and tilt to drop the parcels into the designated chutes based on the sort plan.

Scanner: Equipped with technologies like barcodes, RFID, or dimensional scanning, scanners capture critical data such as parcel ID, size, and weight to enable real-time tracking and precise sorting.

Chute: Chutes are essentially bins that collect parcels for designated sorting zones and parcel characteristics. There are different types of chutes to collect parcels with different characteristics.

Direct chutes: These chutes are for small and lighter parcels, which can be filled without any human supervision. In this case, parcels are dropped directly from the conveyor belt into roller cages, which are placed below the direct chute. Once the cage is filled, it is immediately replaced by a new one by the sorters.

Spiral chutes: These are long metal tubes that connect different levels of the sorting terminal. In these chutes, the dropped parcels travel down from the upper level to the lower-level platform, where a human worker or robot retrieves parcels and places them into roller cages according to their destination. The capacity of these chutes to handle different destinations depends on the number of roller cages they can accommodate. Spiral chutes are mostly used for standard parcels.

Boom conveyors/outbounds: Connected to an outbound gate, boom conveyors load the sorted parcels onto outgoing trucks. Parcels are loose-loaded or placed into roller cages and loaded into truck up to a certain volume based on the type of truck (e.g., swap body, trailer, link). Boom conveyors are usually used during collection or if the terminal is connected to a warehouse with a lot of return parcels (e.g., retail).

Reject chutes: Reject chutes are chutes specifically designed to handle parcels that have been rejected. Parcels can get rejected for various reasons (e.g., missing labels or too many recirculations). At the reject chute, each parcel is handled manually, with the process differing depending on the reject reason. The reject chute is typically connected to an infeed so that the processed parcels can be reintroduced to the system and be sorted correctly.

Carriers, such as roller cages and totes, are used to move parcels within the terminal and prepare them for outbound transportation. Roller cages are commonly employed to consolidate parcels for dispatch, allowing easy loading onto vehicles and efficient handling.

Algorithms: The major algorithm that controls sorting terminal operation is sort plan. It uses predefined rules and real-time data to direct parcels to specific destinations within the terminal. It accounts for factors such as delivery timelines, parcel characteristics, and availability of sorting infrastructure to ensure optimized routing and minimal delays.

Resources: Two types of resources are chiefly considered in sorting terminal operation: sorters and loaders. Sorters manage roller cages, clear chute blockages, and oversee manual sorting of special parcels. Loaders ensure that parcels are correctly unloaded from vehicles and packed into outbound vehicles.

Operational Efficiency

The primary goal of key stakeholders in a sorting terminal is to enhance operational efficiency in a cost-effective manner while addressing the growing demand for parcel delivery and managing inherent uncertainties. Achieving high operational efficiency is extremely critical for maintaining competitiveness, especially in a context where customers expect faster deliveries, demand fluctuates, and parcel volumes continue to grow. This requires the optimum utilization of the infrastructure (e.g., mechanical systems), alignment of processes and algorithms, and effective resource allocation to maximize parcel throughput and accelerate parcel processing.

We define the objectives of contemporary sorting terminals using a goal-means-lever (GML) [3] diagram, as illustrated in Fig. 4.5. As shown in the figure, the top-level goal of improving operational efficiency in a cost-effective manner is systematically decomposed into two sub-goals: enhancing operational efficiency and reducing operational costs. The subgoal of enhancing operational efficiency can be achieved through a set of micro-level goals, such as improving parcel dwell time, reducing chute blockages, and minimizing recirculation counts. Minimizing operational costs, on the other hand, is directly linked to better resource utilization. We consider that each of these leaf-level goals is typically associated with specific measures or KPIs, which can be influenced through various interventions or levers. The leaf-level goals in the GML diagram depicted in Fig. 4.5 are typically evaluated

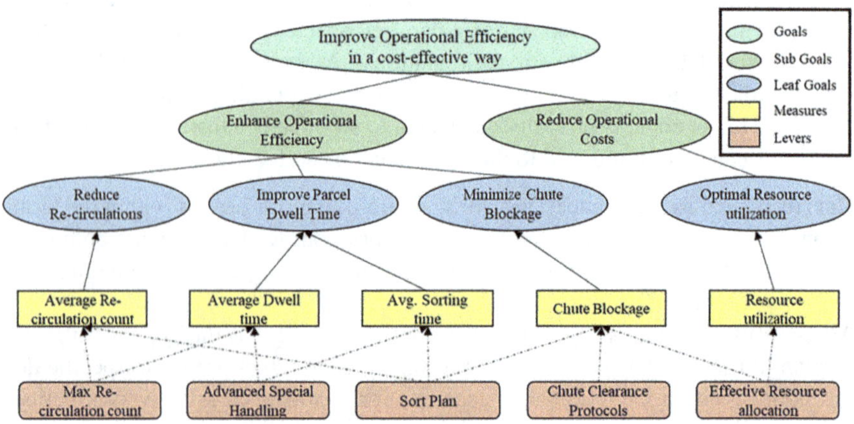

Fig. 4.5 Mapping sorting terminal objectives with GML

using a set of KPIs, with the relevant levers that are typically employed in contemporary sorting terminals of logistics companies also illustrated in the figure. The primary KPIs for sorting terminal efficiency include:

Average sorting time: The average sorting time is the mean duration required for a parcel to move through the sorting process, from its entry into the infeed to its designated chute. This KPI is an indicator of the efficiency of sorting mechanism, including scanning, routing, and parcel movement within the conveyor belt.

Average parcel dwell time: Average dwell time measures the average time a parcel spends in the sorting terminal, from entry to exit. This KPI considers all phases of sorting process including unloading, special handling, sorting, consolidation, and dispatch time. High dwell times indicate inefficiencies in processing and resource allocation. Reducing average dwell time is an important subgoal, as it directly impacts the speed of deliveries and potentially leads to delays in the overall network.

Chute blockage: Chute blockage measures the frequency of obstructions in the chutes due to stagnant parcels in cages. Blockages can disrupt the flow of parcels, causing delays and recirculations. Monitoring and minimizing chute blockages are essential for maintaining smooth operations and avoiding bottlenecks.

Average recirculation count: the mean number of times parcels are re-circulated on the conveyor belt before they are successfully processed. High recirculation count of parcel signify wasted time and resources, as parcels stay on the conveyor belt for longer duration. Reducing recirculations is critical to improve throughput and minimize operational costs.

Resource utilization: This KPI evaluates how effectively human resources (i.e., loaders and sorters), equipment, and infrastructure are utilized during sorting operations. Low resource utilization indicates underused assets, while overutilization can lead to burnout, equipment wear, and decreased operational stability. Achieving the right balance ensures that resources are used optimally to achieve maximum throughput without overburdening the system.

To optimize sorting terminal performance and address operational challenges, a variety of interventions or levers can be considered. These levers typically involve changes in the configurations of the sorting terminal or its components. A list of sorting terminal parameters and their components that influence the desired KPIs are highlighted using dark- and light-blue boxes in Fig. 4.6. As shown, parameters such as belt capacity, number of infeeds, and number of chutes (those highlighted in light-blue color) are associated with fixed infrastructure. These are not operational parameters; rather, they need to be considered during the design or major transformation of a sorting terminal. On the other hand, configurations, such as the number of resources, maximum recirculation count, and sort plan, highlighted in dark-blue color, are often considered for operational interventions by contemporary logistics companies. The most prominent operational interventions are described below.

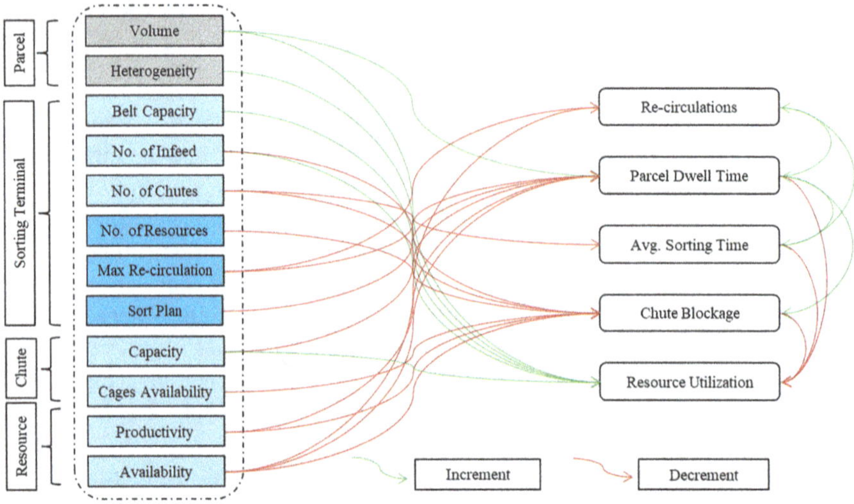

Fig. 4.6 High-level dynamics and influencing factors

Max recirculation count: Defining a threshold for the maximum number of times a parcel can circulate on the conveyor belt before redirecting to the rejection chute for manual intervention.

Effective resource allocation: Allocation of sufficient number of loaders and sorters considering potential parcel load, distribution of parcel profile, and service-level requirements can improve resource utilization and reduce dwell times.

Sort plan (i.e., parcel to chute mapping): A data-driven sorting algorithm tailored to parcel profiles, destinations, and service-level requirements as opposed to static sort plan may minimize sorting time and prevents chute blockage.

Chute clearance protocols: Establishing automated or manual protocols to address chute blockages promptly helps maintain flow and avoids delays. Additional resource allocation for chute clearance could be a useful intervention for peak hours and seasons.

Advanced special handing phase: Use of advanced pre-screening systems to detect oversized or special parcels early in the process ensures they are diverted appropriately to avoid disruptions in standard sorting operations.

Key Challenges

Until now, the logistic companies have managed to fulfil shipment demands with a relatively static network of collection centers, sorting terminals, and destination centers along with relatively static transportation links. However, this traditional static network with pre-configured sorting terminals is no longer capable of handling increased volume and variation in parcel flow with the customer expectation of reducing delivery time. The shift in customer behavior (e.g., C2C business opportunities) and growing shipment demands, particularly during peak times like Black Friday and Cyber Monday, often lead to operational inefficiencies at sorting terminals, thus resulting in disruptions across the entire supply chain. These inefficiencies result in transport delays, missed parcel collections, ineffective resource allocation, inefficient use of mechanical systems and automation aids, and parcels being left at terminals unsorted. Sorting terminal will deliver optimal throughput when the parcels spend as less time on the sorting belt as possible, the chutes get emptied as fast as possible, and as few packets remain on the belt unsorted as possible, which necessitates human intervention.

However, sorting terminal operations face several key challenges due to misalignment between parcel inflow volume (which is beyond the control of sorting terminal stakeholders), design-time capabilities (which cannot be altered once the terminal is operational), and operational configurations (the only pragmatically adjustable parameters). In real-world operations, these elements exhibit complex, non-linear, and often uncertain interdependencies with the KPIs, as illustrated in Fig. 4.6. Design-time parameters, such as belt capacity and the number of chutes, directly impact throughput and sorting efficiency. However, these static configurations interact with dynamic operational parameters, such as resource allocation and sort plans, to shape real-time performance. For instance, increasing the number of chutes can reduce chute blockages under optimal conditions but may also lead to inefficiencies if not paired with sufficient resource levels or a well-optimized sort plan. Similarly, adjustments to operational levers, such as reducing maximum recirculation counts, can influence sorting time but may inadvertently increase manual interventions and resource requirements. These interdependencies create feedback loops, where changes in one parameter can cascade unpredictably through the system, thus amplifying uncertainties across the entire operation.

To address these complexities and uncertainties, it is essential to move beyond traditional decision-making approaches, which often rely heavily on historical data or experiential judgments. Such conventional methods can hinder the achievement of desired goals and optimal KPI outcomes, as discussed below.

Workforce planning: Workforce planning in sorting terminals primarily relies on forecasted data and production planners. Typically, workforce planning is done a week in advance, estimating parcel volumes across each zone and specific chutes and allocating a fixed number of personnel to each zone accordingly. However, this static approach can lead to inefficiencies, particularly when dealing with unexpected changes in parcel volumes, which leads to underutilized or overburdened zones causing delays in sorting operations and reduced overall productivity. These challenges highlight the critical need for balanced and optimal workforce allocation strategies to achieve better terminal performance.

Machine control parameters: Key control parameters, such as maximum recirculation count and dimension criteria for specific chutes, are determined based on historical data. This method is insufficient for making informed and dynamic decisions.

Parcel blockage: Parcel blockage is recorded during instances of chute unavailability and chute jams because of workforce inefficiencies on the floor. The blockage count reflects the severity of the issue, which may involve a smaller number of parcels being blocked multiple times or unique parcel counts, summing up to the total blockage count. This is a critical problem in sorting terminals, significantly affecting sorting efficiency and increasing parcel rejection rates. A key parameter contributing to this problem is the recirculation count, which varies across shifts but is often not optimized. During collection sorting (day shift), a minimal recirculation count of 2 is preferred, as parcels are routed into boom conveyor chutes for truck loading, which cannot handle excessive congestion of parcels. However, distribution sorting (night shift) utilizes a wider array of chutes, allowing for a higher recirculation count of 40. Despite assuming effective use of the conveyor belt to minimize parcel rejection and reduce multiple sorting attempts, significant blockage still occurs, accounting for approximately 40–80% of the total blockage instances relative to the total parcels sorted, leading to inefficient use of sorting machines. This inability to maintain optimal recirculation settings highlights these inefficiencies, making machine parameter optimization, such as the maximum recirculation count, a key challenge for sorting terminals.

Lack of a test environment for sort planners: When sorting planners need to make significant changes to the terminal sorting plan to accommodate changes from other terminals, they lack a dedicated environment to test these modifications. Setting up a live testing environment can create problems when the suggested modification ends up worsening the situation. Moreover, the setup takes a lot of time to set up, thus making it impossible to experiment with all possible candidate suggestions in the live production environment.

Legacy system for sorting process: The sorting process currently relies on a legacy software system that is 15 to 20 years old, responsible for generating sorting decisions. The main challenge is having this outdated system makes it difficult to modify the changes on an occasional basis, causing delays and inefficiencies when changes are required.

State of the Art

Improving the operational efficiency of sorting terminals in a cost-effective manner for varying demands is a complex multivariate optimization problem. However, this challenge is rarely formulated as a single large-scale optimization problem due to the significant number of parameters involved and the inherent complexities of such systems. Moreover, most pragmatic solutions require trade-offs between achieving the desired level of certainty for effectiveness (e.g., incorporating redundancy) and the degree of cost optimization (e.g., resource recruitment).

At the highest level, there are studies that focus on optimizing the layout of sorting terminals focusing on the design aspect to maximize efficiency [4]. However, these studies typically consider only a few predefined structural parameters and fail to address operational parameters in a comprehensive manner. At the next level, given a fixed sorting terminal layout, the operational efficiency problem is typically divided into multiple manageable optimization problems with localized objectives by adopting a divide-and-conquer paradigm. These local optimization problems mostly focus on (i) allocating resources to chutes, (ii) assigning chutes to destinations, and (iii) mapping individual parcels to chutes. Most of the literature addressing these problems adopts one of two types of techniques: conventional optimization techniques and historical data-centric AI approaches.

Conventional optimization techniques, such as a linear programming-based planning approach presented by Khir, Erera, and Toriello [5] for two-phase sort planning or an optimized sorting algorithm for forecasted demand presented by Ghosh et al. [6], are grounded in two key assumptions: (a) the inflow of parcels during a shift or day is accurately estimated and matches the forecast, and (b) the parcels are nearly identical or exhibit limited variation. These techniques tend to produce sub-optimal solutions when these assumptions deviate in practice. In reality, actual parcel flows deviate from forecasts not only in terms of quantity but also in size, destination, characteristics (e.g., hard/soft, bendable/perishable), and the order of arrival at the sorting terminal. Consequently, even the most optimized parcel-to-chute allocation strategy can result in chute blockages, thus necessitating on-the-fly adjustment. Failure to promptly address such disruptions can lead to undesired micro-level inefficiencies. Accumulation of these micro-disruptions (e.g., chute blockages), combined with other uncertainties, such as temporary resource unavailability or machine faults, can lead to significant disruptions at macro-level, i.e., for sorting terminal. Additionally, the use of multiple localized solutions often fails to ensure global robustness. For example, independently optimized solutions for sort plans and resource allocations, based on slightly differing assumptions, may lead to misalignments and inefficiencies when applied to a holistic context.

AI-based approaches, such as neural network-based learning methods, have also been explored [7]. Since these techniques use historical data for training, they perform well when the future can be reasonably extrapolated from past trends. However, they falter in dynamic and evolving contexts, such as changing business models (e.g., the rise of C2C commerce) and shifting customer expectations (e.g., one-day delivery requirements).

To address these pragmatic challenges, a few studies have employed simulation-based approaches using tools like FlexSim and AnyLogic [8–10]. While these simulations offer insights into sorting terminal operations, their flexibility is often insufficient to address the inherent complexity, heterogeneity, uncertainty, and evolving nature of modern logistics.

Our Approach

We adopt the concept of a purposive agent-based digital twin that accurately captures the properties and behaviors of sorting terminal components and their interactions. In our approach, components and sub-components of the sorting terminal are represented as configurable "agents" [11] at a fine level of granularity, while their interactions are modeled through event interactions between these agents as discussed in [12]. The what-if simulation capabilities of our digital twin facilitate the evaluation of operational interventions while accounting for constraints imposed by fixed design-time parameters, such as belt capacity and the number of chutes. Additionally, it enables the continuous alignment of operational strategies with growing parcel volumes and evolving service-level demands. Furthermore, such in silico experimentation enhances the resilience and adaptability of the sorting terminal by identifying optimal configurations and predicting future system responses.

Modeling Abstraction

We use an extended form of agent abstraction as shown in Fig. 4.7a as a metamodel. As shown in our metamodel, we use a core abstraction, termed as "agent." An agent can hierarchically decompose into finer agents. Each agent contains a unique set of attributes that capture its state and has a behavior aimed at achieving its stated objectives. A set of interacting agents are typically required for capturing the heterogeneity and variations of system elements. These agents can interact with other agents through the consuming and producing events. Behavioral aspect dictates that an action is executed if certain events occur and specific conditions in the agent's state are met. Moreover, we support specialization associations to refine the attributes and behaviors for capturing specialized behavior of the system components.

A representation of sorting terminal as a set of interacting agents is shown in Fig. 4.7b. In this topology, the Parcel Feeder agent is tasked with introducing parcels into the infeed, positioning them into designated slots for sorting. Each action of the Parcel Feeder is triggered by specific events, such as the arrival of new parcels, and its state is updated accordingly. This mimics the behavior of the environment of the sorting terminal, i.e., parcel inflows from network to sorting terminal. The Parcel Feeder agent introduces parcels to the infeed, and the infeed agent places these parcels to the slots of conveyor belt. Scanner agents interact with the slots to scan parcels, capturing essential information, such as the next destination, which dictates how parcels should be sorted by sorting logic. The system's composition is further exemplified by the multiple agents working in conjunction, such as the parcels that are then directed to various chutes: direct chutes facilitate the immediate transfer of parcels into cages, while boom conveyors transport parcels directly to vehicles. Sorters retrieve parcels from spiral chutes and subsequently place them into cages; once the cages are filled, the loaders transfer the parcels from the cages

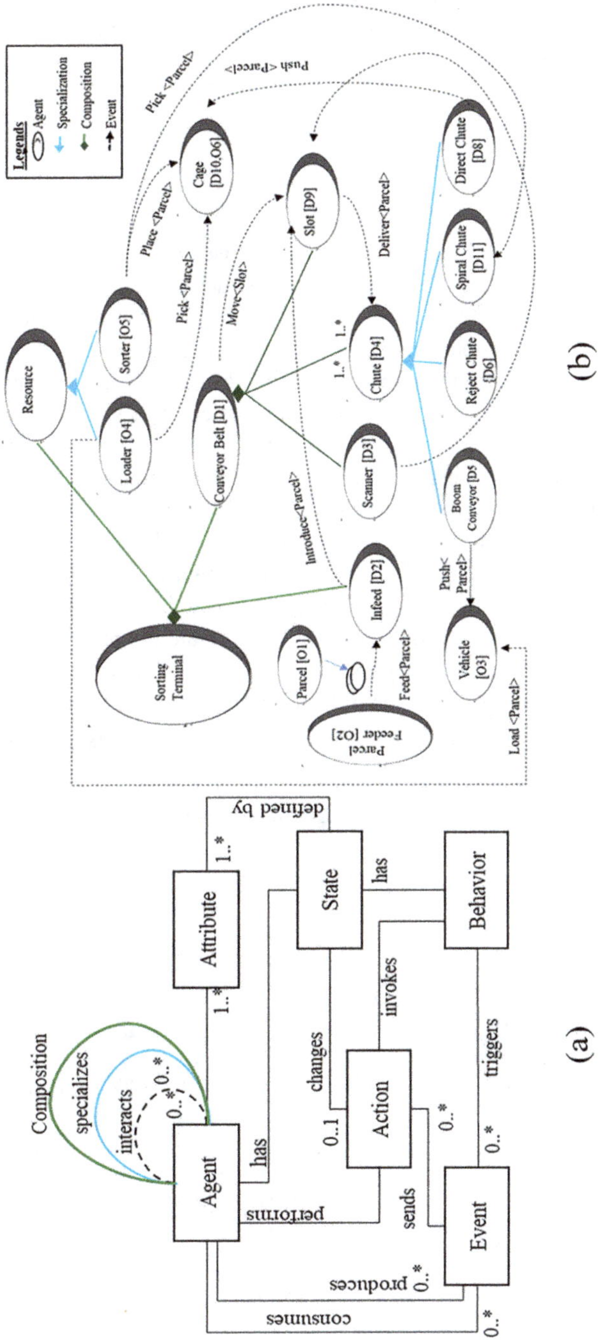

Fig. 4.7 **(a)** Agent metamodel. **(b)** Agent topology

to the vehicles. This seamless interaction among agents not only highlights the dynamic nature of their behavior but also shows how these agents collectively manage complex tasks, with each agent's state and actions influencing the overall efficacy of the sorting process.

Models

The proposed sorting terminal digital twin comprises a federated digital twin that revolves around four key digital twins, the infrastructure twin, parcel twin, orchestration twin, and resource twin, as shown in Fig. 4.8. Each component is designed to be configurable and adaptable, enabling a comprehensive simulation of specific aspect of sorting terminal operations as illustrated in Fig. 4.3. The construction of the digital twin follows a systematic approach that combines these four key twins into a unified and functional virtual representation.

The *infrastructure twin* serves as a digital representation of the physical infrastructure and mechanical systems. It encompasses critical assets such as conveyor belts, chutes, and cages, each of which is carefully modeled to capture their operational characteristics using agent abstraction as shown in Fig. 4.7b. For instance, conveyor belts are modeled with key characteristics such as length, speed, and tray dimensions, utilizing historical data patterns to replicate the physical movement of parcels and factors affecting throughput and efficiency. Chutes are modeled based on specifications such as dimensions like width, length, and sorting characteristics, ensuring accuracy in parcel flow dynamics by incorporating positioning data.

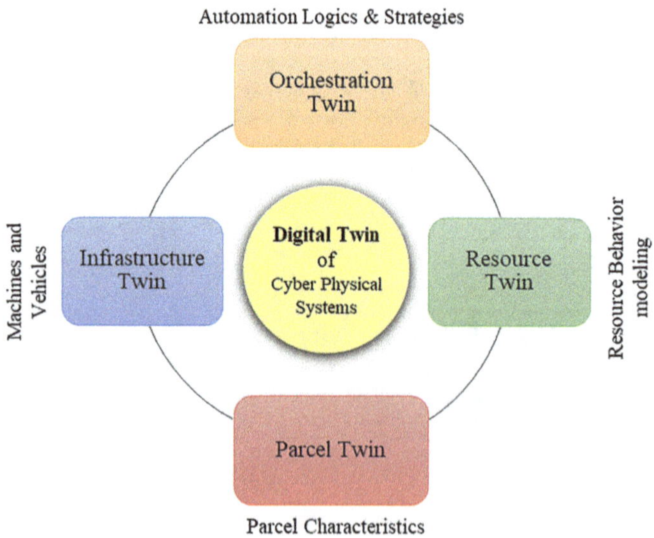

Fig. 4.8 Cyber-physical system twins of twins

Additionally, cage volume and weight capacities are integrated, alongside heuristic approaches that simulate realistic cage-filling patterns categorized into loosely packed, balanced, and tightly packed configurations, aiding effective decision-making in operational contexts. We make this model configurable to mimic real situations or hypothetical cases.

The *parcel twin* plays a key role in representing parcels with varying inflow and heterogeneity in terms of physical characteristics and service-level requirements. By capturing dimensions such as length, width, height, weight, and handling requirements, it is understood how various parcel types engage with the sorting terminal. Each parcel is assigned with unique identifiers, including parcel IDs, pin codes, and service codes, which play critical roles in the sorting workflow. As mentioned in the special handling sorting phase earlier, the distinction between machinable and non-machinable parcels is essential; machinable parcels can be efficiently handled by automated systems, whereas non-machinable items need special processing due to their oversized, heavy, or fragile nature. This differentiation is reflected in the operational design, directing specific parcel categories to manual handling sections. Ultimately, this modeling ensures that parcels are recognized as dynamic entities within the digital twin, capable of interacting dynamically with components such as the conveyor belt, chutes, cages, and resources. As shown in Fig. 4.7b, we consider an additional agent, term as Parcel Feeder, to mimic real situation or experiment with hypothetical parcel inflow scenarios.

The *resource twin* captures two aspects: (a) resource allocations, i.e., allocation of loaders and sorters to the designated area, and (b) availability and productivity of the workforce. Allocation of workforce may change for each shift (modelled as operational configuration), whereas the characteristics and behavior of the workforce within the sorting terminal are complex non-deterministic phenomena. By employing probabilistic and spatiotemporal models, we capture this inherently complex and uncertain human behaviors. In practice, the allocation of loaders to infeed and outbound area and assignment of sorters to designated chutes are done for a shift or slot; therefore, we model them as configuration. A specific configuration must reflect realistic workflow assignment. On the other hand, the factors quantifying workload metrics such as the number of parcels handled and total weight lifted per resource that can be tracked are uncertain to an extent—they may differ within a range. We model them as non-deterministic spatiotemporal behavior with certain bound, which are determined through heuristics.

The *orchestration twin* models complex workflows and operational directives critical to the sorting processes. It incorporates data regarding parcel volumes and routing requirements into a sort plan, which is crafted by anticipated parcel volumes, forecasted demand, and available destinations. This dynamic model adjusts by continuously assessing parcel characteristics and constraints to apply optimal sorting logic. Moreover, it employs multi-destination sorting techniques to distribute workload across multiple chutes, thereby enhancing sorting efficiency. Integrating with these components creates feedback loops that improve simulation accuracy. For instance, changes in resource efficiency immediately influence the handling capacity assessments within the parcel twin and the sorting strategies in the orchestration twin.

Ultimately, this constructed digital twin not only reflects the operational capabilities of the sorting terminal but also serves as a powerful tool that provides insights for continuous improvement and optimization, facilitating data-driven decision-making aligned with the terminal's operational goals, as depicted in Fig. 4.5.

Configuration

The agents representing a sorting terminal digital twin are configurable through a set of parameters, which are broadly categorized to reflect two types of changes: design time and operational changes. Some of these parameters are shown in Fig. 4.10. These parameters primarily define how the agents structure their properties and dynamic responses to an extent. *Design-time parameters* are static in nature and define the foundational structure of the sorting terminal. The examples include the number of slots or tilt trays on conveyor belt, the number and positioning of chutes, chute capacities, and the layout of other fixed components. They are determined during the construction phase and are typically fixed unless significant modifications or redesign of the terminal are considered. For agents representing the terminal, design-time parameters serve as the blueprint, dictating their structural characteristics and interactions within the system. On the other hand, *operational parameters* are dynamic and change based on real-time changes in the sorting terminal. Operational parameters include factors like the occupancy levels of chutes and the routing decisions for parcels based on system's status, i.e., sort plan. Unlike design-time parameters, operational parameters may need constant updated to reflect real sorting process. These parameters allow agents to adapt to real-time changes, such as fluctuations in the number of parcels or shifts in sorting priorities.

Together, these two categories of parameters provide a comprehensive configuration for the agents. Design-time parameters establish the structural framework, while operational parameters enable the agents to respond to real-time changes in the system. This precise configuration ensures the constructed digital twin is a reliable representation of the physical terminal, laying the groundwork for validation and simulation processes.

Simulation-Led Experimentation

The configurable sorting terminal digital twin enables experimentation with various configuration scenarios facilitating evidence-based decision-making as illustrated in Fig. 4.9. As shown in the figure, constructed digital twin allows the configuration of parcel loads including their characteristics and arrival sequences, in addition to

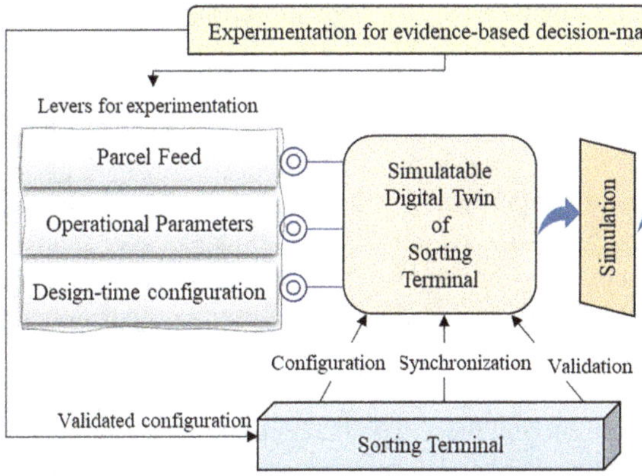

Fig. 4.9 Simulation leading to evidence-based decision-making

design time and operational parameters as discussed before. By simulating different parcel loads along with operational settings, constructed digital twin helps observe system behavior and evaluate operational efficiencies under diverse conditions.

Simulations with different set of configuration parameters, i.e., what-if scenarios, help identify potential bottlenecks, chute blockages, and inefficiencies in operational by observing simulated KPIs. It also aids in experimenting and determining the optimal operational parameters to address inefficiencies under specific load situations. For instance, operational parameters can be adjusted to evaluate short-term interventions, such as reallocating resources, modifying recirculation limits, or refining sort plans to optimize the performance of the sorting terminal.

Configurable design-time parameters, in contrast, provide an aid for evaluating strategic and long-term changes, such as designing new sorting terminals or assessing the impact of large-scale infrastructure transformations. By allowing for controlled experimentation with both short-term and strategic interventions, the digital twin serves as a decision-making aid for addressing immediate operational challenges while also supporting long-term planning.

Validation

The validation of the constructed sorting terminal digital twin is critical to ensuring its accuracy and reliability in supporting evidence-based decision-making with a degree of certainty. We adopt three established validation techniques from simulation research: data validity, conceptual validity, and operational validity as presented by Sargent [13].

Conceptual validity ensures that the digital twin accurately reflects the core elements of the sorting terminal encompassing infrastructure, resources, parcels, and process aspects. During the construction phase, domain experts rigorously evaluate the model to verify that all relevant business elements are appropriately captured as agents, agent behaviors, and agent interactions. For instance, components such as conveyor belts, chutes, and scanners are modeled as agents. Their interactions, such as parcels being routed from the conveyor belt to the appropriate chute based on the sort plan, are represented with appropriate detail. Uncertainties, such as parcel arrival rates and variability in resource productivity, are also incorporated into the model. Conceptual component diagram as shown in Fig. 4.4 and agent specification shown in Fig. 4.7 serve as initial reference points for this validation. Typically, this validation is conducted through interviews and discussion sessions with domain experts.

Data validity is established by configuring agent variables using data from the real system and periodically synchronizing these parameters to maintain alignment with actual operations. For example, the model captures design-time parameters such as belt capacity and the number of chutes from the infrastructure, alongside operational data like real-time parcel inflow rates and resource allocation. This synchronization ensures the twin remains a reliable proxy for the real system and capable of adapting to fluctuations in parcel volumes or evolving operational strategies.

Operational validity involves comparing the simulation results with historical data from known past scenarios to ensure realistic system performance. For instance, if historical data shows chute blockages under specific inflow volumes and resource configurations, the simulation results are expected to replicate these behaviors within a tolerable range to account for certain uncertainties.

Case Study

We illustrate the utilization and efficacy of the proposed sorting terminal digital twin using a real sorting terminal of a Nordic logistics company, where we contextualized the proposed digital twin and leverage to explore operational scenarios aimed at optimizing the sorting process and improving system performance. The company was aiming to achieve operational efficiency with optimum resources while navigating inherent complexity and uncertainties of logistic domain. They need to manage large and fluctuating parcel delivery demands, especially during the holiday seasons, such as Black Friday and Cyber Monday. It is often accompanied by irregular arrival patterns that create significant challenges for maintaining an even distribution across sorting terminals. Additionally, physical infrastructure and its downtime pose inherent bottlenecks. For instance, the placement of chutes and scanners often result in extended travel times for parcels, leading to frequent recirculations. In addition, the dynamic nature of the workforce and their availability make the situation furthermore complex.

We found that the logistics company was aiming to improve operational efficiencies while utilizing resources optimally to address inherent complexities and adapt to market uncertainties. These objectives align closely with the GML model depicted in Fig. 4.5, which emphasizes operational efficiency and cost-effectiveness as core goals.

To support this initiative, the proposed sorting terminal digital twin was configured using real-world data from one of the sorting terminals of the company. This configuration ensured that the digital twin accurately reflected the design time, such as belt capacity and chute numbers, and operational parameters, such as sort plan and resource allocation.

Using supported simulation capabilities, the relevant stakeholders, such as operation head, sort planners, and floor managers, analyzed operational performance under various scenarios and uncertainties to identify bottlenecks and inefficiencies, such as chute blockages or excessive parcel recirculation. By experimenting with different resource allocations, recirculation count thresholds, and sort plans, the simulation provided sufficient insights into potential improvements. Illustrative configuration, validation, and simulation-led experimentations are discussed below.

Terminal Configuration

The company's sorting terminal under analysis consisted of a sophisticated setup, including a conveyor belt with 522 tilt trays, 6 infeeds, 2 scanners, and 18 chutes, comprising 4 direct chutes, 8 spiral chutes, 5 boom conveyor chutes, and 1 reject chute. The workforce at the terminal consisted of 30 workers strategically allocated across four distinct operational zones based on parcel inflow forecast. Further details of the terminal's configuration are depicted in Fig. 4.10.

To evaluate the performance of this sorting terminal and assess the impact of proposed interventions, several KPIs were monitored. These included parcel dwell time, chute blockage frequency, average sorting time, infeed parcel waiting queue, and parcel recirculations. These measures aimed to align system performance with operational goals, driving improvements in throughput and efficiency as discussed in the earlier section using Fig. 4.5. In parallel, experimental levers were configured to address these challenges, such as physical infrastructure adjustments like repositioning high-utilization chutes to optimize parcel travel distances, reconfiguring the resource allocations for optimal resource utilization, and adjusting recirculation count for faster parcel processing.

Validation

Before applying the digital twin model to explore different operational scenarios, the company's operations manager, in collaboration with domain experts, thoroughly reviewed the model's parameters to ensure its validity. They conducted an operational validity using actual operational data spanning 66 months, confirming that the model accurately represented real-world dynamics. This validation process

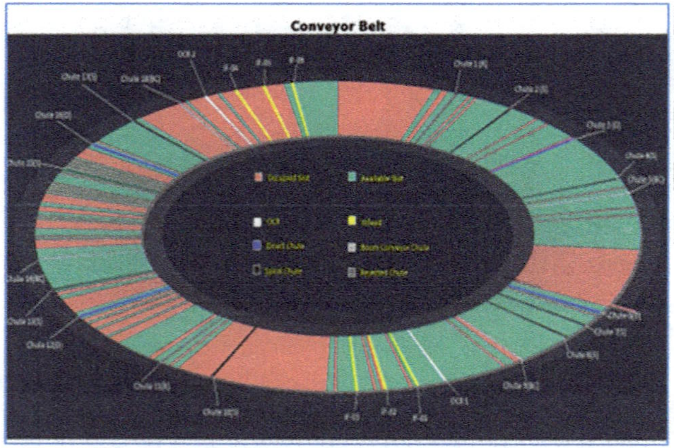

Simulation Configuration

Key	Value	Details(if any)
Simulation Time	1440	60*24*1
Scale of Tick	1	

Resource Configuration

Resource allocation per Zone	3,3,3,4	
Resource Productivity		
	Min Value	Max Value
Resource productivity Range	0.3	1

Cage Configuration

Cage length	1150 mm	
Cage width	700 mm	
Cage height	1500 mm	
Packaging	**Density**	**Blockage Probability**
Loosely Packed	42	30
Balanced Packed	63	50
Tightly Packed	90	20

TOPOLOGY CONFIGURATION

Key	Value
No Of Slots	522
No Of Infeeds	6
No Of Zones	4
Zone Names	Red, Blue, White, Yellow
Infeed Location ZoneWise	[10, 15, 20], [], [165, 170, 175], [176]
Chutes Location Zone Wise	[55, 65, 75, 85], [115, 125, 135, 145], [190, 200, 210, 220, 230], [260, 270, 280, 290,310]
Chutes Type Zone Wise	[1, 0, 1, 2], [0, 1, 1, 2], [1,3,0,1, 2], [1, 0,1,2,4]
Scanners	[25], [], [180], []
Length Of Slot	1.5
Width Of Slot	3.5
Distance b/w Slots	0.5
Distance Per Minute	120
Max Recirculation's	3
Max Parcels Per Tick Per Infeed	40

Chute Configuration

Chute	No. of Cages	Width	Height
Direct Chute	10	NA	NA
Spiral Chute	10	1000	10000
Boom Conveyor	NA	NA	NA
Packaging		**Probability of Blockage**	
Loosely Packed	42	30	
Balanced Packed	63	50	
Tightly Packed	90	20	
Spiral Pushing Probability	10		

Truck Configuration

Truck Width	3000 mm	
Truck Height	2000 mm	
Truck Length	3000 mm	
Packaging	**Density**	
Loosely Packed	42	30
Balanced Packed	63	40
Tightly Packed	90	10

Sorting Logic

Location	Weight	Chutes
0-10000	0-1000	3
0-10000	1001-5000	2,4, 7,8,10,13,15,17
10001-50000000	0-1000	5,9
10001-10000000	1001-5000	14
0-200000000	5001-1000000	18
*	*	18

Fig. 4.10 Sorting terminal topology configuration

ensured that the simulations and proposed adjustments were operationally feasible, making the model a reliable tool for data-driven decision-making.

By systematically monitoring KPIs and configuring the levers, the analysis on this validated digital twin provided actionable insights into optimizing the terminal's performance. The subsequent scenario analyses illustrate how these interventions were applied to explore how different operational adjustments could impact sorting terminal performance.

Scenario Analysis and Interventions

We used the configured and validated sorting terminal digital twin to systematically explore the impact of both operational and design-time parameters on sorting terminal performance. In this section, we present a set of sample experiments focused on operational parameters to demonstrate the practical application of simulation capability.

Scenario 1: Exploring Impact of Chute Positioning

The initial analysis identified a critical bottleneck in the form of Chute 3, which exhibited high utilization but was located far from the scanner. This configuration led to extended travel times and frequent recirculation of parcels. To address this, an experiment is formed where Chute 3 is relocated closer to the scanner. In simulation, this intervention yielded significant improvements as the average sorting time dropped noticeably as shown in Fig. 4.11. These outcomes demonstrated the impact of aligning physical infrastructure with operational needs to optimize parcel movement.

Scenario 2: Adjusting Recirculation Count

The second analysis aimed to optimize the maximum recirculation count for parcels on the sorting belt, which significantly influences the efficiency of parcel processing. In the initial configuration, parcels were allowed a maximum of five recirculations before being sorted. Subsequently, the operational team decided to test the impact of reducing the maximum recirculation count from five to three. This intervention was rooted in the understanding that excessive recirculation could contribute to unnecessary dwell times and increased queue formation at the infeed. The simulation results indicated a substantial reduction in infeed queue formation, as shown in Fig. 4.12. With the new recirculation limit, the average number of parcels

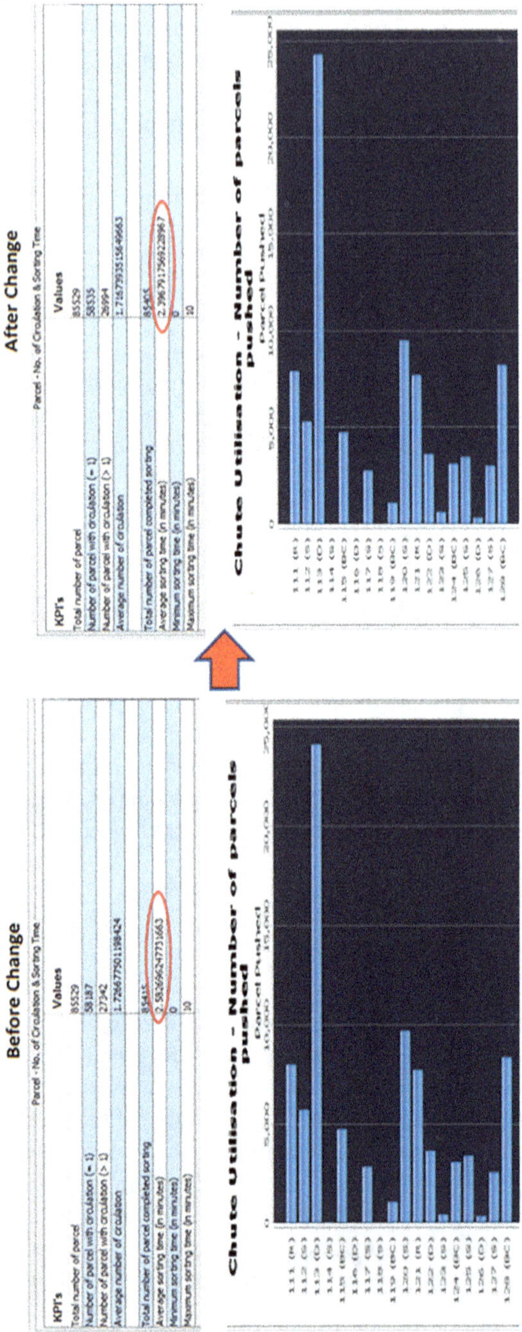

Fig. 4.11 Changing more utilized chute location

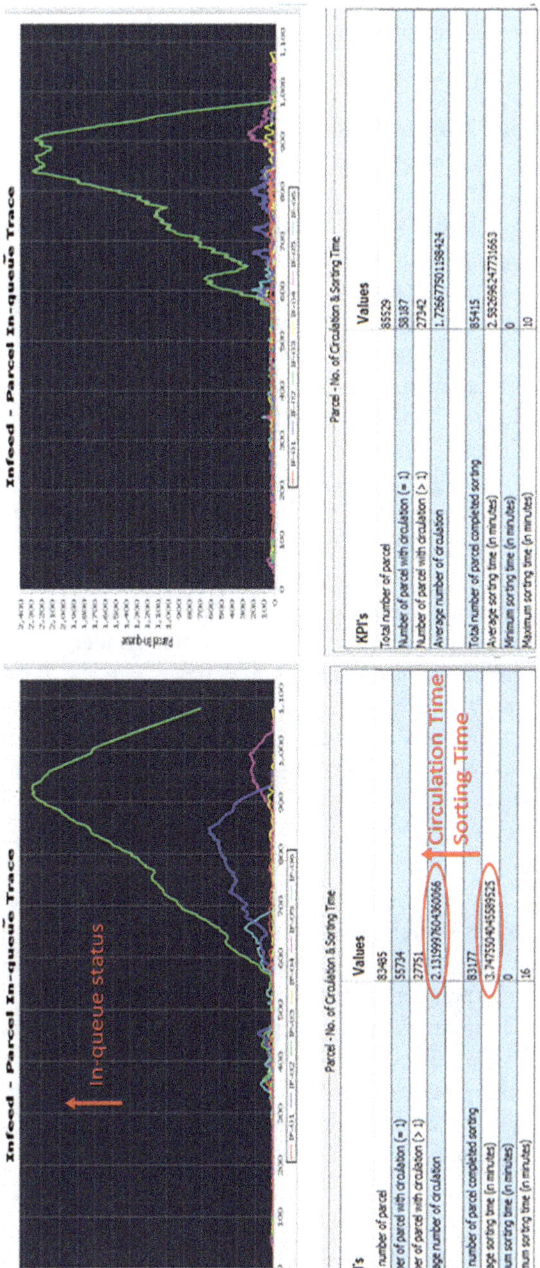

Fig. 4.12 Adjusting recirculation count

processed per cycle improved, alongside a decrease in the average sorting time. Notably, this adjustment led to a more streamlined flow of parcels through the terminal, ensuring a more efficient use of the conveyor belt.

Scenario 3: Exploring Various Resource Allocations

In the final scenario, we shifted our focus to evaluating and optimizing workforce resource allocation across the sorting terminal. The initial assessment revealed that the existing workforce of 13 employees were not being utilized to their full potential, given the current and anticipated parcel volumes as shown in Fig. 4.13a. This insight prompted a deeper analysis into how resource allocation impacts overall sorting efficiency. The first adjustment involved reducing the workforce from 13 to 9 employees, with a strategic reallocation implemented as follows: Zone 1, 2; Zone 2, 2; Zone 3, 2; and Zone 4, 3. This redistribution allowed for improved resource utilization and facilitated a smoother operational flow without compromising the overall performance, as depicted in Fig. 4.13b. The simulation confirmed that this reduction enhanced efficiency while maintaining chute blockage at acceptable levels. Conversely, the effects of further reducing the workforce from 9 to 5 employees (with allocation of Zone 1, 1; Zone 2, 1; Zone 3, 1; Zone 4, 2) were evaluated in the simulations. This adjustment resulted in an increase in chute blockages, as illustrated in Fig. 4.13c. As chute utilization became strained under the reduced staffing conditions, the simulations highlighted the delicate balance between resource counts and operational throughput. These findings highlighted the critical role of effective resource management in sustaining operational efficiency within sorting operations, serving as a fundamental insight into the optimal allocation strategies for the logistics company.

By simulating real-world scenarios and potential levers, we could identify inefficiencies, understand the implication of potential interventions prior to their implementation, and achieve measurable improvements in performance. The findings are encouraging and provide sufficient insights for an evidence-driven approach to terminal optimization. Relocating infrastructure components proved effective in reducing parcel dwell times and recirculation rates. Strategic resource allocation emphasized the need for careful resource planning to improve resource utilization and prevent blockages, while increasing recirculation count showcased the potential for system-wide sorting time enhancements. The results highlight the scalability of this approach, providing a robust framework for enhancing logistics operations in dynamic and complex environments.

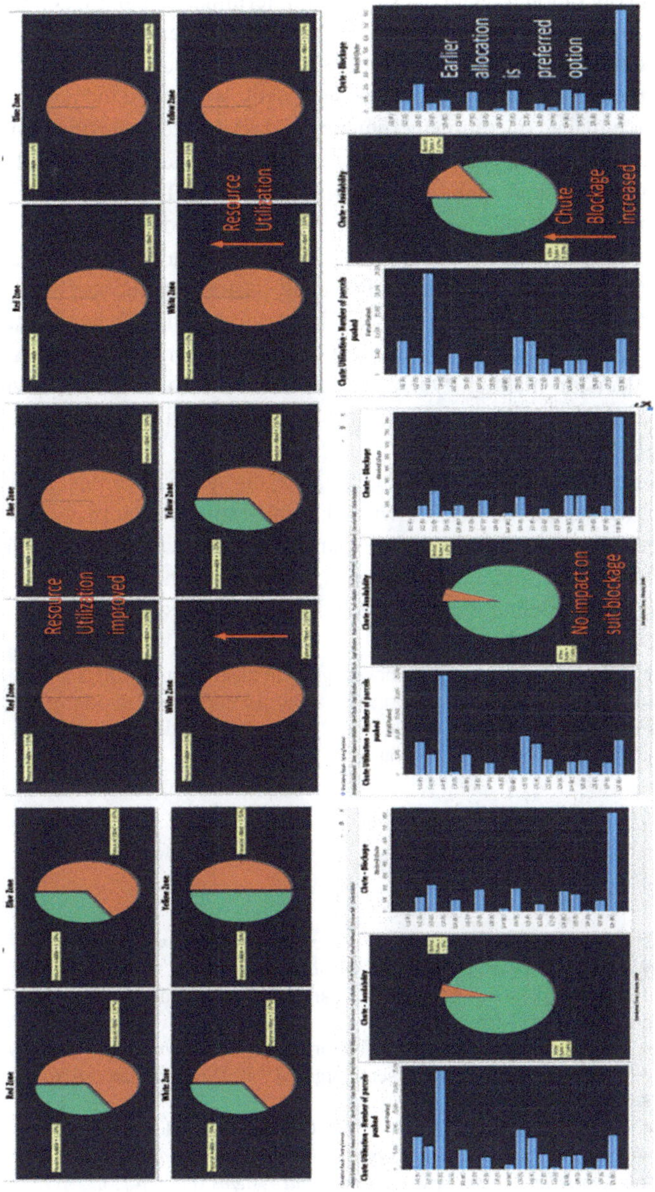

(a) [Z1:3, Z2:3, Z3:3, Z4: 4] (b) [Z1:2, Z2:2, Z3:2, Z4: 3] (c) [Z1:1, Z2:1, Z3:1, Z4: 2]

Fig. 4.13 Experimenting with various resource allocations

Conclusion

This chapter explored the complexities of modern logistics operations with a specific focus on the operational challenges of sorting terminals arising from growing parcel volumes; fluctuating customer demands in B2B, B2C, and C2C contexts; and inherent uncertainties within sorting terminals, such as resource productivity and misaligned configurations. To address these challenges, we argued the potential use of digital twins to enhance operational efficiency and resilience in sorting terminals.

We presented a comprehensive digital twin for sorting terminals detailing its construction, validation, and ability to experiment with real-world market situations, disruptions, and enhancement options. The proposed digital twin leverages configurable agents to model key components, interactions, and parameters at finer level of granularity to enable in-depth in silico analysis and simulation-based experimentation. Through a real-life case study, we demonstrated the efficacy of the digital twin in identifying bottlenecks, optimizing operational parameters, and guiding evidence-based decision-making. Our early experience with the digital twin has been highly encouraging with a major postal company, finding it invaluable as a decision-support aid.

Building on this success, we are extending the digital twin to encompass the broader logistics network as a "twin of twins" by integrating digital twins of sorting terminals and vehicles. We envision this expanded digital twin as a technological enabler for transforming logistics companies, helping them achieve their goals while navigating the ever-changing landscape of modern logistics.

Acknowledgment The authors sincerely acknowledge Christian Østergaard, Christian Edfjäll, and Ravi Kiran Kotty for their invaluable support and insightful contributions during the configuration and validation of the sorting terminal digital twin. Moreover, their critical review of this chapter has been instrumental in enhancing its relevance.

References

1. Bowes, P. (2021, September 14). *Pitney Bowes parcel shipping index reveals 37 percent parcel volume growth in US for 2020*. Business Wire. Retrieved from https://www.businesswire.com/news/home/20210914005274/en/Pitney-Bowes-Parcel-Shipping-Index-Reveals-37-Percent-Parcel-Volume-Growth-in-US-for-2020
2. Council of Supply Chain Management Professionals. (n.d.). *Importance of supply chain management*. Retrieved from https://cscmp.org/CSCMP/Develop/Starting_Your_Career/Importance_of_Supply_Chain_Management.aspx
3. Barat, S., Kulkarni, V., Clark, T., & Barn, B. (2022, October). Digital twin as risk-free experimentation aid for techno-socio-economic systems. In *Proceedings of the 25th international conference on model driven engineering languages and systems* (pp. 66–75).
4. Werners, B., & Wülfing, T. (2010). Robust optimization of internal transports at a parcel sorting center operated by Deutsche Post World Net. *European Journal of Operational Research, 201*(2), 419–426.

5. Khir, R., Erera, A., & Toriello, A. (2021). Two-stage sort planning for express parcel delivery. *IISE Transactions, 53*(12), 1353–1368.
6. Ghosh, S., Pal, A., Kumar, P., Ojha, A., Paranjape, A. A., Barat, S., & Khadilkar, H. (2021, December). A simulation driven optimization algorithm for scheduling sorting center operations. In *2021 winter simulation conference (WSC)* (pp. 1–12). IEEE.
7. Feng, C. (2024). Design of logistics sorting algorithm based on deep learning and sampling evaluation. *International Journal of Computational Intelligence Systems, 17*(1), 82.
8. Li, X., Hong, Y. T., Zheng, H., & Chen, X. J. (2009). FlexSim system simulation software in the distribution center sorting system design. *Logistics Engineering and Management, 31*(1), 37–39.
9. Zhang, F., & Tian, C. (2017, September). Study on modeling and simulation of logistics sorting system based on FlexSim. In *2017 international conference on computer network, electronic and automation (ICCNEA)* (pp. 504–506). IEEE.
10. Changzheng, Z., & Guangpeng, J. (2024, August). Studies on the simulation optimization of distribution center operations for cold chain logistics using petri nets and AnyLogic. In *2024 12th international conference on traffic and logistic engineering (ICTLE)* (pp. 219–223). IEEE.
11. Clark, T., Kulkarni, V., Barat, S., & Barn, B. (2017). ESL: An actor-based platform for developing emergent behaviour organisation simulations. In *Advances in practical applications of cyber-physical multi-agent systems: The PAAMS collection: 15th international conference, PAAMS 2017, Porto, Portugal, June 21-23, 2017, proceedings 15* (pp. 311–315). Springer International Publishing.
12. Barat, S., Kulkarni, V., Paranjape, A., Dhandapani, S., Manuelraj, S., & Parameswaran, S. P. (2022). Agent based digital twin of sorting terminal to improve efficiency and resiliency in parcel delivery. In *International conference on practical applications of agents and multi-agent systems* (pp. 24–35). Springer International Publishing.
13. Sargent, R. G. (2020, December). Verification and validation of simulation models: An advanced tutorial. In *2020 winter simulation conference (WSC)* (pp. 16–29). IEEE.

Chapter 5
Digital Twins for Process Optimization and Predictive Maintenance in Manufacturing Industries

Venkataramana Runkana, Ratnamala Manna, Anagha Deshpande, Sandipan Maiti, Nital Shah, Sri Harsha Nistala, Aditya Pareek, Sivakumar Subramanian, and Rajan Kumar

Abstract Manufacturing industries face challenges in meeting targets with respect to profitability, sustainability, and safety on a daily basis. With the advent of technologies like Internet of Things, artificial intelligence, and hyper-scaler cloud platforms, industries are adopting these new technologies to transform their operations. Digital twins are at the heart of such digital transformations. They are being developed and deployed more often as the technology is becoming mature. Challenges faced by manufacturing industries in adopting digital twins, methodologies, and frameworks for development and deployment of digital twins are described in detail in this chapter. A few real-life examples from power utilities and mineral-processing industries on process optimization and predictive maintenance are presented. Recent developments covering physics-informed neural network models, dynamic root cause identification, and security of digital twin models are briefly discussed. Suggestions for future research on digital twin systems for manufacturing industries are provided.

Introduction

Continuous and discrete manufacturing industries such as chemicals and fertilizers, oil and gas, petrochemicals, drugs and pharmaceuticals, pulp and paper, cement, minerals and metals, automotive, semiconductors, consumer packaged goods, and food processing essentially transform raw materials into products. By-products,

---

V. Runkana (✉) · R. Manna · A. Deshpande · S. Maiti · N. Shah · S. H. Nistala · A. Pareek · S. Subramanian · R. Kumar
Tata Research Development and Design Centre, TCS Research, Tata Consultancy Services Limited, Pune, Maharashtra, India
e-mail: venkat.runkana@tcs.com; ratnamala.manna@tcs.com; anagha.deshpande@tcs.com; sandipan.maiti@tcs.com; shah.nital2202@gmail.com; sriharsha.nistala@tcs.com; pareek9590@gmail.com; sivakumar.subramanian1@tcs.com; rajan48108@gmail.com

V. Kulkarni et al. (eds.), *Digital Twins for Simulation-Based Decision-Making*,
https://doi.org/10.1007/978-3-031-89654-5_5

solid wastes, liquid effluents, and gaseous emissions are also generated in the process. Typically, manufacturing happens in an industrial plant (alternatively referred to as "plant"). The plant comprises of multiple components or equipment, and many industrial processes are carried out in the plant, by one or more of these plant components. A simplified schematic of a typical process manufacturing plant comprising of multiple process units (equipment) interconnected in a complex manner is shown in Fig. 5.1. The process units differ for each plant depending on the products that are manufactured. For the plant to perform at expected efficiency levels and to deliver intended results, the processing units that constitute the plant and different processes that occur within these units need to perform as desired. If any of these components and/or processes do not perform as expected, due to their interconnected nature, it can adversely affect various key performance indicators (KPIs) of an industrial plant, such as overall throughput and productivity, product quality, energy efficiency, rate of release of emissions or wastes or effluents, availability of the plant, cost of maintenance of equipment, number of safety related incidents, etc., and can reduce the overall efficiency at which the plant is operating. These industries face a multitude of challenges in terms of uncertainties in the availability and quality of raw materials and components, production targets, market demand for products, condition and health of the equipment, or assets that are used for transforming raw materials into products, environmental conditions, regulations with respect to emissions and personal safety, etc. Optimization of manufacturing operations and predictive maintenance of equipment are the two key challenges faced by the industries in this dynamic business environment. Continuous monitoring, diagnosis, optimization, and control of various processes and equipment involved in an industrial manufacturing plant hold the key to address these challenges and maintain or improve the efficiency of production operations.

Continuous monitoring helps in timely diagnosis of any of the aforementioned challenges, which in turn enables appropriate actions/corrective measures based on prior knowledge and experience and/or simulation, optimization and control. Instruments or sensors are installed on each and every processing unit in a plant for

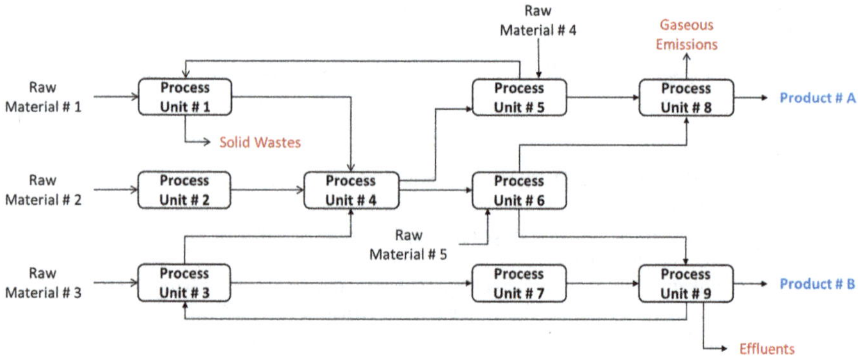

Fig. 5.1 Schematic of a typical process manufacturing plant

this purpose. The number of sensors on each unit may range from a few hundreds to a few thousands, whereas the number of sensors in each manufacturing plant may range from a few thousands to several thousands. These sensors are installed typically for measurement of process variables such as temperatures, pressures, and flow rates. These sensors are usually calibrated regularly to ensure the measurements are accurate. However, despite this, it becomes necessary to carry out data reconciliation [1] to deal with malfunctioning of sensors and erroneous measurements before the faulty sensors are detected, recalibrated, or replaced with freshly calibrated sensors.

Real-time data collected through online sensors is usually sent to automation and control systems such as Supervisory Control and Data Acquisition (SCADA) or Distributed Control System (DCS) or Manufacturing Executing System (MES) or Manufacturing Operations Management (MOM) system and stored and archived in what are usually referred to as Historians. In order to perform a plant-wide performance monitoring, it is important that all such variables or parameters corresponding to processes, materials, sensors, automation systems, actions of plant operators, environmental conditions, and equipment health are monitored and their corresponding values are collected. However, the industrial plants typically have complex architectures, and it may be difficult to monitor certain parameters. For example, temperature inside a multi-phase reactor or a boiler may be too high to be measured using temperature sensors, or even if capable temperature sensors are installed, they may get damaged due to constant exposure to high temperatures and pressures. In such scenarios, the existing plant monitoring systems fail to perform the monitoring as desired, and this in turn affects efficiency with which corrective measures are taken. To a certain extent, soft sensors, based on data-driven/physics-based/hybrid models are developed and utilized for this purpose, provided they can be deployed for real-time monitoring and control. Soft sensors are also critical for carrying out mass and energy balances across individual processing units or for the whole plant [2].

Characterization of materials is another important and critical activity in manufacturing industries as properties of materials have a strong influence on the KPIs mentioned above. This is usually done in-line, at-line, or off-line. In-line sensing is carried out if appropriate sensors are available to measure the properties online in real time. On the other hand, at-line and off-line measurements are done by collecting samples of materials and measuring their properties like density, viscosity, chemical composition, etc. At-line analysis is done on the shop-floor itself, whereas off-line analysis is carried out in the laboratory using appropriate instruments and characterization equipment such as rheometer, x-ray diffractometer (XRD), gas chromatograph-mass spectrometry (GC-MS), high-performance liquid chromatograph (HPLC), scanning electron microscope (SEM), etc. The data from these instruments consists of both structured and unstructured data (images). Structured data related to materials is usually captured and stored in a laboratory information and management system (LIMS), whereas the images are stored within the software systems connected with each characterization equipment.

Condition and health monitoring of equipment is another activity that is important in manufacturing operations as maintenance of equipment in good condition is paramount to achieving targeted KPIs. Parameters like voltage, current drawn, vibration, power drawn, etc. are commonly measured, and periodic inspection and maintenance are also carried out for this purpose. While measured parameters are stored in databases, inspection and maintenance reports are usually stored in the form of documents, images, and videos.

Process automation and control systems in manufacturing industries ensure that the plant operates at the set points of various operating process variables maintained and controlled within their desired limits based on sensor data. The control systems consist of single input-single output (SISO) or multiple input-multiple output (MIMO) systems designed for specific control loops in a processing unit. The control systems are commonly based on proportional-integral-derivative (PID)-type control algorithms, although many advanced process control (APC) systems employ model predictive control (MPC) algorithms. Majority of them do not take the data or information related to materials or equipment condition into account. Also, the control systems have a predefined input-output structure involving the manipulated and controlled variables.

Prediction, simulation, and forecasting of the behavior of the plant is another important requirement as data from sensors or from laboratory analyses is not sufficient to understand and control the manufacturing operations. The control systems are commonly deployed for process control and are not designed to track equipment health. Often, they do not consider material properties, especially those obtained by off-line analysis. Typically, the control models are data-driven and obtained through system identification. Steps tests are usually carried out on the process for a set of operating conditions for obtaining appropriate data that is utilized for system identification. The accuracy of these models beyond the region of operation is generally poor, and one has to carry out system identification again to update the control models for any new operating regime.

One potential solution to these problems is the application of digital twins that emulate working of the plant, which can be then used to monitor, assess, and improve its performance [3]. It is imperative to develop methods or techniques that can quantitatively capture information related to the behavior and status (operating performance, health, etc.) of a plant at any instance, the ingredients/raw materials used, the influence of the control settings, and so on to build a digital twin of an industrial process and/or equipment. A digital twin of the system is expected to describe the current state of the corresponding industrial process and/or equipment and predict or forecast values of one or more process variables or asset health parameters in the future and recommend necessary actions for its improvement. With the advent of artificial intelligence and machine learning algorithms and abundance of data supported by advanced sensors and IoT platforms, industries are embracing these technologies to build and deploy digital twins or self-organizing cyber-physical systems for online optimization of manufacturing operations and for predictive maintenance of the assets so as to optimize the performance of the entire industrial plant. A detailed review of the recent work on application of artificial intelligence and machine learning for process systems engineering is available elsewhere [4].

We have been involved in the development and deployment of digital twins for manufacturing industries. Details of the frameworks developed along with a few industrial applications are described in this chapter. It is not intended here to review the current literature on digital twins. Rather, our objective is to share the knowledge and experience of developing and deploying industrial analytics and digital twin solutions for production operations. This chapter is organized as follows: The basic definition of a digital twin for manufacturing operations is discussed in the next section followed by descriptions of the frameworks for development and deployment of digital twins. Industrial applications of digital twins are explained through three real-life examples, namely, boiler performance optimization, plant-wide optimization of mineral processing, and predictive maintenance of an air preheater. Recent developments on physics-informed neural networks, real-time root cause identification, and security of digital twin models are briefly covered subsequently. Summary and suggestions for future research are presented last.

Digital Twin Framework

We define the digital twin as an autonomous cyber-physical system of systems that is in continuous synchronization with the industrial plant, ingesting all the data from the plant in real time and providing solutions to optimize the KPIs of a plant in real time [3]. A digital twin is essentially a system that provides a mechanism for monitoring plants, determining whether performance of the plant as a whole or of any of the plant components, including sensors, actuators, and controllers and plant automation systems, is meeting a desired performance level, and accordingly determines and triggers corrective action in real time. The digital twin at its core has a mathematical or computational representation of the process unit or plant it is representing, which can be used to predict the variables of interest that are mapped to measured/unmeasured physical quantities or an abstract condition such as its health. It also provides a means to temporarily or otherwise substitute the lack of good-quality data through soft sensors in case the physical sensors are found to be faulty or non-functional. The soft sensors, in turn, are also monitored continuously to ascertain their performance, and their behavioral models are updated, if found necessary, through self-update algorithms, to be explained subsequently. In a general sense, the soft sensors are the digital twins of the physical sensors or instruments as well as sensors for parameters that are not measured.

The key elements of an industrial plant are raw materials, products, by-products, wastes or effluents or emissions, main and auxiliary equipment, sensors or instruments, plant automation systems, the environment in which the industrial plant is operating, and the people operating the plant. The digital twin system is expected to monitor the current condition and performance of these elements of the industrial plant, diagnose the reasons for any deviations in their behavior or performance, predict KPIs for real-time validation of the predicted behavior, forecast the future behavior and performance of the elements as well as the industrial plant as a whole, and provide recommendations to improve the behavior and the performance of the industrial plant through various components of the system. The key component of such a system is the behavioral model of the industrial plant. In a general sense, the behavioral model may represent a prediction model, a classification model, an optimization model, or any similar model that is used to represent the behavior of an industrial plant. The models themselves may be physics- or first principles-based models, data-driven models derived through statistical or machine learning or deep learning techniques, hybrid physics-based plus data-driven models, or qualitative models that may utilize techniques such as fuzzy logic or agent-based modeling for circumstances or situations that cannot be described using physics-based or data-driven models.

There are three important stages in the realization of digital twins, namely, development, deployment, and maintenance. Development of necessary algorithms and models is usually carried out using historical data to train, validate, and test the models before they are deployed online. On the other hand, the digital twin systems, when deployed online, have to deal with streaming real-time data from sensors as well as data from other sources like LIMS. After deployment, it is important to continuously monitor the performance of the digital twin system, especially the models, and maintain or update them through self-learning. Additionally, since the main purpose of digital twins is to improve the plant performance, one needs to identify the business goals to be achieved through digital twins and define the scope before embarking on development. Similarly, once a digital twin system with a defined scope and objectives has been developed and deployed, based on the knowledge and experience gained, one may intend to scale the system in terms of enhancing the scope or features of the digital twin system already developed, expand the scope to the entire manufacturing plant, and also replicate the same for multiple processing lines or plants. The framework for development of digital twins is described first.

Framework for Development of Digital Twins

A typical manufacturing plant consists of a number of interconnected processing units for transforming raw materials into final products (see Fig. 5.1). While the raw materials go through multiple processing units in a sequential manner, some intermediate products may be recycled to previous processing steps in order to improve efficiency of operations and the product quality. Typical processing units in a manufacturing plant may consist of blending or mixing units, reactors, boilers, turbines, heat exchangers, distillation columns, evaporators, extruders, furnaces, etc. Additionally, auxiliary units like pumps, blowers, conveyors, and compressors would also be required for transportation and processing of gases, liquids, solids, and their mixtures. It is necessary to handle a plurality of data that consists of process variables, environmental variables, market demand, availability of raw materials, condition of process equipment, and characteristics of raw materials, intermediate products, by-products, final products, emissions, wastes, and effluents. These datasets are acquired and stored in multiple systems such as a SCADA, DCS, LIMS, MES, Historians, etc.

The general framework for development of various algorithms and models required for developing digital twins, starting from raw data to coming up with implementable recommendations through prescriptive analytics, is shown in Fig. 5.2 [5]. Initially, data is combined at a process unit level to obtain unit-wise dataset of all the industrial processing units, wherein the unit-wise dataset of each processing unit is sampled at a different frequency. The unit-wise datasets are integrated and synchronized, taking into account the time lags due to residence times in various units and times of transportation of materials between one or more industrial processing units and response time of one or more sensors of the processing units. In the next step, the integrated unit-wise dataset is checked for quality, for example, presence of unrealistic values, percent availability, standard deviation and interquartile range of all the variables of the processing unit, etc. Subsequently, the raw data is pre-processed to obtain clean datasets of each of the industrial processing units, wherein pre-processing is an iterative process comprising the steps of outlier removal, imputation of missing values, and clustering [6]. Next, the data for each process unit is integrated to obtain data for the whole plant, combining the pre-processed data of each of the industrial processing units. This data can also be supplemented with additional data obtained through simulations using physics-based or data-driven models, if available, for variables that are not available through sensors or laboratory analyses and can be predicted through such models. This provides us with the final set of data that is available and suitable for subsequent descriptive, diagnostic, predictive, and prescriptive analytics at the enterprise level.

Descriptive analytics is carried out mainly for knowledge discovery through data mining. It is important to identify the regime of operation of the plant as it keeps changing based on availability of raw materials, production targets, environmental conditions, etc. This can be carried out using clustering techniques such as distance-based clustering, density-based clustering, and hierarchical clustering. Baseline statistics are also extracted to determine ranges of each variable corresponding to the KPIs of the enterprise level dataset, based on predefined baseline statistics and the one or more operating regimes. These operating ranges of variables are useful in various activities subsequently, for example, steady-state identification, process monitoring and diagnostics, constrained optimization, etc.

Diagnostic analytics is one of the most sought-after tasks in manufacturing industries as process engineers usually need to understand the reasons for any deterioration or improvement of plant performance through root cause analysis. In this context, dynamic root cause analysis is very important as one could use various feature selection techniques to determine the relationship between KPIs and manipulated and disturbance variables and identify the key variables for each KPI in a dynamic fashion. Feature selection could be carried out for each regime of plant operation as well as with the overall dataset at the enterprise level to obtain a set of

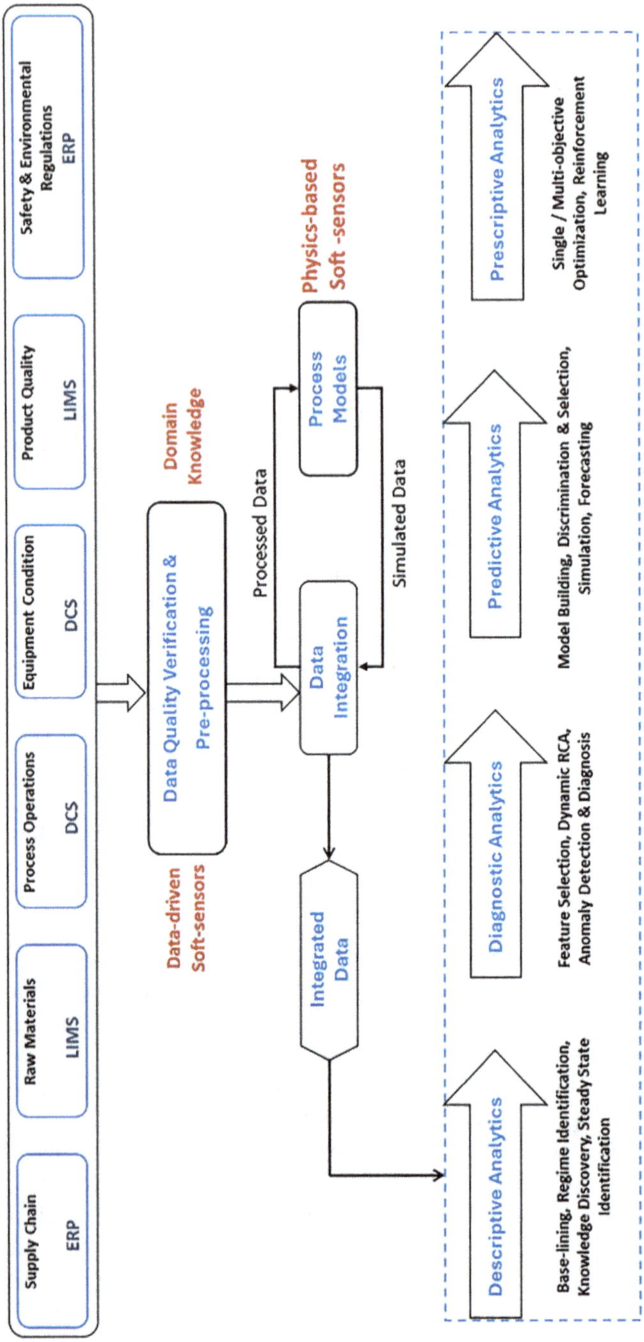

Fig. 5.2 Framework for development of digital twin models

global features. This helps in dimensionality reduction as well. Additionally, diagnostics is also carried out to detect anomalies in both process and equipment health or performance and diagnose the reasons for the same in this step. Ground-truth data or information available in maintenance records and operator logs along with sensor data will be useful for validation of such diagnostics models.

The key variables identified in the diagnostic analysis are utilized in the predictive analytics step for developing the models. The objective here is to identify an appropriate ML/DL algorithm from the available set of algorithms to build an accurate model for each variable based on various model performance metrics such as mean absolute error, hit rate, R^2, precision, recall, etc. The steps described above are followed for both regression and classification models, and the models are tested with historical data rigorously to ensure that the models meet the accuracy and robustness requirements. These models are utilized to act as soft sensors for monitoring and control, for carrying out what-if and if-what simulations, for forecasting and prognostics, and for taking optimization and control actions or decisions.

Finally, prescriptive analytics is carried out through single or multi-objective optimization using the ML/DL models derived in the previous step with appropriate constraints for all KPIs and process variables, derived in the descriptive analytics step. Here again, one could employ a multitude of optimization techniques including gradient search, linear programming, goal programming, simulated annealing, and evolutionary algorithms and choose an appropriate algorithm based on the success of convergence under different operating regimes, computational costs, and the optimization results obtained.

Once all the models, workflows, and algorithms are tested with sufficient good-quality historical data, they are deployed online for real-time monitoring, detection, diagnosis, simulation, forecasting or prognostics, optimization, etc., described next.

Framework for Deployment of Digital Twins

A digital twin system once deployed in a real-time production environment has to work in an autonomous manner, receiving data from all sources in a manufacturing plant and providing actionable recommendations that can be implemented on the physical entity for which it was created. A typical digital twin system consists of various modules that include features such as data ingestion, data quality verification, data pre-processing, data synchronization and integration, simulation, forecasting, and optimization and cognitive features such as self-monitoring, self-diagnosis, and self-learning for updating the workflows and models that are part of the digital twin system in a continuous manner. It will also have modules for data sources management, sensor management, workflow management, model management, and algorithm management as the system has to deal with thousands of sensors, algorithms, and workflows and models for a reasonably complex manufacturing plant. The digital twin is implemented as an independent system and is interfaced with plant automation systems so that it is in continuous synchronization with the plant in real time (see Fig. 5.3) [7].

The digital twin system is configured to collect information related to various variables and parameters associated with different processes and assets in the manufacturing plant that is being monitored. The data ingestion module receives real-time and non-real-time data from a plurality of plant data servers. The plant data servers may store information related to various variables and parameters specific to working of the plant, for example, physical and chemical characteristics of materials (raw materials, final products, intermediate products, by-products, solid wastes, liquid effluents, gaseous emissions, etc.), plant operating conditions (flow rates of materials, temperatures and pressures in a particular equipment or at different locations in the plant), condition of the equipment (power consumed, current drawn, fouling, vibration, etc.), environmental conditions (temperature, pressure, humidity, wind velocity, etc.), uptime of automation systems, heartbeat of an instrument signal, etc. The data sources management module stores information regarding connection to the plant data servers in the databases. Further, the data synchronization and integration module synchronizes and integrates real-time and non-real-time data from all process units in the plant considering time lags due to residence times in various units, time involved in transportation between various units, and response times of sensors.

Soft sensors are the fundamental building blocks of a digital twin system. The soft sensor is used here as a generic term to represent all the models that are part of the system. They may include models of sensors, manufacturing processes, process equipment variables, etc. and can be of various types, that is, data-driven, physics-based, and hybrid. While the soft sensors for physical sensors may act as redundant

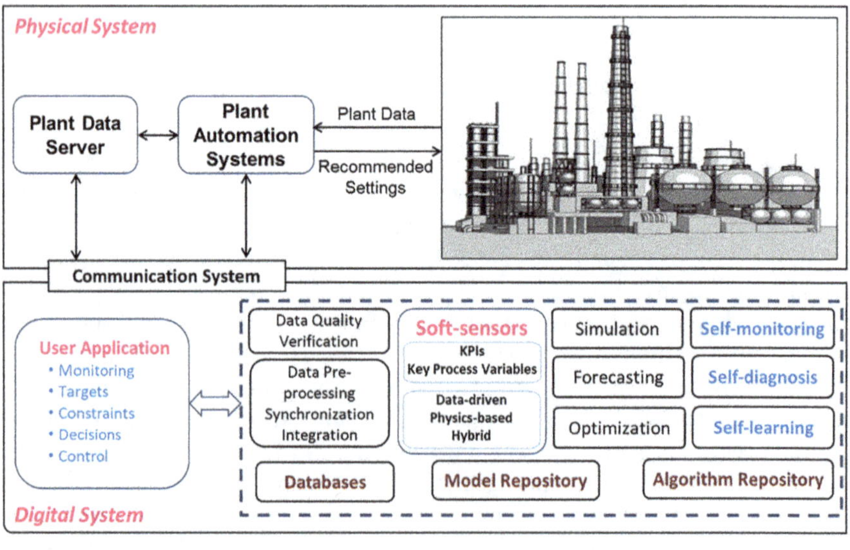

Fig. 5.3 Schematic of a typical digital twin system for manufacturing processes

sensors to deal with failure or malfunctioning of the physical sensor, they are of great value for critical parameters that are difficult to measure and for product quality parameters that are usually obtained through off-line laboratory analyses. The digital twin system utilizes the soft sensors for predictions, for carrying out simulations, for forecasting the behavior, and for process optimization and control. The performance of soft sensors is continuously monitored and compared with actual measurements so as to check the accuracy of predictions and to take corrective actions if needed. This is where the cognitive capabilities of a digital twin system become necessary.

The self-monitoring module monitors the performance of all the soft sensors in terms of prediction accuracy and behavioral patterns, especially with respect to manufacturing processes and equipment health. The functional block diagram depicting components of the self-monitoring module is shown in Fig. 5.4. It includes modules for data quality verification, monitoring of sensors and actuators, soft sensors, data pre-processing, and self-diagnosis. The self-monitoring module is configured to function at multiple levels. At the lowest level, it monitors plant measurements of process variables, actuator signals, or controller outputs using their corresponding soft sensors that are in essence the digital twins of corresponding physical entities. It monitors the assets and their operational behavior as well. At the highest or the global level, the self-monitoring module monitors the complete industrial plant comprising of various assets, the operations/processes that are being carried out in the plant, materials and their flow, environment in which the plant operates, the people/users who operate the plant, and the automation systems that operate at the individual asset or operation level, in order to optimize the performance of the complete industrial plant at the global level. The self-monitoring module makes the whole system integrated, in the sense that it works at the sensor and materials level as well as at the global industrial plant level, and links all the other self-organization

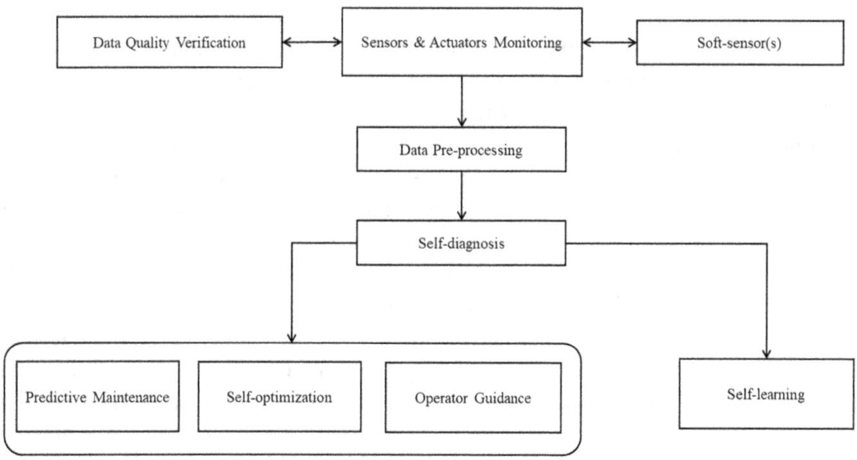

Fig. 5.4 Self-monitoring module in a digital twin system [7]

features, that is, self-diagnosis, self-learning, and self-optimization. The self-monitoring module also uses the plant data as well as predictions of the behavioral models to monitor the soft sensors for any degradation in their predictive capabilities, which may be caused due to a multitude of factors, for example, physical failure of the sensor, inappropriate or infrequent calibration of the sensor, degradation of the predictive capabilities of the behavioral model of a sensor or a process, etc.

The self-monitoring module receives plant data from data synchronization and integration module. Further, the sensors and actuators monitoring module processes the received data to check if characteristics of the data are within predefined acceptable ranges. The sensors and actuators monitoring module may use any suitable data-processing method. If advanced processing of the data is required to verify the data quality, the sensors and actuators monitoring module invokes data quality verification module, which performs advanced-quality verification involving multivariate analysis or any other similar data-processing technique. Further, the sensors and actuators monitoring module may invoke soft sensors module to obtain information related to key internal process variables that may not be measured or measured in non-real time or difficult to measure or when a physical sensor is malfunctioning. The soft sensors module makes predictions of such variables with the help of a behavioral model and available data from the industrial plant. The data-preprocessing module further processes the data to determine if there are gaps, outliers, anomalies, etc. and imputes the missing data or performs outlier removal. Further, the self-diagnosis module monitors the process and equipment conditions based on data received from the industrial plant and the historical data and invokes different modules to perform appropriate actions.

By processing the collected information, the self-monitoring module determines performance of each of the plant components separately and performance of the plant as a whole and also the behavioral models of the industrial plants and its various components. It monitors both the physical industrial plant and its digital counterpart continuously. Monitoring of the physical plant is carried out using the data coming from the physical plant, whereas monitoring of the digital plant is done using the data coming from the predictions of the behavioral model or models of the physical plant. Further, monitoring the performance separately at component level and at plant level allows to detect the deterioration in performance, if any, at the component level and at the plant level, so that the performance correction action(s) can be triggered at the individual component level as well. Also, multiple components of the plant may together constitute different "sections" of the plant. By processing groups of data from different components that form a section, performance measurement/assessment can be done at a section level as well. Values or range of values of different variables, or of a combination of variables, that represent an expected/desired performance of each of the components and that of a whole section are stored in the database. The self-monitoring module compares the estimated performance with the expected performance and determines the deviation(s). If deviation up to a certain limit may be allowed, a threshold of performance may be configured with the self-monitoring module. If the estimated performance is matching the desired performance or if the deviation is below the threshold of deviation, then working of the component/process may be considered to be in a "normal range" of operation. If the estimated deviation exceeds the threshold of deviation for any component or process, then the self-monitoring module determines that the component/process is outside the normal range of operation.

Upon detecting that the operation of at least one of the components is outside the defined normal range of operation, the self-monitoring module triggers self-diagnosis. When self-diagnosis is triggered, the self-diagnosis module determines one or more actions to be executed in response to the determined deviation. The self-diagnosis module is configured to detect triggers corresponding to different actions. The triggers may be detected in terms of values of different variables or combination of variables, as configured. Similarly, different triggers may be defined in terms of variables such as, but not limited to, model quality parameters, based on whether a new regime has been flagged, based on whether any new raw materials change has been detected, and so on.

If the performance of one or more of the process or equipment behavioral models is below a threshold of performance, a trigger for executing self-learning of one or more behavioral models is initiated by the self-diagnosis module. For example, predictions generated by one or more of the behavioral models may be below a threshold of quality of the behavioral model. In such cases, the models may be interpreted as being underperforming models by the self-diagnosis module. Upon identifying this trigger, the self-diagnosis module invokes the self-learning module to perform a self-update/self-learning mechanism to update one or more behavioral models [8]. Similarly, if the performance level of the industrial plant is below a defined benchmark of performance of the industrial plant, a trigger for executing optimization of the industrial plant is initiated by the self-diagnosis module. Similarly, if deviation in performance or health of one or more of the plant components from a defined benchmark of performance or health indicator of the components exceeds a threshold, a trigger is initiated for executing the predictive maintenance of the plant components. The maintenance of the behavioral models of the plant and its components, and the self-learning of the behavioral models, is repeated till their performance reaches a desired level to ensure the plant and its components perform at the expected levels.

The self-diagnosis module includes modules for steady-state/unsteady-state identification, steady-state estimation, time lag identification, regime shift analysis, raw material identification, remaining useful life (RUL) estimation, real-time root cause analysis, feature extraction, feature strength estimation, alarm diagnosis, and so on. It monitors the process operating conditions and invokes different modules to perform appropriate actions. It is to be noted that the components/blocks of the self-diagnosis module may change depending on types of trigger conditions defined. For example, the regime shift analysis module is to be included in the self-diagnosis module only if any trigger in terms of the regime shift is to be detected.

Based on the data and information received from the data pre-processing module, the self-diagnosis module carries out several activities that may comprise identification of the current state of the plant in terms of steady or unsteady state and determination of time lags that provide an estimate of the effect of a particular independent process variable or a set of variables on a dependent variable or a set of dependent variables [9]. This is of immense help to provide answers to commonly asked questions, for example, how long does it take to see the effect of physical or chemical characteristics of a particular raw material on productivity of a process or quality of a product is one of the key inputs required by plant operators for optimization and control of a plant, identification of the regime of operation of a plant [10] to understand whether to trigger the self-update module, detection of anomalies in the health or condition of an equipment to provide appropriate advice to the operators when to carry out maintenance activities of that equipment, identification of key factors that are causing degradation of the plant performance through real-time root cause analysis, extracting features from signals or time series data from the sensors, and utilizing these extracted features either to provide insights to the plant operators or to provide inputs to behavioral models of the digital twin system.

The self-learning module (Fig. 5.5) is one of the key components of a digital twin system. Based on triggers from the self-monitoring and self-diagnosis modules, the self-learning module is activated to update the models. The self-update may involve model re-tuning (updating the parameters in the ML/DL algorithm used for building model) or model re-building (exploring multiple ML/DL algorithms but keeping the set of features or independent variables unchanged) or model re-creation (developing the ML/DL model ab initio, with new features exploring all available algorithms and identifying the best suitable algorithm for the given set of data). In case of physics-based models, re-tuning is carried out first to determine the best-fit values of model parameters. Model re-building may also be utilized to explore multiple numerical algorithms in case convergence is not achieved with the previously used numerical algorithm [11]. Automatic model re-creation of physics-based models is not feasible as it requires complete re-development of the model if the set of features has to be modified and new phenomena have to be incorporated into the model.

The databases in a digital twin system may store structured data like numerical values and unstructured data like text, images, sound, and videos. Further, the

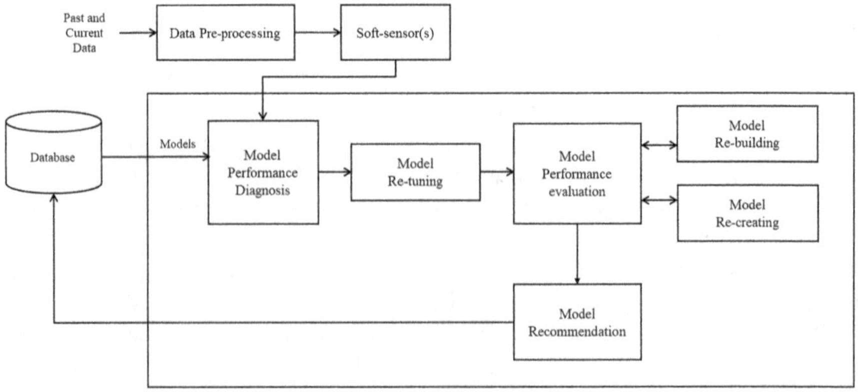

Fig. 5.5 Self-learning module in a digital twin system [7]

databases contain information that includes but not limited to data used by a plurality of services running in the monitoring framework, logs generated by the services running in system, prebuilt domain knowledge, raw data from various plant data sources and the corresponding processed data, knowledge extracted from the plant data, knowledge acquired from publicly available sources, etc.

The model repository stores a plurality of models that are invoked by the digital twin system. These models capture the behaviors of a component or a process or the plant KPIs, which may include one or more of models for soft sensors, optimization models, classification models, anomaly detection models, causal or sensitivity models, correlation models, etc. Based on the scope and requirements of the digital twin system, the complete model for a process or an asset may be composed by combining multiple models that represent the behavior, and the total number of models for a process may consist of several hundreds or even thousands of models.

The algorithms repository stores a plurality of ML or DL and numerical algorithms. The numerical algorithms are required for solving equations that represent physics-based models or for solving optimization and control problems. The physics-based models may consist of a set of linear or nonlinear algebraic or differential equations, and they may be solved using appropriate numerical algorithms such the Newton-Raphson method, Runge-Kutta method, finite difference method or finite volume method, etc. On the other hand, deterministic or stochastic optimization algorithms such as quadratic programming, genetic algorithms, and particle swarm optimization are employed to solve the single/multi-objective optimization and optimal control or model predictive control problems when the plant engineers seek to improve the KPIs of the plant with several business constraints that are expressed by the behavioral models. Additionally, the digital twin system will also have a workflow repository that contains workflows related to various activities required to build and deploy a digital twin. When the digital twin is deployed in a production environment, data flows from databases in the industrial plant to the monitoring module. The digital twin processes the real-time data as well as the historical data and reverts with real-time actionable recommendations to improve the working of the asset or a process unit or the complete industrial plant, depending on the scope and purpose for which it has been created.

The digital twin system may generate the data-driven behavioral models automatically in real time using the self-learning capabilities [8, 11], by executing the following steps. It collects real-time data representing the characteristics of working of the industrial plant and by monitoring its performance. It also collects and stores data representing working of the industrial plant in past instances as historical data and generates pre-processed data by pre-processing the real-time data and the historical data. It then simulates values of non-measurable parameters of the industrial plant by using physics-based or data-driven or hybrid models. The term "non-measurable" may represent certain data that cannot be measured in real-time due to complexities of the industrial plant. It may also represent certain data that could not be measured for an instance due to any temporary technical challenges. Further, the integrated data is generated by combining the pre-processed data and the simulated data. The integrated data is then used to generate each of the one or more data-driven models using the algorithms available in the repository. The digital twin system at the time of deployment may have certain capabilities to address the needs at the time of deployment. However, it can be updated to enhance the decision-making capabilities in order to address any future requirements, accessing the real-time as well as historical data, through off-line analyses and simulations. The process of updating the digital twin system as per new requirements may be manually triggered as and when needed or may be created as an automatic process (like periodic maintenance). For example, simulations using physics-based models that take relatively long time for execution may be invoked at predefined intervals so as to provide simulated or forecasted data from the physics-based models, and this data from the physics based models are used along with the real-time data from the plant, to generate the data-driven behavioral model(s), which are then used for determining/estimating the plant performance. The simulated data may also be archived along with the corresponding real-time data in the knowledge base of that plant for future use.

Based on the framework described above, we have developed a platform called TCS INTWIN™ for development and deployment of digital twin systems [7, 12]. While the generic features or components and working of a digital twin system are discussed here, detailed descriptions of specific examples of digital twins can be found elsewhere [13–17]. A few industrial applications are presented in the next section.

Industrial Applications

The TCS INTWIN™ platform has been used extensively not only for solving real-life industrial problems off-line but also for deploying digital twin systems across diverse industries such as power utilities, iron and steel, chemicals, pulp and paper, oil and gas, semiconductors, etc. for real-time monitoring, diagnostics, and optimization of manufacturing operations and for predictive maintenance of equipment. Three use cases related to performance optimization of a coal-fired boiler in a thermal power plant, plant-wide optimization of a mineral-processing plant, and predictive maintenance of an air pre-heater in a power plant are described briefly in this section.

Boiler Performance Optimization

Coal-fired boilers are important process units in a thermal power plant as the economics of power production and greenhouse gas emissions depend strongly on thermal efficiency of the boiler [18]. They are employed to generate steam from water using coal as fuel. Coal is combusted with air at high temperatures and results in release of gases such as carbon dioxide (CO_2), carbon monoxide (CO), and oxides of nitrogen (NOx) and sulfur (SOx). A simplified process flow diagram of a thermal power plant consisting of a pulverizer, boiler, selective catalytic reduction (SCR), and air pre-heater (APH) is shown in Fig. 5.6. The roles of SCR and APH are discussed later. The power plant engineers have to deal with challenges like dynamic changes in load and variations in coal quality in their day-to-day operations. Additionally, they have to conduct what is commonly referred to as combustion tuning if there is a major change in quality of coal or the condition of the boiler because the coal characteristics and boiler condition have a strong influence on boiler KPIs such as thermal efficiency and emissions [19]. Combustion tuning is also carried out at the time of commissioning of a boiler to determine the optimum operating conditions for a given type of coal or set of coals. A large number of tests are conducted on the industrial scale boiler by a team of combustion tuning experts to determine the optimum operating conditions for achieving high thermal efficiency while meeting the environmental and safety regulations. Process variables such as air-to-fuel ratio, flow rates of primary and secondary air, and their distributions are varied over their permissible ranges and their effects on boiler tube temperatures and pressures, and concentrations of O_2, NOx, and CO in the flue gases are evaluated during these tests to identify the optimum conditions for the given type of coal.

We have developed and deployed a digital twin system using the TCS INTWIN® platform to assist the combustion tuning team to reduce the time or the number of tests required. The generic framework was customized for a coal-fired boiler to suit the requirements of the power plant engineers. Data from more than 2000 sensors was collected along with coal characteristics (% fixed carbon, % volatile matter, %

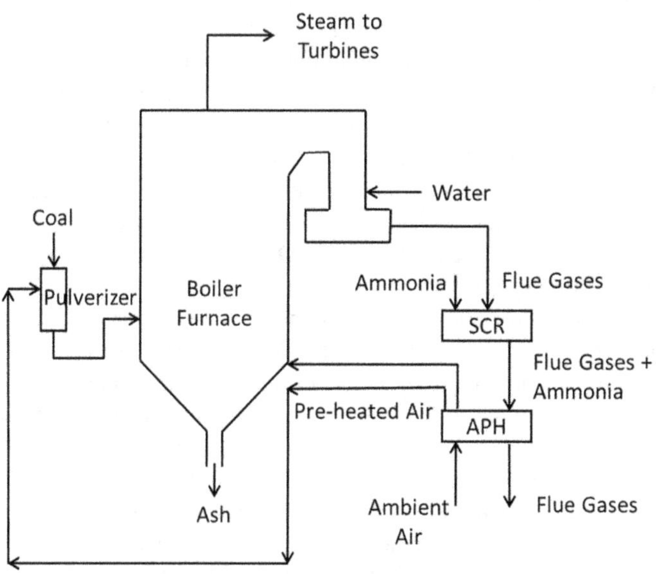

Fig. 5.6 Schematic of a coal-fired boiler along with additional units in the process (pulverizer, selective catalytic reduction (SCR), and air pre-heater (APH))

moisture content) to build ML models and to conduct multi-objective optimization in a dynamic manner during the commissioning of the boiler. ML models were developed for parameters like boiler thermal efficiency, boiler tube temperatures and pressures, concentrations of pollutants like NOx, CO, etc. Maximizing boiler efficiency and minimizing emissions were the two main objectives. The boiler tube temperatures and pressures were incorporated as constraints to ensure optimization results meet the safety requirements. Complete details of this implementation cannot be provided here due to confidentiality. Subsequently, the scope of the digital twin system was enhanced for optimization of day-to-day operations and for additional units in the power plant by customizing the INTWIN® platform specifically for power plants [20].

Plant-Wide Optimization of Mineral Processing

Metals such as iron, aluminum, copper, lithium, silicon, and nickel are intricately woven in our lives with a wide range of applications, for example, domestic appliances, automobiles, batteries, solar cells, wind turbines, electronic devices, medical devices, etc. Mineral processing is a critical step in the extraction of metals from the ores. Usually, ores containing the key mineral(s) are mined and processed to obtain a concentrate that is rich in the desirable mineral. Subsequently, the concentrate is further processed to extract the metal. For example, metallic iron (Fe) is available in iron ores in the form of minerals like hematite (Fe_2O_3) and magnetite (Fe_3O_4). It is extracted from the ore by reducing the mineral with reducing agents like carbon monoxide and hydrogen. The ore is first mined through operations such as blasting, fragmentation, crushing, and screening to obtain what is usually termed Run of the Mine (ROM) ore. This is transported to the mineral-processing plant where the ROM is purified to produce the mineral concentrate. As the ores generally contain both desirable and undesirable minerals, it's necessary to separate the former from the latter through mineral processing to obtain a relatively pure concentrate that is rich in the desirable mineral. The digital twin framework was applied for an industrial-scale mineral-processing plant. Details of this use case are briefly described here. More details can be found elsewhere [21].

A mineral-processing plant consists of continuous operations where mined ore in the form of rocks (0.2 m or above) is broken down to fine particles (50–100 μm) by passing it through a comminution circuit consisting of crushers and grinding mills. These fine particles are fed to the flotation circuit of the plant, which consists of a series of flotation cells. Flotation is essentially a separation process in which desirable minerals are floated out in a bubbly environment from the undesirable minerals present in the ore using a mixture of chemical reagents. The final output of the flotation circuit is in the form of a mineral concentrate (primary product) and tailings (waste). A representative process flow diagram of the industrial mineral-processing plant is shown in Fig. 5.7 [21, 22]. The ore is processed through a sequence of unit operations like crushing (in gyratory and cone crushers), grinding (in a

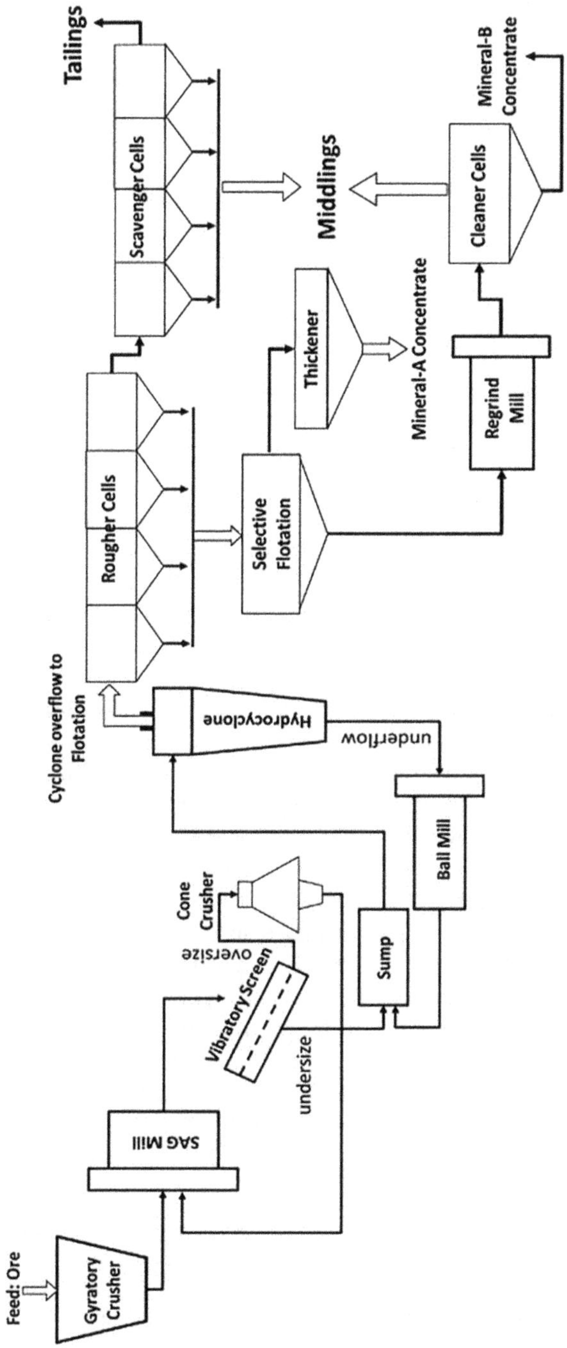

Fig. 5.7 Schematic of a typical mineral-processing plant [21]

semi-autogenous grinding or a ball mill), screening, solid-liquid separation in cyclones (for separating coarse particles from fine particles based on their size and specific gravity), flotation (rougher cells, scavenger cells, cleaner cells), and thickening (for separating solid particles from liquid using chemical reagents like dispersants, flocculants, and thickening agents). Depending on the geological nature, the ore may contain more than one desirable mineral, and it is possible to obtain two concentrated products separately. In the process, middlings (containing both desirable and undesirable minerals but with low purity) and tailings (essentially a waste that has low levels of desirable minerals) are also generated. It is important to achieve a high concentration of the desirable mineral in the concentrate and a low concentration in the tailings so as not to lose the valuable mineral through the tailings.

The aim of mineral-processing operations is to maximize both recovery or yield and purity of the desired mineral in the concentrate. However, there is a trade-off as it's not possible to maximize both yield and purity at the same time. As the quality of ores keeps changing with time, it is necessary to identify the optimum conditions to achieve high yield and purity. The common practice is to manipulate flow rate of raw ore to the grinding circuit to achieve a high yield, compromising the plant throughput and potentially neglecting the purity of mineral concentrate as well. Hence, there is a need to improve purity of the mineral concentrate too while attempting to achieve a high yield by identifying and controlling other important variables in different units of the plant.

All relevant data for more than 1200 process variables, including data from sensors and laboratory analyses, from the industrial plant was collected for about a year, and the framework described in the previous section was used for building models of plant KPIs as well as key process variables and for model-based process optimization. After carrying out data quality verification and pre-processing steps, feature selection algorithms were employed to identify manipulated variables other than feed rate of the ore that affect both yield and concentrate purity, for example, pH, air flow rates to different flotation cells, and reagent addition rates. ML models were developed for KPIs of the plant using the ML algorithms available in the TCS INTWIN® platform. Model predictions of yield and purity for one of the desirable minerals are compared with actual plant data in Fig. 5.8.

A multi-objective optimization problem was formulated with two objectives, maximize yield and concentrate purity with appropriate constraints, and solved using the Non-dominated Sorting Genetic Algorithm (NSGA)-II [23] to determine the set points of manipulated variables such that the KPIs of the plant can be improved. The results of optimization are shown in Fig. 5.9. It can be noticed that there is a trade-off between yield and concentrate purity, and it is also strongly influenced by the grade or purity of ore being processed. As the ore quality degrades, the scope for improving recovery and purity decreases. Suggestions in the form of look-up tables were provided to the plant operators to assist them in changing the set points at regular intervals based on the quality of ore being processed.

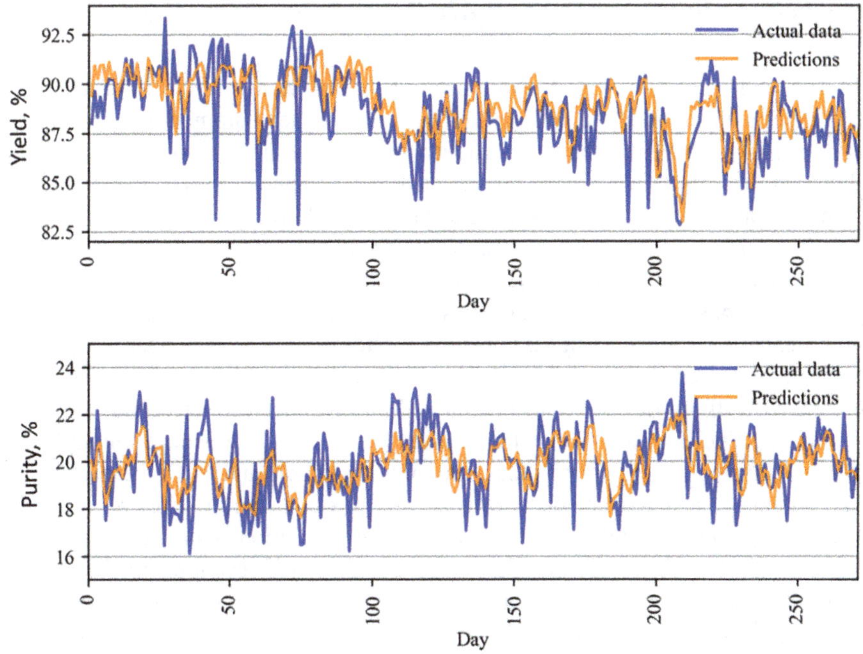

Fig. 5.8 Comparison of model predictions with industrial mineral-processing plant data [21]

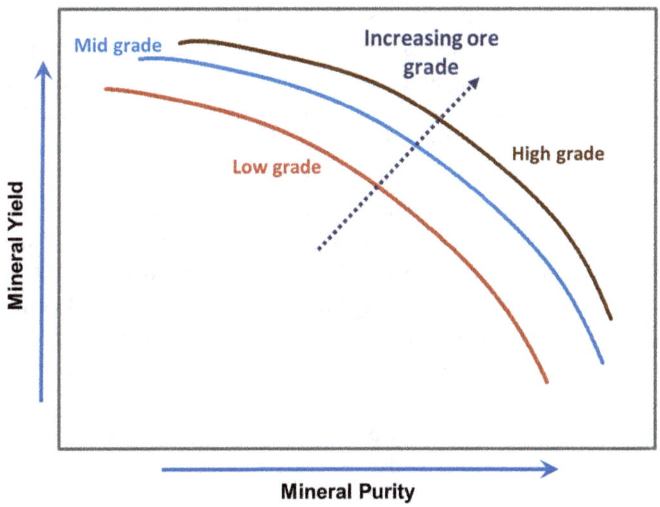

Fig. 5.9 Pareto optimal profiles of yield vs purity for a mineral-processing plant

Predictive Maintenance of an Air Pre-heater

The raw materials are converted into useful products using various industrial process equipment or assets. It is important to maintain the equipment in good condition to achieve KPIs like plant throughput and product quality. Unplanned outage or shutdown of critical equipment can result in huge financial losses. Rotary equipment such as pumps, compressors, and turbines are relatively more prone to damage due to continuous movement of rotating elements or components. The health and performance of equipment depend strongly on the materials being processed, operating conditions, and the environment as well. For example, equipment that handle multiphase materials like slurries containing solid particles or materials at high temperature and pressure are more likely to have health and performance issues as compared to those dealing with liquids and gases under ambient conditions. For example, particles in slurries and dust-laden gases can erode equipment surfaces. Manufacturing industries keep redundant units for simple and less expensive assets like pumps. But that is not the case with complex and more expensive units like boilers and turbines, and it's important that their condition is monitored continuously to take corrective actions in a proactive manner to prevent equipment failure and unplanned outages. Detection and diagnosis of faults, prognosis of potential failures, and estimation of remaining useful life of key components are crucial not only for designing the equipment maintenance schedules but also for procuring the necessary replacements in time [24].

The important points to be considered when it comes to maintenance of critical assets are mean-time and expected cost to repair an asset and impact of asset failure on the whole plant. The goals of a predictive maintenance program commonly include fault detection (detect and report an abnormal equipment condition), fault diagnosis (determine the root cause, mode and severity of detected fault), and prognostics (estimating time-to-failure of the faulty component and suggesting remedial actions). An industrial use case on predictive maintenance of an air pre-heater in a thermal power plant is presented here to illustrate the basic approach.

Air pre-heater (APH) is a key unit in a thermal power plant (Fig. 5.6) as it helps in improving thermal efficiency of a boiler by recovering heat from flue gases and increasing the temperature of incoming air used for combustion of coal [25]. APH helps in increasing the boiler efficiency by about 10–12%, which results in reducing the coal consumption. Generally, every 22 °C rise in air temperature is likely to improve the boiler efficiency by almost 1% [26]. APH is essentially a heat exchanger rotating along its axis with a metallic or ceramic packing inside that enhances the efficiency of heat transfer (Fig. 5.10).

Fouling is a major problem faced in the operation and maintenance of an APH. It occurs due to the deposition of ash present in the flue gases and a sticky compound, ammonium bisulfate (ABS). The flue gases from a coal-fired boiler contain carbon monoxide, carbon dioxide, sulfur oxides (SOx), and nitrogen oxides (NOx) besides ash and unburnt carbon. The flue gases are usually treated in a unit called selective catalytic reduction (SCR) to minimize NOx. Ammonia is used as a reagent for this

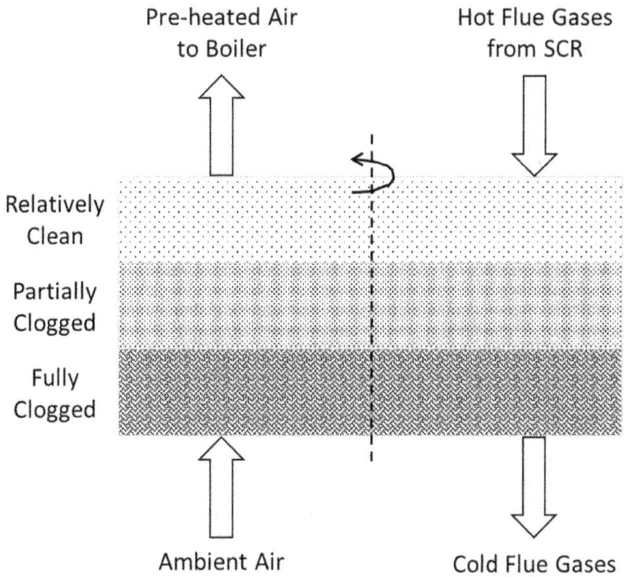

Fig. 5.10 Schematic of an air pre-heater

purpose, and trace amounts of ammonia exit the SCR with the flue gases. Sulfur oxides react with ammonia in the APH to form ABS. When NH_3 concentration is low and sulfur trioxide concentration is high, the tendency to form ABS is usually high [27]. When the flue gas temperature drops below a certain temperature in the APH, ABS deposits along with fly ash. Continuous deposition of ash and ABS results in blocking of passages in the metallic packing for flow of air and flue gases, and hence the pressure drop across the APH keeps increasing, initially slowly but rapidly later on. The electric current required for transporting air and flue gases through the APH also increases due to the higher pressure drop. Ultimately, beyond a certain limit, it is no longer possible to push the gases through the packing, and the plant operators are forced to take a shutdown to clean or regenerate the APH. A typical pressure drop profile during one cycle of start-up and shutdown of an APH is shown in Fig. 5.11. The effect of fouling is mitigated by blowing steam at high pressure through the packing at periodic intervals using equipment known as soot blowers to remove the deposited solids [28]. This is, however, a partial remedy as soot blowing does not reach all regions of the packing and the deposited material does not get removed completely.

Fouling of APH has major economic implications for power plants. First, the frequency and intensity of soot blowing every day have to be increased to minimize deposition of solids on packing. This increases APH operating costs. Second, thermal efficiency of the APH also keeps decreasing due to fouling, which leads to higher fuel usage. Third, fouling is unpredictable because it is influenced by multiple factors such as weather, coal characteristics, and upstream operating conditions in the boiler and the selective catalytic reduction unit. Complete blockage of the

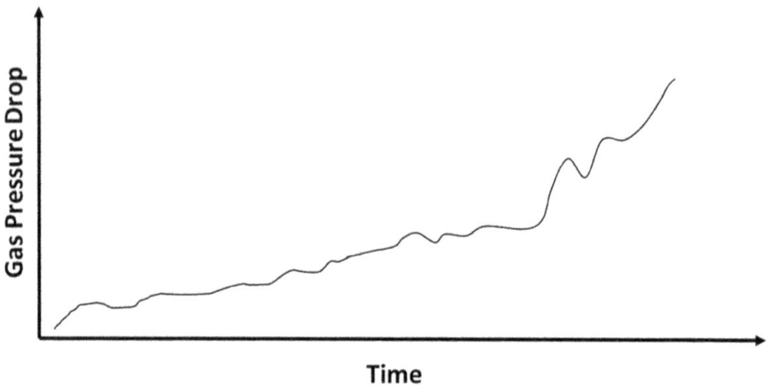

Fig. 5.11 Typical profile of gas pressure drop across the air pre-heater in a thermal power plant

APH due to fouling may take anywhere between a few months to a few years [29] depending on the factors mentioned above. Fouling usually results in forced or unplanned outages, ranging from 15 to 30 days, and causes additional maintenance expenses and economic losses. Since fouling is unpredictable, planning maintenance schedules for an APH is also challenging. Currently, fouling cannot be detected or monitored in situ as sensors do not exist. The extent of fouling is essentially inferred from pressure drop across the APH. Hence, there is need for a system that can help in monitoring and forecasting the level of fouling to optimize soot blowing conditions daily and to design maintenance schedules in a predictive manner.

We have conceptualized a digital twin solution to address this need. The key component of this solution is the model for APH fouling. A multi-step methodology was developed to build a hybrid model combining physics-based and data-driven models (Fig. 5.12). First, sensor data from the APH for process variables like flow rates, pressures, and temperatures of air and flue gases is integrated with coal characteristics (e.g., ash content, percent sulfur, etc.), ambient air conditions (temperature, humidity, etc.), and sensor data from upstream units like boiler and SCR (ammonia content in flue gases). Since the APH is a rotating unit, sensors for measurement of internal temperatures cannot be installed. Hence, a physics-based model that predicts heat transfer between air, flue gases and metallic packing, and pressure drop across the APH was developed and validated with actual data [30]. The physics-based model is utilized as a soft sensor to provide internal temperature and pressure profiles that are employed along with inlet ammonia concentration and other sensor data to predict the ABS Deposition Index along the height of APH, which indicates the extent of fouling [31].

One of the main challenges faced during the model development is that the rise in pressure drop due to fouling does not follow a common pattern across cycles. It varies from cycle to cycle because coal characteristics, condition of the metallic packing, power plant operating conditions, and the environment change with time. An adaptive data transformation methodology was developed first to deal with

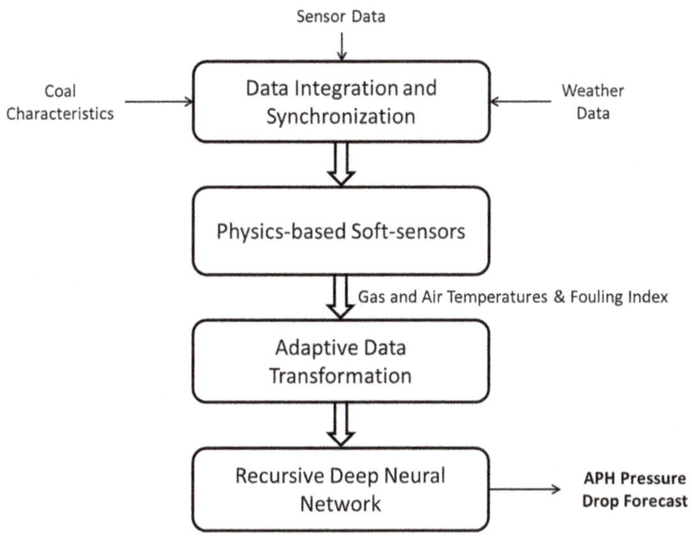

Fig. 5.12 Multi-step methodology for developing air pre-heater fouling model

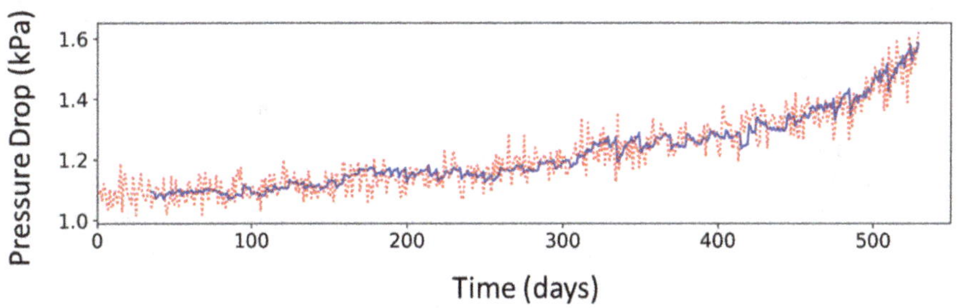

Fig. 5.13 Comparison of predicted (continuous line) pressure drop across an APH with actual data (dotted line) [31]

varying pressure drop—time patterns [30]. The transformed data was employed to build a long-short-term-memory (LSTM) network model for long-term forecasting of pressure drop across the APH. In order to evaluate the utility of incorporating physics-based models in the methodology, different variants of the LSTM model, namely, data-driven LSTM, data-driven autoregressive LSTM, physics-assisted LSTM, and physics-assisted autoregressive LSTM network, were explored, and it was found that physics-assisted LSTM network models performed better than purely data-driven counterparts. This is not surprising because predictions from physics-based soft sensors provide additional valuable information in the form of temperature, pressure, and ABS Deposition Index, which are not available to pure data-driven models. A representative figure for validation of the APH model is shown in Fig. 5.13. The digital twin system of the APH provides effective predictive maintenance augmenting human experience and expertise. It can assist in increasing plant availability by eliminating forced outages due to fouling and in optimizing soot blowing on a daily basis, thus reducing fuel usage and prolonging the cycle time.

Recent Developments

While the application of digital twins is progressing steadily, there are many areas in which there is a need for improvement. Some of the recent developments that are relevant and important are described briefly in this section.

One of the main differentiators of manufacturing industries as compared to other industries is that the phenomena are governed by fundamental principles of physics. Hence, there is a need to ensure that the causal relationships or correlations drawn through data-driven approaches follow the governing phenomena and the predicted results satisfy the laws of conservation. While physics-based models have been in use for off-line simulation, they are not well suited for real-time applications as they are computationally expensive and may not also account for some of the stochastic aspects of the phenomena. On the other hand, data-driven or artificial intelligence approaches address some of the limitations, but do not provide the insights and explainability that one can derive from physics-based models. Hybrid digital twins that combine physics-based models with data-driven models have been developed as well as deployed for industrial systems [14, 16] with reasonable success. However, majority of them utilize predictions from physics-based models as inputs to the data-driven models or the other way round. Similarly, data-driven models are developed using synthetic data generated using the physics-based models and combined with purely data-driven models. Recently, physics-informed neural networks (PINNs) that combine deep neural networks (DNNs) with physics-based models have been developed and solved in a coupled manner [32]. The coordinates are taken as inputs, and process variables are predicted. They are trained by minimizing residuals originating from partial differential equations. Industrial use cases with simplified physics-based models have been proposed and demonstrated with limited industrial-scale data or benchmark datasets [33]. One of the limitations of PINNs is that their training is computationally intensive and they need to be retrained if the boundary conditions change. A hypernetwork-based PINN model was proposed recently for real-time monitoring of an industrial heat exchanger to avoid retraining the PINNs [34]. Similarly, neural operators have also been employed to combine physics with DNNs. They provide rapid, scalable, and efficient solutions for systems described by high-dimensional partial differential equations [35, 36].

Manufacturing plant engineers usually face the challenge of carrying out root cause analysis (RCA) not only in diagnosing process and equipment anomalies or faults or failures but also in understanding variations in KPIs because the number of variables is quite large and their interrelationships are highly nonlinear. It is also equally important to determine time-dependent causal relationships because a majority of the industrial processes have relatively long residence times and transportation lags make it complex to understand these relationships. Recently, a fault traversal and root cause variable identification approach for industrial systems was proposed to determine the causal structure of faults completely using sensor data without any prior process knowledge and to automatically determine the fault traversal paths and variables that caused the fault [37]. Multivariate time delayed transfer entropy, which can capture nonlinearities and incorporate time delays between variables, was used to learn the causal relationships among the fault variables. The proposed algorithm was tested with data for the benchmark Tennessee Eastman process [38] and for RCA of a fault in a coal pulverizer in a thermal power plant. Root cause identification of faults is critical from the perspective of industrial safety as well because it helps in detecting the source of faults and addressing the root cause before they propagate and lead to a catastrophic failure. Manufacturing plants consist of thousands of interconnected networks of sensors, and one has to deal with a high-dimensional time series data. Since the sensor network can be represented as a graph, a hypergraph learning–based recommender system was developed for anomaly detection [39]. As large language models (LLMs) gained prominence recently, an agentic Retrieval-Augmented Generation (RAG) framework was proposed for time series analysis tasks such as forecasting, classification, anomaly detection, and imputation [40]. It consists of a hierarchical, multi-agent architecture in which the master agent orchestrates specialized sub-agents and delegates the end-user request to the relevant sub-agent. The sub-agents employ smaller, pre-trained language models that are configured for specific purposes by fine-tuning using instruction tuning and direct preference optimization. The sub-agents retrieve relevant prompts from a repository of prompts that contain distilled knowledge about historical patterns and trends to improve predictions when applied to new data. This framework was tested with data related to traffic. However, this can be gainfully utilized for time series analysis tasks in process industries as plant engineers grapple with time series analysis of sensor data. A detailed review of recent literature on time series anomaly detection through deep learning is available elsewhere [41].

Cybersecurity is one of the critical challenges faced by the industries as they move data to cloud-based systems. Deep learning models that are part of digital twin systems deployed on the cloud are vulnerable to adversarial attacks [42] that can mislead the plant engineers and potentially lead to catastrophic events. Adversarial attacks are carried out by appending an imperceptible noise to the inputs. They are classified according to their goals, knowledge, and scope of perturbation [43]. These attacks can be targeted or untargeted. In case of targeted attacks, the attacker tries to misguide the model to predict a particular class other than the true class. On the other hand, in case of untargeted attacks, the attacker attempts to misguide the model to predict any of the incorrect classes. Similarly, the attacks can be on individual samples in a dataset or on the whole dataset. In case of attacks on individual samples, the perturbation is estimated by solving an optimization problem for that particular sample. Universal attacks are executed by determining the perturbation by solving the optimization problem for the whole dataset. Addition of same perturbation to different input samples can make the model predict incorrect class for each of the samples, and the accuracy of model predictions decreases as the strength of perturbation increases [44]. These attacks can be carried out in a single step or in multiple steps iteratively. The fast gradient sign method (FGSM) [45] belongs to the class of single-step attacks, whereas the basic iterative method (BIM) [46] belongs to the class of multi-step attacks. Multi-step methods result in stronger attacks than single-step attacks because smaller step sizes taken iteratively result in strong adversarial samples. Adversarial training is one of the strategies followed as a defense against such attacks. The training data is augmented with adversarial samples during training as these samples act as regularizers. It was found that adversarially trained models trained using FGSM were able to defend well against both FGSM and BIM attacks [47]. Adversarial machine learning is developing as an active area of research, and recent developments in this field can be found elsewhere [48–50].

Summary and Suggestions for Future Research

Manufacturing industries face challenges in meeting targets linked to plant productivity and availability, product quality, asset maintenance, emissions, safety, energy consumption, resource utilization, etc. Availability of skilled and knowledgeable workforce is also becoming scarce. As industrial operations are influenced by global events and supply chain disruptions happen relatively frequently, new technologies such as digitalization, Internet of Things, hyper-scaler platforms, and artificial intelligence are being employed to address the above challenges as well as to monitor, diagnose, optimize, and control the manufacturing operations remotely. Several industries are embarking on digital transformation of their operations. Digital twin, an autonomous cyber-physical system that can work in tandem with a physical entity taking real-time data and providing real-time decisions, is one of the key components of this transformation. Digital twin technology has matured to a level that it is being gainfully deployed in several operating plants globally. It can be used for a variety of applications in operating plants in real time, both for optimization of plant performance and for an efficient and cost-effective maintenance of plant assets. The utility and transformative potential of digital twins are discussed in this chapter.

The frameworks and platforms for development and deployment of digital twin systems for manufacturing operations are described in detail. Three industrial use cases, performance optimization of coal-fired boilers in power plants, plant-wide optimization of mineral-processing plants, and predictive maintenance of an air preheater in thermal power plants, are explained. Recent developments related to physics-informed neural networks, real-time root cause identification, and adversarial attacks and defenses for time series models relevant for manufacturing industries are also briefly discussed.

Despite the advances in ML and DL algorithms, one of the key challenges for manufacturing industries today is the availability of good-quality data for building accurate and robust models. Data quality verification, pre-processing, and integration of data from multiple sources require considerable amount of time, efforts, and knowledge of the industry domain. Focused research needs to be carried out to leverage developments in knowledge engineering and potentially the large language models.

Since manufacturing of materials is governed by first principles, there is a need to develop hybrid models combining physics-based models with data-driven models. This area is still at a nascent stage, and more research is required on PINNs and neural operators to address challenges such as long training time, huge computational resources, and generalization to unseen data, especially dynamic operating conditions. Similarly, development of physics-based models itself is also a major challenge. Application of LLMs leveraging the vast knowledge and resources available publicly in books and journals for this purpose would greatly facilitate development of hybrid digital twin systems.

Predictive maintenance of assets is an industry-wide problem. Despite years of research, this problem is still unwieldy, especially for complex and critical assets. Their failure is relatively rare but quite expensive. While DL models have been developed for this purpose with limited success, it is important to address this problem using a multipronged approach involving both structured and unstructured data and, again, leveraging recent developments in LLMs.

Security of DL models built using time series data from sensors has been shown to be susceptible to adversarial attacks. This topic has received considerable attention recently, but focused efforts are required, especially to ensure reliability and robustness of forecasting models as incorrect decisions can result in catastrophic events.

Manufacturing industries spend quite a lot of time, effort, and money in testing of materials in laboratories. This data is very critical for digital twin systems. Application of artificial intelligence for testing and characterization of materials is receiving attention recently [51], but more research in this direction will certainly be of great value not only for digital twin systems but also for industries in general as availability of knowledgeable workforce is a major challenge.

Acknowledgments The authors thank the management of Tata Consultancy Services Limited for the permission to publish this work and Dr. Harrick Vin, Mr. K Ananth Krishnan, Dr. Gautam Shroff, and Dr. Sachin Lodha for their support.

References

1. Narasimhan, S., & Jordache, C. (1999). *Data reconciliation and gross error detection: An intelligent use of process data*. Gulf Professional Publishing.
2. Masampally, V., Pareek, A., Nadimpalli, N. K. V., & Runkana, V. (2023). *Method and system for material balance and data reconciliation in a plant*. Patent No. IN202021016143.
3. Runkana, V. (2018). Digital twins. In *Reimagining research* (pp. 97–103). Tata Consultancy Services Ltd..
4. Puliyanda, A., Srinivasan, K., Thosal, D., Bhakte, A., Sngh, K., Addo, P., Srinivasan, R., & Prasad, V. (2024). Artificial intelligence and machine learning at various stages and scales of

process systems engineering. *Canadian Journal of Chemical Engineering, 103*, cjce.25525. https://doi.org/10.1002/cjce.25525
5. Biswas, J., Kumar, R., Mynam, M., Nistala, S., Panda, A., Pandya, R., Rathore, P., & Runkana, V. (2017). *Method and system for data based optimization of performance indicators in process and manufacturing industries*. Patent No. US10636007B2.
6. Runkana, V., Pandya, R., Kumar, R., & Panda, A. (2016). *System and method for data preprocessing*. Patent No. JP6568565B2.
7. Subramanian, S., Runkana, V., Parameswaran, S., Shah, N., Sandipan, M., Mehrotra, A. N., Padsalgi, M. S., Manna, R., Kumar, R., Nistala, S., Pandya, R., Pareek, A., Baikadi, A. K., & Deodhar, A. (2020). *System and method for development and deployment of self-organizing cyber-physical systems for manufacturing industries*. India Patent Application No. 202021021089.
8. Nistala, S., Kumar, R., Biswas, J., Jadhav, C., Baikadi, A., Runkana, V., & Pandya, R. (2019). *Method and system for adaptive learning of models for manufacturing systems*. Patent No. IN201921019548.
9. Kumar, R., Parihar, M., Kumar, V., and Runkana, V. (2020). *Method and system for time lag identification in an industry*. Patent Application No. 202021004042.
10. Kumar, V., Kumar, R., Parihar, M., & Runkana, V. (2019). *Method and system for identification and analysis of regime shift*. Patent Application No.: 201921039286.
11. Singh, K., Runkana, V., & Nistala, S. (2021). Method and system for adaptive learning of models in manufacturing systems. Patent No.: 4102311.
12. TCS INTWIN® is a registered Trademark of Tata Consultancy Services. (2020). Retrieved from https://www.tcs.com/what-we-do/services/iot-digital-engineering/solution/tcs-intwin-ai-techniques-agile-sustainable-plants.
13. Majumder, S., Natekar, P. V., & Runkana, V. (2009). Virtual Indurator: A tool for simulation of induration of wet iron ore pellets on a moving grate. *Computers and Chemical Engineering, 33*, 1141–1152.
14. Nistala, S., Singh, K., Vakkantham, P., Pareek, A., Masampally, V., Kumar, R., & Runkana, V. (2022). Virtual sinter®: Digital twin for integrated sinter plants. *Transactions of the Indian National Academy of Engineering, 7*, 943–955.
15. Nistala, S., Kumar, R., Parihar, M. S., & Runkana, V. (2024). Metafur: Digital twin system of a blast furnace. *Transactions of the Indian Institute of Metals, 77*, 4383–4393. https://doi.org/10.1007/s12666-024-03374-0
16. Runkana, V., & Majumder, S. (2009). *On-line optimization of induration of wet iron ore pellets on a moving grate*. Patent No. US8571715B2.
17. Runkana, V., Majumder, S., Desai, V. J., Arunprasath, J., Kumar, R., Nistala, S., Parihar, M., Singh, K., & Kumar, V. (2024). Digital twins for optimization of ironmaking operations. *CSI Transactions on ICT, 12*, 57–70.
18. Dukelow, S. G., Liptak, B. G., Cheng, X., & Meeker, R. H. (2006). Boiler control and optimization. In B. G. Liptak (Ed.), *Process control and optimization, Vol. II, Instrumentation engineers' handbook* (4th ed.). Taylor & Francis.
19. Cheng, Y., Huang, Y., Pang, B., & Zhang, W. (2018). ThermalNet: A deep reinforcement learning-based combustion optimization system for coal-fired boiler. *Engineering Applications of Artificial Intelligence, 74*, 303–311.
20. TCS Intelligent Power Plant (TCS IP2™) is a registered Trademark of Tata Consultancy Services. (2018). Retrieved from https://www.tcs.com/what-we-do/services/iot-digital-engineering/solution/intelligent-power-plant-enabling-sustainability.
21. Masampally, V., Pareek, A., Nadimpalli, N., & Runkana, V. (2024). Artificial intelligence for monitoring and optimization of an integrated mineral processing plant. *Transactions of the IIM, 77*, 4231–4240. https://doi.org/10.1007/s12666-023-03093-y
22. Crundwell, F. K. (2011). *Extractive metallurgy of nickel, cobalt and platinum-group metals*. Elsevier.

23. Deb, K., Pratap, A., Agarwal, S. and Meyarivan, T. (2002). A fast and elitist multiobjective genetic algorithm: NSGA-II. In *IEEE transactions on evolutionary computation* (Vol. 6). https://doi.org/10.1109/4235.996017.
24. Sikorska, J. Z., Hodkiewicz, M., & Ma, L. (2011). Prognostic modelling options for remaining useful life estimation by industry. *Mechanical Systems and Signal Processing, 25*, 1803–1836.
25. Heidari-Kaydan, A., Hajidavalloo, E., & Mehrzad, S. (2022). Three-dimensional simulation of leakages in rotary air preheater of steam power plant. *Heat Transfer Engineering, 43*(17), 1512–1528.
26. Shi, Y., Jingcheng, W., & Jie, W. (2017). On-line monitoring of ash fouling for air pre-heaters in coal-fired power plant boiler. In *Proceedings, 2017 29th Chinese control and decision conference (CCDC)* (pp. 1386–1390). IEEE.
27. Zhou, C., Zhang, L., Deng, Y., & Ma, S. (2016). Research progress on ammonium bisulfate formation and control in the process of selective catalytic reduction. *Environmental Progress & Sustainable Energy, 35*(6), 1664–1672.
28. Pena, B., Teruel, E., & Diez, L. I. (2011). Soft-computing models for soot-blowing optimization in coal-fired utility boilers. *Applied Soft Computing, 11*(2), 1657–1668. https://doi.org/10.1016/j.asoc.2010.04.023
29. Hovland, A., Lyter, F. G., & Truchot, C. (2011). Innovative cleaning of air preheater coils with pressurized liquid nitrogen (LN2). *ASME Power Conference, 44601*, 159–171.
30. Gupta, A., Jadhav, V., Patil, M., Deodhar, A., & Runkana, V. (2021). Forecasting of fouling in air pre-heaters through deep learning. In *Proceedings, ASME 2021 power conference (power 2021), July 18–22, 2021, Anaheim, CA, USA*.
31. Gupta, A., Jadhav, V., Deodhar, A., Runkana, V. (2022). Physics-assisted long-short-term-memory network for forecasting of fouling in a regenerative heat exchanger. In *Proceedings, ASME 2022 Heat transfer summer conference (SHTC 2022), July 11–13, 2022, Philadelphia, PA, USA*.
32. Raissi, M., Perdikaris, P., & Karniadakis, G. (2019). Physics-informed neural networks: A deep learning framework for solving forward and inverse problems involving nonlinear partial differential equations. *Journal of Computational Physics, 378*, 686–707.
33. Jadhav, V., Deodhar, A., Gupta, A., & Runkana, V. (2022). Physics informed neural network for health monitoring of an air preheater. In *Proceedings, PHM Society European conference* (Vol. 7, p. 219).
34. Majumdar, R., Jadhav, V., Deodhar, A., Karande, S., Vig, L., & Runkana, V. (2024). HxPINN: A Hypernetwork-based physics-informed neural network for real-time monitoring of an industrial heat exchanger. *Numerical Heat Transfer B: Fundamentals, 1–2*, 1. https://doi.org/10.1080/10407790.2024.2325648
35. Li, Z., Zheng, H., Kovachki, N., Jin, D., Chen, H., Liu, B., Azizzadenesheli, K., & Anandkumar, A. (2024). Physics-informed neural operator for learning partial differential equations. *ACM/JMS Journal of Data Science, 1*, 1.
36. Rosofsky, S., Al Majed, H., & Huerta, E. A. (2023). *Applications of physics informed neural operators* (Vol. 4, p. 025022). Machine Learning: Science and Technology.
37. Zope, K. B., Singhal, T., Nistala, S., & Runkana, V. (2023). Transfer entropy based automated fault traversal and root cause identification in complex nonlinear industrial processes. *Industrial & Engineering Chemistry Research, 62*, 4002–4018.
38. Downs, J. J., & Vogel, E. F. (1993). A plant-wide industrial process control problem. *Computers & Chemical Engineering, 17*, 245.
39. Sakhinana, S., Sarkar, R., & Runkana, V. (2022). Hypergraph learning based recommender system for anomaly detection, control and optimization. In *Proceedings, IEEE international conference on big data (IEEE big data 2022), Osaka, Japan, Dec 17–20, 2022*.
40. Ravuru, C., Sakhinana, S., & Runkana, V. (2024). Agentic retrieval-augmented generation for time series analysis. In *Proceedings, undergraduate consortium, knowledge discovery and data mining(ACM KDD)-2024, August 25-29, 2024, Barcelona, Spain*.

41. Darban, Z. Z., Webb, G. I., Pan, S., Aggarwal, C., & Salehi, M. (2024). Deep learning for time series anomaly detection: A survey. *ACM Computing Surveys, 57*(1), 15.
42. Szegedy, C., Zaremba, W., Sutskever, I., Bruna, J., Erhan, D., Goodfellow, I., & Fergus, R. (2013). Intriguing properties of neural networks. *arXiv preprint arXiv:1312.6199*.
43. Wu, J., & Fu, R. (2022). *Universal, transferable and targeted adversarial attacks*. Retrieved from https://arxiv.org/abs/1908.11332v4.
44. Basak, A., Rathore, P. Nistala, S.H., Srinivas, S., & Runkana, V. (2021). Universal adversarial attack on deep learning based prognostics. In *Proceedings, IEEE 2021 international conference machine learning applications (ICMLA2021), 13–15 December 2021*.
45. Goodfellow, I. J., Shlens, J., & Szegedy, C. (2014). Explaining and harnessing adversarial examples. *arXiv preprint arXiv:1412.6572*.
46. Kurakin, A., Goodfellow, I., & Bengio, S. (2016). *Adversarial examples in the physical world*. Retrieved from https://arxiv.org/abs/1607.02533.
47. Rathore, P., Basak, A., Nistala, S., & Runkana, V. (2020). Untargeted, targeted, universal adversarial attacks and defenses on time series. In *Proceedings, paper id. 20727, international joint conference on neural networks (IJCNN 2020), Glasgow, UK, July 19–24, 2020*.
48. Akter, K., Rahman, M. A., Rashidul Islam, M., Sheikh, M. R. I., & Hossain, M. J. (2025). Attack-resilient framework for wind power forecasting against civil and adversarial attacks. *Electric Power Systems Research, 238*, 111065.
49. Bairaktaris, J. A., Johannssen, A., & Tran, K. P. (2024). Security strategies for AI systems in industry 4.0. *Quality and Reliability Engineering International., 41*, 897. https://doi.org/10.1002/qre.3678
50. Shen, Z., & Li, Y. (2025). Temporal characteristics-based adversarial attacks on time series forecasting. *Expert Systems with Applications, 264*, 125950. https://doi.org/10.1016/j.eswa.2024.125950
51. Sakhinana, S., Sannidhi, G., Ravuru, C., & Runkana, V. (2024). Parameter-efficient quantized mixture-of-experts meets vision-language instruction tuning for semiconductor electron micrograph analysis. In *AI for science: Scaling in AI for scientific discovery workshop, international conference on machine learning (ICML) 2024, July 21st–28th, Vienna, Austria*.

Chapter 6
Development of Digital Twins for Chemical Reactors to Predict the Catalysis Conversion Efficiency

Vishwesh Kulkarni and Evgeny Rebrov

Abstract We consider the problem of how digital twins can improve the process of synthesising catalysts so that the carbon monoxide conversion efficiency of chemical reactors can be improved in general. Six key steps in the life cycle of such a digital twin are outlined, and new results are presented for the first two steps, viz. conceptualisation and model development, using published data from 96 well-referenced publications on such chemical reactors. A range of machine learning algorithms is considered as a candidate for developing the digital twin that can accurately predict the conversion efficiency of the chemical reactor for a variety of operational conditions. It is shown that Gaussian process regression models outperform linear regression models, support vector machine models, decision trees and ensemble trees in this context.

Steps in the Life Cycle of Digital Twins

A digital twin has been defined as "a set of virtual information constructs that mimics the structure, context, and behaviour of an individual or unique physical asset, is dynamically updated with data from its physical twin throughout its life cycle, and ultimately informs decisions that realize value" [1]. This definition highlights the ways in which a digital twin goes beyond traditional modelling and simulation to bring value, through the bidirectional feedback flows between the physical asset and its virtual representation. The physical system for which the digital twin is developed may be called its Physical Twin. Attempts to emulate the behaviour of

V. Kulkarni (✉)
King's College, London, UK
e-mail: vishwesh@kcl.ac.uk

E. Rebrov
University of Warwick, Coventry, UK
e-mail: E.Rebrov@warwick.ac.uk

V. Kulkarni et al. (eds.), *Digital Twins for Simulation-Based Decision-Making*,
https://doi.org/10.1007/978-3-031-89654-5_6

physical systems are a key component of engineering and science. However, the difference between the digital twin and a computer model is that the digital twin updates itself to track the physical twin using sensors, data analysis, machine learning and the Internet of things. The digital twin may also direct changes to the physical twin through signals sent to actuators on the physical twin. Ideally, physical and digital twins must achieve temporal synchronisation. The flow of data from physical to virtual enables the virtual representation to be dynamically updated, thus tailoring it to the specific behaviour of its physical counterpart, while the flow from virtual to physical induces changes in the physical asset, through control, sensor steering or other manipulations of the physical system. The virtual representation typically comprises a disparate set of models representing different disciplines, subsystems and components of the physical system. These models may be based on an understanding of the physical principles (for instance, analytical and empirical models that are grounded in physical governing laws). These models may also be purely numerical, such as statistical models that fit from data and machine learning. These models may also be hybrid combinations of physics-based and data-driven models.

Decades of advances in modelling and simulation are powerful precursors to digital twins. A digital twin builds on these advances but goes beyond them, as a capability to provide a physical asset with a unique digital identity [2]. Underlying this unique identity are the requirements to digitally capture relevant asset aspects, such as actual geometry, realised performance and other physical state observations. Also required is the ability to present and manipulate the digital twin view to humans for complex decision-making. These aspects may be achieved by a data-centric approach that measures and stores asset-specific information or by a model-centric approach that combines analysis, models and data from other indirect measurements. These analyses can leverage well-known simulation technologies, such as behavioural simulation, computational fluid dynamics, finite-element analysis and computer-aided design, combined with additional numerical methods to twin the model with the physical asset. The digital twin development can be broken down into six key steps (see [1]):

Step 1: Digital twin conceptualisation: Define requirements, constraints, architecture, internal and external conditions, use cases and related expectations. This step should identify existing models, existing data sources and modelling gaps.

Step 2: Digital twin development: Develop a set of models theoretically, code those models in software, add graphical user interfaces, integrate the relevant software/hardware packages and streamline the workflows. Surrogate modelling may play an important role in this step due to the need to satisfy stringent computational constraints in operation in real time that require fast response time.

Step 3: Digital twin validation: Determine how accurate the model is in the context of its intended use. As argued in [1, 2], a digital twin must balance the fidelity of predictions, as defined in the digital twin's conceptual design phase, with the computational demands (such as time, power and complexity).

Step 4: Digital twin operation: In the operation phase, the digital twin is evaluated to support the decision-making process. It is composed of two major aspects: (1) a digital framework to execute, evaluate and visualise the digital twin and (2) business processes that integrate the digital twin information for decision-making. The digital framework collects data from the different authoritative sources, such as sensor data and other context information or product configurations, and provides the storage and computational services to execute the digital twin.

Step 5: Digital twin update: Updating is a critical element of a digital twin and a key distinguishing factor that enables a digital twin to bring added value. Whatever the extent and timescale of the updates, the notion of continuous validation is critical. Updates that take place in real time or near real time (for instance, via data assimilation or parameter-estimation algorithms) must be accompanied by a form of certification that the components of the digital twin virtual representation remain within acceptable bounds.

Step 6: Digital twin disposal: The disposal of a digital twin must follow the end of life of the physical assets.

In this chapter, we present new results concerning the first two steps outlined above for the application of catalyst synthesis using chemical reactors.

Problem Specification

Catalytic products have a significant influence on energy (petrochemicals), healthcare (pharmaceuticals), new materials (polymers), transportation (catalytic converters) and the environment (water, air quality, renewable and bio-produced materials). It is estimated that nearly 90% of all chemical processes are catalysed, implying that the economic effect of catalysts is enormous, with the catalysis process accounting for 30–40% of global GDP. Catalysts may be expected to play an even bigger role in protecting our social well-being as the world shifts toward more sustainable industries and feedstocks to ensure a cleaner future. One of the most promising energy conversion systems is fuel cell technology, which electrochemically transforms hydrogen and oxygen to electricity and water. Because of the difficulties in storing hydrogen, on-site hydrogen production is seen as the most viable option. It has a disadvantage in that the reforming mechanism produces toxic and unnecessary CO and CO_2. The WGS water gas shift reaction will reduce CO levels to as low as 1%, followed by preferential CO oxidation (PROX) for complete elimination. Water gas shift (WGS) is a two-step process, high-temperature shift (573–723 K) and low-temperature shift (473–523 K), all of which require a metal catalyst; in this case, noble metal catalysts are used because they are more durable and ideal for fuel cell applications, so Fe-Cr- and Cu-Zn-based catalysts are removed as they are more reactive and unstable.

$$CO + H_2O \rightleftharpoons CO_2 + H_2$$

WGS activity, i.e. the flowrate of hydrogen, depends on catalyst preparation variables such as the type and the amount of noble metal, type of support, etc. and the operational variables such as reaction time, temperature, the space time and feed composition (ratio of carbon monoxide to water). Different variables have influences at the different gas shift operations.

Traditionally, as has been the case with hundreds of WGS publications, the solution to the problem of catalyst synthesis is approached by first searching for promising catalysts families though empirical rules. However, hurdles and difficulties such as non-uniformities, gaps, mismatches and even conflicts in the publications spark a more systematic way to approach the problem where the application of machine learning and data minding tools allows for more useful insight. We chose 96 highly reputed and relevant publications and extracted from those the data correlating catalyst preparation and operational variables with CO conversion. This dataset consists of (1) the weight proportions of 7 different base metals, (2) indicators of which 21 different support types are used and in what proportions, (3) indicators of which 29 promoter type and with what weight proportions, (4) the calcination temperature, (5) incubation time, (6) the amount of catalyst synthesised, etc. Using this dataset, we executed the first two steps of the digital twin life cycle for the chemical reactor of interest. For the digital twin development, we decided to train a variety of machine learning models and then choose the machine learning algorithm that gave the best prediction on the amount of the synthesised catalyst.

Digital Twin Conceptualisation and Development

Computational Models of the Physics and Chemistry of the Chemical Reactors

Empirical laws and equations were first studied to obtain valid mathematical equations to test the performance of the machine learning algorithms. Standard references such as [3–6] were used in this process. For the physical and chemical reactions, including WGS, the Arrhenius equation defines the relationship between reaction rate and temperature. The WGS reaction can be modelled as a first-order reaction with a rate that is proportional to the reactant concentration. Differential rate laws were used to explain what happens at the molecular level during a reaction, while combined rate laws were used to determine the reaction order and rate constant value from experimental data.

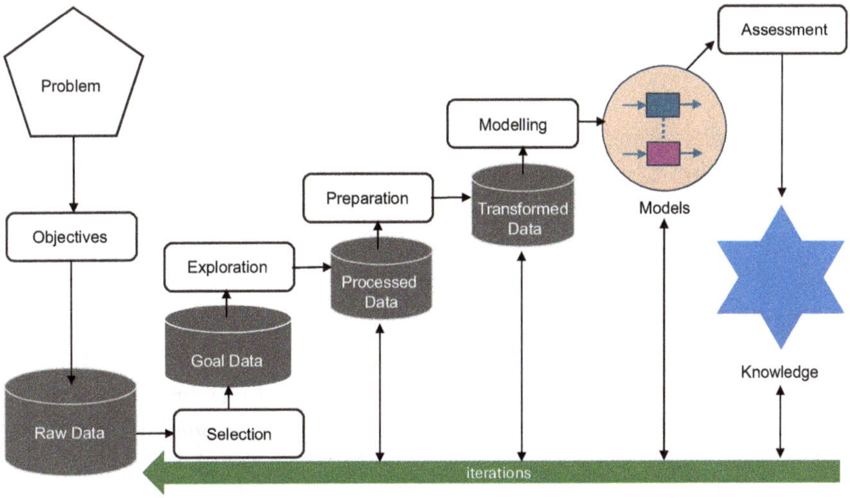

Fig. 6.1 This figure illustrates the "knowledge discovery in databases" (KDD) pipeline used by us to develop the digital twin of the chemical reactor. This pipeline illustrates the process of discovering useful knowledge from data and is reproduced from [7]

Rules for Creating Knowledge Database from Published Data

Our process of extracting useful knowledge from the data collected from the 96 publications (see [3]) followed the standard "knowledge discovery in databases" (KDD) pipeline that is summarised in Fig. 6.1.

Feature Selection

Feature selection is an important step in the KDD process where the number of attributes in a dataset are reduced so that only the ones relevant to the predictive modelling problem being solved are retained [7]. Feature selection methods include and exclude attributes present in the data without changing them, which differs from dimensionality reduction where new combinations of attributes are created. There are many advantages to feature selection that relate to different aspects of data analysis such as better visualisations, better understanding of the data, less taxing on the computational system that is processing the code, faster results analysis and more accurate predictions. There are three main methods of conducting feature selection on datasets. The first is the filter method where an independent assessment is conducted based on the general characteristics of the data. The features are scored using a statistical measure and ranked before the unneeded features are removed. The second approach is the wrapper method where a predictive model is used to evaluate different combinations of features and assign scores based on model accuracy. The third method is the embedded method, which learns which features best contribute to the accuracy of the model while the model is being created. The most common method is regularisation. We used all three methods and observed that regularisation gave the best results as far as the prediction of the amount of catalyst synthesised is concerned.

Choice of Machine Learning Algorithms

We decided to develop the prediction models using the following set of machine learning algorithms: linear regression, regression trees, regression tree ensembles, support vector machines and Gaussian process regression (GPR). Baseline information about these algorithms can be obtained from standard references such as [8–12].

Regression trees are decision trees in which the target variable may take continuous values (typically real numbers). They are made using a technique known as recursive partitioning, which involves recursively separating each derived subset. The recursion ends when the goal variable values in the subset node are all the same or when branching no longer adds value to the forecasts. Overfitting is controlled by the maximum number of splits. Generally, there are three types of regression trees: coarse, medium and fine trees. All of these have fast prediction speed, use up small memory and are easy to interpretate. The three types of trees are differentiated by its maximum number of splits with 4, 20 and up to 100, respectively. Ensembles of trees are trees sets combined by multiple regression trees to achieve greater statistical utility than a single tree alone. This is done by promoting randomness to gain independence and low-bias, high-variance classifiers.

Gaussian process regression (GPR) is a generalised supervised learning approach intended to solve problems of regression and probabilistic classification. One of the benefits of Gaussian processes are forecasts interpolates the findings for regular kernels. The prediction is probabilistic (Gaussian) so that one can compute empirical confidence intervals and decide based on those if one should refit (online fitting, adaptive fitting) the prediction in some region of interest. GPR is versatile as different kernels can be specified. Common kernels are provided, but it is also possible to specify custom kernels. It also comes with drawbacks such as, for example, non-sparse properties, meaning that GPR uses the whole samples/features information to perform the prediction. Subsequently, these methods lose efficiency and high computation time in high-dimensional spaces, namely, when the number of features exceeds a few dozens. GPR entails a Gaussian process, which is a stochastic process, meaning that any finite set of such random variables has a multivariate normal distribution, a measure of the correlation between points (the kernel function) to predict the value of an unknown point from the training data. Basic aspects that the covariance function can be defined through the covariance function are the process stationarity, isotropy, smoothness and periodicity. We experimented with variations of GPR such as rational quadratic GPR, exponential GPR, square exponential GPR and Matern 5/2 GPR that are well described in [12]. A GP model is a nonparametric model which is flexible enough to fit many kinds of data, including geospatial and time series data. At the core of GP regression is the specification of a suitable kernel function or measure of similarity between data points whose locations are known—this constitutes the *model selection* (MO) step. The tractability of the Gaussian distribution means that one can find closed-form expressions for the posterior predictive distribution conditioned on training data. Though well-established, GPs are an area of ongoing research: recent developments span multi-output GPs, variational inference for GP regression and scalable GPs. GP regression packages are readily available for use with R, Python and MATLAB. We opted to use the package with MATLAB.

Estimation of the Cost of Production

We did not factor in fixed cost and external factors such as labour cost, factory operation cost, economies of scale, geographical location, etc. The marginal cost of CO production is determined mainly by the choice of the base metal, the support metal and the operational conditions. To simplify, it can be assumed that the cost on different settings of operational condition is negligible other than operational temperature. Then, the first step in arriving at the relative marginal cost is to use the following logic: *Relative Marginal Cost = (amount of metal% × Price/gram) + Difference in temperature*. In this cost computation, the difference in temperature is used because higher temperature comes with higher energy consumption costs. However, this cost should not include temperature linearly but exponentially owing to the mathematics governing the Arrhenius equation and the first-order kinetic models. Hence, we estimated the cost as follows:

$$\text{Relative Marginal Cost} = \alpha\left(\text{amount of metal\%} \times \text{Price} / \text{g}\right) + \beta e^{kT},$$

where α, β and k are the constants to be calibrated (Fig. 6.2).

Family	Models	RMSE
Linear Regression	Linear Regression	23.628
	Robust Linear Regression	25.442
Regression Tree	Fine Tree	16.636
	Medium Tree	18.477
	Coarse Tree	21.209
Support Vector Machine	Linear SVM	24.939
	Quadratic SVM	30.348
	Fine Gaussian SVM	12.515
	Medium Gaussian SVM	20.247
	Coarse Gaussian SVM	23.749
Ensemble	Boosted Trees	20.19
	Bagged Trees	15.574
GPR	Squared Exponential GPR	**9.5682**
	Matern 5/2 GPR	**9.2446**
	Exponential GPR	**9.72**
	Rational Quadratic GPR	**8.9786**

Fig. 6.2 RMSE values for various machine learning algorithms used on our dataset

Results and Discussion

We adopted the root mean square error (RMSE) as the metric to evaluate the prediction accuracy of various machine learning algorithms on our dataset. The RMSE is a standard deviation of the residuals, which are a measure of how far actual data points are from the regression line. In addition, we also chose several other standard metrics to evaluate the prediction performance of our machine learning algorithms: mean absolute error (MAE), mean squared error (MSE), R-squared value, speed of computation, etc.

As shown in Fig. 6.3, GPR outperformed all other machine learning algorithms used by us on our dataset as far as the RMSE value is concerned. So, for further analysis, we chose to work with the GPR models and trained those on selected features which are chemically related to CO directly. For example, the inputs are taken as (1) the presence/weight of the catalyst metals Pt, Au, Ru, etc., (2) CeO_2, (3) ZrO_2, (4) temperature in Kelvin, (5) initial CO and H_2O volume in percentages and (6) flowrates. The output was taken as the CO conversion. We now present simulation

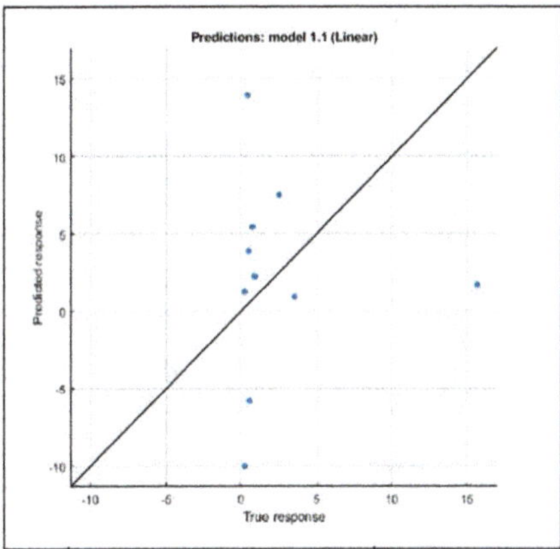

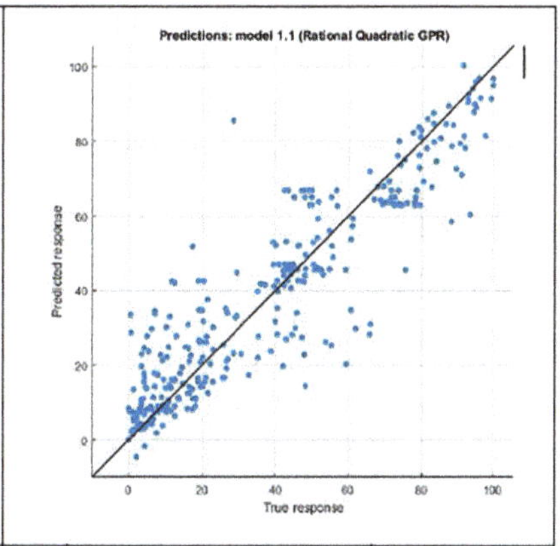

Ir	SVM	RMSE: 4.106 R^2:-1.18	Pt	Rational Quadradic GPR	RMSE: 17.712 R^2:0.73

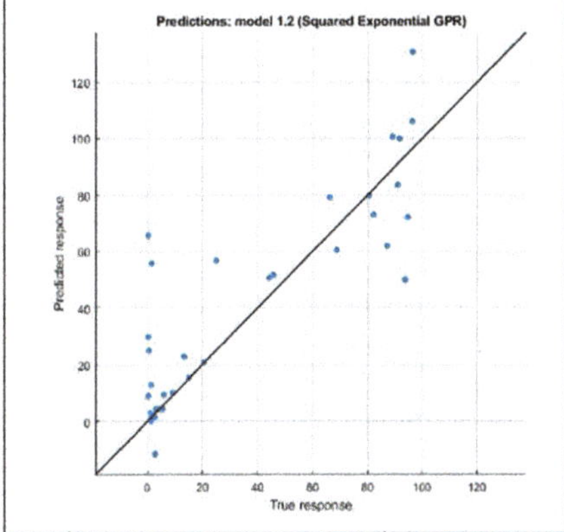

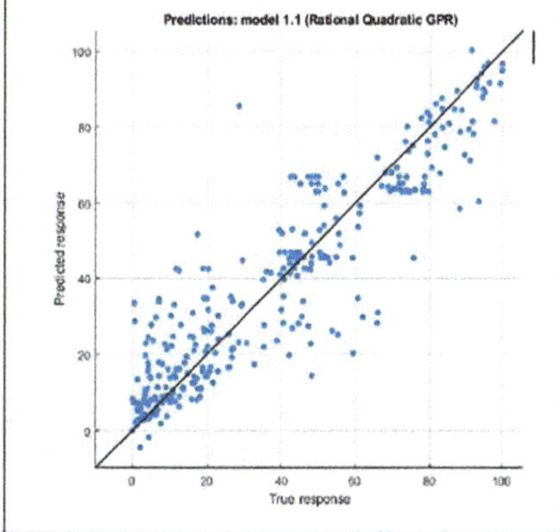

Rh	Square Exponential GPR	RMSE: 21.106 R^2:0.71	Ru	Matern 5/2 GPR	RMSE: 14.412 R^2:0.82

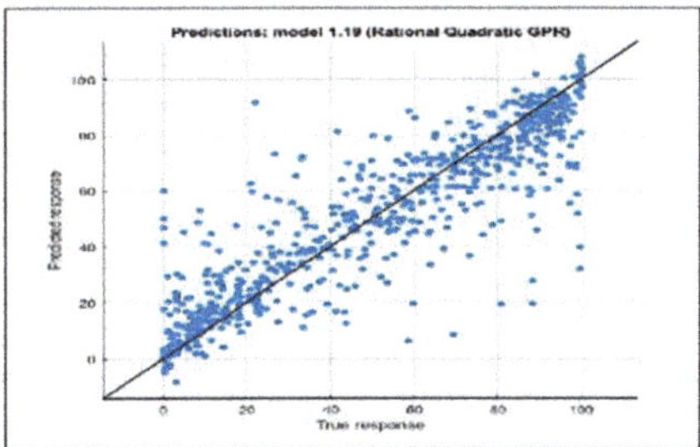

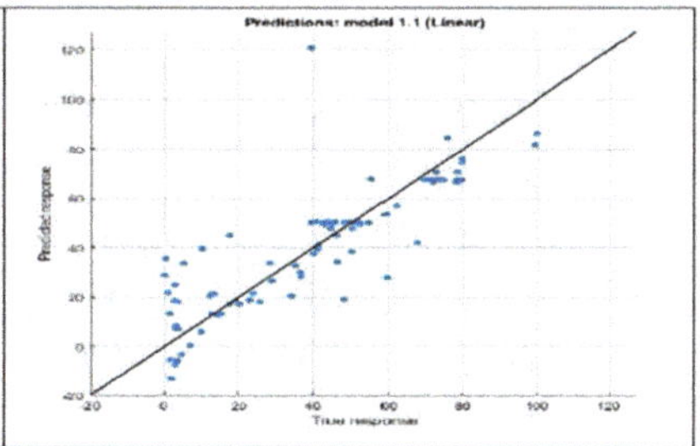

Au	Rational Quadradic GPR	RMSE: 14.106 R^2:0.82	Cu	Exponential GPR	RMSE: 10.115 R^2:0.74

Fig. 6.3 Predicted values with temperature raised to k, where $k = 1.1$, for different base metals and for different machine learning algorithms. The best results for the machine learning algorithms are shown

results wherein the operating temperature was raised to k for different values of k for a variety of base metals. As shown in Figs. 6.3, 6.4 and 6.5, the GPR models outperform other predictive models significantly. The R-squared value obtained for the best fit model was 0.92. This means that the model can explain 92% statistical variation in the given dataset. Because the R-squared value is >1 for the SVM model, it follows that the SVM model is a very poor predictor for the catalyst synthesis using this dataset.

Of course, a higher R-squared value in the range of [−1, 1] does not necessarily mean that the model is a better fit. For example, non-random residual patterns

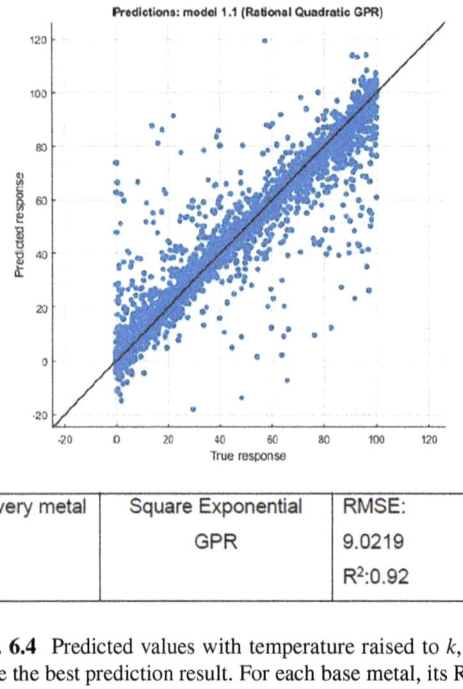

Results
RMSE 9.0219
R-Squared 0.92
MSE 81.394
MAE 4.9052
Prediction speed ~6800 obs/sec
Training time 205.69 sec

Model Type
Preset: Rational Quadratic GPR
Basis function: Constant
Kernel function: Rational Quadratic
Use isotropic kernel: true
Kernel scale: Automatic
Signal standard deviation: Automatic
Sigma: Automatic
Standardize: true
Optimize numeric parameters: true

Optimizer Options
Hyperparameter options disabled

Feature Selection
All features used in the model, before PCA

PCA
PCA disabled

Every metal	Square Exponential GPR	RMSE: 9.0219 R^2:0.92

Fig. 6.4 Predicted values with temperature raised to k, where k = 1.1. Square exponential GPR gave the best prediction result. For each base metal, its R-squared value was 0.92

	(k)^0.8	*(k)^0.9*	*(k)^1.1*	*(k)^1.2*
RMSE	9.1139	9.1089	9.1669	9.4424
R-squared	0.92	0.92	0.92	0.92
MSE	83.063	82.973	84.031	89.159
MAE	4.9229	5.0491	4.934	5.1299
Prediction Speed	16000 obs/sec	17000 obs/sec	16000 obs/sec	17000 obs/sec
Training Time	97.411 sec	98.863 sec	99.976 sec	99.632 sec

Fig. 6.5 Statistical metric values for the performance of the square exponential GPR for different values of k

indicate a bad fit despite a high R-squared value. This type of specification bias occurs when the model is underspecified. So, one should check the residual plots. To produce random residuals, one could try adding terms to the model or fitting a nonlinear model.

Although GPR gave the best prediction results, we would like to point out that GPR is computationally expensive. In MATLAB, running GPR on the given dataset took us nearly 300% more time compared to SVM or ensemble methods.

By keeping uniform operational condition and features for the base metals, we can estimate the effectiveness of each base metal by putting them into a comparison. This is conclusive as the relative importance of the operational condition is not properly explored as different settings of operational conditions might impact different base metals differently. However, it can provide a good estimate on how well one base metal performs in high-temperature shift (573–723 K) and low-temperature shift (473–523 K).

Critical information can be extracted from Fig. 6.6. Firstly, that in low-temperature shift, rhodium excels and performs significantly better than all other

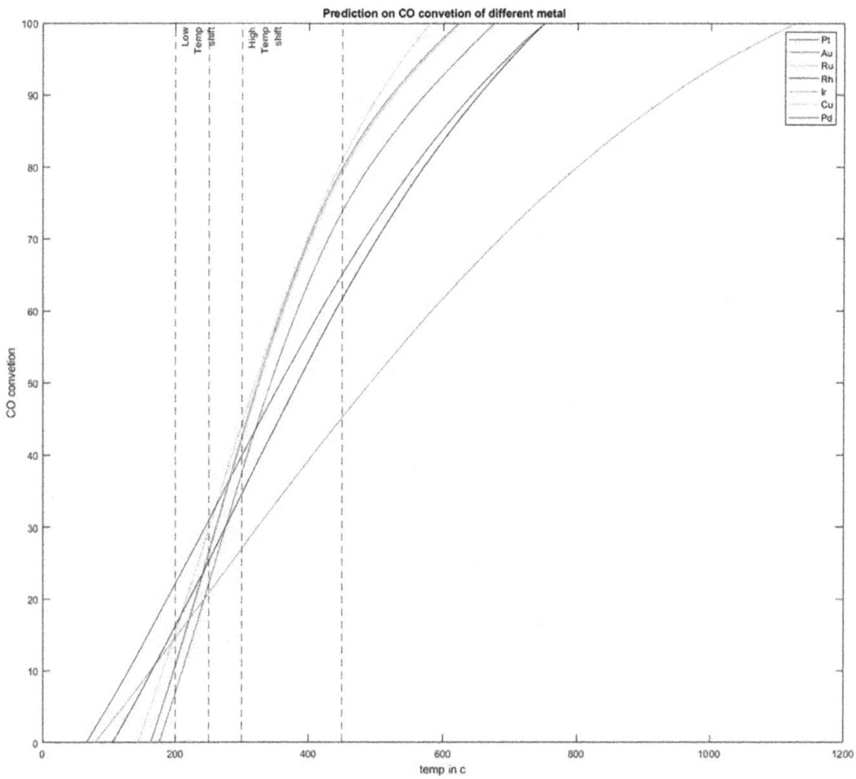

Fig. 6.6 This figure illustrates a comparison of the performance of base metals where Au excels in low-temperature shift, while the three base metals Ru, Pt and Cu perform similarly in the region of high-temperature shift

	Pt	Au	Ru	Rh	Ir	Cu	Pd
Price/gram In usd	$39.70	$58.54	$14.15	$681.60	$141.46	$0.01	$53.14
Temp (C)	627	678	581	725	1130	627	725
Relative Marginal Cost	**82.7**	155.54	**14.15**	825.6	690.146	**56.01**	197.14

Fig. 6.7 Prediction of the cost of production

base metals. However, in high-temperature shift ruthenium, platinum and copper perform similarly. When aiming for a 100% rate of conversion, the prioritisation of metal used should be as follows for lowest temperature: ruthenium over platinum, platinum over copper, copper over gold, gold over rhodium, rhodium over palladium, etc. The table in Fig. 6.7 summarises the predicted cost of production. The best-performing base metals in cost efficiency are copper, ruthenium and platinum, which is reasonable as they are the cheapest and reaches 100% conversion at low temperatures.

Conclusion

We have explored the problem of how digital twins can improve the process of synthesising catalysts so that the carbon monoxide conversion efficiency of chemical reactors can be improved in general. Six key steps in the life cycle of such a digital twin are outlined, and new results are presented for the first two steps, viz. conceptualisation and model development, using published data from 96 well-referenced publications on such chemical reactors. A range of machine learning algorithms is considered as a candidate for developing the digital twin that can accurately predict the conversion efficiency of the chemical reactor for a variety of operational conditions. The algorithms are implemented in MATLAB. It is shown that Gaussian process regression models outperform linear regression models, support vector machine models, decision trees and ensemble trees in this context. Our Gaussian process regression models achieve an excellent R-squared value of 0.92 in predicting the efficiency of catalytic conversion. We show that choosing copper, ruthenium or platinum as the base metal will reduce the cost of operation.

Acknowledgements Dr. Vishwesh Kulkarni is a Senior Lecturer at the Department of Biomedical Engineering and Imaging Science of King's College London (London, UK) and the Programme Lead of Biomedical Engineering at the SUSTech-King's School of Medicine (Shenzhen, China). Professor Evgeny Rebrov is a Professor at the School of Engineering of the University of Warwick (Coventry, UK) and a Full Professor at the Eindhoven University of Technology (Eindhoven, the Netherlands). Emails: vishwesh.kulkarni@kcl.ac.uk, E.Rebrov@warwick.ac.uk.

References

1. Wilcox, K., & Segundo, B. (2024). The role of computational science in digital twins. *Nature Computational Science, 4*, 147–149.
2. Ferrai, A., & Wilcox, K. (2024). Digital twins in mechanical and aerospace engineering. *Nature Computational Science, 4*, 178–183.
3. Odabaşi, Ç., Günay, M. E., & Yildirim, R. (2014). Knowledge extraction for water gas shift reaction over noble metal catalysts from publications in the literature between 2002 and 2012. *International Journal of Hydrogen Energy, 39*(11), 5733–5746. https://doi.org/10.1016/j.ijhydene.2014.01.160
4. Ashter, S. A. (2014). *Thermoforming of single and multilayer laminates: Plastic films technologies, testing, and applications*. Elsevier.
5. Petrucci, R., et al. (2016). *General chemistry: Principles and modern applications* (11th ed.). Pearson College Div.
6. Zhang, Y., & Xu, X. (2021). Predictions of adsorption energies of methane-related species on cu-based alloys through machine learning. *Machine Learning with Apple, 3*, 100010.
7. Fernández, A., et al. (2018). *Learning from imbalanced data sets*. Springer Nature Switzerland AG.
8. Bishop, C. M. (2006). *Pattern recognition and machine learning* (Information science and statistics series). Springer Science + Business Media.
9. Hastie, T., et al. (2009). *The elements of statistical learning: Data mining, inference, and prediction* (Springer series in statistics) (2nd ed.). Springer Verlag.
10. James, G., et al. (2013). *An introduction to statistical learning: With applications in R* (Springer texts in statistics series) (2nd ed.). Springer Verlag.
11. Breiman, L. (2001). Random forests. *Machine Learning, 45*, 5–32.
12. Zhang, N., Xiong, J., Zhong, J., & Leatham, K. (2018). Gaussian process regression method for classification for high-dimensional data with limited samples. In *The Eighth International Conference on Information Science and Technology (ICIST), Cordoba, Spain.*

Chapter 7
Harnessing Digital Twins for Building Resilient Food Supply Chains

Abhishek Yadav, Parijat Deshpande, Shankar Kausley, Beena Rai, and Souvik Barat

Abstract The need to feed a population of ~10 billion by 2050 and growing concern of food wastage have collectively prompted diverse stakeholders, including producers, logistics companies, governments and food health enforcement bodies to explore various strategies for establishing robust food supply chains to ensure food availability and reduce wastage. In addition, food quality and safety are becoming critical from the consumer perspective. However, reducing food wastage while ensuring food availability, safety and quality is a challenging task due to the uneven demand patterns, unique perishability dynamics of the food, uncertain environmental factors and a wide range of supply chain complexities. Better demand forecasting, continuous monitoring of food throughout their life cycles, timely interventions, better storage and distribution systems and seamless movements of food throughout the supply chain network conforming to food characteristics are essential to achieve the desired objective of reducing food wastage while ensuring food availability, safety and quality. We adopted food digital twin (FDT) technology in combination with enterprise digital twin (EDT) to establish a resilient and sustainable food ecosystem addressing existing challenges. FDT, a multi-modal sensing and combined-physics- and AI-based model, helps monitor food condition and assess the remaining shelf life of food by considering its unique biochemical characteristics and degradation patterns. EDT, in contrast, is leveraged for supply chain specific to the unique characteristics of food. A seamless integrated use of both types of digital twins, i.e. FDT and EDT, ensures food safety and establishes a resilient and sustainable food supply chain to reduce food wastage and ensure food availability to the consumers without compromising on nutritional food value. This chapter discusses the challenges related to food safety and food supply chain, introduces the foundational concepts of FDT and EDT and illustrates our integrated approach using a case of post-harvest supply of fresh climacteric fruits and vegetables.

A. Yadav (✉) · P. Deshpande · S. Kausley · B. Rai · S. Barat
Tata Consultancy Services, Pune, Maharashtra, India
e-mail: y.abhishek1@tcs.com; parijat.deshpande@tcs.com; shankar.kausley@tcs.com; beena.rai@tcs.com; souvik.barat@tcs.com

V. Kulkarni et al. (eds.), *Digital Twins for Simulation-Based Decision-Making*,
https://doi.org/10.1007/978-3-031-89654-5_7

Introduction

Meeting growing food demands and food wastage have remained significant global concerns for a long time. Ensuring food quality and safety throughout the food supply chain from the production or harvesting of food to consumption is becoming crucial for protecting public health[1,2,,3] However, achieving the balance between reduction of food wastage and maintaining food quality for varying environmental conditions is highly complex as characteristics of food are diverse and they have varying degradation patterns, shelf life and storage requirements. These variations, combined with unpredictable demands and environmental uncertainties including temperature fluctuations and humidity, pose unique challenges in maintaining food quality and controlling food wastage while ensuring food demands. Moreover, conventional logistics and storage management with limited focus on food characteristics contribute to excessive food wastage.

To overcome these challenges in the food supply network, several key requirements must be considered, including better sensing, specific food supply chain and dynamic adaptation. Real-time sensing capability is crucial for continuous monitoring of food quality and environmental conditions, serving as spoilage indicators to enable proactive interventions before food degradation occurs. A resilient supply chain tailored to specific food characteristics and having complete knowledge of necessary interventions to control food degradation at various stages is critical. Additionally, effective demand prediction and precise inventory management that account for the remaining shelf life of stocked food are also essential to align supply with demand and reduce wastage. We believe that these measures collectively ensure consistent food availability, maintain quality standards, reduce food wastage and enhance the overall efficiency of the food supply network.

A synergistic use of state-of-the-art sensing technologies, predictive nature of AI and simulation-led what-if capability of digital twins offer transformative potential for developing food supply chains with desired characteristics. Sensing and AI-driven predictive analyses enable spoilage detection, prediction of remaining shelf life of food and optimum storage management. Digital twin technology of food supply network helps evaluate potential interventions of food supply chains using in silico what-if analyses to support evidence-based decision-making, ensuring overall operational efficiency. By leveraging these two types of digital twins, food systems can achieve greater sustainability, reduce waste and improve food quality management, leading to a more resilient and efficient food network. We

[1] https://www.fao.org/home/en/

[2] https://www.un.org/sustainabledevelopment/hunger/

[3] https://www.fao.org/fileadmin/templates/wsfs/docs/expert_paper/How_to_Feed_the_World_in_2050.pdf

propose a seamless integration of a food digital twin (FDT)[4,5] with an enterprise digital twin (EDT) [1] as a comprehensive digital twin platform. The FDT, a multi-model AI framework, acts as a real-time monitoring system that enables precise sensing of food quality and helps in predicting the remaining shelf life by analysing spoilage patterns that are specific to different food types. By understanding these spoilage dynamics, the FDT can recommend necessary interventions for maintaining food quality.

EDT, on the other hand, serves as a comprehensive platform for evaluating the broader supply chain dynamics. It considers prediction on food demand, required interventions for maintaining food quality (from FDT) and accounts for key logistics and environmental factors that influence food as well as food systems. The integrated digital twin platform, therefore, enables simulations for evaluating the efficacy of various interventions aimed at reducing food waste and ensuring consistent food availability and better food quality. By incorporating environmental variables such as temperature fluctuations, humidity and transportation efficiency, EDT helps in assessing the overall impact of supply chain disruptions and proposing corrective actions from supply chain perspective. In this context, FDT and EDT complement each other in a holistic manner. FDT focuses on the micro-level factors of food quality, spoilage and demand forecasting, while EDT operates at the macro-level, considering the complex interplay of logistics, inventory management and environmental conditions. This integrated approach not only improves food quality management and reduces waste but also aligns with broader sustainability goals by considering both the economic and social implications of food systems. The synergy between these two digital twins allows for an optimized, adaptive food supply chain capable of responding to both predictable and unforeseen challenges, ultimately fostering a more resilient and sustainable food system.

This chapter focuses on fresh fruits and vegetables as illustrative examples to discuss key aspects, such as food characteristics, spoilage dynamics and other critical factors that impact food quality including nutritional value, taste, aroma and safety standards. Furthermore, it discusses the correlations between these unique food factors and their influence on food wastage, quality, availability and distribution efficiency. The rest of the chapter is organized as follows. The next section discusses food characteristics and their inherent complexities. It also highlights food supply chain–related complexities. We then present the foundational concepts of FDT and EDT. The subsequent section presents an integrated food supply chain digital twin, followed by a set of case studies. The next section highlights the applicability of the proposed approach for the food ecosystem. Finally, we conclude this chapter with a brief summary and our early experiences.

---

[4] https://www.tcs.com/what-we-do/research/article/digital-twin-technology-food-freshness-monitoring

[5] https://www.youtube.com/watch?v=CrD7MoSXxhI&t=73s

Food Dynamics and Supply Chain Complexities

Food Shelf Life and Inherent Uncertainties

The shelf life and spoilage dynamics of fresh fruits and vegetables are multifaceted physico-chemical phenomenon characterized by an array of physiological, biochemical and developmental transformations [2]. Categorically, they are influenced by intrinsic and extrinsic factors coupled with inherent uncertainties. Globally, around 13.2% of food produced is lost between harvest and retail due to the ineffective management of these intrinsic and extrinsic factors. This not only generates substantial greenhouse gas emissions[6] but also impedes advancements toward achieving the Zero Hunger Sustainable Development Goal (SDG). The intrinsic factors typically include the release of biogases during the food degradation process. For fruits, especially climacteric fruits, intrinsic factors are fruit's ripening rate, respiration pattern and release of gases, such as CO_2 and ethylene. These factors further accelerate the ripening process and bio-chemical degradation. Extrinsic factors such as temperature, relative humidity, handling conditions and exposure to contaminants affect the shelf life and spoilage. For example, mangoes are highly sensitive to temperature fluctuations, ripening rapidly under warm conditions. Similarly, bananas are prone to ethylene-induced over-ripening when stored with other fruits, leading to softening, discolouring, loss of taste and aroma. Uncertainties arise from variability in cultivation practices, harvesting times and the effectiveness of post-harvest preservation techniques, making it challenging to predict shelf life and spoilage timelines accurately.[7]

In addition to the uncertainty around these intrinsic and extrinsic factors, significant challenges arise from the brief duration of the optimal edible phase of perishable food, limited viable options to regulate bio-chemical degradation within food safety norms and the prohibitive costs of viable treatment options. Ineffective management of these factors can lead to considerable waste.

According to the Food and Agriculture Organization (FAO)[1,6] [3] of the United Nations, global food wastage amounts to 1.3 billion tons annually, with fruits and vegetables accounting for approximately 40% of this waste. In response to this challenge, the FAO has outlined a path toward achieving zero hunger and aims to transform food systems to meet the Sustainable Development Goals (SDGs) by 2030. The focus is on reducing global food loss and waste, particularly in relation to SDG #2 (Zero Hunger) and SDG #12.3 (Responsible Consumption and Production).

---

[6] https://www.un.org/en/observances/end-food-waste-day

[7] https://www.fao.org/newsroom/detail/FAO-UNEP-agriculture-environment-food-loss-waste-day-2022/en

Supply Chain Complexities Due to Spoilage Dynamics

Managing the supply chains for perishable food is inherently challenging due to the complex interplay of bio-degradation, spoilage dynamics and the limited shelf life of these products. These dynamics, as illustrated using a causal loop diagram (CLD) in Fig. 7.1, introduce significant nonlinearity and uncertainties across multiple stages of the supply chain, from production to retail. Extrinsic factors such as temperature, transit times and handling practices directly influence the freshness and quality of food items, thereby affecting demand and pricing. For instance, inadequate transportation or poorly managed storage conditions can accelerate spoilage, thus leading to wastage. A delay in transporting bananas, for example, can speed up ripening to the point where they are unsellable upon arrival at retail outlets. Similarly, suboptimal storage conditions for apples may lead to visible spoilage, reducing consumer appeal and lowering market value that directly affect consumer demand. These issues disrupt supply chain planning, pushing retailers to either overstock to prevent lost sales opportunities or understock to avoid wastage. Both strategies come with their own set of inefficiencies, leading to excessive investment in cold storage infrastructure and food-specific handling protocols, which drive up operational costs and complexity.

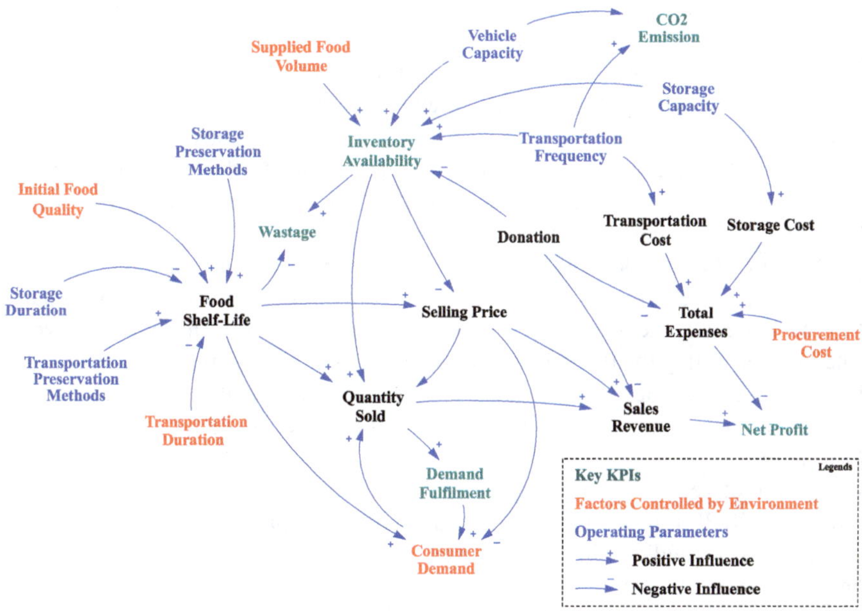

Fig. 7.1 High-level dynamics and influencing factors in the food supply chain

To address these challenges, it is essential to understand the key stakeholder groups—supply, storage and transportation, and demand—and their interconnected roles in the supply chain.

Supply: The supply end of the chain is primarily influenced by extrinsic factors, including the geographic location of production, the timing of harvests and the agricultural practices employed at individual farms. These factors collectively determine the quality and quantity of food entering the supply chain, as well as its residual shelf life.

The procurement cost is shaped by demand-supply dynamics and the quality of the harvested produce. However, because supply is an uncontrollable variable, adaptability is key to managing fluctuations. During peak harvest periods, for instance, the supply chain must efficiently handle increased production volumes, requiring well-coordinated systems for packaging, storage and transportation. Conversely, during off-peak seasons, operators may need to source produce from alternative regions or rely on preservation techniques to ensure a consistent supply of high-quality produce.

Storage and transportation: The storage and transportation phase of the supply chain plays a crucial role in maintaining product quality. Proper management of environmental factors, such as temperature and humidity, is essential for reducing spoilage and maximizing customer satisfaction. The remaining shelf life of food at any stage—whether in storage or transit—is directly influenced by the preservation techniques used and the duration of these phases as depicted in Fig. 7.1.

To minimize spoilage and operational inefficiencies, warehouses must be strategically located and appropriately sized, and transportation systems must be carefully selected to align with the perishability of the goods. However, these improvements come with associated costs. Despite these efforts, a portion of the produce is inevitably lost at each stage, highlighting the importance of optimizing these processes to reduce waste while controlling expenses.

Demand: On the demand side, market dynamics such as consumer demand and selling price directly influence decision-making across the supply chain. Pricing is heavily dependent on supply chain performance and plays a pivotal role in determining the demand-fulfilment ratio, which measures the chain's ability to meet market needs. For example, disruptions in quality or availability can lead to unmet demand or reduced sales, ultimately impacting revenue and profitability.

The effectiveness of food supply chains is evaluated using key performance indicators (KPIs), including demand fulfilment, net profit and net wastage, all of which are visualized in Fig. 7.1. These metrics are influenced by the freshness and nutritional quality of produce at every stage of the supply chain. In addition, adherence to food safety standards and maintaining affordability are critical for meeting consumer expectations and achieving broader sustainability goals.

Background Technologies

This section presents two foundational digital technologies, FDT[4,5] and EDT [1], which act as essential building blocks for developing holistic and comprehensive digital twin technology for food supply chain, specifically tailored for perishable foods.

Food Digital Twin (FDT)

FDT is a platform that leverages cutting-edge technologies, such as the Internet of Things (IoT), data analytics and machine learning (ML), to sense and predict the quality and freshness of food throughout its life cycle—from the farm to the consumer. FDT offers three core capabilities—sense, predict and simulate. The sense module integrates a wide range of IoT-enabled sensors that monitor key parameters such as visible and near-infrared (NIR) imaging, ultrasound scanning, galvanic skin resistance (GSR), air quality, gas composition (e.g. CO_2, C_2H_4, O_2), weight, various volatile organic compound (VOC) content and chemically analysed food properties. The sense module works in tandem with advanced data analytics, image processing and cloud computing technologies for real-time prediction of food quality and remaining shelf life.

The simulation module helps simulate the environmental conditions that food can be exposed to, during the supply chain and conditions in the field, during storage or while in transit. It helps understand how different extrinsic factors may affect the shelf life and quality of food.

When deployed in real-world scenarios, FDT offers significant benefits to stakeholders across the food supply chain by producing real-time insights about food items and possible trajectories under different conditions. The insights into localized stage-specific variations in food qualities, combined with food demand data and a global overview of the supply chain, help better decision-making for optimized logistics and minimize food spoilage, enhancing overall efficiency and sustainability.

Models

At the heart of the system are hybrid models that combine AI/ML techniques with physics-based models. These models use both non-invasive sensor data and offline laboratory data to develop FDT models and simulate various supply chain scenarios. By integrating multivariate, multimodal and time-series data, the platform continuously refines its predictions and adapts to new information. The predictive models generate a digital signature of the food that allows for accurate forecasting of food quality, freshness index and remaining shelf life. This capability enables the creation of a feedback system that can dynamically adjust environmental conditions to extend shelf life or repurpose food that may otherwise go to waste by redirecting it to alternate locations or channels.

The FDT platform performs a time series analysis where data is collected at discrete intervals. Each time step incorporates sensory inputs (such as temperature, humidity and gas measurements), visual data from high-resolution cameras and chemical analysis results. This multi-dimensional data is used to train machine learning models that predict the freshness of food over time.

To process visual data, the platform employs a pre-trained convolutional neural network (CNN). The CNN extracts features from the images, converting them into a vectorized representation of the food. This vector, or visual embedding, acts as a digital signature that characterizes the food's freshness. A single CNN network is shared across all time steps of the recurrent neural network (RNN) model used in the analysis, ensuring consistency in feature extraction.

The visual embeddings generated by the CNN are compared with a standardized representation for freshness. This comparison is performed using vector similarity measures, which allows the system to assess and predict the freshness index or remaining shelf life of the food. By integrating visual content through CNNs, the platform enhances the accuracy of freshness predictions, providing a more comprehensive evaluation thereby creating a food quality monitoring soft-sensor.

Realization

The FDT platform is implemented using state-of-the-art sensing, IoT and cloud technologies. It utilizes a multimodal sensor suite that collects data from multiple IoT sensors interfaced via Bluetooth Low Energy (BLE) or Wi-Fi modules. The real-time data is then transmitted to the cloud, allowing stakeholders to monitor food quality from anywhere in the world. This cloud-based architecture facilitates continuous tracking and provides actionable insights for decision-making, particularly in adjusting storage or transportation conditions to optimize food freshness.

The proposed solution is a platform designed for real-time assessment and prediction of food freshness, incorporating multi-modal sensing, food chemistry and AI techniques. Central to developing this system is a custom-designed parameter-controlled enclosure, which is capable of simulating diverse environmental conditions such as temperature, humidity and light intensity. This setup accurately replicates conditions experienced during storage and transit, thus providing a realistic assessment of environment for food storage and transport.

Inside this enclosure, these modular sensors are integrated to conduct comprehensive assessments and gather data. These sensors include a range of devices such as near-infrared (NIR) sensors, galvanic skin resistance (GSR) sensors, gas sensors (for CO_2, O_2, NH_3, C_2H_4, etc.), temperature and humidity sensors, pH sensors and volatile organic compound (VOC) sensors. Additionally, multiple high-resolution cameras are deployed to capture visual data from various angles.

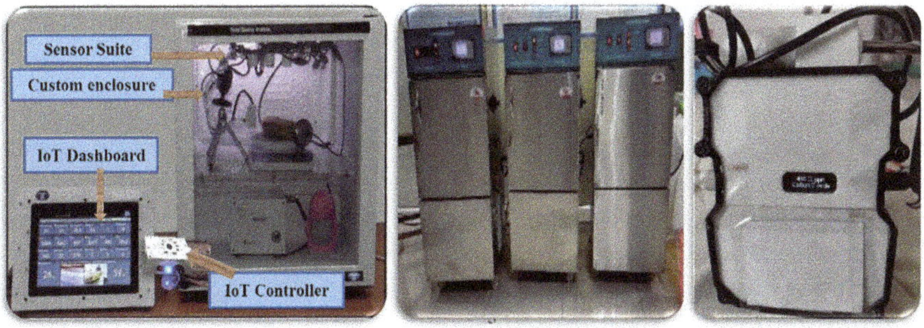

a) Custom Designed Enclosure b) Environmental Chambers c) Handheld Diagnostic Device

Fig. 7.2 Food digital twin development and implementation through measurement of food quality

The system operates through synchronized data collection facilitated by these sensors and cameras. The NIR reflectance spectra is employed for non-destructive detection of damaged spots on food items, while the GSR sensor, modified for this purpose, detects minute changes in skin resistance indicative of food degradation. The modular framework of the sensors allows for flexibility; sensors can be added or removed based on the specific needs of the food being monitored.

The sensed signals are converted to digital outputs by a microcontroller, which interfaces with various devices such as PCs, laptops, tablets and smartphones via a BLE module. The data collected is then transmitted to an internal cloud-based system, enabling real-time online monitoring of quantitative parameters and model building.

The FDT platform leverages advanced analytical techniques and machine learning models to assess these data and develop models to predict the freshness of perishable food items[4,7]. The system collects sensory and image data over time, combined with periodic chemical analyses, and build soft sensors to identify correlations and develop predictive models for remaining shelf life and quantitative freshness with limited data availability.

This solution offers a powerful tool for multiple stakeholders to make informed decisions regarding food quality, thereby enhancing the efficiency and sustainability of the food supply chain. Figure 7.2 shows the laboratory setup to measure variations in the food quality under different supply chain scenarios, which plays an important role in the development of FDT.

Enterprise Digital Twin (EDT)

Conceptually, Enterprise Digital Twin (EDT) [1] is a purposive digital replica of enterprise that helps perform what-if and if-what analyses leading to evidence-based informed decision-making in the face of uncertainty. It captures purpose-specific and related aspects of enterprise that may include strategies, processes, resources, systems and other core elements along with the environment of the enterprise, such as supplies and demands (i.e. customers), and external environmental factors (i.e. micro- and macro-uncertainties). Creating an EDT involves modeling the enterprise at the appropriate level of granularity, using techniques such as agent-based modeling, system dynamics, AI or other paradigms that effectively capture behaviours, interactions and inherent uncertainties. The construction process leverages domain knowledge and historical data to enhance the fidelity of the digital twin. The construction process can employ traditional methods, such as interviewing domain experts, or adopt a human-in-the-loop generative AI–based approach as proposed in [4].

Once constructed for a purpose, EDT serves as powerful aid for in silico experimentation, enabling enterprises to evaluate the potential impacts of strategic changes, optimize operations and evaluate effectiveness of the potential interventions for realizing higher objectives before real-world implementation. By simulating "what-if" scenarios, such as process optimizations, or market strategies, EDT provides evidence-backed insights, fostering informed decision-making while reducing risks and costs. They are particularly effective in addressing multi-objective trade-offs and navigating uncertainties, making them invaluable across industries, such as telecom [1], logistics [5] and social domains like digital twin of city for controlling COVID-19 pandemic [6].

Modeling and Analysis Approaches

Modeling and analysis techniques for representing complex systems like enterprise are broadly classified into two categories: historical data-centric and domain knowledge-centric approaches. Historical data-centric models, primarily driven by AI and ML models, are highly effective when enterprises have access to comprehensive, high-quality and relevant datasets. These models excel in predictive tasks of static systems but falter in systems characterized by high flux and fragmented data. Conversely, domain knowledge-centric approaches rely on understanding the behavioural aspects and characteristics of enterprise along with its operating environments. Mathematical modeling techniques like linear programming (LP) and operational research (OR) techniques are capable of capturing behavioural aspects of complex systems in precise forms; however, they are found to be effective when systems are relatively bounded, exhibit low uncertainty and have well-defined objective functions. Enterprise modeling techniques, such as ArchiMate [7], i* [8] and BPMN [9], help modeling large systems from different perspectives, but they have limited analysis support and are often inadequate in addressing high uncertainty.

Machine-processible enterprise modeling techniques, including system dynamics models [10] and agent-based modeling [11], are widely used to represent complex systems. These approaches align with the two primary paradigms of enterprise modeling: top-down and bottom-up. Stock-and-flow models, conforming to the system dynamics paradigm, adopt a top-down approach, focusing on capturing enterprise dynamics at an aggregated level. They are particularly useful for modeling systems where macro-level trends and behaviours, such as resource flows and accumulation, are key. In contrast, agent-based models follow a bottom-up approach and offer simulation of micro-level interactions among individual elements or agents within the enterprise. While agent-based modeling offers detailed insights into localized behaviours and emergent phenomena, it demands extensive domain knowledge about enterprise components, making digital twin construction a time- and resource-intensive effort.

In this chapter, we utilize a stock-and-flow model to develop a digital twin for a supply chain by leveraging its strength in capturing system-wide behaviours and dependencies at a strategic level. However, for a more precise representation of digital twins, especially in scenarios with high uncertainty or fragmented data, hybrid approaches are recommended. Combining AI with agent-based modeling and system dynamics can bridge the gap between detailed micro-level dynamics and overarching enterprise-wide patterns.

Stock and Flow Modeling

Stock-and-flow modeling is a powerful system dynamics modeling technique for understanding and simulating the behaviour of complex systems at coarser level of granularity. It represents systems as interconnected stocks (quantities or accumulations) and flows (rates of change), capturing the dynamic interplay between feedback loops, delays and nonlinear relationships. This modeling technique is well suited for analysing systems with nonlinear temporal behaviours, such as supply chains, population dynamics or resource management.

To construct a stock-and-flow model, key variables are identified and represented as stocks, with flows modeled to reflect the processes that alter these stocks. Relationships between variables are captured using differential equations, enabling the simulation of system behaviour under different scenarios. This approach facilitates exploration of cause-and-effect relationships, feedback structures and policy impacts.

Our Approach: Food Supply Chain Digital Twin

The perishable food supply chain is a multi-stage network designed to transport food efficiently from harvesting locations to consumption points, such as distributed retailers. As illustrated in Fig. 7.3, the supply chain begins at harvesting sites, which serve as the initial supply sources, and progresses through a network of distribution centres (DCs) that act as intermediaries. These DCs, such as warehouses, are equipped with advanced storage facilities that extend food shelf life by maintaining controlled storage environments. Strategically positioning these DCs and seamless connectivity with efficient transportation ensure that food quality is preserved throughout its journey.

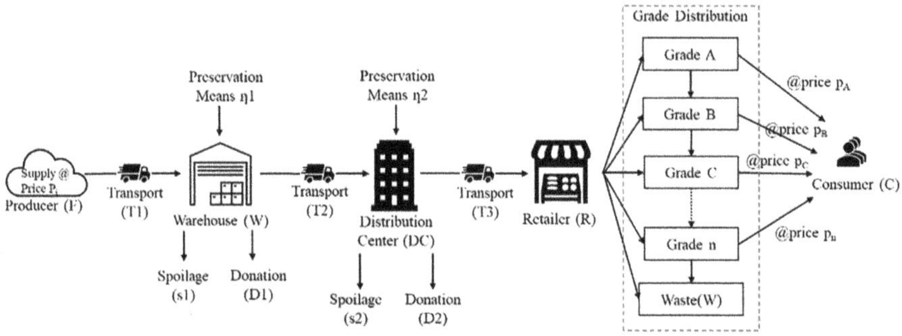

Fig. 7.3 A multi-stage view of food supply chain

At the other end of the supply chain, retailers receive food in various grades based on its perishability and remaining shelf life. For climacteric fruits, these grades typically include pre-climacteric peak (Grade A), climacteric peak (Grade B) and post-climacteric peak (Grade C). Perishable food exhibits complex dynamics as it degrades from one grade to another at varying rates due to intrinsic (e.g. biochemical properties) and extrinsic factors (e.g. temperature and humidity). Retailers employ various strategies, such as dynamic pricing, inventory management, promotional campaigns and localized preservation techniques, to maintain steady sales flow, maximize profits and minimize wastage. Additionally, when potential wastage is detected early, selling food at low price and donation are often considered as a proactive measure to ensure economic efficiency and social responsibility.

The efficiency of such a food supply chain relies heavily on strategic decisions and timely operational interventions at each stage. Efficacy of these decisions helps balance food availability, minimize wastage and maintain food quality and safety while meeting key business performance indicators (KPIs) such as profitability.

Conforming to the canonical digital twin framework [12] and presented EDT concepts, our food supply chain digital twin (FSCDT) is realized using three core components:

1. Model for Food Supply Chain (**M4FSC**): This component serves as a virtual model that accurately mimics the physical supply chain, capturing its structure and flow dynamics along with their complexities and uncertainties using the concepts of enterprise digital twin (EDT).
2. Physical to food supply chain digital twin (**P2FSCDT**): Equipped with FDT, this component facilitates the continuous collection of real-time data providing insights into the perishability status and remaining shelf life of food at various stages of the supply chain.
3. Food Supply Chain Simulation (**FSCSim**): This component enables what-if analyses leading to evidence-based decision-making using EDT technology.

Together, these components form a comprehensive purpose-specific EDT for food supply chain, specifically tailored for perishable food as shown in Fig. 7.4. We term this EDT as food supply chain digital twin (FSCDT) that acts as an aid for both

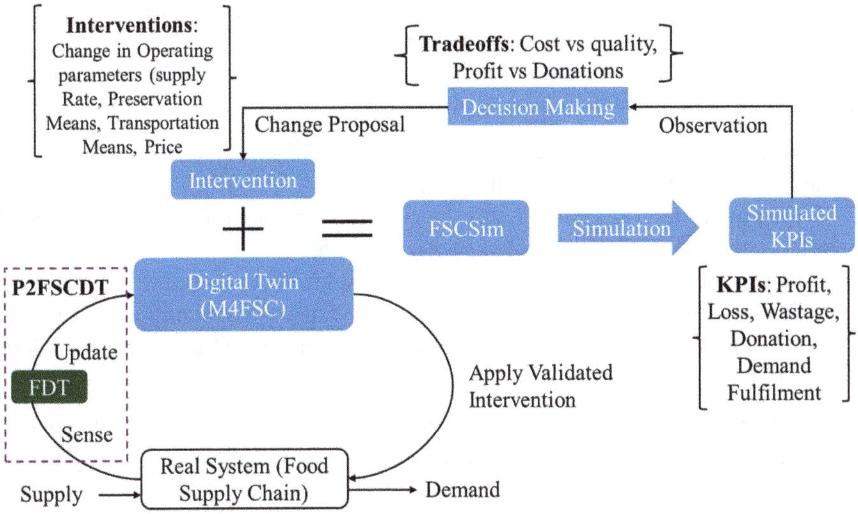

Fig. 7.4 FSCDT-based design and exploration

strategic and operational decision-making to introduce efficiency and resilience in the perishable food supply chain. The strategic design exploration focuses on optimizing the configuration of warehouses, distribution networks and vehicle routing policies. Operational interventions involve real-time sensing and control, such as regulating supply rates, implementing preservation techniques, optimizing food donation strategies and planning transportation to improve efficiency and reduce waste. The rest of this section discusses the core components of FSCDT.

Model for Food Supply Chain (M4FSC)

The dynamics of the conceptual food supply chain depicted in Fig. 7.3, referred to as perishable food supply chain, can be effectively modelled using a stock-and-flow framework. In this model, **stocks** represent various storage facilities, including warehouses, distribution centres (DCs) and retailers, while **flows** correspond to the movement of food between these storage points. Additional flows account for spoilage at different locations and the donations made to minimize wastage. Decision factors influencing food movement are incorporated as auxiliary variables within the model.

While the aggregated properties of food during storage and transportation align well with the system dynamics paradigm, the inclusion of perishability aspects—such as food quality and remaining shelf life—introduces additional complexity. The ripening process dynamics, spanning all stages of the supply chain, and their interaction with preservation methods are inherently nonlinear. Furthermore, a feedback loop exists between the extent of ripening (or remaining shelf life) and the duration and methods of storage and transportation.

To capture and analyse these nonlinear dynamics with precision, we introduce three key modeling abstractions as shown in Fig. 7.5:

1. **Storage dynamics**: Representing the behaviour of facilities such as warehouses and distribution centres shown in Fig. 7.5a
2. **Transportation dynamics**: Capturing the movement of food and associated effects on quality and shelf life shown in Fig. 7.5b
3. **Retailer dynamics**: Addressing the more complex behaviour of retailers, which differs significantly from that of warehouses and distribution centres due to additional considerations such as pricing, demand management and rapid food degradation as shown in Fig. 7.5c

These abstractions enable a comprehensive representation of the supply chain's multifaceted dynamics, ensuring accurate modeling and analysis of its operations.

Storage Dynamics

The storage dynamics in the food supply chain are critical for maintaining food quality and managing inventory levels throughout the network of warehouses and distribution centres. These storage units function as nodes where food is collected from harvesting sites, stored under controlled conditions and redistributed to meet downstream demand. Modeling these storage units within a stock-and-flow system dynamics framework involves capturing both the quantity of food and their quality over time, accounting for perishability and degradation.

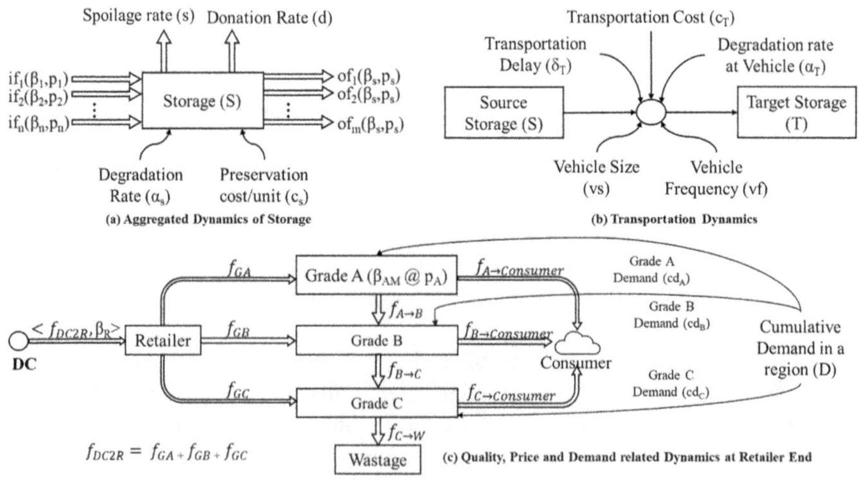

Fig. 7.5 Dynamics in M4FSC

The quantity of stock in a storage unit at any given time t, denoted as S_t, changes based on the balance of inflows and outflows, adjusted for spoilage and donations. This relationship is expressed by the differential equation:

$$\frac{dS_t}{dt} = \sum_{i=1}^{N} I_i - \sum_{j=1}^{M} O_j - s - d$$

In this equation:

$\frac{dS_t}{dt}$ represents the rate of change of the stock at time t.

I_i are the inflows to the storage unit, such as purchases from harvesting sites or transfers from other storage units.

O_j are the outflows from the storage unit, including shipments to other storage units or to retailers.

s is the spoilage rate within the storage unit.

d is the donation rate to minimize wastage.

The quality of the food in storage is captured by the aggregated remaining shelf life, denoted as β_t which represents the average remaining shelf life of all food in the storage unit at time t. This value is updated by considering the shelf life of incoming food, the degradation of existing stock due to storage conditions and the quantities involved. The aggregated remaining shelf life at time $t + 1$ is calculated using:

$$\beta_{(t+1)} = \frac{\sum_{i=1}^{N} \left(I_i \beta_{I,i}\right) + \beta_t \left(1 - \alpha_s\right) S_t}{\sum_{i=1}^{N} I_i + S_t}$$

Here:

$\beta_{(t+1)}$ is the average remaining shelf life at time $t + 1$.

β_t is the average remaining shelf life at time t.

$\beta_{I,i}$ are the average remaining shelf-lives of the inflows I_i.

S_t is the current stock level at time t.

α_s is the degradation rate during storage ($0 \leq \alpha_s \leq 1$), representing the fraction of shelf life lost per unit time due to storage conditions.

The degradation rate α_s can be adjusted through preservation methods that reduce the rate at which food degrade while in storage. The effectiveness of preservation is represented by η_s, with $0 \leq \eta_s \leq 1$, where a higher η_s indicates more effective preservation. The adjusted degradation rate is calculated as:

$$\alpha_s = \alpha_s^{\text{base}} \left(1 - \eta_s\right)$$

where α_s^{base} is the base degradation rate without any preservation techniques applied.

Spoilage within the storage unit is modelled as a fraction of the current stock that becomes unsuitable for sale due to degradation beyond acceptable quality levels. The spoilage rate is given by:

$$s = \gamma_s \times S_t$$

where γ_s is the spoilage fraction per unit time, influenced by factors such as handling practices, storage conditions and environmental factors.

Implementing preservation techniques to reduce the degradation rate incurs a cost, which is calculated as:

$$c_s = c_s^{\text{unit}} \times S_t$$

In this formula:

c_s is the *total* preservation cost at time t.

c_s^{unit} is the cost of preservation per unit of stock.

Decision-making in storage management involves balancing several factors to optimize operations. One key aspect is determining the optimal purchase rate, f_P, and the quality of incoming food, β_I, balancing higher-quality purchases with potentially higher purchase costs. Another important factor is the level of investment in preservation methods, η_s, which reduces the degradation rate but increases preservation costs. Additionally, managing the donation rate, d, helps minimize wastage by distributing excess stock nearing the end of its shelf life while considering the impact on revenue and food availability.

By carefully managing these variables, storage units can optimize their operations to preserve food quality, meet downstream demand and minimize losses due to spoilage. This involves continuous monitoring of stock levels and shelf life, adjusting inflows and outflows and effectively employing preservation techniques to enhance the overall efficiency of the supply chain.

Transportation Dynamics

Transportation dynamics are a critical component of the food supply chain, influencing not only the movement of food between different stages but also the quality of food upon arrival at their destinations. In the stock-and-flow system dynamics model, transportation is represented by flows connecting various storage units, such as warehouses and distribution centres. The flow rate of food from a source S to a target T, denoted as $f_{S \to T}$, is determined by the transportation policies, which include the selection and utilization of different types of vehicles.

In this model, V represents different vehicle types, each characterized by specific attributes: size ($v_{S,k}$), transportation delay ($\delta_{ST,k}$), degradation rate during transit ($\alpha_{V,k}$) and count (n_k) of vehicles available for each type k. These vehicle types vary in their capacities, speeds, preservation capabilities and operational costs, providing flexibility in transportation strategies.

The flow rate $f_{S \to T}$ is calculated based on the combined capacity of the vehicles used and their operating frequencies. This relationship is expressed by:

$$f_{S \to T} = \sum_{k=1}^{K} n_k \times v_{S,k} \times v_{F,k}$$

Here:

K is the number of different vehicle types.

n_k is the count of vehicles of type k available for dispatch.

$v_{S,k}$ is the capacity or size of vehicle type k.

$v_{F,k}$ is the frequency at which vehicles of type k depart from the source S.

This equation quantifies the total volume of food transported from the source to the target per unit time, considering all available vehicle types and their counts.

During transit, food undergo quality degradation due to factors like time, temperature fluctuations and handling conditions. The average remaining shelf life of food upon arrival at the target T, denoted as β_T, is reduced from the initial shelf life at the source β_S due to degradation occurring during the transportation delay associated with each vehicle type. The degradation is modeled by:

$$\beta_T = \beta_S - \sum_{k=1}^{K} \left(\alpha_{V,k} \times \delta_{ST,k} \times \frac{f_{S\to T,k}}{f_{S\to T}} \right)$$

In this equation:

$\alpha_{V,k}$ represents the degradation rate per unit time during transportation in vehicle type k.

$\delta_{ST,k}$ is the transportation delay between S and T for vehicle type k.

$f_{S\to T,k}$ is the flow rate contributed by vehicle type k.

$\frac{f_{S\to T,k}}{f_{S\to T}}$ is the proportion of the total flow carried by vehicle type k, ensuring that the degradation contribution of each vehicle type is weighted accordingly.

Transportation costs impact overall supply chain efficiency and profitability. The total transportation cost c_T for moving food from S to T is calculated as:

$$c_T = \sum_{k=1}^{K} c_{V,k} \times f_{S\to T,k} \times \delta_{ST,k}$$

Here:

$c_{V,k}$ is the cost per unit per time associated with operating vehicle type k, encompassing expenses such as fuel, labour, maintenance and any additional costs for temperature control systems.

Decision-making within transportation dynamics involves balancing several factors to optimize both cost and food quality. Selecting the appropriate mix of vehicle types is crucial. Different vehicles have varying capacities, speeds, degradation rates and costs. For example, refrigerated trucks (vehicle type k_1) may have higher operating costs (c_{V,k_1}) but can significantly reduce the degradation rate (α_{V,k_1}), resulting in food arriving with a higher remaining shelf life. Non-refrigerated trucks (vehicle type k_2) may be less costly but have higher degradation rates.

Adjusting the frequency of shipments ($v_{F,k}$) and the allocation of food to different vehicle types (n_k) can impact freshness and responsiveness to demand but may affect transportation costs due to increased operational activities. The availability and counts of each vehicle type (n_k) impose constraints on transportation capacity and scheduling. For instance, a limited number of refrigerated trucks may necessitate careful planning to prioritize high-value or highly perishable shipments.

Transportation delay ($\delta_{ST,\,k}$) plays a significant role in food quality upon arrival. Strategies to reduce $\delta_{ST,\,k}$ include utilizing faster transportation modes or optimizing routes, albeit potentially at increased costs. Vehicles with higher speeds may reduce delays but might have different cost structures and capacity limitations.

Preservation techniques during transit, such as controlled atmosphere packaging or temperature regulation, can mitigate degradation but require additional investment and may influence the choice of vehicle type. Implementing these techniques affects the degradation rate ($\alpha_{V,\,k}$) and the operational cost ($c_{V,\,k}$) for the corresponding vehicle type.

Overall, transportation dynamics necessitate careful consideration of trade-offs between cost, time and quality. By optimizing variables such as the selection and allocation of vehicle types (V and n_k), shipment frequencies ($\nu_{F,\,k}$), degradation rates during transit ($\alpha_{V,\,k}$) and transportation delays ($\delta_{ST,\,k}$), supply chain managers can enhance the efficiency of food movement. This optimization ensures that food reach their destinations promptly and with minimal quality loss, thereby reducing spoilage, meeting consumer demand effectively and maintaining profitability throughout the supply chain.

Retailer Dynamics

Retailers operate within a complex and uncertain environment, managing the dual challenge of maintaining sufficient availability to meet consumer demand while avoiding the economically and environmentally detrimental effects of over-availability. Retailers categorize produce into multiple quality-based grades, assigning distinct pricing strategies to each grade. This approach aims to enhance consumer satisfaction, minimize waste and sustain profitability. The conceptual abstraction of a retailer is illustrated in Fig. 7.5c.

A retailer R receives food from distribution centres at a rate f_{DC2R}, with an average remaining shelf life denoted as β_R. The ideal shelf life of the food, corresponding to their climacteric peak, is represented as β_I, while the estimated (and potentially variable) demand at the retailer is denoted as D.

Retailer R classifies (for the purpose of illustration) food into three grades to implement quality-based pricing. **Grade A** includes food in the pre-climacteric stage, **Grade B** represents food at the ideal stage (climacteric peak) and **Grade C** encompasses food in the post-climacteric stage that are still consumable but not ideal. Formally, β_{AL}, β_{BL} and β_{CL} denote the lower threshold remaining shelf life values for Grades A, B and C, respectively. Consequently:

- The shelf life range for Grade A is $[100, \beta_{\mathrm{AL}}]$.
- For Grade B, $[\beta_{\mathrm{AL}}, \beta_{\mathrm{BL}}]$
- For Grade C, $[\beta_{\mathrm{BL}}, \beta_{\mathrm{CL}}]$.

Additionally, β_{AM}, β_{BM} and β_{CM} represent the median remaining shelf life values for Grades A, B and C, respectively.

Although the rate at which food are received from the distribution centre (f_{DC2R}) can be controlled relatively easily, managing the remaining shelf life (β_R) is more challenging in practice. As a result, the internal distribution of inflows among Grades A, B and C (referred to as grade distribution) cannot be precisely determined. Moreover, food continuously degrade, transitioning from Grade A to Grade B, Grade B to Grade C and finally to Wastage. These transitions, known as grade flows, follow a standard degradation rate (α_L), which is influenced by local environmental factors and is typically beyond operational control at the retail level.

Additionally, the demand for each grade (A, B, and C) depends on the prices set for those grades, denoted as p_A, p_B and p_C, respectively. To model these interdependent dynamics, we employ three estimator functions, which are detailed further in the discussion.

Grade Distribution and Grade Flow

The grade distribution dynamics for food with an average remaining shelf life (β_R) into Grade A, Grade B and Grade C are inversely proportional to the difference between β_R and the median shelf life of each respective grade. The total inflow from the distribution centre to the retailer (f_{DC2R}) is divided into f_{GA}, f_{GB} and f_{GC}, representing the proportions allocated to Grades A, B and C, respectively. This distribution is mathematically expressed as:

$$< f_{GA} : f_{GB} : f_{GC} >= \frac{1}{|\beta_R - \beta_{AM}|} : \frac{1}{|\beta_R - \beta_{BM}|} : \frac{1}{|\beta_R - \beta_{CM}|}$$

The flows between grades, representing the transitions of food from Grade A to Grade B, Grade B to Grade C and Grade C to Wastage, are modeled using a conventional decay function based on the stock-and-flow principle. These flows are defined as:

$$\frac{1}{|\beta_{AM} - \beta_{BM}|} : \frac{1}{|\beta_{BM} - \beta_{CM}|} : \frac{1}{|\beta_{CM}|}$$

These dynamics capture the natural progression of food through grades as their shelf life diminishes, ultimately leading to spoilage.

Demand Distribution

The demand for a particular food at a retail outlet is influenced by multiple factors, including geographic location, the proximity of other retail shops, the historical track record of food quality at the store, seasonal variations and socio-economic conditions. In this analysis, we assume the overall demand (D) for a specific food at a retailer is a known constant.

The primary challenge addressed here is estimating how this demand is distributed across various food grades. While this distribution may also be affected by the pricing of other complementary items that consumers frequently purchase, we approximate it based on the quality of each grade (derived from its definition) and the respective grade prices. The demand distribution for Grade A, Grade B and Grade C is represented as $<c_{dA} : c_{dB} : c_{dC}>$, where:

$$c_{d\{k\}} = \left(\frac{1}{\left|\beta_I - \beta_{\mathrm{KM}}\right|^{\phi_1}}\right)\left(\frac{1}{p_K^{\phi_2}}\right), K \in \{A,B,C\}$$

The fractional demand is inversely related to two weighted values: ϕ_1, representing the average degraded remaining shelf life relative to the ideal condition (β_I), and ϕ_2, associated with the price of the grade. The parameters ϕ_1 and ϕ_2 are introduced to quantify the consumer's preference for quality and price, respectively, which may vary across individuals or consumer personas. For this study, it is assumed that price sensitivity outweighs quality sensitivity for most consumers.

Physical to Food Supply Chain Digital Twin (P2FSCDT)

This component bridges the gap between the physical supply chain and its virtual counterpart by leveraging the core capabilities of the FDT as outlined in the Background section. It enables real-time insights into the status and dynamics of perishable food products. Essentially, the IoT-enabled sensors and advanced data acquisition systems embedded in the FDT continuously capture critical parameters, such as temperature, humidity and biochemical indicators, across various stages of the supply chain. These real-time inputs are utilized to generate dynamic digital replicas of food items by accurately reflecting their ripeness levels, freshness and degradation properties.

Through detailed modeling of the physical and chemical degradation processes of the food items, the FDT provides precise quality predictions by simulating the unique degradation patterns of food items under different environmental conditions. These insights allow the supply chain digital twin to assess the evolving state of food items, thus enabling proactive measures to preserve quality and minimize losses effectively.

Moreover, by harnessing the real-time insights generated by the FDT, the supply chain digital twin facilitates informed decision-making including adjusting logistics strategies, such as re-routing shipments or altering storage conditions, to extend shelf life and optimize resource utilization. It also helps support adaptive responses to potential wastage by suggesting alternative strategies, such as redirecting food for donation or alternative uses, thereby aligning operational efficiency with broader sustainability objectives.

Overall, it enhances visibility and predictability of perishable food dynamics while enabling data-driven and agile decision-making for enhancing supply chain resilience, minimizing wastage and optimizing the overall value chain.

Food Supply Chain Simulation (FSCSim)

This component is built on a stock-and-flow modeling approach that conforms to system dynamics simulation principles. We use Vensim for modeling and simulation of perishable food supply chain including supply, storages, transportations, retailers and market demands introduced in M4FSC. Real-time data from FDT is seamlessly integrated to ensure accurate and responsive simulation outcomes. In addition to Vensim [13], PySD [14] is used for two core capabilities:

1. Integrating real-time data from the FDT into Vensim for simulation. This ensures that the model reflects the evolving state of the physical system.
2. Enabling the configuration of variables for designing and performing what-If experiments.

   Collectively, these capabilities help evaluate the impacts of various strategic and operational decisions, such as changes in item price, logistics, storage practices and supply chain policies.

An illustrative Vensim model of food supply chain (i.e. a realization of M4FSC), comprising one supply site, one warehouse, one DC and one retailer, is shown in Fig. 7.6 [2]. In this model, we use two types of interconnected stocks: (a) primary stocks to represents the quantity of items and their flows and (b) shadow stocks to mimic aggregated values of remaining shelf life of the food items conforming to perishability dynamics. Details of the model are described below.

Figure 7.6a depicts the primary stocks and flows, including donations and spoilage at different stages. It also shows the movement of food across grades at the retailer level.

Figure 7.6b illustrates the shadow stocks and their perishability dynamics.

Figure 7.6c demonstrates the implementation of demand distribution logic.

Figure 7.6d calculates the supply chain's economic aspects, using auxiliary variables to compute costs (e.g. purchase, transportation, preservation) and evaluate revenue and profit margins.This Vensim-based simulator with FDT as sensing means realizes FSCDT, which facilitates simulations of both current ("as-is") and potential future ("to-be") supply chain models, with or without interventions, where interventions can focus on strategic or operational aspects.

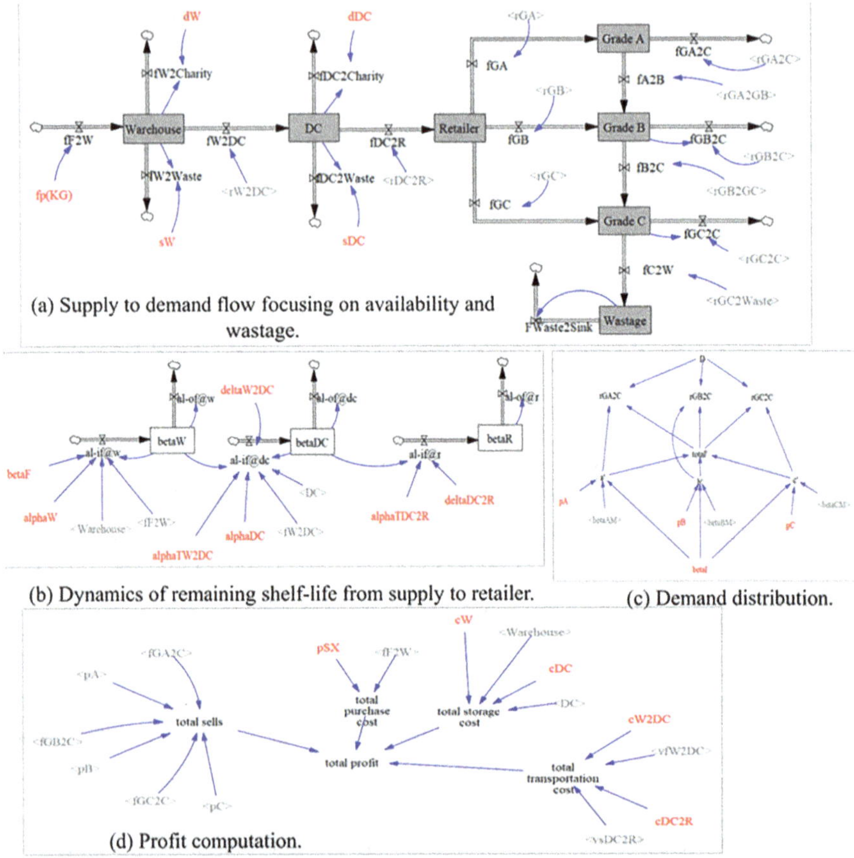

Fig. 7.6 Part of Vensim model of food supply chain digital twin

Table 7.1 outlines a non-exhaustive list of scenarios that can be explored using the supply chain digital twin. Simulating multiple scenarios involving different design choices and interventions provides valuable insights, aiding informed decision-making. A selection of these scenarios is illustrated as a use case in further section.

Case Studies

This section presents three case studies with distinct focus on the proposed food supply chain digital twin. The first two case studies illustrate the utility and effectiveness of the FDT, which serves as a critical interface between the physical and digital worlds and enables seamless synchronization with real-world data. The third case study focuses on proposed food supply chain digital twin and demonstrates the

Table 7.1 Interventions and design exploration possibilities

Aspect	Parameters to explore	Description
Supply	Purchasing Rate (fSX), Moderate Price (pSX) and remaining shelf life (αSX)	Investigate combination of Purchasing Rate (fSX), Moderate Price (pSX) and remaining shelf life (αSX). Consider relocating warehouse closer to harvesting site for better shelf life
Storage	Preservation cost (c), Degradation rate (α), Donation Rate (d)	Explore improving product quality by investing more on preservation or donating excess stock at the early stage
Storage	Addition, removal and relocation of warehouses and distribution centers	Assess the impact of altering the number or position of storage and distribution facilities
Transport	Vehicle size (vs), frequency (vf), speed (δT), degradation rate (αT) and vehicle cost (cT)	Experiment with changes in transport frequency or vehicle size to optimize supply chain efficiency. Evaluate using different vehicle types with varying cost and preservation facilities
Retailer	Grade definition (i.e., βAL, βBL and βCL) and price for different grades (i.e., pA, pB and pC)	Investigate new pricing strategies and grade definition to match customer affinities about quality and price

efficacy of its capabilities in optimizing supply chain operations and strategic decision-making.

Case Study 1: Management of Potato Supply Chain

The potato (*Solanum tuberosum* L.) is the world's third most important food crop, after rice and wheat. Known for its versatility, the potato is widely consumed as a staple food and features prominently in daily meals worldwide. Potatoes are processed into a variety of popular products, including French fries, chips, mashed potatoes and various snacks, helping meet the dietary needs of a vast global population. A typical potato supply chain is shown in Fig. 7.7. This includes harvesting and curing of potatoes at farm, storage in cold storage, transportation to processing units, processing into chips (i.e. frying of potato chips), packaging of potato chips and consumption. Alternatively, after harvest, potatoes may be directly sold to consumers for domestic consumption, or potatoes from cold storage may be sold to consumers for different applications such as starch production and seed applications.

The stakeholders face several challenges across different stages of the supply chain, including deciding right time for harvesting, temperature and humidity control during storage, maintaining consistent chips quality during processing and avoiding wastage at each stage. The food digital twin addresses these issues by predicting the real-time quality of potatoes and enables stakeholders in taking dynamic decisions including repricing, maintaining optimized storage conditions, optimizing process conditions, reducing waste, enhancing product consistency and streamlining inventory management, ultimately leading to better resource efficiency, cost reduction and sustainability across the entire supply chain (shown in Fig. 7.7).

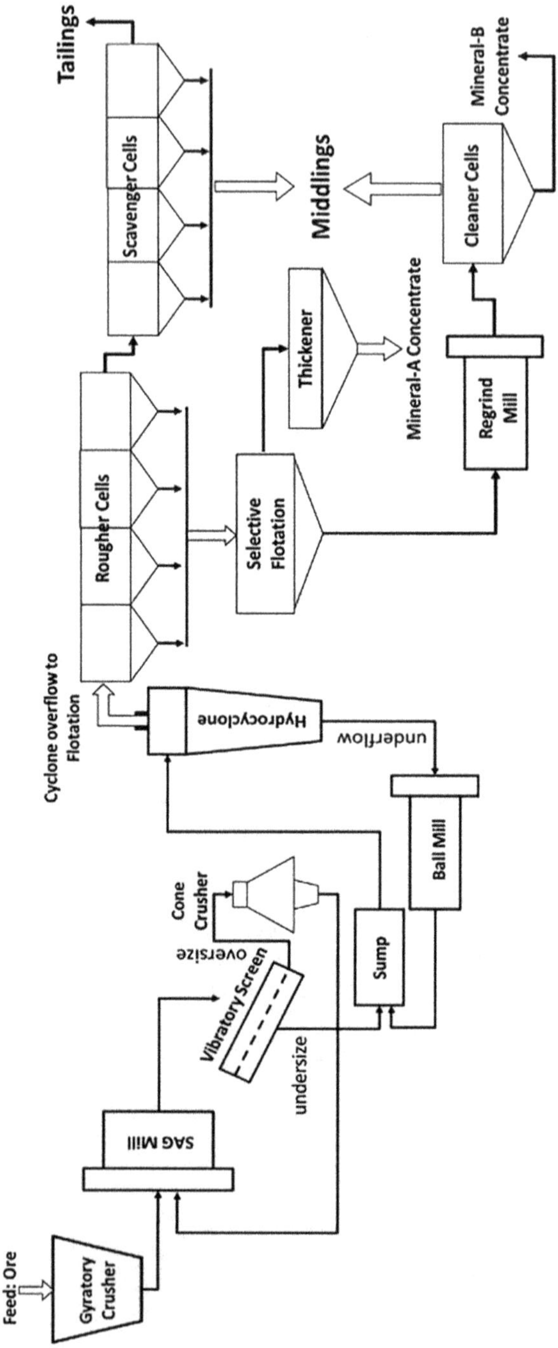

Fig. 7.7 A typical food supply chain and application of FDT

The following section describes in detail how the FDT can be used to predict potato quality in the cold storage and help in design and operation of cold storage.

Potatoes are stored in cold storage to prolong their shelf life and maintain their quality by slowing down their respiration process. Depending on the targeted end use, potatoes are stored under different environmental conditions, mainly temperature and humidity. For example, the temperature and humidity conditions required for domestic consumption, chip production and seeding applications differ. Cold storage facilities face several challenges, including temperature fluctuations, humidity control and the management of gases like carbon dioxide (CO_2) and ethylene, which can negatively affect the quality of stored potatoes. Conventional methods for addressing these challenges include manual monitoring of storage conditions and the use of rudimentary ventilation systems. However, these approaches often fail to provide precise control and real-time data analysis. By employing FDT, operators can predict the quality of potatoes at various sections of the storage facility. It can, therefore, identify hotspots, moisture spots and gas concentrations, enabling precise adjustments to storage conditions and preventing spoilage. FDT also aids in inventory management by forecasting demand for different potato applications, such as chip production, starch extraction, seeding and table consumption. By optimizing storage conditions and predicting quality degradation, operators can enhance the efficiency of their facilities, ensure potatoes meet the specific requirements for diverse uses and ultimately improve profitability while reducing waste.

Different supply chain scenarios were created by storing potatoes under different environmental conditions (as shown in Fig. 7.8) and collected image, sensory and compositional data. The collected time-series data were used to develop both first-principle and database models to predict changes in potato quality. First-principle models were developed to understand transpiration, respiration and the interaction with the environment [15]. Image-based models were developed to predict weight loss in potatoes and remaining shelf life. The models were developed to predict changes in reducing sugar content, which is a critical parameter for chip production, under different environmental conditions. Considering the variety of potato cultivars across the globe, two generic models were developed: one for cultivars sensitive to temperature and another for cultivars not sensitive to temperature [16].

In cold storage, in addition to monitoring the biochemical changes occurring in the potatoes, such as variations in starch, sugar and moisture content, it is essential to understand the flow of air and the gases released by the potatoes. During storage, potato release gases such as carbon dioxide and ethylene, which can impact their respiration rate and influence quality parameters such as texture, colour and sprouting. Properly managing the air circulation and gas exchange is critical for maintaining optimal storage conditions, reducing spoilage and extending the shelf life of the potatoes.

The packing of potatoes in jute bags and their stacking—whether on top of each other or on racks—can affect air circulation and the gases released, impacting potato quality. While jute bags are breathable, tight packing or stacking restricts airflow, especially in lower layers, leading to gas build-up (e.g. carbon dioxide and ethylene). This can accelerate respiration and cause issues like sprouting or increased

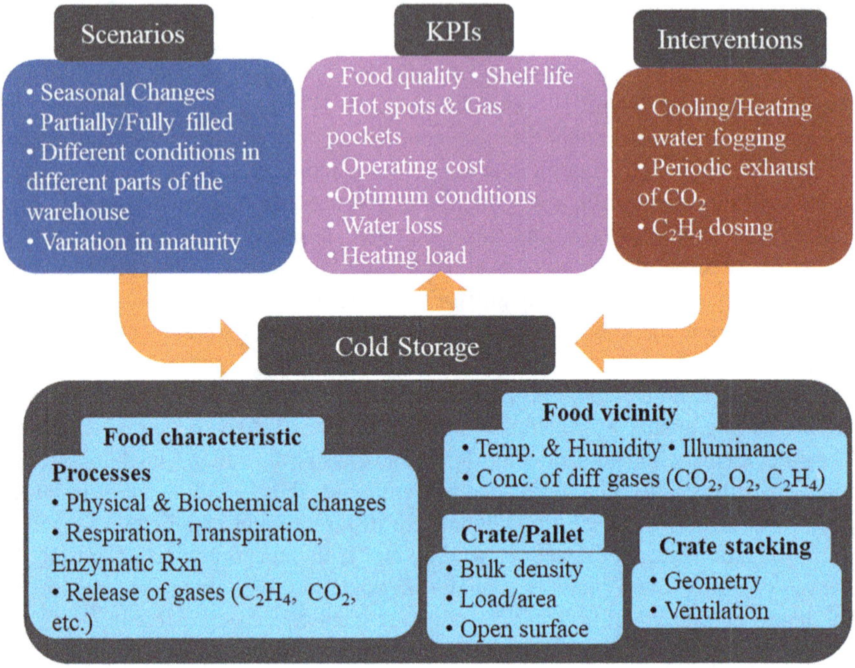

Fig. 7.8 Application of food digital twin in design and operation of cold storage

sugar conversion, deteriorating quality. Variations in temperature and humidity within the cold storage further exacerbate this, creating localized conditions that affect different lots of potatoes unevenly. Poor ventilation in certain areas can result in inconsistent quality, influencing factors like texture, moisture and shelf life. Figure 7.8 shows different factors affecting the food quality in the cold storage under different scenarios and possible interventions to maintain the food quality. We employed a combination of computational fluid dynamics (CFD) and kinetic models to predict temperature and gas concentrations in the cold storage. Further, mapping variations in temperature, moisture and gas concentrations across different environmental scenarios (such as seasonal conditions) will help develop a surrogate model for predicting food parameters in a short time. The models developed using supply chain scenarios act as soft sensors for predicting a range of information from minimal data obtained from inexpensive sensors in the field.

In real time, depending on the available data, we can predict potato quality. For example, image data can be used to estimate weight loss and remaining shelf life for table consumption under specific environmental conditions. If we know the initial reducing sugar content in the potatoes or the cultivar type, we can calculate the change in reducing sugar content over time at given environmental conditions and predict the remaining shelf life for chip production [16]. Similarly, gas release patterns over a few minutes can predict the current health of potatoes and their remaining shelf life for different applications. In cold storage, FDTs help identify gas accumulation in specific regions of the facility. This can improve inventory management, such as by removing lots from areas with high CO_2 concentrations that are deteriorating faster. The technology can also be applied to portable cold storage units, such as those mounted on vehicles. Based on gas and temperature hotspots, one can rank crates in moving cold storage as premium, good, moderate, average or poor quality. Potatoes that are deteriorating faster could be repurposed for different applications or sold at discounted prices to prevent waste and provide appropriate returns to supply chain stakeholders (e.g. farmers and cold storage owners).

Case Study 2: Predicting the Shelf Life of Bananas

This case study explores the prediction of ripeness levels and shelf life for the 'Robusta' variety of bananas by analysing their respiration rate and ripeness levels under varying storage conditions. To achieve this, initially, FDT is developed using the in-house multi-modal sensing system, paired with a temperature-controlled enclosure. This system monitors key indicators of banana metabolism, such as carbon dioxide (CO_2) release, oxygen (O_2) consumption and ethylene (C_2H_4) emission during the bananas' respiration as shown in Fig. 7.9. Additionally, the system tracks the changes in peel colour as bananas ripen, transitioning from yellow to brown, which provides valuable insights into their ripeness stage. These synchronized multi-modal inputs are used to develop models specific to the 'robusta' cultivar of bananas.

The banana samples are subjected to different storage environments to simulate real-world conditions: (1) a household refrigerator maintained at 4 °C, (2) ambient temperatures of 18 °C and 20 °C and (3) elevated temperatures of 25 °C and 30 °C, typical of large-scale storage facilities. To refine the classification of banana ripeness, machine learning and physics-based models, initially developed and fine-tuned with banana images, are employed [17–19]. These models categorize bananas into ripeness stages such as "unripe", "early ripe", "partially ripe" and "ideally ripe".

Respiration rate ($RRCO_2$) is calculated by monitoring the variation in released CO_2 and consumed O_2, utilizing principles from enzyme kinetics and the Michaelis-Menten eq. A strong correlation between $RRCO_2$ and ripeness levels is established across the different storage conditions. The FDT model is then leveraged to predict the shelf life of bananas by integrating their current respiration rate and ripeness stage, factoring in the storage conditions. The models developed serve as a soft sensor, enabling real-time predictions of banana shelf life as they move through various stages of the supply chain, ultimately optimizing storage and reducing waste.

It helps farmers, retailers and suppliers to take dynamic decisions on repricing, rerouting or re-purposing of bananas based on the remaining ripening duration such that the stock can be cleared in time and wastage can be minimized. Further, it assists in controlling and altering the transport and warehouse conditions of the bananas in bulk to get the desired ripening rate and accordingly enhance shelf life of these fruits. Moreover, in the case of large consignments when bulk of bananas are kept together, it is extremely difficult to get images of individual fruits

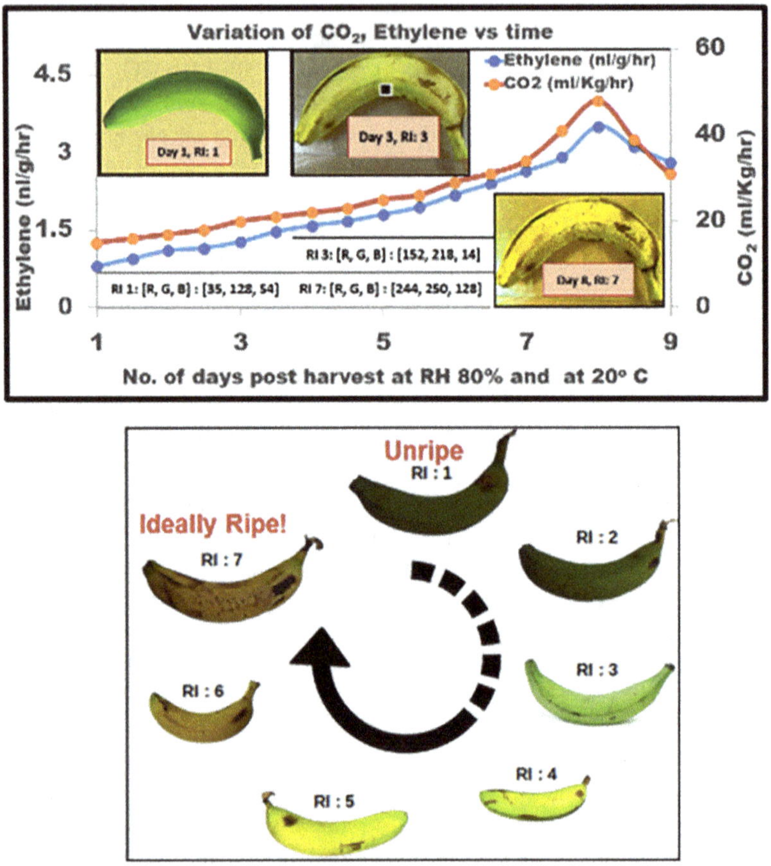

Fig. 7.9 Prediction of ripeness level and ripening duration of banana

especially when they are transported in trucks. Therefore, in such scenarios, inexpensive CO_2 and O_2 sensors can be easily deployed, and CO_2 respiration rate can be measured. Once the respiration rate is measured in real time, it can be correlated to the ripeness levels, and dynamic decisions can be taken on the consignment to maximize profits and reduce wastage based on the ripeness level of bananas. In order to use these food digital twins for field applications, a portable device is developed as shown in Fig. 7.2c to facilitate end users to easily ascertain the storage temperature, released CO_2 and consumed O_2 by the fruits and assist the stakeholders to take these dynamic decisions.

Case Study 3: Supply Chain of Climacteric Fruits

This case study focuses on the apple supply chain (a climacteric fruit) by contextualizing the constructed FSCDT [3]. The auxiliary variables of the stock-and-flow model representing M4FSC are configured using the values provided in Table 7.2,

Table 7.2 Exploration details

Exp #	Description	f_p (KG)	d_W	d_{DC}	p_A	p_B	p_C	c_W	c_{DC}	c_{W2DC}	c_{DC2R}	αW	α_{DC}	α_{TW2DC}	α_{TDC2R}	δ_{W2DC}	δ_{DC2R}
	Base configuration	10000	0	0	175	200	100	1	1	1000	1000	0.02	0.04	0.075	0.075	4	2
1	Decreasing α_{DC} by increasing preservation cost c at DC	10000	0	0	175	200	100	1	**2**	1000	1000	0.02	**0.01**	0.075	0.075	4	2
2	Decreasing α_T by increasing transportation cost c_T	10000	0	0	175	200	100	1	1	**1500**	**1500**	0.02	0.04	**0.05**	**0.05**	4	2
3	Decreasing $\boldsymbol{\delta}_\mathbf{T}$ by increasing transportation c_T on Exp 2	10000	0	0	175	200	100	1	1	**4000**	**4000**	0.02	0.04	**0.05**	**0.05**	**2**	**1**
4	Decreasing Grade C price p_c	10000	0	0	175	200	**75**	1	1	1000	1000	0.02	0.04	0.075	0.075	4	2
5	Increasing Grade A and B price	10000	0	0	**250**	**300**	100	1	1	1000	1000	0.02	0.04	0.075	0.075	4	2
6	Decreasing purchase rate	**8000**	0	0	175	200	100	1	1	1000	1000	0.02	0.04	0.075	0.075	4	2
7	Donating 2% stock/day from warehouse and DC	10000	**0.02**	**0.02**	175	200	100	1	1	1000	1000	0.02	0.04	0.075	0.075	4	2
8	Applying Exp 6 and 7	**8000**	**0.02**	**0.02**	175	200	100	1	1	1000	1000	0.02	0.01	0.075	0.075	4	2
9	Increasing donation on top Exp 8	**8000**	**0.04**	**0.04**	175	200	100	1	1	1000	1000	0.02	0.04	0.075	0.075	4	2
10	Applying Exp 5 and 9	**8000**	**0.04**	**0.04**	**250**	**300**	100	1	1	1000	1000	0.02	0.04	0.075	0.075	4	2
11	Applying Exp 2, 5, and 6	**8000**	0	0	**250**	**300**	100	1	1	**1500**	**1500**	0.02	0.04	**0.05**	**0.05**	4	2

and simulation component, i.e. FSCSim, is configured, to observe key performance indicators (KPIs) such as wastage, revenue, profit margin, demand fulfilment and grade distribution (i.e. quality). The primary parameters explored include purchase rate (f_P); degradation rates at the warehouse (α_W); distribution centre (α_{DC}); during transit from warehouse to DC (α_{TW2DC}) and from DC to the retailer (α_{TDC2R}); preservation costs at the warehouse (c_W) and DC (c_{DC}); unit vehicle costs for transit from warehouse to DC (c_{W2DC}) and DC to retailer (c_{DC2R}); unit prices of Grade A, Grade B and Grade C (p_A, p_B and p_C); and donation rates from the warehouse (d_W) and DC (d_{DC}). The KPIs are visualized in Fig. 7.10.

In the baseline scenario, we observed substantial wastage (Fig. 7.10a), a low fulfilment ratio for high-quality fruits (Grades A and B, Fig. 7.10c) and a high inflow of Grade C fruits (Fig. 7.10d), negatively affecting overall fruit quality, consumer satisfaction and shelf life at the retailer. The baseline also indicated low-to-moderate revenue and profit, as shown in Fig. 7.10b.

To address these challenges, we focused on improving the degradation rate at the DC (α_{DC}) by investing in enhanced preservation measures, increasing c_{DC} from 1 to 2 USD/lb. This intervention yielded better-grade distribution, reducing daily wastage from 23% to 13%, increasing overall demand fulfilment from 76 to 90% and achieving revenue and profit growth of 24% and 50%, respectively, compared to the baseline.

In Experiment 2, we evaluated the impact of better degradation rates during transportation. While this reduced daily wastage from 23% to 18%, the improvement was less pronounced than in Experiment 1, indicating that investing in storage enhancements was more beneficial than transportation.

Experiment 3 explored the use of high-speed vehicles with increased transportation costs. Although this approach resulted in lower wastage, improved demand fulfilment and better shelf life at the retailer, profitability emerged as a concern.

Experiments 4 and 5 assessed the effects of grade-specific pricing strategies on the baseline. In Experiment 4, reducing the price of low-grade fruits (Grade C) did not significantly improve demand fulfilment or profitability. Conversely, Experiment 5 showed that optimizing prices for higher-quality fruits (Grades A and B) produced better outcomes.

Experiment 6 examined the impact of purchase rate adjustments on the baseline scenario. The results were promising but indicated the need for further investigation to determine the optimal purchase rate for varying demand levels.

Experiment 7 focused on donations from warehouses and DCs. Comparing the KPIs of Experiment 7 with the baseline revealed significant reductions in wastage and improved profitability. This suggests that timely donations can enhance business KPIs while simultaneously supporting sustainability goals.

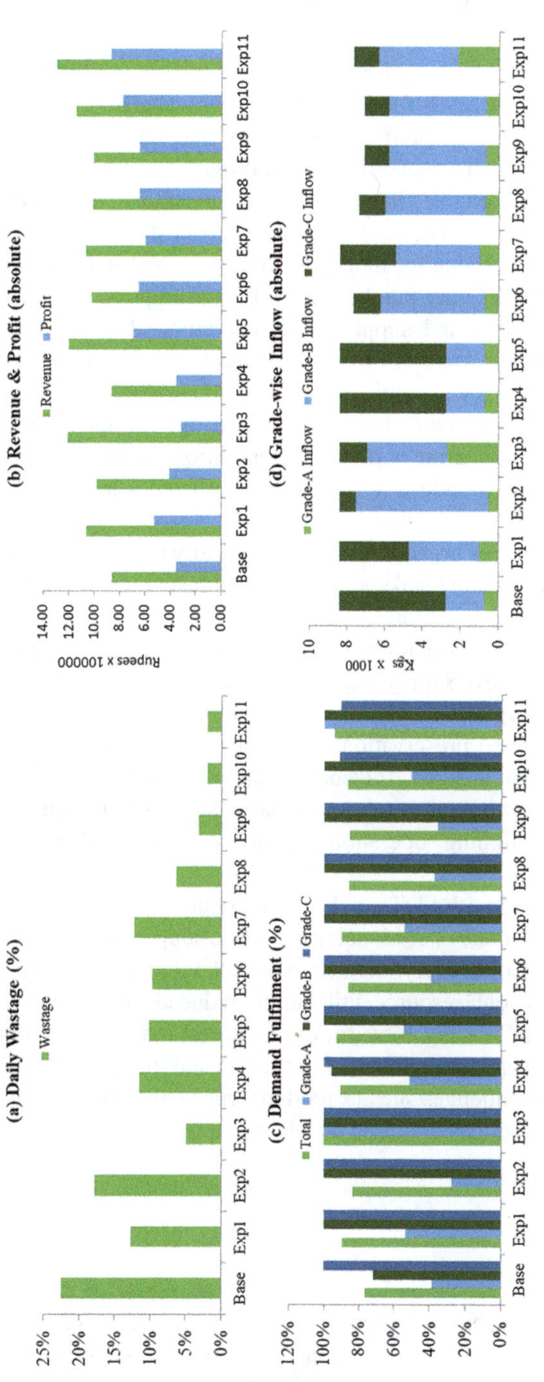

Fig. 7.10 Experimentation results

Exploring Practical Applications

The presented FDT, M4FSC and FSCDT offer significant utility both as individual component and in synergy for the food ecosystem. The FDT is a novel capability that accurately senses and predicts the quality and remaining shelf life of food items. For retailers, such as supermarkets, it provides real-time monitoring of food freshness, which can enable them to optimize inventory, minimize spoilage and refine pricing strategies. These capabilities help customers receive high-quality products, maximizing value for money of their purchase and ensuring food safety. Consumer can use FDT after purchase for safe consumption.

For food processors and supply chain operators, the FDT offers predictive insights into the quality and shelf life of food items. By continuously tracking critical parameters, it enables dynamic adjustments to logistics, such as rerouting shipments or modifying storage conditions, ensuring optimal food handling and transportation. Experimenting with these interventions helps the key stakeholders of the food supply chain to reduce waste, enhance efficiency and maintain food safety standards.

The M4FSC provides broader insights by virtually representing the entire supply chain and all its associated stakeholders. Policymakers and sustainability enthusiasts can leverage this to explore the future of food supply chain and evaluate the impacts of supply chain policies on food availability, demand fluctuation and environmental uncertainties. Supply chain managers may use it for scenario analysis and strategic planning. By simulating different configurations of warehouses, transportation networks and preservation techniques, M4SFC with realistic data helps identify solutions that balance efficiency, profitability and sustainability. It also supports proactive interventions to minimize waste, such as redirecting surplus food to alternative uses, aligning operational goals with societal and environmental objectives.

M4FSC combined with FDT, i.e. FSCDT, creates a comprehensive decision aid for addressing immediate operational needs while supporting long-term sustainability and resilience. Collectively, they equip stakeholders to reimagine the food system, enabling efficient resource utilization, reduced waste and improved food security worldwide. Moving forward, the proposed integrated approach presented in this chapter has significant potential to explore and implement strategies addressing critical global challenges such as food insecurity and greenhouse gas emissions while promoting practices like food donation and repurposing.

Summary

In this chapter, we introduced three novel interconnected concepts and capabilities that are necessary for transforming contemporary food systems: food digital twin (FDT), Model for Food Supply Chain (M4FSC) and a comprehensive realization of the food supply chain digital twin (FSCDT). We argued the real-time monitoring and predictive capabilities of FDT help a wide range of stakeholders, such as retailers, food processors and consumers, to proactively reduce spoilage, maintain safety and optimize resource use. The M4FSC, as a configurable stock-and-flow model, enables simulation and experimentation of supply chain dynamics supporting strategic planning and decision-making. The integration of these components within FSCDT delivers a comprehensive, multi-scale, multi-perspective representation of food supply chains combining real-world data and virtual simulations to drive both operational and strategic interventions.

We illustrated the utility of these capabilities through three case studies: the optimization of potato cold storage using predictive FDT capabilities, the application of a food digital twin to monitor ripeness in bananas and a representation of the apple supply chain through FSCDT. Each case study highlighted specific benefits offered by these components. For instance, the potato case study demonstrated how real-time sensing and shelf life prediction help cold storage management, while the banana FDT case provided an insight into the role of biochemical and environmental monitoring in minimizing waste. The apple supply chain case showcased the power of FSCDT in strategic decision-making, such as configuring supply chain parameters to balance efficiency and sustainability.

We discussed how FSCDT, when it is collectively used with FDT, redefine food systems to become more adaptive, efficient and sustainable, where the FDT can provide localized micro-level food quality insight and M4FSC can provide a macro-level perspective of the supply chain. We believe these capabilities will pave a new way to reimagine food supply chains for a more sustainable and resilient future.

References

1. Barat, S., Kulkarni, V., & Bhattacharya, K. (2022). Enterprise digital twins for risk free business experimentations. In *2022 winter simulation conference (WSC)* (pp. 2864–2875). IEEE.
2. Barat, S., Deshpande, P., Yadav, A., Paranjape, A. A., Kulkarni, V., Rai, B., Vora, H. K., Kumar, S., Pahare, I., Mittal, P., Bansal, M., & Sai, V. (2024). Digital twin as an aid for optimizing climacteric fruit supply chains. In *2024 annual modeling and simulation conference (ANNSIM)* (pp. 1–14). https://doi.org/10.23919/ANNSIM61499.2024.10732353
3. Ranganathan, V., Kumar, P., Kaur, U., Li, S. H., Chakraborty, T., & Chandra, R. (2022). Re-inventing the food supply chain with iot: A data-driven solution to reduce food loss. *IEEE Internet of Things Magazine, 5*(1), 41–47.
4. Kulkarni, V., Reddy, S., Barat, S., & Dutta, J. (2023). Toward a symbiotic approach leveraging generative AI for model driven engineering. In *2023 ACM/IEEE 26th international conference on model driven engineering languages and systems (MODELS)* (pp. 184–193). IEEE.
5. Barat, S., Kulkarni, V., Paranjape, A., Dhandapani, S., Manuelraj, S., & Parameswaran, S. P. (2022). Agent based digital twin of sorting terminal to improve efficiency and resiliency in parcel delivery. In *International conference on practical applications of agents and multi-agent systems* (pp. 24–35). Springer International Publishing.
6. Barat, S., Paranjape, A., Parchure, R., Darak, S., & Kulkarni, V. (2022). Agent based simulatable city digital twin to explore dynamics of covid-19 pandemic. In *2022 winter simulation conference (WSC)* (pp. 557–568). IEEE.

7. Josey, A., Lankhorst, M., Band, I., Jonkers, H., & Quartel, D. (2016). *An introduction to the ArchiMate® 3.0 specification*. White Paper from The Open Group.
8. Franch, X., López, L., Cares, C., & Colomer, D. (2016). The i* framework for goal-oriented modeling. In *Domain-specific conceptual modeling: Concepts, methods and tools* (pp. 485–506).
9. Chinosi, M., & Trombetta, A. (2012). BPMN: An introduction to the standard. *Computer Standards & Interfaces, 34*(1), 124–134.
10. Forrester, J. W. (1995). The beginning of system dynamics. *McKinsey Quarterly*, 4–17.
11. Agha, G. A., Mason, I. A., Smith, S. F., & Talcott, C. L. (1997). A foundation for actor computation. *Journal of Functional Programming, 7*(1), 1–72.
12. Singh, M., Fuenmayor, E., Hinchy, E. P., Qiao, Y., Murray, N., & Devine, D. (2021). Digital twin: Origin to future. *Applied System Innovation, 4*(2), 36.
13. Eberlein, R. L., & Peterson, D. W. (1992). Understanding models with Vensim™. *European Journal of Operational Research, 59*(1), 216–219.
14. Martin-Martinez, E., Samsó, R., Houghton, J., & Solé Ollé, J. (2022). Pysd: System dynamics modeling in python. *The Journal of Open Source Software, 7, num. 78*, 4329.
15. Kedia, P., Kausley, S. B., & Rai, B. (2021). Temperature and humidity based models for the prediction of transpiration rate in potatoes during storage. *Journal of Food Process Engineering., 44*(3), e13626.
16. Kedia, P., Kausley, S. B., & Rai, B. (2022). Development of kinetic models for prediction of reducing sugar content in potatoes using literature data on multiple potato varieties. *LWT., 155*, 112986.
17. Rai B., Dutta J., Deshpande P., Kausley, S. B., Karande, S. S., Patwardhan, M. S., Deshmukh, S. M., & Tata Consultancy Services Ltd. (2022). System and method for monitoring and quality evaluation of perishable food items. U.S. Patent 11,488,017. Retrieved from https://patents.google.com/patent/US11488017B2/en.
18. Kapse, S., Kedia, P., Kausley, S., & Rai, B. (2023). Nondestructive evaluation of Banana maturity using NIR AS7263 sensor. *Journal of Nondestructive Evaluation., 42*(2), 30. https://doi.org/10.1007/s10921-023-00943-z
19. Dutta, J., Patwardhan, M., Deshpande, P., Karande, S., & Rai, B. (2023). Zero-shot transfer learned generic AI models for prediction of optimally ripe climacteric fruits. *Scientific Reports, 13*(1), 7347.

Chapter 8
Digital Twin of Fuel Cell

Ming Zhang, Nasser Amaitik, Amirpiran Amiri, Yuchun Xu, and Lucy Bastin

Abstract Fuel cells are an innovative technology that converts chemical energy directly into electrical energy through electrochemical reactions, offering a clean and efficient alternative to conventional energy sources. Unlike traditional combustion-based power generation, fuel cells produce electricity with minimal emissions, primarily water and heat, making them highly attractive for applications in various fields, such as transportation, where they power hydrogen fuel cell vehicles; stationary power generation, where they provide reliable backup and grid support; and portable energy, where they offer power solutions for remote or off-grid locations. Despite their significant advantages, fuel cells face challenges related to durability and long-term performance, which are critical for their widespread adoption and reliable operation. The digital twin of fuel cell (DTFC) technology represents a ground-breaking approach to managing and optimizing fuel cell systems, specifically addressing the critical challenge of durability. A digital twin is a sophisticated virtual model that mirrors the physical fuel cell, integrating real-time data, historical records, and advanced computational techniques. The digital model is continuously updated with information from embedded sensors and external sources, offering a comprehensive view of the fuel cell's performance and operational characteristics. By utilizing this real-time simulation, the digital twin provides profound insights into how various factors affect the fuel cell's behaviour. This enables more accurate predictions, enhanced optimization, and predictive and proactive maintenance strategies. Specifically, the digital twin approach addresses fuel cell durability issues by revealing degradation patterns and facilitating timely interventions. This capability significantly improves the efficiency and reliability of fuel cell systems, making it a vital tool for advancing their performance across a range of applications. By reading this chapter, readers will gain a comprehensive understanding of the fundamental principles of fuel cell operation, the challenges

M. Zhang (✉) · N. Amaitik · A. Amiri · Y. Xu · L. Bastin
College of Engineering and Physical Sciences, Aston University, Birmingham, UK
e-mail: m.zhang21@aston.ac.uk; n.amaitik@aston.ac.uk; a.p.amiri@aston.ac.uk; y.xu16@aston.ac.uk; l.bastin@aston.ac.uk

V. Kulkarni et al. (eds.), *Digital Twins for Simulation-Based Decision-Making*,
https://doi.org/10.1007/978-3-031-89654-5_8

related to their durability and maintenance, and how digital twin technology offers innovative solutions to these issues. Key sections cover the technical aspects of fuel cell modelling, degradation prediction, real-time monitoring, and predictive maintenance, providing insights into how the DTFC can optimize fuel cell systems in electric vehicles. This chapter serves as a valuable resource for researchers, engineers, and industry stakeholders looking to explore the role of digital twins in the advancement of hydrogen-powered fuel cell technology for sustainable transportation solutions.

Introduction of Fuel Cells

Basic Principles

Fuel cells operate by converting chemical energy directly into electrical energy through an electrochemical reaction. The core process involves combining hydrogen and oxygen to produce electricity, water, and heat. In a typical fuel cell, hydrogen is fed into the anode, where it is split into protons and electrons. The protons move through an electrolyte to the cathode, while the electrons travel through an external circuit, generating electricity. At the cathode, oxygen combines with the protons and electrons to form water and complete the reaction. The essential components of a fuel cell include two electrodes (anode and cathode) and an electrolyte that separates them. The anode facilitates the hydrogen oxidation process, and the cathode supports the reduction of oxygen. This setup ensures that ions can move between the electrodes, while the electrons flow through an external circuit, producing continuous electrical energy. Proton-exchange membrane fuel cells (PEMFC) are one type of fuel cell, and their mechanism is shown in Fig. 8.1. Fuel cells are

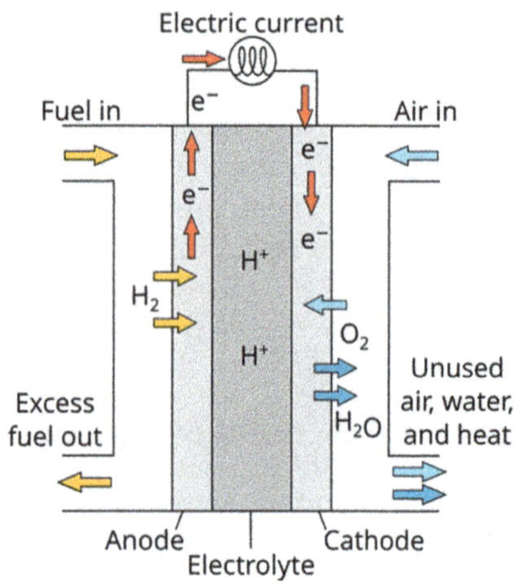

Fig. 8.1 Proton-exchange membrane fuel cells (PEMFC) diagram [1]

known for their high efficiency and environmentally friendly operation, as they primarily emit water and heat, making them a promising technology for clean energy applications.

Fuel Cell Types and Their Applications

The type of fuel cell used depends on the application, operating conditions, and specific requirements of the system. Here's a brief overview of various fuel cell types and their applications:

Proton Exchange Membrane Fuel Cells (PEMFCs): PEMFCs use a solid polymer membrane as an electrolyte to transport protons from the anode to the cathode, generating electricity. They operate at low temperatures (60–80 °C) and offer high power density and quick start-up times. Commonly used in transportation and portable power applications, PEMFCs are ideal for vehicles, backup power systems, and small-scale electronics due to their compact size and efficiency.

Solid Oxide Fuel Cells (SOFCs): SOFCs feature a solid ceramic electrolyte that conducts oxygen ions at high temperatures (600–1000 °C). They provide high efficiency and can utilize a variety of fuels, including hydrogen and hydrocarbons. SOFCs are predominantly used in stationary power generation and combined heat and power systems, offering reliable and efficient power for industrial and residential applications.

Molten Carbonate Fuel Cells (MCFCs): MCFCs use a molten carbonate salt as the electrolyte and operate at high temperatures (600–700 °C). They can efficiently convert various fuels, such as natural gas and biogas, into electricity. MCFCs are suited for large-scale stationary power generation and industrial processes, where their high efficiency and fuel flexibility make them a strong choice.

Alkaline Fuel Cells (AFCs): AFCs utilize an alkaline electrolyte, typically potassium hydroxide, to facilitate the electrochemical reaction at moderate temperatures (50–200 °C). Known for their high efficiency and reliability in specific contexts, AFCs have been used in space missions and are considered for stationary power and military applications due to their effective performance in various conditions.

Direct Methanol Fuel Cells (DMFCs): DMFCs operate similarly to PEMFCs but use methanol directly as fuel, simplifying the system by avoiding the need for complex fuel processing. They work at relatively low temperatures (50–120 °C) and are mainly employed in portable power applications, providing energy for devices like laptops, mobile phones, and other small electronics.

Fuel Cells Modelling and Simulation

Fuel Cell Physical Model

In this section, we introduce the physical model of Proton Exchange Membrane Fuel Cell (PEMFC), capturing the fundamental electrochemical and physical processes that govern its behaviour. The model aims to provide an accurate representation of the fuel cell's voltage output by accounting for key losses, including activation, ohmic, and concentration overpotentials.

The key assumptions of the model are as follows:

- The fuel cell is fed with hydrogen and air only.
- The ideal gas law is applicable to all gases in the system.
- The fuel cell temperature remains stable.
- The model is zero-dimensional.

The fuel cell voltage (V_{fc}) is calculated by subtracting the fuel cell losses, or overpotentials, from the thermodynamic potential (E), and is given by the following in Eq. (8.1):

$$V_{\text{fc}} = E - V_{\text{act}} - V_{\text{ohm}} - V_{\text{conc}} \tag{8.1}$$

where E defines the voltage at open circuit conditions and is calculated from the ideal cell voltage ($\Delta E^0(T)$) and the Nernst voltage as shown in Eq. (8.2). V_{act} is the activation overpotential, V_{ohm} is the ohmic overpotential, and V_{conc} is the concentration overpotential.

$$E = \Delta E^0 \left(T\right) - \frac{R \bullet T}{2 \bullet F} \bullet \ln\left(\frac{\mathrm{C}_{\mathrm{H_2O}}}{\mathrm{C}_{\mathrm{H_2}} \bullet \mathrm{C}_{\mathrm{O_2}}^{0.5}}\right) \tag{8.2}$$

where F is the Faraday constant, R is the universal gas constant, and $\mathrm{C}_{\mathrm{H_2O}}$, $\mathrm{C}_{\mathrm{H_2}}$, and $\mathrm{C}_{\mathrm{O_2}}$ are the concentrations of water, hydrogen, and oxygen, respectively. T denotes the cell operating temperature. ΔE^0 can be obtained from Eq. (8.3):

$$\Delta E^0 = \frac{1}{2F}\left(\Delta G + \Delta S\left(T - T_r\right)\right) \tag{8.3}$$

where ΔG is the change in Gibbs free energy, ΔS is the entropy change, and T_r is the reference temperature.

The activation overpotential (V_{act}), including both anode and cathode contributions, can be calculated from Eq. (8.6) as follows:

$$V_{\text{act}} = -\left\{\mu_1 + \mu_2 \bullet T + \mu_3 \bullet T \bullet \ln\left(\frac{\mathrm{CO_2}}{5.1\times10^6 \bullet \mathrm{e}^{\frac{-498}{T}}}\right) + \mu_4 \bullet T \bullet \ln\left(i_{\text{fc}}\right)\right\} \tag{8.4}$$

where μ_1, μ_2, μ_3, and μ_4 represent parametric coefficients for the cell model and i_{fc} is the cell operating current.

Ohmic losses are determined by proton transport across the membrane, which mainly affects ionic conductivity. The ohmic overvoltage is given by the Eq. (8.5):

$$V_{\mathrm{ohm}} = i_{\mathrm{FC}} \left(\rho_m \bullet t_m \bullet A_{\mathrm{fc}}^{-1} + C \right) \tag{8.5}$$

where constant "C" is the resistance to proton transfer through the membrane, ρ_m is the specific resistivity of the membrane for electron flow, t_m is the thickness of the membrane, and A_{fc} is the cell active area.

The concentration overvoltage (V_{conc}), which is due to mass transport limitations, can be determined by Eq. (8.6):

$$V_{\mathrm{conc}} = -B \bullet \ln(1-\theta) \tag{8.6}$$

where:

$$\theta = \left(i_{\mathrm{fc}} \bullet A_{\mathrm{fc}}^{-1} \right) \left(\left(i_{\mathrm{fc}} \bullet A_{\mathrm{fc}}^{-1} \right)_{\max} \right)^{-1} \tag{8.7}$$

and B is a parametric coefficient that depends on the cell and its operating state as shown in Table 8.1.

Degradation Modelling

Degradation modelling is a vital component of fuel cell analysis and maintenance, offering valuable insights into the gradual wear and performance decline of fuel cells over time. As fuel cells operate, they are subjected to various degradation mechanisms that affect their efficiency, lifespan, and reliability. These mechanisms include catalyst degradation, membrane deterioration, and other operational stresses. Accurate understanding and prediction of these degradation patterns are essential for optimizing fuel cell performance and ensuring long-term operational success. Effective degradation modelling is a core function in the development of

Table 8.1 Bounds of PEMFC model parameters

Parameters	Lower bound	Upper bound
μ_1	−0.952	−0.944
μ_2	0.001	0.005
μ_3	7.4×10^{-5}	7.8×10^{-5}
μ_4	-1.98×10^{-4}	-1.88×10^{-4}
B	0.016	0.5
C	0.0001	0.0008

digital twins for fuel cells, as it enables real-time monitoring and proactive management of fuel cell health.

There are several approaches to degradation modelling in fuel cells:

Empirical models are based on historical data and observed degradation trends. These models use statistical techniques to predict future performance based on past behaviour. Empirical models are valuable for their practicality and ease of use in real-world conditions but may lack detailed insights into the underlying degradation mechanisms.

Physical models, on the other hand, are grounded in the fundamental principles of chemistry and physics. These models simulate the detailed processes that lead to degradation, such as the chemical reactions in the fuel cell and the physical wear of its components. By using detailed descriptions of the fuel cell's components and their interactions, physical models provide a deeper understanding of degradation mechanisms, although they can be complex and computationally intensive.

Hybrid models combine elements of both empirical and physical approaches. They integrate real-time data with theoretical insights, providing a more comprehensive and dynamic prediction of fuel cell performance. Hybrid models leverage the practical applicability of empirical data with the detailed understanding of physical models, offering a balanced approach to predicting and managing degradation. In summary, degradation modelling is vital for the effective management of fuel cell systems, which serve as the core digital model in the DTFC design. By employing empirical, physical, and hybrid models, researchers and engineers can better understand and predict how fuel cells degrade over time. This knowledge enables improved design, maintenance, and operational strategies, ultimately enhancing the reliability and efficiency of fuel cell technologies in various applications.

Digital Twins of Fuel Cells

System Design and Key Features

The architecture of digital twins for fuel cells integrates a physical fuel cell system with its virtual counterpart to create a dynamic, data-driven model that optimizes performance in real-time, which is shown in Fig. 8.2. The physical system, which operates based on parameters like temperature, pressure, and flow rate, generates output metrics such as voltage and current. This real-world data is continuously fed into the virtual representation, or digital twin, which simulates the fuel cell's operations under current and potential future conditions. The virtual model mirrors the physical system's behaviour, allowing for accurate predictions and adjustments. This interconnectedness forms a bidirectional feedback loop, where data from the physical system informs the virtual model, and insights from the virtual model guide adjustments in the physical system.

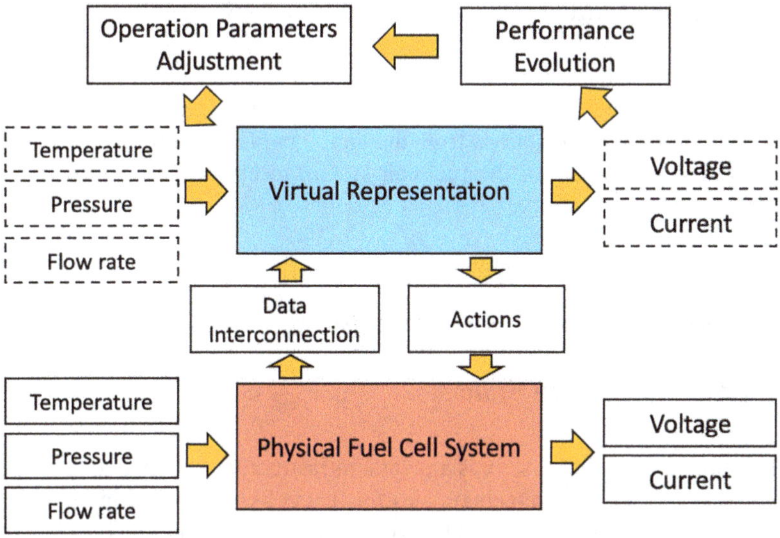

Fig. 8.2 Architecture of the digital twin for fuel cells

This architecture offers substantial benefits, including real-time monitoring, system behaviour and degradation prediction, and performance optimization while also facilitating predictive maintenance and more informed decision-making. The digital twin evaluates the fuel cell's performance, predicts potential issues before they arise, and estimates its remaining useful life (RUL), thus enabling proactive maintenance strategies and effective life cycle management. In addition, the digital twin allows for dynamic adjustment of operational parameters, ensuring that the fuel cell consistently operates at peak efficiency. By continuously updating the virtual model with real-world data, the system supports data-driven decision-making, reduces downtime, and extends the fuel cell's lifespan. This sophisticated integration of virtual and physical components highlights how digital twins can enhance the management and optimization of complex systems like fuel cells, ultimately leading to more efficient and reliable energy solutions.

The key features of proposed DTFC are outlined as follows:

Bidirectional feedback loop: Continuous exchange of data between the physical fuel cell system and its digital model, ensuring synchronization and enabling real-time adjustments

Real-time monitoring: Constant observation of the fuel cell's operational parameters and outputs, allowing for immediate responses to any changes in the system's performance

Performance evaluation: Involves fault detection and diagnosis to identify issues within the system and RUL prediction to estimate how long the fuel cell can continue operating before requiring maintenance

Predictive maintenance: Utilizes data from the digital twin to anticipate potential failures and plan maintenance activities in advance, minimizing downtime and extending the system's life cycle

Decision-making and life cycle management: Data-driven decision-making based on simulations and predictions from the digital twin, supporting comprehensive life cycle management of the fuel cell system to ensure optimal performance over time

Monitoring, Diagnostic, and Prognostic

Real-Time Monitoring System

The real-time monitoring system is a pivotal infrastructure designed to enhance the effectiveness of digital twin technologies for fuel cells. By integrating this system into current fuel cell setups, we can bridge the gap between physical operations and digital simulations, enabling a more accurate and dynamic digital retrofit of existing systems. At its core, the real-time monitoring system continuously captures and transmits data from fuel cells, including critical parameters such as temperature, pressure, flowrate, current, and voltage. This real-time data is essential for feeding into digital twins, sophisticated virtual models that simulate the behaviour and performance of fuel cell systems under various conditions.

The primary advantage of incorporating a real-time monitoring system is its ability to provide up-to-the-minute information on the operational state of fuel cells. This continuous data flow allows digital twins to reflect the most current conditions, leading to more precise simulations and analyses. Consequently, it enhances the ability to predict performance, detect anomalies, and optimize operations in real time. With real-time data, the digital twin of a fuel cell system can dynamically adjust its simulations, providing valuable insights for improving operational efficiency and reliability. This capability not only aids in fine-tuning existing fuel cell systems but also supports proactive management and timely interventions based on live data.

Fault Detection and Diagnosis

Fault detection and diagnosis (FDD) is a crucial function for maintaining the reliability and performance of fuel cell systems and their associated components [2]. This sophisticated process involves identifying, isolating, and diagnosing faults in the fuel cell and its critical subsystems, including the water pump, compressor, motor, and tanks. Fuel cells are complex systems that rely on precise chemical and physical processes to generate electricity. Any deviations or malfunctions in these processes can lead to reduced efficiency, performance degradation, or even complete system failure. Effective FDD helps mitigate these risks by providing real-time insights into the operational state of the fuel cell and its components. Water pumps, compressors, motors, and tanks are integral to the fuel cell system's functionality. Water pumps circulate coolant to maintain optimal operating temperatures, compressors supply the necessary air pressure, motors drive various mechanical functions, and tanks store and supply reactants. Each component must operate correctly to ensure the overall system's efficiency and safety. FDD systems utilize a combination of sensors, data analytics, and diagnostic algorithms to continuously monitor and evaluate these components. By analysing data from sensors, FDD systems can detect anomalies such as abnormal vibrations, pressure drops, or temperature fluctuations. These anomalies are then assessed to identify potential faults or performance issues. The diagnostic component of FDD further isolates the source of the problem, whether it's a malfunctioning pump, a failing compressor, or a leak in the tank. Early detection allows for timely maintenance or repairs, reducing downtime and preventing more severe damage.

Remaining Useful Time Prediction

Remaining useful life (RUL) prediction is a pivotal function of the DTFC system, distinguished from fault detection and diagnosis by its focus on forecasting future conditions rather than merely assessing the current state. While FDD is concerned with identifying and diagnosing existing faults or deviations in the fuel cell and its components, RUL prediction is aimed at predicting the future health state and estimated the remaining operational lifespan of the system and its parts [3].

Remaining useful life (RUL), also named as remaining service life, residual life, or remnant life, refers to the time left before machinery loses its operation ability given the current age and condition and the past operation profile. The RUL is generally defined as the conditional random variable specified in relative or absolute time units, for instance, load cycles or flight hours, etc. The RUL l_k at current time t_k is denoted as

$$l_k = \inf\left\{l_k : x\left(l_k + t_k\right) \geq \lambda | x_{0:k}\right\}$$

where $x(l_k + t_k)$ represents the health state at the future time $l_k + t_k$, $x_{0:k}$ represents the health states observed at previous time index $t_{0:k}$, and λ is a prespecified failure thresholds. The principles of RUL prediction are shown in Fig. 8.3.

Key Benefits of RUL Prediction

- **Predictive maintenance**: By estimating the time left before a component or the entire fuel cell system reaches the end of its useful life, RUL prediction allows for scheduling maintenance activities proactively. This approach reduces the

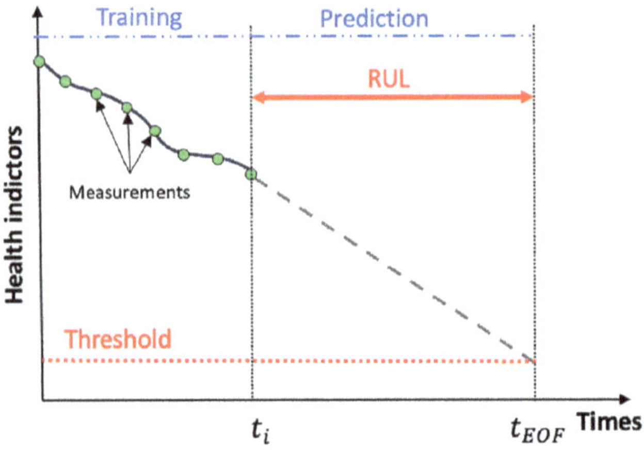

Fig. 8.3 Principles of remaining useful lifetime prediction

likelihood of unexpected failures and minimizes unplanned downtime, ensuring that the system operates smoothly and efficiently.

Life cycle management: Accurate RUL estimates help in planning the life cycle of the fuel cell system more effectively. Operators can optimize maintenance schedules, plan component replacements, and manage spare parts inventory based on predicted needs, leading to cost savings and enhanced system reliability.

In summary, RUL prediction within a digital twin framework provides a proactive approach to managing fuel cell systems, offering significant advantages in predictive maintenance and life cycle management.

Maintenance and Life Cycle Management

The integration of digital twin technology in fuel cells offers significant opportunities for optimizing maintenance schedules and managing the life cycle of fuel cell components. By utilizing real-time data and advanced predictive analytics, digital twins can significantly enhance the reliability, efficiency, and extending the lifespan of fuel cell systems.

Maintenance Practices

Effective maintenance strategies are critical for ensuring the reliability, efficiency, and lifetime of fuel cell systems. Maintenance practices for fuel cells can generally be classified into three types [4]:

Reactive maintenance: Reactive maintenance involves repairing components only after a failure has occurred. While this approach may seem cost-effective in the short term, it often leads to significant downtime and damage to other system components. For example, if a fuel cell membrane fails unexpectedly, the entire system could be compromised, resulting in expensive and time-consuming repairs.

Preventive maintenance: This involves performing scheduled maintenance activities to prevent failures. Preventive maintenance follows a fixed schedule based on historical performance data and component lifetime estimates. While this approach ensures some level of reliability, it can lead to unnecessary servicing of components that may still be functioning optimally, thereby increasing downtime and costs.

Predictive maintenance: Predictive maintenance utilizes real-time data and predictive analytics to assess the current condition of fuel cell components and predict potential failures. This approach, often enabled by digital twin technology, allows for maintenance to be performed only when necessary, based on the actual state of the components. By continuously monitoring key parameters such as temperature, pressure, and voltage, predictive maintenance minimizes unexpected failures and reduces unnecessary servicing, optimizing both performance and cost efficiency.

Implementing an effective maintenance strategy that balances preventive and predictive practices can significantly enhance the reliability of fuel cell systems. By adopting predictive maintenance, fuel cells can be maintained with precision, ensuring timely interventions that prevent more severe issues. This approach extends the lifetime of fuel cell systems and ensures optimal performance and cost savings over time.

Life Cycle Management

Life cycle management plays a pivotal role in maximizing the operational lifetime and sustainability of fuel cell systems. It involves overseeing the entire life cycle of fuel cell components, from design and manufacturing to operation, maintenance, and end-of-life management. Effective life cycle management ensures that components are used efficiently, replaced timely, and disposed of in an environmentally friendly manner [4, 5].

Benefits of life cycle management in fuel cells:

Maximizing component lifetime: By analysing real-time data on the performance and degradation of fuel cell components, life cycle management helps optimize the use of each component, ensuring that it operates efficiently until it reaches the end of its useful life.

Informed decision-making: With the help of digital twin technology, life cycle management can provide insights into how operational conditions, such as temperature fluctuations or varying load demands, affect the durability of critical components like the fuel cell stack, catalysts, and electrodes. This data-driven approach allows for informed decisions regarding component replacements, ensuring the system's performance is maintained.

Sustainability and recycling: Life cycle management also addresses the end-of-life phase of fuel cells, identifying which components can be refurbished or recycled. This reduces waste and supports the development of more sustainable energy solutions by reusing materials where possible.

Stakeholders benefiting from life cycle management:

Manufacturers: By analysing component degradation patterns, manufacturers can improve future designs to enhance the durability and performance of fuel cell systems.

Maintenance providers: With real-time insights into the system's health, maintenance providers can plan for proactive interventions, reducing system downtime and operational costs.

Operators/end users: Operators benefit from increased reliability and extended system lifetime, allowing for more efficient use of resources and reduced operating expenses.

Figure 8.4 demonstrates how digital twin technology integrates with life cycle management practices to enhance the performance and sustainability of fuel cells.

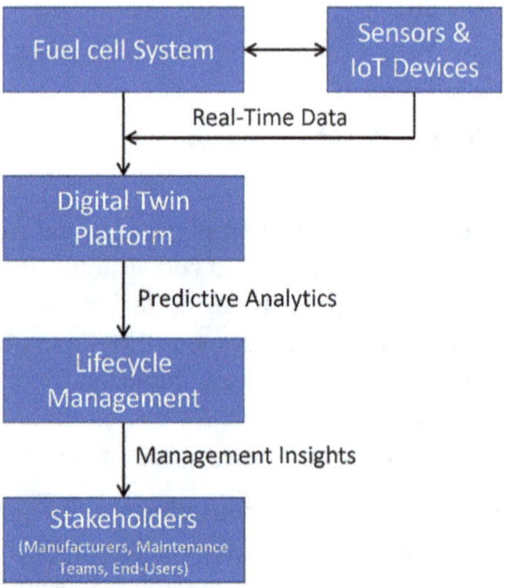

Fig. 8.4 Fuel cell digital twin-enabled maintenance and life cycle process flow

Digital Twins Platform for Fuel Cell

Introduction to Digital Twin Platforms

Digital twin platforms have emerged as a pivotal technology in the digital transformation of industries. They serve as the foundation for creating, managing, and analysing digital twins, which are virtual replicas of physical systems. These platforms enable organizations to simulate, monitor, and optimize the performance of their assets in real time, driving efficiencies and innovation across various sectors.

Definition and Importance of Digital Twin Platforms

A digital twin platform is a comprehensive software environment that facilitates the development and deployment of digital twins. It integrates various technologies, including the Internet of Things (IoT), data analytics, cloud computing, and artificial intelligence (AI), to create a dynamic and accurate representation of physical assets. This virtual model is continuously updated with real-time data from the physical system and may also aggregate this data as time series, enabling it to mirror the physical system's current state, learn from historical patterns, predict future behaviours, and provide insights for decision-making [6].

The importance of digital twin platforms lies in their ability to enhance operational efficiency, reduce costs, and improve decision-making processes. By utilizing digital twin platforms, industries can perform predictive maintenance, optimize resource utilization, and conduct scenario planning without disrupting actual operations. These platforms also enable organizations to innovate by testing new strategies and designs in a virtual environment before implementing them in the real world so that risks are minimized [7].

Overview of Existing Digital Twin Platforms

Several digital twin platforms have gained significance across various industries, each offering unique capabilities fitted to specific industrial needs. Below is an overview of some of the most widely used digital twin platforms:

Azure Digital Twins: Microsoft's Azure Digital Twins is a comprehensive platform that enables the creation of digital models of physical environments. It allows organizations to model complex systems, from individual assets to entire environments, using real-time data from IoT devices. Azure Digital Twins has been used in various smart city initiatives, including projects in Dublin and Birmingham. These cities are utilizing the platform to manage urban infrastructure, monitor pollution levels, and optimize traffic flow. By using real-time data, both cities aim to improve the overall quality of life for their citizens [8].

Ansys Twin Builder: Ansys Twin Builder is a specialized platform designed for engineering and simulation purposes. It allows users to create detailed digital twins of products and processes, simulating their behaviour under various conditions. The platform is particularly popular in the automotive and manufacturing industries. For example, BOSCH has utilized Ansys Twin Builder to create digital twins of its automotive components, enabling engineers to simulate the performance and durability of products under different operational conditions. This has allowed BOSCH to optimize product designs and reduce physical testing costs [9].

IBM Digital Twin: IBM's Digital Twin platform focuses particularly on industries like manufacturing, energy, and infrastructure management. For example, the Port of Rotterdam, one of the largest ports in the world, uses IBM's Digital Twin technology to create a virtual replica of its operations. This digital twin helps manage and monitor the port's vast infrastructure, optimizing shipping routes, predicting maintenance needs, and reducing downtime. By utilizing this technology, the port has improved its efficiency and reduced operational costs, making it a benchmark for other global ports [10].

Key Features of a Digital Twin Platform for Fuel Cells

Digital twin platforms designed for hydrogen fuel cells should include several key features to effectively model, monitor, and optimize these complex systems. These features are essential for ensuring that the digital twin can provide accurate insights, enabling the efficient operation and maintenance of fuel cell technology.

Real-Time Data Acquisition and Processing

One of the most critical features of a digital twin platform for fuel cells is real-time data acquisition and processing. Fuel cells operate under dynamic conditions, with performance parameters such as temperature, pressure, and voltage continuously fluctuating based on load demands and environmental factors. To accurately reflect the current state of the fuel cell system, the digital twin platform must be capable of collecting and processing data in real time. This can be achieved through the integration of IoT devices and sensors embedded within the fuel cell components [7]. By utilizing this real-time data, the platform can monitor system performance, detect anomalies, and provide immediate feedback, which is crucial for maintaining optimal operation and preventing potential failures.

High-Fidelity Modelling and Simulation Capabilities

High-fidelity modelling and simulation are central to the effectiveness of a digital twin platform. For fuel cells, this involves creating detailed and accurate virtual models that can simulate the electrochemical reaction and degradation process of the system under various operating conditions. High-fidelity models are essential for predicting the performance and lifetime of fuel cells, as they can replicate the complex interactions within the system [5]. For example, these models can simulate how changes in operating temperature affect the performance of the fuel cell, enabling engineers to test different scenarios and optimize system design without the need for extensive physical testing. The ability to run these simulations in a virtual environment saves time and resources and allows for more innovative approaches to fuel cell development.

Example of Integrated Digital Twin Architecture for Fuel Cell in Electric Vehicle

To illustrate how these key features come together in an application, we present an example of an integrated digital twin architecture for a fuel cell in an electric vehicle (EV), as shown in Fig. 8.5. This example demonstrates how real-time data acquisition, high-fidelity modelling, and IoT integration are integrated in a comprehensive digital twin platform.

The digital twin architecture for a fuel cell in an EV is composed of three main layers:

Data collection: This layer includes the fuel cell, sensors, and data acquisition (DAQ) devices, all integrated to collect real-time data on key performance parameters. The data is then sent to a cloud data repository, where it can be accessed for further analysis.

Cloud-based condition monitoring, simulation, and maintenance planning: In this layer, the real-time data is processed and analysed to assess the current condition of the fuel cell. The condition monitoring module tracks the health status, while the simulation and predictive analytics module predicts future performance and remaining useful life (RUL). The maintenance planning module uses this information to schedule necessary maintenance activities, ensuring the fuel cell's optimal performance and reliability.

Visualization and dashboard: The final layer provides a user-friendly interface where stakeholders, including drivers, fuel cell manufacturers, and maintenance providers, can visualize real-time performance data, health status, and maintenance schedules. This visualization is crucial for making informed decisions that enhance the overall efficiency and reliability of the fuel cell system.

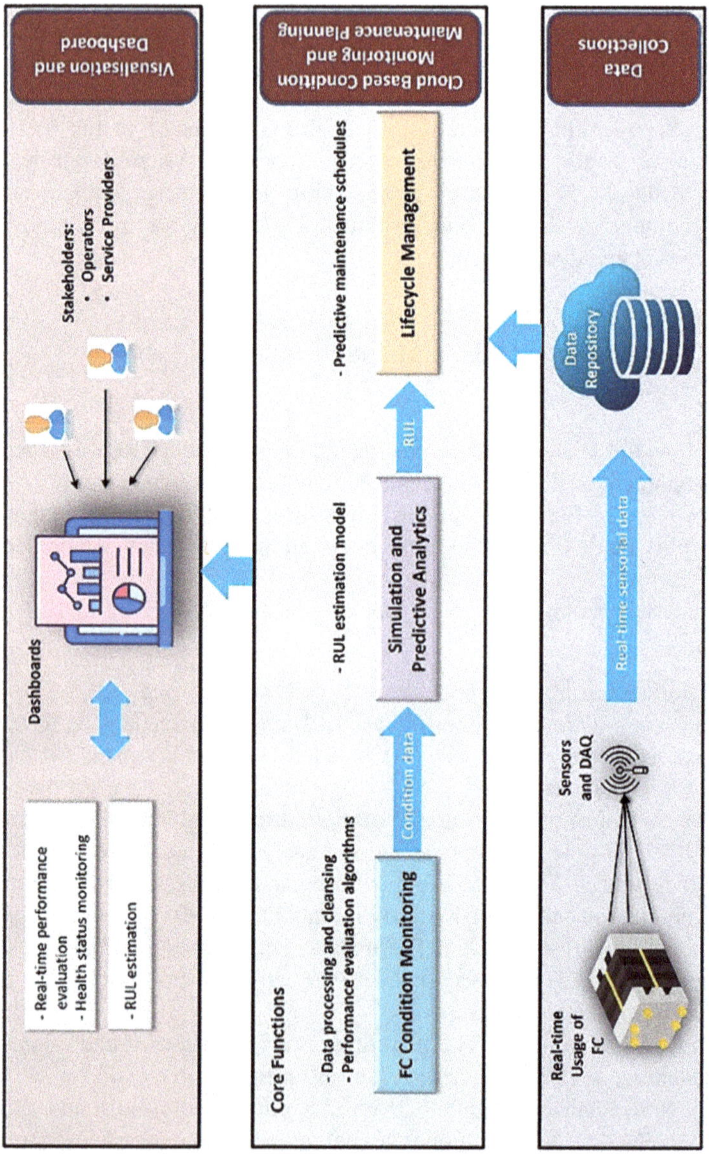

Fig. 8.5 Integrated digital twin architecture for fuel cell in electric vehicle, illustrating the three main layers: data collection, cloud-based condition monitoring and simulation, and visualization and dashboard

Data Management and Integration

In the case of the fuel cell digital twin, the formats and protocols of incoming and outgoing data streams may follow bespoke industrial standards specific to an individual system. However, in order to ensure the long-term utility of a digital twin, it often becomes necessary to consume data from a new type of sensor or send parameters to a new kind of actuator. It may also be necessary to integrate digital twins with other models and digital twins to simulate and monitor more complex systems. The discourse around digital twins exhibits many parallels with that on "data spaces" [11], including concerns such as standardization, semantic and technical harmonization, and quality control for heterogeneous data streams. We briefly discuss these topics with reference to some recent domain research.

Data Ingestion and Use: The Importance of Metadata and Standards

Commercial sensor data are often available via a variety of incompatible protocols and formats. To tackle this challenge, open standards have been developed, including the OASIS-standardized Message Queuing Telemetry Transport (MQTT; https://mqtt.org/) and the Open Geospatial Forum's SensorThings API (STA; https://www.ogc.org/standard/sensorthings/). In order to integrate heterogeneous data sources, transformations, resampling, and conceptual mappings are usually needed, and this requires good metadata on the nature and uncertainty of the data and the phenomena and sampling procedures which it represents. Most digital twin prototypes are built to address a very specific concern, with these aspects of data assumed or hard-coded in the models, and it is only when interoperation becomes necessary that the inadequacy of documentation becomes apparent.

To counter this challenge, data managers can use universally accepted definitions of units, phenomena, and sampling methods, in the form of agreed online vocabularies and ontologies which supply accepted definitions. Examples that are relevant for digital twins include the Smart Data Models initiative (https://github.com/smart-data-models) and the Smart Applications REFerence (SAREF) suite of ontologies [12]. The open-source nature of these resources allows them to be not only referenced but also adapted and extended to support emerging sensors and systems. For example, SAREF has been adapted to support digital twins for building monitoring, "to ensure interoperability by using existing classes, concepts, and relations" [13].

Uncertainty and Data Quality

Many digital twins involve multivariate process and data-driven models which allow the representation and modelling of non-linear and context-dependent relationships. The statistical nature of these models allows the handling and consideration of some (but not all) aspects of the epistemic uncertainty, which stems from incomplete knowledge and model generalizations, and the aleatory uncertainty that results from the natural variability in real-world systems [14, 15]).

Data quality information is important in order to allow propagation of uncertainty through such complex models, to allow for an estimation of confidence. Some of this can be deduced from patterns in the incoming data—for example, by explicit uncertainty quantification [16] or by the detection of outliers and instrument artefacts. However, an element of less-detectable uncertainty remains, and therefore, it is valuable, when possible, to have a quantified estimate of the reliability of incoming data in the form of metadata. Quality information is not often available at the individual observation level but may be inferred from dataset or sensor-level metadata.

At dataset level, standards such as ISO 19157 allow encoding of quality summaries capturing aspects such as misclassification rate and representativity, supported by open repositories of quality metrics [17]. At the level of the generic sensor type, there are a range of developing standards for defining data quality characteristics and conformance (e.g. ISO/FDIS 8000-210 and ISO/CD 8000-220). At the time of writing, mature and open information models such as the Semantic Sensor Network ontology (https://www.w3.org/TR/vocab-ssn/) can already be used to capture known sensor characteristics, using the system capability terms to report accuracy, range, known bias, and limits to precision. This approach may also be used to characterize individual sensor instances where a quality evaluation against ground truth is available and to associate the relevant information with the sensor data stream.

Advanced Data Analytics and Machine Learning

Advanced data analytics and machine learning (ML) are novel technologies driving to support digital twin platforms for fuel cells. These technologies leverage vast amounts of data to provide deeper insights, enhance operational efficiency, and optimize maintenance strategies. By integrating real-time data with sophisticated analytical methods, digital twins can simulate, predict, and manage fuel cell systems with unprecedented accuracy.

Advanced Data Analytics

Advanced data analytics plays a crucial role in optimizing the performance, maintenance, and overall management of fuel cells through the digital twin technology. By analysing complex datasets derived from various sources, advanced analytics methods provide insights that enhance decision-making, predict performance issues, and optimize operational efficiency. Here are several key data analysis methods used in the context of digital twin of fuel cells:

Statistical analysis: This method focuses on collecting, interpreting, and presenting data to reveal underlying patterns and insights. By examining both historical and real-time data, statistical analysis identifies trends, correlations, and key performance metrics. Techniques such as regression analysis and hypothesis testing provide a foundational understanding of fuel cell behaviour. This approach not only enhances the comprehension of operational data but also supports optimization and informed decision-making, making it a critical tool in analysing and improving fuel cell performance.

Time-series analysis: Time-series analysis examines data collected at regular intervals to uncover patterns, trends, and seasonal variations. In the context of the DTFC, this approach is essential for tracking how fuel cell performance changes over time. By analysing sequential data—such as temperature, pressure, and output—time-series analysis enables accurate forecasting, anomaly detection, and strategic optimization. This method enhances predictive maintenance and overall system management by providing insights into performance dynamics and helping anticipate future behaviour.

Monte Carlo simulation and what-if analysis: Monte Carlo Simulation uses random sampling to explore a range of possible outcomes and assess the likelihood of various scenarios. What-if analysis evaluates the impact of hypothetical scenarios on fuel cell performance. Combined, these methods provide a comprehensive approach to understanding potential performance variations and assessing the effects of different operational conditions, enabling more informed decision-making and risk management.

Multivariate analysis: Multivariate analysis investigates multiple variables simultaneously to uncover complex relationships and interactions. Key techniques include principal component analysis (PCA) and factor analysis. PCA reduces dimensionality by converting data into a set of linearly uncorrelated components, making complex datasets more manageable. Factor analysis identifies the underlying factors that drive correlations among observed variables, providing insights into the fundamental drivers of fuel cell performance and behaviour. These methods are crucial for understanding the intricate dynamics of fuel cell systems.

Machine Learning

Machine learning (ML) is a branch of artificial intelligence that develops algorithms capable of learning from data and making predictions or decisions without explicit programming. Within the realm of digital twins, ML enhances predictive capabilities by analysing historical and real-time data. Supervised learning models can forecast the RUL of fuel cell components based on past degradation patterns, while unsupervised learning identifies hidden anomalies or emerging degradation modes. This predictive capability allows for optimized maintenance scheduling, improved resource allocation, and enhanced overall system performance.

While both machine learning and data analysis are vital to the digital twin of fuel cells, they fulfil distinct roles. Data analytic focuses on exploring and interpreting historical and real-time data to identify trends, correlations, and insights about fuel cell performance. It utilizes statistical methods and visualizations to understand the current and past state of the system. Conversely, ML extends beyond descriptive analysis by employing algorithms to forecast future behaviour, detect anomalies, and optimize operations. While data analysis provides essential foundational knowledge, ML offers advanced predictive capabilities and proactive management, crucial for the dynamic adaptation and optimization of the DTFC.

Supervised learning: Supervised learning is a machine learning approach where models are trained on labelled datasets, with input-output pairs provided to the algorithm. The goal is for the model to learn the mapping from inputs to outputs, allowing it to make accurate predictions or classifications on new, unseen data. This method involves training on historical data with known outcomes, enabling the algorithm to identify patterns and relationships. In the context of digital twins for fuel cells, supervised learning techniques, such as regression and classification, are used to predict performance metrics, identify potential faults, and optimize system operations based on historical and real-time data.

Unsupervised learning: Unsupervised learning is a machine learning approach where models are trained on datasets without labelled outcomes. The goal is to identify hidden patterns, structures, or relationships within the data. Unlike supervised learning, which uses predefined input-output pairs, unsupervised learning explores the inherent structure of the data to uncover insights. Techniques such as clustering, dimensionality reduction, and anomaly detection are commonly used. In the context of digital twins for fuel cells, unsupervised learning helps in discovering unknown operational states, grouping similar performance patterns, and reducing data complexity, thereby providing deeper insights into system behaviour and performance.

Deep learning: Deep learning, a subset of machine learning, leverages neural networks with multiple layers to model complex patterns and representations in large datasets. It is highly effective in tasks where traditional algorithms struggle, particularly in recognizing intricate patterns and relationships. Deep learning models automatically learn feature representations from raw data, making them highly effective for tasks such as image recognition, natural language processing, and time-series forecasting. In the context of digital twins for fuel cells, deep learning enhances predictive accuracy and optimizes system performance by analysing vast amounts of operational data.

Reinforcement learning: Reinforcement learning (RL) is a machine learning paradigm where agents learn to make decisions by interacting with their environment and receiving feedback through rewards or penalties. Unlike supervised learning, which relies on labelled datasets, RL employs a trial-and-error approach, allowing agents to explore various actions and learn optimal strategies through their experiences. In the context of digital twins for fuel cells, RL can enhance control strategies, boost operational efficiency, and adapt to evolving conditions by leveraging real-time feedback. This continuous learning process enables more precise management and optimization of fuel cell systems.

Ensemble methods: Ensemble methods are sophisticated machine learning techniques that enhance predictive performance and stability by combining multiple models. By aggregating the outputs of various models, ensemble methods typically achieve superior accuracy and generalization compared to individual models. This approach capitalizes on the strengths of diverse algorithms while compensating for their individual weaknesses, leading to more robust and reliable predictions. In the context of fuel cells, ensemble methods significantly improve predictive accuracy, optimize system performance, and strengthen fault detection.

Visualization Tools

Visualization tools are essential for effectively interacting with and interpreting the data generated by the DTFC. These tools help transform complex datasets and predictive models into intuitive graphical formats, providing insights into system behaviour, performance, and potential issues. By offering real-time and historical data visualization, they enable stakeholders to monitor fuel cell operations, predict maintenance needs, and make data-driven decisions that optimize performance and longevity. While no current DTFC system has been specifically deployed using these tools, the following commercial platforms have the capability to support DTFC applications:

Microsoft Power BI: A user-friendly business intelligence tool, Power BI provides real-time data visualization and customizable dashboards. Its integration with IoT devices allows for efficient monitoring of digital twin models, making it a strong candidate for supporting DTFC platforms by visualizing fuel cell performance and degradation trends.

Siemens MindSphere: Siemens MindSphere is an industrial IoT platform tailored to digital twin applications. It offers comprehensive tools for real-time monitoring, simulation, and optimization of systems like fuel cells. MindSphere's robust capabilities make it well suited to support DTFC applications, enhancing data analysis and operational decision-making.

AWS IoT TwinMaker: AWS IoT TwinMaker provides a cloud-based infrastructure for creating and managing digital twins. It integrates real-time data from physical systems and offers 3D visualizations, making it a powerful tool for enhancing DTFC by supporting real-time monitoring and predictive analytics.

Tableau: Known for its interactive dashboards, Tableau is a leading data visualization tool that can handle complex datasets. Its ability to visually represent fuel cell performance makes it a strong tool for supporting DTFC platforms, enabling the monitoring of fuel cell trends and facilitating informed maintenance decisions.

Prospects

As fuel cells continue to gain prominence in the global transition toward clean and sustainable energy, the role of digital twin technology is expected to expand significantly. The future of digital twins for fuel cells is promising, driven by advancements in technology and the increasing demand for efficient, reliable, and eco-friendly energy systems. This section explores the potential future developments and trends for digital twins in the context of hydrogen fuel cells:

Integration with emerging technologies: One of the most exciting prospects is the integration of digital twins with cutting-edge technologies such as the Internet of Things (IoT), edge computing, and advanced machine learning algorithms. These advancements will enable real-time data collection, analysis, and decision-making at unprecedented speeds, enhancing the overall efficiency of fuel cell systems.

Improved real-time monitoring and responsiveness: Future developments will focus on enhancing the real-time capabilities of digital twins, allowing them to monitor and respond to changes in fuel cell performance more effectively. This will result in more accurate predictions of system behaviour, early identification of potential issues, and faster adjustments to optimize operations.

User-friendly interfaces and greater accessibility: As digital twin technology matures, there will be a greater emphasis on creating intuitive user interfaces and improving accessibility. This will make it easier for engineers, operators, and decision-makers to interact with digital twins, harnessing their full potential for improving fuel cell performance and decision-making.

Heightened security and privacy focus: As digital twins become more deeply integrated into critical energy systems, the importance of security and privacy will increase. Future developments will likely emphasize safeguarding data and ensuring the integrity of digital twin platforms, particularly as they handle sensitive operational and performance data.

In conclusion, the future of digital twins for fuel cells holds tremendous potential, spurred by technological advancements and expanding applications. As digital twins continue to evolve, they will play a crucial role in optimizing fuel cell performance, integrating with emerging technologies, and meeting the growing demand for clean, efficient energy. The ongoing development of digital twin platforms will further enhance their capabilities, making them an indispensable tool in the pursuit of sustainable energy systems.

References

1. https://en.wikipedia.org/wiki/Proton-exchange_membrane_fuel_cell

2. Abid, A., Khan, M. T., & Iqbal, J. (2021). A review on fault detection and diagnosis techniques: Basics and beyond. *Artificial Intelligence Review, 54*(5), 3639–3664. https://doi.org/10.1007/s10462-020-09934-2
3. Ferreira, C., & Gonçalves, G. (2022). Remaining useful life prediction and challenges: A literature review on the use of machine learning methods. *Journal of Manufacturing Systems, 63*, 550–562. https://doi.org/10.1016/j.jmsy.2022.05.010
4. Zonta, T., et al. (2020). Predictive maintenance in the industry 4.0: A systematic literature review. *Computers & Industrial Engineering, 150*, 106889. https://doi.org/10.1016/j.cie.2020.106889
5. Simons, A., & Bauer, C. (2015). A life-cycle perspective on automotive fuel cells. *Applied Energy, 157*, 884. https://doi.org/10.1016/j.apenergy.2015.02.049
6. Lehner, D., et al. (2022). Digital twin platforms: Requirements, capabilities, and future prospects. *IEEE Software, 39*(2), 53. https://doi.org/10.1109/MS.2021.3133795
7. Mohsen Attaran and Bilge Gokhan Celik. (2023). Digital twin: Benefits, use cases, challenges, and opportunities. *Decision Analytics Journal, 6*, 100165. https://doi.org/10.1016/j.dajour.2023.100165
8. Microsoft Azure. (2023). *Azure digital twins documentation*. Retrieved from https://azure.microsoft.com/en-us/services/digital-twins/.
9. Ansys. (2023). *Ansys Twin Builder*. Retrieved from https://www.ansys.com/products/digital-twin.
10. IBM. (2023). *IBM Maximo Application Suite: Digital Twin*. Retrieved from https://www.ibm.com/products/maximo/digital-twin.
11. Noardo, F., Atkinson, R., Bastin, L., Maso, J., Simonis, I., Villar, A., Voidrot, M.-F., & Zaborowski, P. (2024). Standards for data spaces building blocks. *Preprint*, 2024072264. https://doi.org/10.20944/preprints202407.2264.v1
12. Daniele, M. L., Garcia-Castro, R. Lefrançois, M., & Poveda-Villalon, M. (2023) *Saref: The smart applications reference ontology*. Retrieved 03 August, 2024, from https://saref.etsi.org/core/.
13. Bjørnskov, J., & Jradi, M. (2023). An ontology-based innovative energy modeling framework for scalable and adaptable building digital twins. *Energy and Buildings, 292*, 113146. https://doi.org/10.1016/j.enbuild.2023.113146
14. Deantoni, J., Muñoz, P., Gomes, C., Verbrugge, C., Mittal, R., Heinrich, R., Bellis, S., & Vallecillo, A. (2024). *Quantifying and combining uncertainty for improving the behavior of Digital Twin Systems*. Retrieved 24 August, 2024, from https://arxiv.org/abs/2402.10535.
15. Abdoune, F. Rifi, L., Fontanili, F., & Cardin, O. (2022). Handling uncertainties with and within digital twins. In *SOHOMA 2022—Service Oriented, Holonic and Multi-Agent Manufacturing Systems for Industry of the Future, Sep 2022, Bucharest, Romania* (pp. 118–129). Retrieved 24 August, 2024, from https://imt-mines-albi.hal.science/hal-0396800.
16. Thelen, A., Zhang, X., Fink, O., et al. (2023). A comprehensive review of digital twin—Part 2: Roles of uncertainty quantification and optimization, a battery digital twin, and perspectives. *Structural and Multidisciplinary Optimisation, 66*, 23. https://doi.org/10.1007/s00158-022-03476-7
17. Peng, G., Lacagnina, C., Downs, R. R., Ganske, A., Ramapriyan, H. K., Ivánová, I., Wyborn, L., Jones, D., Bastin, L., Shie, C.-L., & Moroni, D. F. (2022). Global community guidelines for documenting, sharing, and reusing quality information of individual digital datasets. *Data Science Journal, 21*, 8. https://doi.org/10.5334/dsj-2022-008

Chapter 9
Building Resilient Public Healthcare Systems Using Digital Twins

Vinay Kulkarni, Shrinivas Darak, Ritu Parchure, Aditya Paranjape, and Souvik Barat

Abstract The global healthcare sector is facing a number of challenges in the face of a growing range of infectious and lifestyle diseases, ageing populations in several countries, as well as climate change. The challenge is particularly exacerbated in low- and middle-income countries. The diverse demands on the healthcare system demonstrate the importance of ensuring sustainability and resilience: the healthcare infrastructure must be prepared to manage sudden outbreaks of infectious diseases while providing long-term care for chronic and age-related conditions. In order to achieve this, global healthcare systems must continuously adapt to evolving situations, plan strategically, and optimize the use of available resources to manage acute stressors and chronic illnesses effectively. However, building a sustainable and resilient healthcare system that meets the growing public demand is a complex task. Even as the demand for healthcare services is increasing, with individuals becoming ever more reliant on healthcare systems to improve their quality of life and longevity, economic constraints have limited the growth of healthcare infrastructure. As a result, there is a clear need to optimize the medical infrastructure holistically through improved planning, smarter resource utilization, and more efficient workflows. This chapter explores the design and use of digital twins to provide a comprehensive perspective of the public healthcare system, identify operational gaps, and facilitate in silico experimentation to develop effective strategies for intelligent real-time as well as for long-term planning and resource management.

V. Kulkarni · S. Darak · R. Parchure
Prayas Health, Pune, Maharashtra, India
e-mail: vinay@prayaspune.org; shirish@prayaspune.org; ritu@prayaspune.org

A. Paranjape
Monash University, Melbourne, VIC, Australia
e-mail: aditya.paranjape@monash.edu

S. Barat (✉)
Tata Consultancy Services Research, Pune, Maharashtra, India
e-mail: souvik.barat@tcs.com

V. Kulkarni et al. (eds.), *Digital Twins for Simulation-Based Decision-Making*,
https://doi.org/10.1007/978-3-031-89654-5_9

Introduction

The COVID-19 pandemic simultaneously showed the fragility of healthcare systems when faced with a sudden and large-scale crisis as well as their ability to adapt and recover over time to deliver quality healthcare in the middle of a crisis. It served as a visible and clear reminder of the challenges facing public healthcare systems worldwide and more so in low- and middle-income countries (LMICs). It signaled the necessity for creating robust healthcare systems that are capable of responding rapidly to evolving threats even as they deal with chronic medical issues and diseases induced by age and lifestyle in a crowded and rapidly warming world.

Among other things, the COVID-19 pandemic was marked by a widely publicized use of epidemiological models, with predictions and model-based interventions communicated to the public on a regular basis by individual governments for the very first time in the history of epidemics. The resulting collective experience demonstrated the value as well as the limitations of model-based planning in the realm of public healthcare. The objective of this chapter is to build upon the very specific context of the COVID-19 pandemic and discuss the manner in which a model-based approach employing digital twins can be used for planning and optimizing the healthcare system. We take a holistic view of a healthcare system and discuss how digital twins can be employed gainfully in order to make it robust and sustainable in the face of long-term trends and threats while being able to withstand short-term shocks such as outbreaks of highly infectious and virulent diseases.

The rest of the chapter is organized as follows. We start by reviewing the challenges facing the contemporary healthcare systems. This review motivates the development of the conceptual ingredients of a healthcare-oriented model, which we use to define the conceptual structure of a digital twin. Next, we present a generic healthcare digital twin for sustainable and resilient healthcare system, which brings together the aforementioned ingredients. We present a real-life use case involving a city digital twin for managing the COVID-19 pandemic in the Indian city of Pune as an illustrator to demonstrate the efficacy of digital twin in healthcare before concluding the chapter.

Challenges in Public Healthcare Systems

Uncertainty

The unpredictability of health crises and the wide range of required healthcare services to address them are primary obstacles toward a sustainable and resilient healthcare system. For example, a sudden outbreak of infectious diseases such as COVID-19, Ebola, or Zika presents acute short-term shocks that demand immediate attention, rapid scaling of healthcare services such as specialized hospital beds and trained personnel, and an ability to control the spread. On the other hand, non-communicable diseases such as cancer, diabetes, and heart conditions place continuous and growing pressures on healthcare systems worldwide. These chronic stressors evolve over time and require sustained capacity building in terms of more efficient healthcare infrastructure and trained human resources. For instance, the increasing prevalence of lifestyle-related diseases and aging-related conditions, such as Alzheimer's and dementia, demands long-term care, specialized facilities, and trained healthcare workers. Addressing acute as well as chronic conditions simultaneously requires that the healthcare systems be flexible and adaptable.

Environment and Climate

Climate change has impacted the availability of food, potable water, and ambient conditions conducive to human health and productivity, with the situation becoming particularly difficult for LMIC. The burden of infectious as well as non-communicable diseases is linked not only to age profile of the population and its lifestyle but also to environmental stressors, the quality of health infrastructure, nutrition, and the availability of clean drinking water.

Infrastructure and Supply Chains

Accessibility to healthcare systems, especially in rural and remote areas in countries like India, is a major barrier for sustainable healthcare. According to the National Health Profile (NHP) 2022 [1], India has only 1.7 hospital beds per 1000 people, far lower than WHO's recommended 5 beds per 1000 people. Nearly one-third of the population lacks access to an in-patient healthcare facility within 5 kilometers of their residence, creating a barrier to timely medical care. This disparity is pronounced in several remote areas where healthcare infrastructure remains limited. Despite 65% of the population living in rural regions, healthcare services are often concentrated in urban centers. The uneven distribution of healthcare facilities, developed on the basis of historical demand and crisis situations, hampers the provision of quality healthcare to the broader population.

In addition to infrastructure scarcity, healthcare supply chains are a critical concern, especially in rural regions. The distribution of essential medicines, vaccines, and medical supplies is often unreliable leading to delays in treatment and care. These are particularly damaging during times of acute crises, such as during the COVID-19 pandemic when shortages of critical resources such as oxygen, ventilators, and personal protective equipment (PPE) severely hampered the ability of the healthcare system to respond effectively.

Medical Personnel

Existing medical professional constraints further exacerbate the challenges in achieving sustainable and resilient healthcare system. There is a persistent shortage of healthcare professionals, including doctors, nurses, and other health workers. This shortage is particularly acute in rural areas, where attracting and retaining skilled personnel is difficult. Without an adequate and well-distributed workforce, healthcare systems struggle to provide equitable access to care during times of crisis. While this challenge cannot be addressed in the short term as building a skilled workforce takes time, effective resource utilization and distribution considering demand could offer a viable way forward.

According to the World Health Organization, a health system consists of all organizations, people, and actions whose primary intent is to promote, restore, or maintain health. This includes efforts to influence determinants of health and more direct activities that improve health. We believe that significant strategic shifts are necessary in order to achieve sustainable and resilient healthcare systems in this sense in most countries. These shifts can be considered from three different perspectives:

(a) Adaptations: proactive and reactive adaptations
(b) Vision: long-term and short-term objectives
(c) Context: microscopic and macroscopic focus

Healthcare systems must be capable of responding both reactively and proactively to the full spectrum of health crises. Decision-making for reactive adaptation demands flexibility in healthcare systems in order to respond rapidly and effectively to immediate health issues. On the other hand, proactive strategies include anticipating potential health crises and building adequate healthcare systems to handle evolving demands in a sustainable manner. Furthermore, a shift from current treatment-based model to a model that emphasizes preventive and promotive care is becoming critical in this context. This shift should include behavior changes, extensive use of proactive screening, and preventive interventions. A comprehensive healthcare system should consider both a microscopic view, to focus on individuals, and a macroscopic view, which considers community and population-wide needs. By balancing short-term interventions with long-term objectives, public health systems can address the root causes of health issues while remaining prepared for unforeseen crises. These perspectives are essential for building a resilient healthcare system that not only addresses illness-related demands but actively promotes well-being across the population.

We believe that digital twins [2] can play a crucial role in this reimagination and transformation journey of healthcare systems. The ability of digital twins to model and simulate complex systems, identify gaps that prevent the achievement of desired objectives, and provide for a systematic exploration of uncertainties and interventions in an in silico environment makes it a useful aid for creating robust and informed healthcare systems. By providing a virtual model of the healthcare ecosystem, digital twins enable policymakers, healthcare professionals, and researchers to simulate various scenarios, experiment with changes, and improve decision-making processes without disrupting the actual system. The structure of the digital twin and the simulation results are often amenable to a high degree of visualization. This allows domain experts and the key stakeholders to better understand and validate the model as well as the simulation results, which serves to enhance their willingness to optimize their decision-making using a high-fidelity model instead of relying purely on their experience and intuition. Key applications of digital twins can be threefold: understanding the healthcare system, identifying gaps and bottlenecks in infrastructure and resources, and exploring short-term and long-term interventions for addressing reactive and proactive situations.

Public Healthcare Systems from Systems Theory Perspective

A public healthcare system is a complex adaptive network of medical facilities that interoperate dynamically and utilize infrastructure and resources to deliver medical services, manage health conditions, and ensure public well-being. From a systems theory perspective, a healthcare system can be represented using six interrelated aspects of interest—disease, patient, infrastructure (e.g., hospitals, clinics), resources (e.g., medical supplies and workforce), processes (e.g., hospital management, regulations, policies), and the environment (external influences, such as weather and socioeconomic conditions) as shown in Fig. 9.1.

Disease is the core driving force behind the functioning of a healthcare system. However, comprehending the impact of disease on population is not easy. They vary widely from etiology and transmission mechanisms and onset patterns perspective. Infectious diseases, for instance, may spread through airborne, vector-borne, or contact routes, while chronic conditions often arise from genetic, lifestyle, or environmental factors. Moreover, these diseases may follow different pathways and show different characteristics under different spatiotemporal conditions. Spatially they exhibit geographic variability driven by environmental factors, population density, and healthcare access, leading to uneven disease burdens across regions. Temporally, seasonal changes and periodic environmental shifts influence disease transmission and progression rates, particularly for respiratory and vector-borne diseases. Systemic uncertainties, such as fluctuating resource availability, socioeconomic disparities, and evolving pathogen characteristics, further complicate disease management. Combined, these factors create a dynamic and unpredictable demand for a healthcare system.

People are key stakeholders in healthcare systems. While illness often triggers the need for healthcare services, the type and duration of care required depend on factors such as demographics, lifestyle and health behaviors, socioeconomic status, and comorbidities. For example, an aging population typically requires ongoing management for chronic conditions, while an infectious disease outbreak triggers a sudden surge in demand across all age groups.

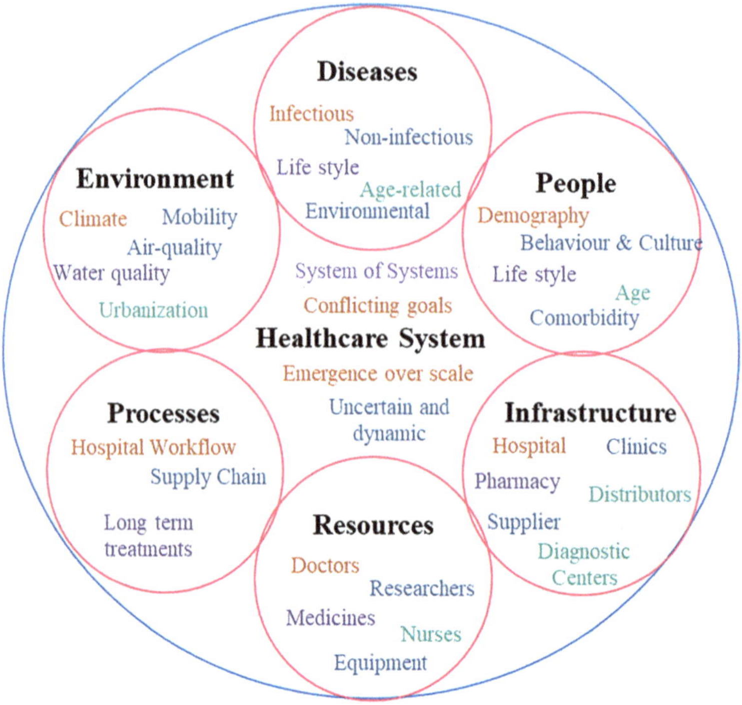

Fig. 9.1 Healthcare system and its components

Infrastructure comprises a network of establishments like hospitals, clinics, and diagnostic centers. They form the supply side of the system. Necessary and adequate infrastructure at appropriate locations is essential for ensuring patient demands, but lack of infrastructure or disparities in distribution across the location often limit access and lead to inadequate healthcare services.

Resource includes medical professionals (e.g., doctors, nurses) and supplies (e.g., medicines, vaccines, equipment), which are crucial for maintaining the healthcare system's functionality. Medical professionals provide their services based on their expertise and experience through the infrastructure. The supplies, on the other hand, flow through the system via processes.

Process encompasses clinical procedures (e.g., patient diagnosis and treatment), administrative workflows (e.g., hospital management, insurance processing), and public health policies. While processes and workflows enable medical services to patients, policies aim to ensure quality of services, equity, and the robustness of the system. Therefore, processes and workflow should be aligned to infrastructure and resource situations so that the expertise of medical professionals is suitably leveraged and supplies are effectively utilized for timely patient care. The policies, on the other hand, should ensure uninterrupted and sustainable services for different situations. For example, streamlined hospital workflows and regulatory policies are essential for quickly scaling up services during health crises like pandemics.

The *environment* serves as an overarching dimension representing all external factors, such as weather and economic conditions, that directly and indirectly influence healthcare systems. They may abruptly or progressively introduce additional constraints, situations, and uncertainties that the system must adapt to. For example, seasonal variations like flu outbreaks during winter or extreme weather events (e.g., floods) can disrupt healthcare system and supply chain. Socioeconomic conditions can affect both the demand for services (e.g., poverty or population density influencing disease spread) and the supply (e.g., affordability of medicines). These factors often become critical for healthcare systems. During the COVID-19 pandemic, an unprecedented rise in demand for medical services put pressure on the healthcare supply (hospitals, beds, equipment), disrupted resources (medical professionals and supplies), and forced rapid changes in processes (such as patient care workflows).

The relationships between these six core aspects are complex and often resemble classic complex systems theory principles of interdependence and feedback loops. Diseases and patients (demand) generate acute or growing stress on the healthcare system, which must be met by infrastructure and resources (supply). Processes manage these interactions, ensuring that resources are allocated efficiently while adhering to environmental constraints and emerging situations. The environment introduces external factors that can abruptly or progressively change demand (e.g., disease outbreaks or ageing population) or affect operational processes (e.g., regulatory changes). Principally, modeling contemporary public healthcare systems face several core challenges that are inherent to large complex systems:

- **System of systems**: Healthcare is inherently a system of systems, where distinct and heterogeneous subsystems, such as hospitals, public health agencies, and suppliers, function with relative autonomy yet interact and orchestrate to achieve their own and system goals.
- **Uncertainty**: Similar to other large systems, healthcare systems operate in an inherently uncertain and dynamic environment, such as disease outbreaks, patient demands, and resource availability.
- **Emergent behavior**: Healthcare systems exhibit emergent properties, meaning that the whole system's behavior often cannot be specified or predicted by analyzing its parts. For example, the interactions between healthcare providers and patients can create new patterns and workflows that are not obvious from purely macroscopic models.
- **Data limitations**: A common challenge across complex systems is incomplete or limited data. In healthcare, data scarcity or inconsistency can hinder decision-making and efficient resource allocation, impacting everything from patient treatment plans to public health interventions. Moreover, the healthcare sector faces additional privacy challenges.
- **Conflicting objectives of stakeholders**: Aligning the objectives of different stakeholders (e.g., patients and hospitals) is essential, but they are complex and

conflicting in many cases. For example, while patients seek the best care, providers are constrained by infrastructure and resource limitations.
- **Mismatched supply and demand**: Demand for healthcare services is increasing steadily (e.g., growing population with chronic healthcare issues) and surges unpredictably (e.g., during disease outbreaks and pandemics), while infrastructure capacity and resources have different growth dynamisms. This requires introducing ad hoc but principled mechanisms for modeling trade-offs that are not inherently measurable in terms of economic costs.
- **Process rigidity**: Most of the healthcare-related processes are designed based on historical contexts. They are not adaptable as expected. Therefore, they often face the challenge of allocating optimum resources. For instance, when vaccines are scarce, deciding how to prioritize populations (e.g., frontline workers vs. elderly) becomes a critical issue.

Conforming to system theory, sustainability in healthcare can be defined as the ability of the system to reliably meet present healthcare needs while being adaptable to future demands despite uncertainty and emerging complexity. In contrast, resilience in healthcare can be referred to a capacity of the system to withstand and adapt to sudden shocks and effectively respond to evolving environmental pressures. Both sustainability and resilience require (a) precise understanding of health demands and anticipation of health crises under different situations and (b) proactive and reactive decision-making for strategic and operational changes in infrastructure, resource capacities, and processes.

Basics of Digital Twins: From Modeling Concepts to Construction Methodology

Development of a comprehensive healthcare digital twin requires sophisticated modeling techniques and supported technologies to capture and simulate intricate dynamics of healthcare systems including patient and disease demands, infrastructure and resource supply, healthcare processes, and involved environmental uncertainties. In this context, we consider a multi-modeling technique involving agent-based modeling (ABM) [3] and AI and coarse-grained models, such as stock and flow models [4] for effectively modeling interdependent dimensions, and their interactions at different levels of granularity. Here, each technique contributes unique strengths that, when combined, allow for a multifaceted and adaptable digital twin of healthcare system and potential interventions supporting desired scenario-playing capabilities.

Agent-based modeling (ABM): ABMs were employed for the very first time in the context of epidemiology for studying the SARS epidemic in the mid-2000s [5]. ABMs offer a fine-grained and detailed modeling technique for capturing individual entities such as patients, healthcare providers, and diseases as autonomous agents. Each agent has its own attributes, behaviors, and ability to handle external events that are triggered by different agents. The uncertainties are modeled as stochastic agent behavior. These agents collectively represent the system where dynamic interactions, feedback loops, and non-determinism lead to emergent behavior. For the demand dimension, ABM allows detailed representation of patients and diseases, enabling the simulation of disease progression, individual patient responses to treatments, and interactions between agents (e.g., disease transmission among populations). In the supply dimension, ABM models the behavior of healthcare resources, such as hospital beds and medical staffs, in response to fluctuating demand. Process modeling, such as patient care pathways, hospital management, and treatment protocols, can also be modeled and simulated using ABM, allowing stakeholders to assess how variations in these processes influence patient outcomes and resource utilization. By incorporating environmental agents that represent external factors like climate or air quality, ABM enables the modeling of environmental uncertainties and their impacts on disease spread and healthcare demand. ABM's ability to simulate bottom-up interactions between agents makes it a powerful aid for understanding complex, emergent behaviors within healthcare systems, especially where individual variability plays a significant role.

Data-driven techniques: data-driven models, including deep learning, are essential for capturing elements of a digital twin wherein domain understanding is limited but ample data is available for predictive modeling and decision support. In the context of demand, AI models can be trained to predict microscopic view of individual patients and also provide estimations about patient inflow and the possibility of disease outbreaks based on historical data, demographic patterns, and environmental factors. Machine learning models are particularly useful in identifying and forecasting demand surges by analyzing large datasets on patient characteristics, disease incidence, and historical healthcare utilization. In the supply dimension, AI-driven optimization algorithms can be applied to resource allocation challenges, enabling dynamic adjustments of healthcare resources like staff scheduling, medical equipment distribution, and hospital bed utilization to meet evolving demands. For process modeling, reinforcement learning techniques can optimize patient care pathways, enhancing treatment efficiency and resource use. Furthermore, AI can improve environmental modeling by analyzing patterns in climate and environmental data, identifying potential health risks, and suggesting preventive measures.

Coarse-grained models: stock-and-flow models, commonly used in system dynamics, offer a coarse-grained, high-level perspective on healthcare systems, emphasizing aggregate flows of resources, patients, and diseases. This technique is particularly useful for modeling supply and demand at a macro-scale, capturing essential system behaviors without requiring fine-grained detail. Stocks represent accumulations such as hospital beds or patient populations, while flows represent the rates at which these stocks increase or decrease (e.g., patient admissions and discharges). In the demand dimension, stock-and-flow models can capture overall disease prevalence and patient populations by region, allowing planners to assess system-wide demand fluctuations. In the supply dimension, stock-and-flow models track the availability of healthcare resources, such as staffing levels, equipment inventories, and pharmaceutical supplies and how they are affected by inflows (procurement) and outflows (usage or wastage). For process modeling, stock-and-flow models can represent aggregate patient movements through the healthcare system, offering insights into bottlenecks and process efficiencies. Although stock-and-flow models are less granular than ABM or AI models, they are invaluable for providing a persona/archetype-level resource distribution and utilization patterns supporting high-level policy and planning decisions.

By integrating three types of modeling technique, we use micro-level modelling details of ABM and predictive power of AI alongside the macro-level aggregated modelling capability of stock-and-flow modeling. For instance, ABM helps simulate individual patient and disease interactions, AI to predict demand surges and optimize resource allocation, and stock-and-flow models to track resource levels and inform long-term capacity planning. This multi-modeling capability enables healthcare planners and policymakers to understand complex system behaviors, evaluate interventions under varying conditions, and make data-driven decisions for optimizing healthcare delivery.

The development of the proposed healthcare digital twin follows a structured three-phase process to systematically capture and translate domain knowledge and integrated data across four key dimensions into a simulatable model. Phases include (a) conceptual modeling, (b) construction of a simulatable specification, and (c) use of digital twin, i.e., experimentation through what-if scenarios as discussed in [6].

Conceptual modeling: The first phase focuses on capturing domain knowledge and data acquisition across four dimensions, i.e., demand, supply, processes, and environmental aspects, along with their interaction patterns. This phase targets two primary information categories: domain knowledge and contextual data. To capture domain knowledge comprehensively, we utilize qualitative research methodologies, including structured interviews and focused study groups with relevant experts, such as healthcare professionals, administrators, epidemiologists, demographic experts, environmental scientists, and policymakers. The key objectives in this context are to gather insights about key domain elements and stakeholders (in the form of agent) across four dimensions that include disease dynamics, resource situations, patient care protocols, and environmental influences. This phase also aims to identify behaviors, relationships, dependencies, and levels of granularity of identified elements (or agents) to construct a comprehensive system model (as a set of interacting elements or agents).

In this phase, we conduct conceptual validation using iterative feedback from various stakeholders through interviews enhancing the faithfulness of the constructed model. This validation step, known as conceptual validation [7], is crucial for aligning the model with real-world context and confirming that it adequately represents the system complexities.

Another task in this phase involves data collection for constructing and training AI models for those elements or agents whose behavior is not known explicitly, but relevant data describing their behavioral trends exist in the system. This data acquisition activity includes a three-step process: identifying data sources, collecting data, and transforming or restructuring them into agent topology. Interviewing with relevant stakeholders is a way forward to identify relevant data sources. Data collection often requires field visits and getting access to information systems. A combination of NLP and AI techniques is used to classify and convert data into target formats, preparing it for subsequent phases.

Construction of a simulatable specification: Second phase translates the constructed conceptual model into a simulatable specification by adopting multi-modeling techniques. This step involves a collaborative effort among domain experts, modelers, and technologists to ensure that conceptual models are accurately translated into simulation models. Primarily, the captured domain knowledge is transformed into ABM and stock-and-flow models depending on the type of knowledge captured in Phase 1. Fine-grained elements are converted into simulated agent specifications, while coarse-grained and aggregated knowledge about conceptual elements is represented as agents encapsulating stock-and-flow models. Additionally, the collected data is used to construct and train agents encapsulating AI models. Throughout this phase, we apply conventional implementation validation techniques to ensure that the simulation specification computationally aligns with the conceptual model and accurately reflects domain insights.

In this phase, we also employ operational validity to ensure the simulation semantics of the multi-modeling specification. This validation involves simulating the constructed specification with historical real-world events and comparing the simulation outcomes with observed historical data to verify the accuracy of the digital twin.

What-if simulations and experimentation: The final phase involves conducting what-if simulations to iteratively evaluate various healthcare scenarios and explore potential interventions to assess their impacts and effectiveness. These simulations help evaluate system responses to different conditions, resource and infrastructure related strategies, disease outbreaks, and environmental changes. By evaluating multiple scenarios using in silico environment, i.e., using healthcare digital twin, stakeholders can gain insights about potential system behavior, identify resource bottlenecks, and evaluate intervention strategies. Simulation results from these experiments provide actionable insights, supporting evidence-based decision-making, capacity planning, and policy adjustments for healthcare systems.

Healthcare Digital Twins

A comprehensive public healthcare digital twin for understanding system, identifying gaps and bottlenecks, supporting effective mitigation strategies and decision-making, and evaluating policies should incorporate all six aspects outlined in Fig. 9.1 along with their constituent elements in a faithful manner. It must account for the dynamic interactions and inherent complexities of the elements including non-determinism.

Figure 9.2 presents a schematic representation of a public healthcare digital twin. It represents six key aspects discussed in Fig. 9.1 along four primary dimensions:

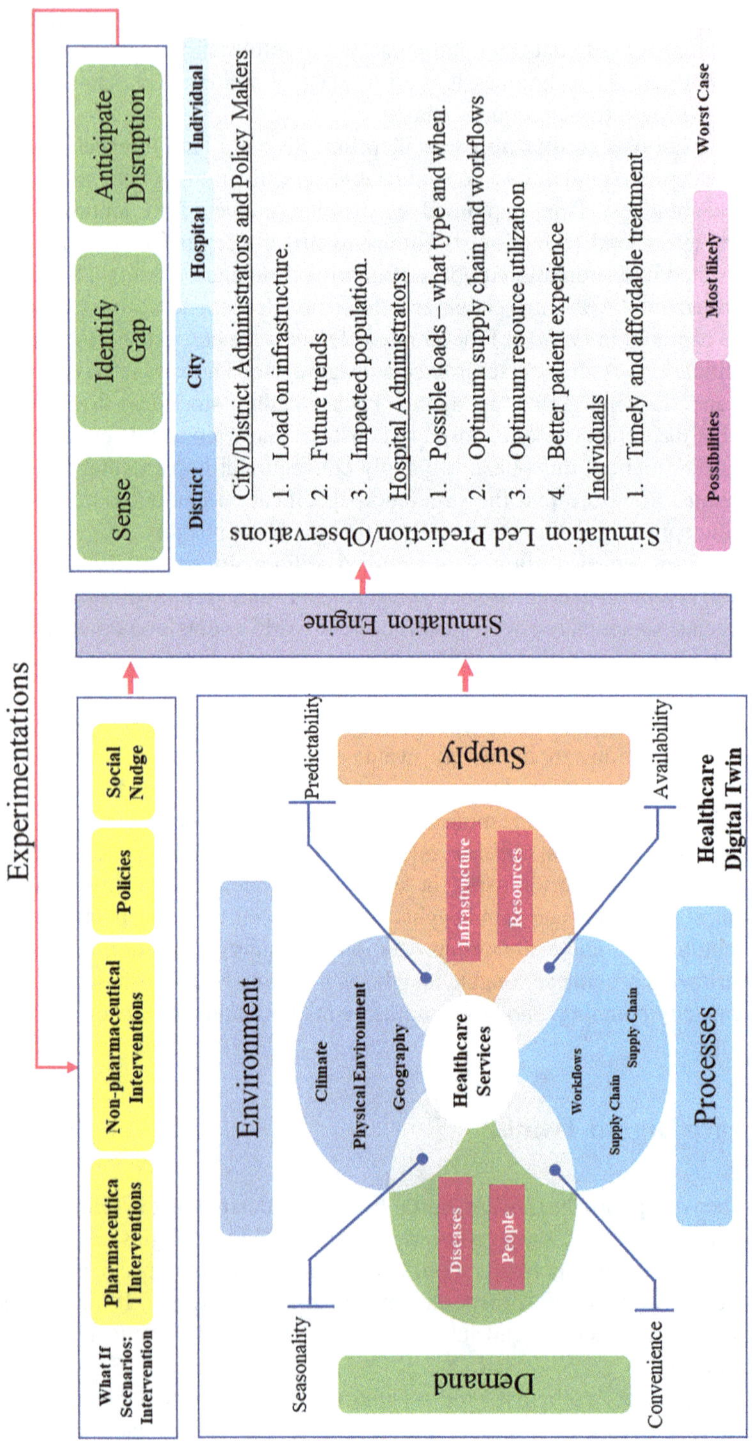

Fig. 9.2 In silico experimentation using digital twin

demand, supply, process, and environment. We summarize the four dimensions before presenting a more detailed description. In this formulation, demand and environment are highly dynamic and uncertain dimensions. Demand primarily arises from two closely interrelated aspects of interest: disease and people, i.e., disease prevalence and characteristics of individuals. The environmental uncertainties, insufficient medical infrastructure and other supplies, and inefficient processes further exacerbate the demand. While the environment represents external factors beyond the control of healthcare systems, infrastructure and processes are key enabling controlled variables from a healthcare system perspective. Infrastructure and processes frequently require alignment, augmentation, redistribution, optimization, or even reimagining to meet the dynamic and uncertain demands of healthcare.

Next, we discuss the key characteristics and inherent complexities of these dimensions and aspects. We also outline how they can be effectively represented with appropriate technologies and the level of methodological rigor required for faithful representations.

Demand dimension involves modeling people and diseases. The key objective for disease modeling is to understand types of healthcare services required, their duration, and the criticality of needs duration. Modeling of disease includes pathogenic characteristics including disease characteristics, progression, pathway, transmission dynamics, and severity. Modeling of people needs attention from two perspectives: individuals (or persona/archetype) and community. Modeling of individuals (or architype of individuals) focuses on distinct characteristics of individuals (e.g., demographic factor, socioeconomic factor and profession) to capture the heterogeneity. Modeling of community deals with aggregated understanding of vulnerable groups (susceptible population), infected population, and spread dynamics (community level transmission).

Disease and individual characteristics are closely related so often that they are modeled together. For example, pathogenic characteristics, such as cause of disease and transmission, decide the people getting affected from disease, whereas the progression, pathways, and severity are strongly influenced by individual factors. They also depend on infrastructure, treatment, and environmental conditions, which we model through interactions with other dimensions.

We consider three main pathogenic factors: source of the disease (etiology), transmission mode, and onset and duration as shown in Fig. 9.3. The source of the disease is fundamental for understanding how diseases develop. Disease origins may be hereditary (e.g., genetic conditions) or acquired from external sources. For example, infectious diseases can be transmitted through air, water, food, blood, or vectors like mosquitoes. Some diseases arise from lifestyle factors (e.g., obesity), prolonged exposure to adverse environments (e.g., cardiovascular diseases due to exposure to air pollution), or aging. This pathogenic classification also decides how a disease spreads among individuals and affects larger populations. For instance, respiratory-transmitted infectious diseases like flu primarily cause lung infections and have high airborne transmission potential within the community. Conversely, genetic diseases like diabetes are generally inherited within families, manifest at certain ages, and progress over time.

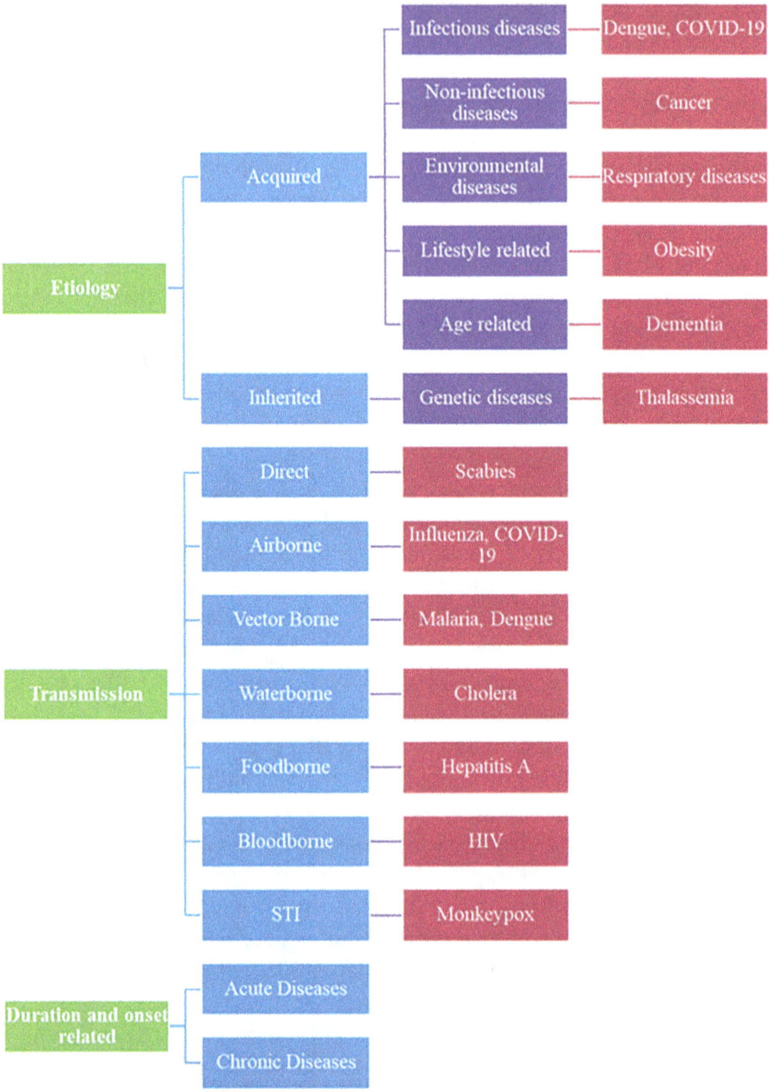

Fig. 9.3 Disease classification

Disease progression and severity are primarily tied to pathogen characteristics, but they also depend on individual characteristics such as age and comorbidity. For example, COVID-19 is airborne or a droplet-borne disease that spreads via the air, causing respiratory infections and advancing quickly for certain age groups. On the other hand, diabetes progresses slowly, often beginning asymptomatically and worsening over time for certain individuals.

Community transmission dynamics and outbreak possibilities are highly complex. For infectious diseases, individual progression (i.e., microscopic view) influences community-level impacts (i.e., influence macroscopic view), which, in turn, affects more individuals within susceptible groups based on spread dynamics. As shown in Fig. 9.4, these interactions can often lead to sudden surges in cases, straining healthcare resources.

Supply dimension encompasses infrastructure and resource aspects of healthcare systems. This includes modeling of various types of hospitals, clinics, healthcare professionals (doctors, nurses, medical staff), and pharmaceutical supplies. The infrastructure of a healthcare system is essentially a network of different types of medical infrastructure, where these infrastructures capture four main aspects: geographic location, the services they provide (e.g., number of beds, ICU availability, diagnostic capabilities), human resources (e.g., the presence and expertise of doctors and nurses), and availability of pharmaceuticals (e.g., medicines). Geographic location captures accessibility of healthcare services, while other infrastructural facilities (e.g., beds), resources, and information about pharmaceuticals determine the quality and scope of healthcare services available.

As an illustration, the Indian healthcare system is chiefly structured across primary, secondary, and tertiary healthcare facilities as shown in Fig. 9.5. Each level offers distinct healthcare services:

Primary healthcare: Primary care facilities include clinics and outreach workforces, with limited resources and basic medical equipment. With a low number of beds and general practitioners as the main healthcare providers, these facilities serve essential, routine care needs and offer basic pharmaceuticals to address common ailments. They also play a crucial role in triage, which helps reduce excessive load on secondary and tertiary healthcare facilities.

Secondary hospitals: Medium-sized, secondary hospitals provide a broader range of services than primary facilities. Equipped with more beds, specialized doctors, and enhanced medical infrastructure, secondary hospitals manage moderate-to-complex health cases. Their pharmaceutical resources are more varied, supporting a wider range of treatments than primary care clinics.

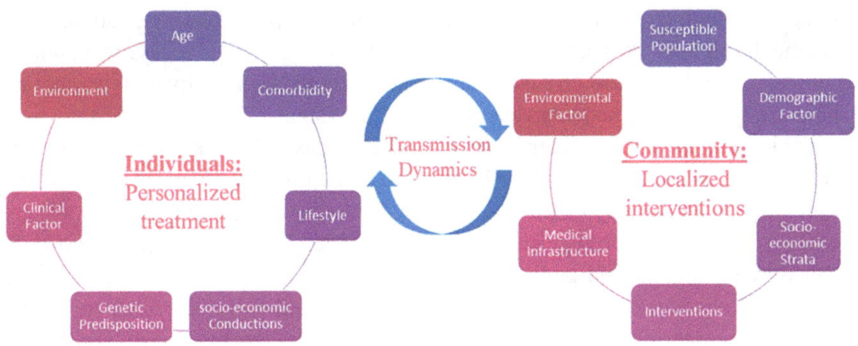

Fig. 9.4 Dynamics of individual and community transmission

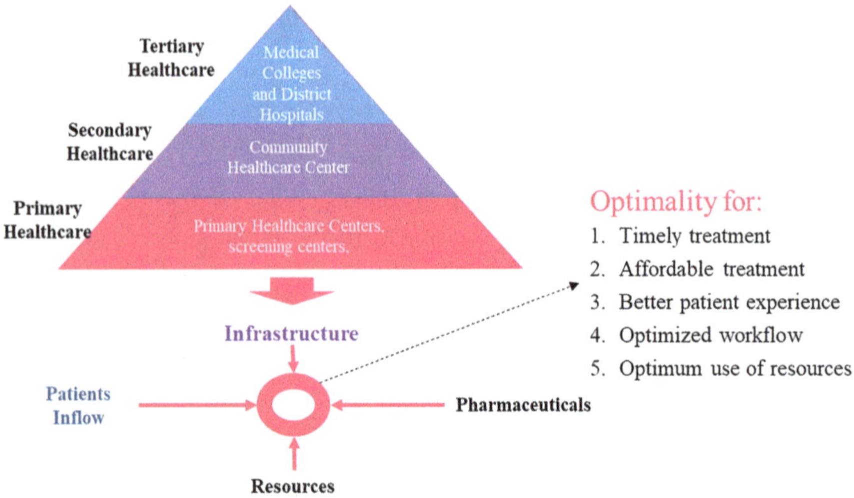

Fig. 9.5 An illustrative healthcare infrastructure model for the Indian context

Tertiary hospitals: Located in urban areas, tertiary hospitals serve as advanced centers for critical and complex treatments. They are equipped with extensive medical resources, numerous types of beds suitable for different types of patients, and highly specialized healthcare professionals, including surgeons and critical care specialists. With sophisticated diagnostics, ICUs, and a wide range of pharmaceuticals, tertiary hospitals manage complex cases that require advanced intervention.

Process dimension models operational and procedural elements of healthcare system. This includes hospital management process that manages patient inflows by utilizing resources and staff ensuring seamless operation and coordination within facilities. Patient care pathways define the step-by-step processes for diagnosis, treatment, and follow-up, creating structured routes that guide patient journeys through the healthcare system based on their specific needs. Treatment protocols establish standardized approaches to medical interventions, ensuring consistency in care and adherence to best practices for quality and safety. Additionally, the healthcare supply chain that manages the flow of medical supplies, pharmaceuticals, and equipment supports uninterrupted care by maintaining timely access to essential resources. Together, these processes shape how healthcare is delivered, promoting efficiency, quality, and responsiveness within the system.

In this context, we consider three types of process elements: (a) patient care pathways and treatment protocols, (b) hospital and clinic management process, and (c) pharmaceutical supply chain. Patient care pathways and treatment protocols are disease-specific and derived from medical science. They should be aligned to demand trends and individual factors. They should be adapted to the severity of the disease and pharmaceutical availability for optimal individual care. Hospital and clinic management processes are unique to each establishment and tailored based on available infrastructure, healthcare staff, and equipment for optimizing facility

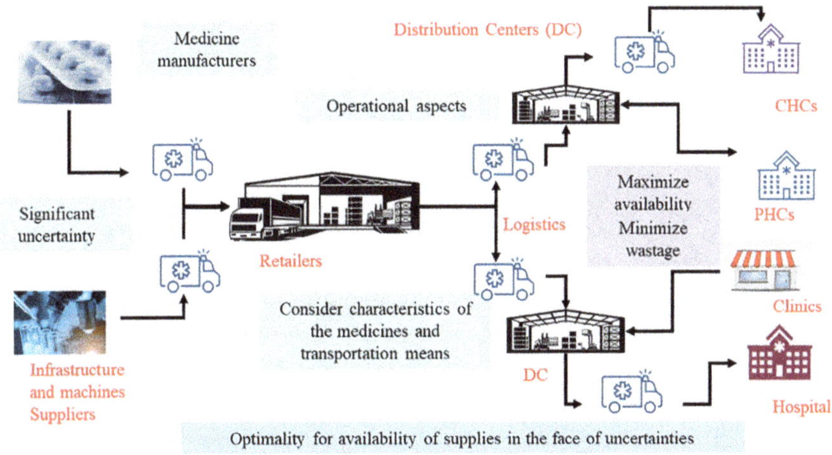

Fig. 9.6 An illustrative healthcare supply chain

operations. They aim to maximize resource utilization to serve the community effectively. In contrast, the supply chain is specific to locality and network of healthcare infrastructure. They should ensure the timely delivery of medical needs to maintain uninterrupted service continuity across the healthcare system. However, maintaining these objectives considering varying patient inflow and type of need care is complex. They need alignment and realignment based on situations for sustainable and resilient healthcare. An illustrative supply chain network model for Indian healthcare system is shown in Fig. 9.6.

Environment dimension models all external factors and their inherent micro- and macro-uncertainties that impact healthcare systems. These include (a) climate, which influences seasonal disease patterns and the prevalence of certain health conditions; (b) physical infrastructure elements such as air and water quality, household structures, and urban architecture, which affect public health outcomes; and (c) geographic diversity, which drives regional differences in healthcare needs and resources. Together, these environmental factors contribute to a complex landscape in which healthcare systems must adapt to dynamic external conditions, addressing varying health risks and challenges across different communities.

Understanding the Healthcare System

Simulation using the constructed digital twin allows stakeholders to understand and visualize how different aspects and components of a healthcare system interact with each other. It offers deeper insights into its dynamics, emergent behavior, and bottlenecks of as-is system. For instance, it can simulate different patient flows with different needs to understand the bottlenecks, inefficiencies, and critical dependencies within the system. A digital twin with distribution of healthcare infrastructure (e.g., hospitals and clinics) and resources (e.g., medical practitioners, and supplies) across regions can help in identifying areas where infrastructure may be insufficient or where demand is likely to exceed capacity during crisis.

Identifying Gaps: Demand Versus Existing Infrastructure

A critical capability of digital twin is its ability to model anticipated healthcare demand versus existing infrastructure capacity under different stressors. It helps stakeholders identify gaps that could impact system resilience. By simulating different healthcare scenarios, such as sudden outbreaks of infectious diseases, surges in non-communicable disease cases, or impact of the growing aging population, a digital twin can show mismatches between healthcare demand and the availability of medical facilities, supplies, and human resources. For example, by modeling infectious disease outbreak, the constructed digital twin can simulate how quickly hospitals will fill up and where shortages in medical staff or equipment may occur. This allows decision-makers to focus on areas with inadequate capacity or insufficient critical care facilities. Similarly, it can assess the demand for long-term care services driven by introducing growing burden of non-communicable diseases, such as diabetes, heart disease, and cancer. Such understanding helps predict future infrastructure needs.

In modeling of rural settings, where healthcare infrastructure and supply chains are often vulnerable, digital twins can reveal infrastructure insufficiency and logistical weaknesses, such as delays in the delivery of medicines. These insights can guide targeted investments in infrastructure and resource allocation to address the most pressing gaps in the system.

Exploring Interventions and Ensuring Sustainability and Resilience

One of the useful applications of digital twin is its ability to simulate and explore the impact and consequence of various interventions before they are implemented in the real world. This capability allows stakeholders to test the efficacy of policies and changes from infrastructure, processes, and resources perspectives. They can be for both proactive and reactive adaptations. From short-term perspective, a digital twin can model immediate interventions during crises, such as optimizing hospital resource allocation, reallocating healthcare staff, or provisioning temporary care facilities to manage surges (i.e., reactive adaptation). For example, during the COVID-19 pandemic, the digital twin helped explore non-pharmaceutical interventions like lockdown and testing uptake. It is also useful in exploring immediate vaccination strategies among different vulnerable groups. This enables a more agile and informed response to public health emergencies leading to resilience.

From a long-term perspective, a digital twin provides comprehensive support to test infrastructural changes and policies aimed at addressing existing chronic health issues (i.e., reactive adaptation). Policymakers and other stakeholders can use constructed digital twin to simulate the effects of reforms along infrastructure and processes by modeling the impact of building new hospitals, upgrading existing facilities, or reforming workflows for the future (i.e., proactive adaptation). They help in achieving sustainability in healthcare.

Our internal evaluation indicates that the proposed healthcare digital twin is better suited to address macroscopic needs, i.e., needs for community and population, whereas the use of sensing of individual indicators and application of analytics (i.e., the digital model) effectively serves microscopic needs, such as predicting outcomes for specific individuals.

Illustration: Digital Twin of a City for Prediction and Controlling the Spread of COVID-19

During the initial phase of the COVID-19 pandemic, public health administrators and healthcare providers were unaware of the mechanisms governing the transmission of the COVID-19 virus within various localities. Lockdowns were imposed to stem the growth in the number of cases while simultaneously building up the capacity of the healthcare system at every level. Lockdowns played a crucial role for saving lives during the early phase of the pandemic but came at a high economic cost. This led authorities to explore alternative strategies to establish a balance between safeguarding public health and supporting economic recovery.

During the later phase of the pandemic, public health administrators sought to minimize movement restrictions. They were tasked to plan localized movement restrictions of shorter durations and explore other forms of non-pharmaceutical interventions (NPIs), such as social distancing, using masks at social gatherings, and increasing testing uptakes. However, there were no universal models to evaluate the efficacy of these potential non-pharmaceutical interventions in individual areas and jurisdictions since the effectiveness depended strongly on local demographic factors and social behavior.

We developed a city digital twin [6, 8, 9], conforming to our proposed digital twin framework, to predict the spread of COVID-19 by considering local factors and evaluate the effectiveness of potential NPIs [8]. Our digital twin was purpose-specific, fine-grained, and capable of capturing local factors such as epidemiological aspects, population heterogeneity, urban infrastructure, mobility patterns, and localized interventions, as shown in Fig. 9.7. Modeling of the environment was limited to city infrastructure (i.e., various places), and the movement allowed within and between the various places was also modeled. Climate-specific variations were

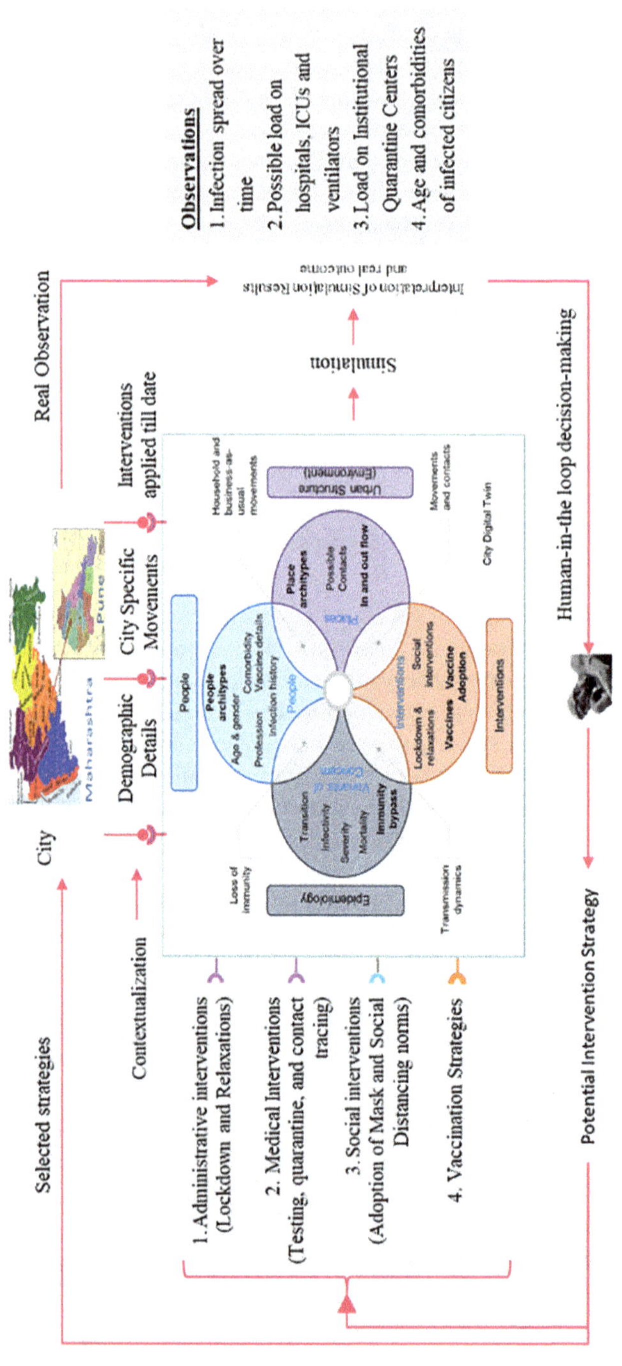

Fig. 9.7 City digital twin

excluded from environment dimension. The process dimension captured different types of interventions, including administrative interventions (e.g., lockdowns, closure of places like schools and offices, closure of non-essential shops), social interventions (e.g., social distancing and mask usage), medical interventions (e.g., testing strategies), and vaccination strategies. In this case, the supply dimension in terms of infrastructure (hospital beds, ICUs, ventilators) and resource (medical staff and medicines) was not modeled explicitly; rather, emerging needs for infrastructure and resources due to evolving situations under different interventions were predicted using digital twin by conducting guided what-if simulations. Our digital twin was configured using known and anticipated virus characteristics, demographic and epidemic-related data collected from Pune (a western Indian city with a population then of four million) for scenario-based simulations.

Models

We consider a city as a coherent unit, i.e., a system with various constituent elements (i.e., agents) as shown in Fig. 9.8. A city in India typically comprises multiple administrative wards, each exhibiting unique characteristics in terms of unique composition of places, households, and people. Places and household compositions represent the environmental aspect of our digital twin.

We capture unique characteristics of environmental aspect using places and household archetypes. Place archetypes, such as schools, colleges, markets, and offices, represent different movements patterns and contact possibilities. Similarly, the variation in household structures that influence household infection possibilities are represented using household archetypes. They capture variations in terms of size, gathering possibilities and socioeconomic status, such as small and crowded homes with many members and large homes with fewer occupants. The places and household archetypes in our digital twin model are illustrated in Fig. 9.9.

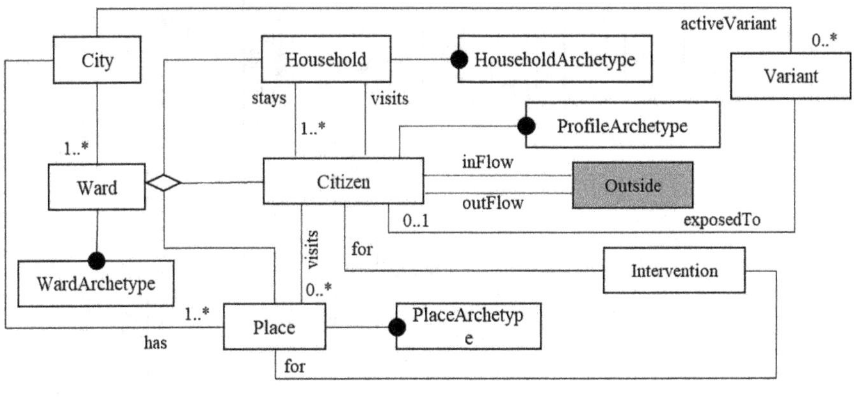

Fig. 9.8 Schematic representation of key agents

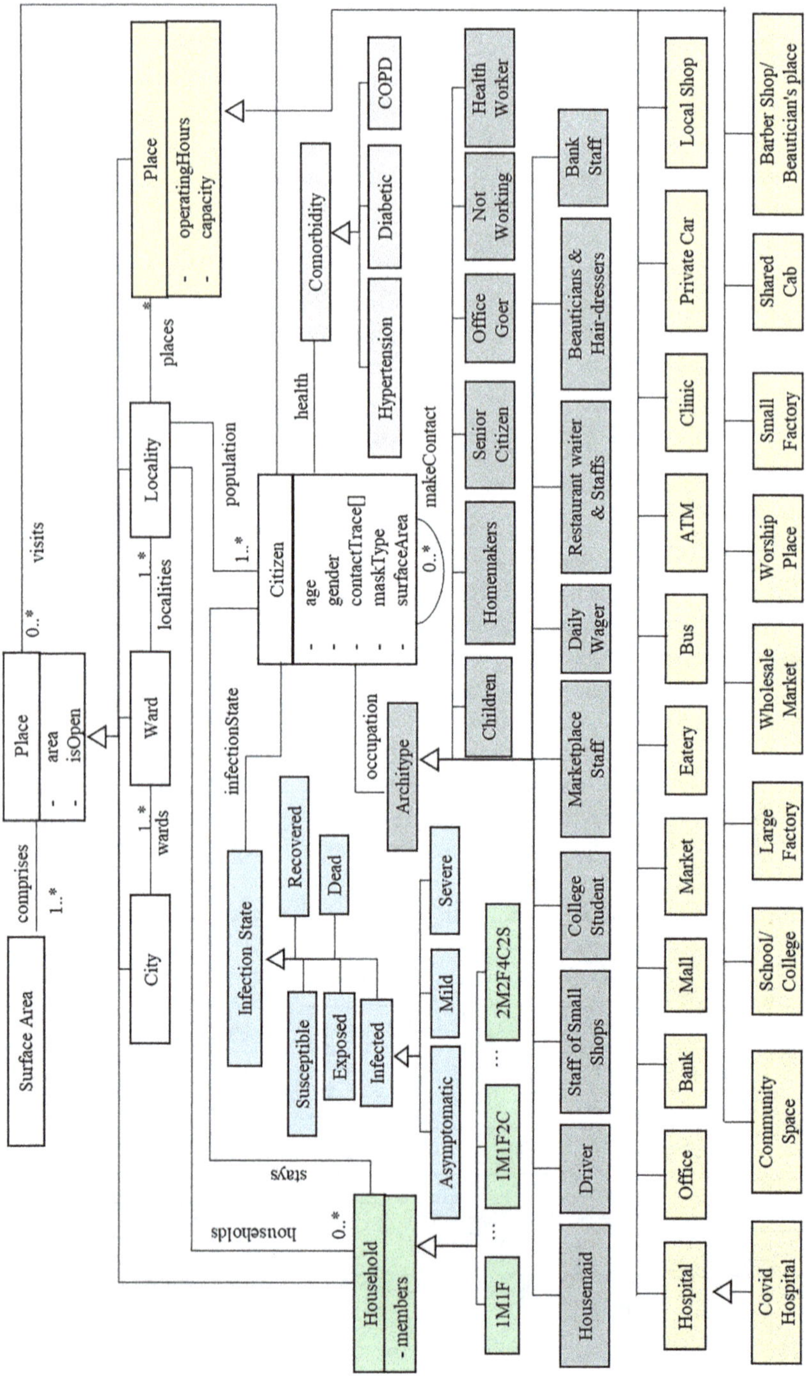

Fig. 9.9 Agent archetypes and classification

People are the key active elements in this system. We capture the heterogeneity of the people using people archetypes (e.g., office workers, shopkeepers, students, drivers), as shown in Fig. 9.9. Each individual belongs to an archetype and has specific characteristics (e.g., age, gender, comorbidities). These individuals exhibit non-deterministic and spatiotemporal behaviors, which are chiefly governed by factors such as their vocation (e.g., archetype, a student or office worker), location (e.g., place archetype, at home, in an office, school, clinic, or restaurant), and the time of the day. Essentially, movement within a place (e.g., inside a household, office, or school) is inherently random but stays with certain predefined patterns and has bounded uncertainty. For instance, a doctor remains in a designated location during clinic hours, while patients wait in the waiting area for a specific period before their consultation. An office worker goes to work if it is open, uses various commuting options, and occasionally visits markets or restaurants.

From an epidemiological perspective, we specifically focus on infection progression and infection transmission. Infection progression for each individual principally follows the conventional SEIR (susceptible-exposed-infectious-removed) model [10] as shown in Fig. 9.10. However, the duration of each phase and severity for each individual vary based on factors like the virus variant, vaccination status, age, and comorbidities of the individual. Infection transmission between individuals depends on the proximity between a susceptible person and an infectious one, the duration of their interaction, the characteristics of the location (e.g., open or closed), and mask usage by both individuals.

We used an extended agent-based model and simulatable specification, termed as ESL [11], to represent elements of a city as interacting agents with their unique and non-deterministic behaviors. In this formulation, the dynamism of city emerges as interacting agents exhibit their nondeterministic and nonlinearity behaviors in a simulation environment.

In our digital twin, we consider three types of interventions—administrative, healthcare-related, and social as change in agent structure and/or behavior. Administrative interventions pertain to citizen movement restrictions, partial or full closure of places, and capacity constraints on public transport. Healthcare-related

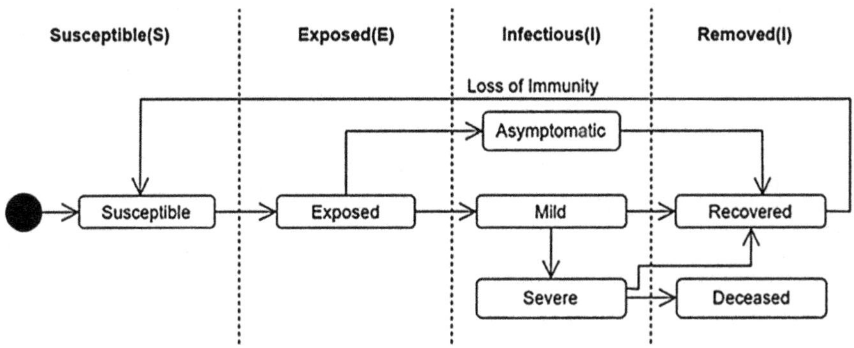

Fig. 9.10 Progression of COVID-19 infection

interventions include testing mildly infected (in addition to severely infected) citizens, contact tracing, and isolation of detected mildly infected individuals. Social interventions encompass measures like mask usage by individuals. These interventions can be active for specific localities or citizen archetypes in a time-bound manner, influencing the behavior of place and citizen agents accordingly.

Experiments

Simulation of a sufficiently contextualized digital twin can help understand the evolution of the COVID-19 pandemic under different situations at different localities. Here, we present a set of illustrative simulation results to demonstrate the usefulness of our digital twin and how they helped different stakeholders understand emerging situations and evaluate the efficacy of different interventions prior to applying them in reality. Figure 9.11a shows infection trends if there is no intervention and under different hypothetical interventions. Infection trends for different wards are shown in Fig. 9.11b, and possible sources of infection from different places are depicted in Fig. 9.11c. The consequence of opening shops vs offices, the efficacy of higher testing uptake, efficacy of wearing mask are shown in Fig. 9.11d–f, respectively. The experimentation can be constructed for various micro- and macro-level interventions (e.g., for opening/closing a specific place archetype) and anticipated/hypothetical scenarios for a for analyzing localized contexts such as a ward or a city.

While city administrators found our analyses useful for making timely decisions for optimum localized timebound interventions in Pune, our post facto analysis confirmed that the simulation results were largely accurate throughout the pandemic. Figure 9.12a shows our simulation predictions alongside the actual reported cases in Pune. The gray line represents our early prediction of critical case numbers, the blue line shows reported cases, and the orange line is our refined prediction after considering the characteristics of the Delta variant and other potential mutations. As shown, the difference between the early prediction (gray line) and the corrected prediction (made in April 2021 at the onset of the Delta variant) is due to two factors: (a) the possibility of virus mutations was known and considered in our model and (b) partial knowledge about the characteristics of the Delta variant. Both predictions supported our goal of estimating healthcare system loads. We also predicted cumulative reported cases (shown in Fig. 9.12b) and deaths (shown in Fig. 9.12c), both of them closely matched with the reported data throughout the COVID-19 pandemic. Our analysis also provided insights to healthcare providers and city administrators on the dynamics and proportions of various COVID-19 variants, as shown in Fig. 9.12d, during the emergence of new variants.

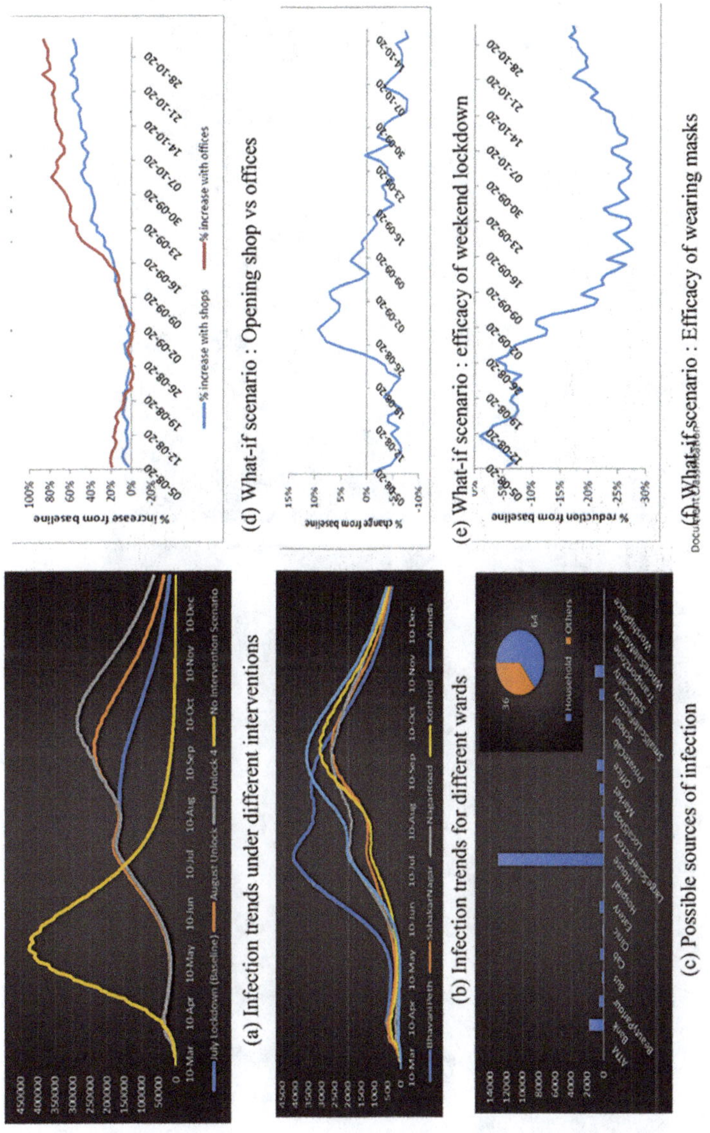

(a) Infection trends under different interventions
(b) Infection trends for different wards
(c) Possible sources of infection
(d) What-if scenario : Opening shop vs offices
(e) What-if scenario : efficacy of weekend lockdown
(f) What-if scenario : Efficacy of wearing masks

Fig. 9.11 Simulation results

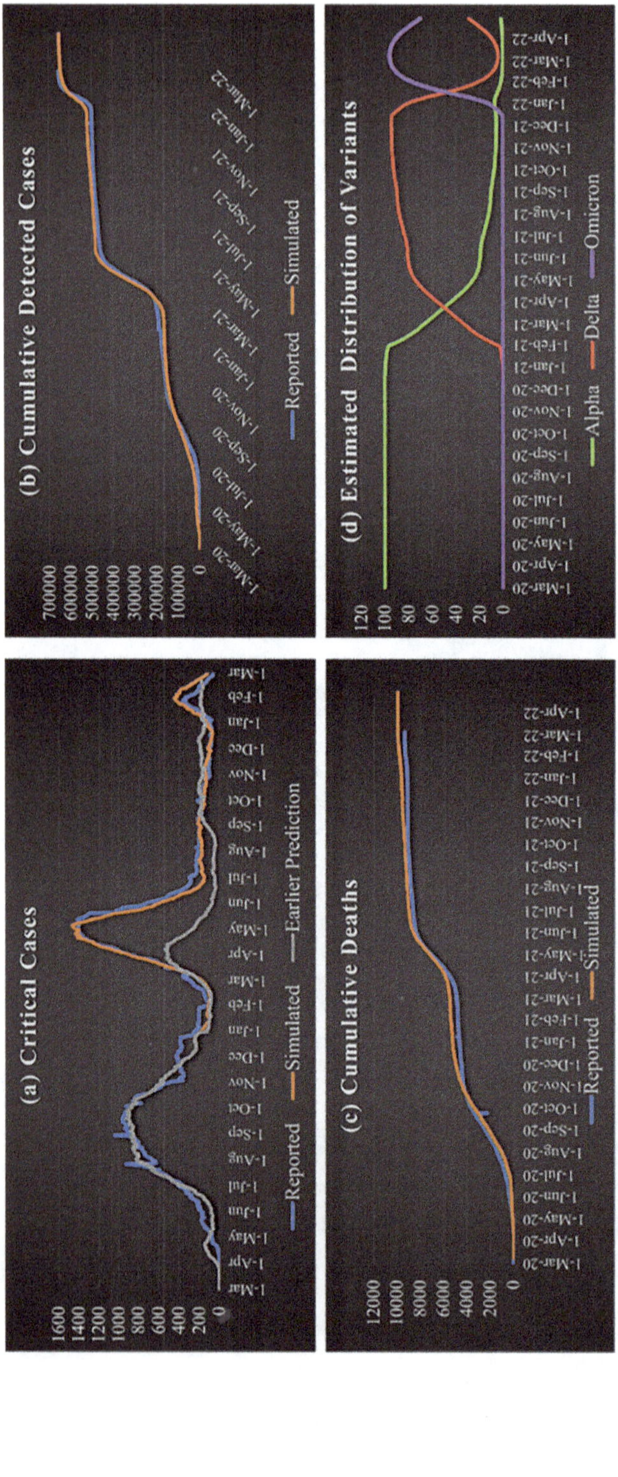

Fig. 9.12 Evaluation of simulation results and justification

Conclusion

In this chapter, we presented a comprehensive approach for constructing healthcare digital twin by seamlessly combining domain knowledge with existing healthcare data using a pragmatic multi-modeling technique. We explained how our healthcare digital twin supports simulation of an integrated view of the healthcare system across four key dimensions, i.e., demand, supply, processes, and environmental aspects, to comprehend complexities and bottlenecks arising from inherent system uncertainties and nonlinear interactions among them. We further highlighted the transformative value of this healthcare digital twin where stakeholders can quantitatively identify current system gaps, conduct pre-implementation evaluations of potential interventions, and experiment with various anticipated scenarios. We believe these capabilities are crucial for assessing healthcare resilience and operational robustness. Furthermore, the predictive insights possible through this healthcare digital twin support evidence-based decision-making for better alignment of infrastructure, resource optimization and allocation, and streamlining supply chain processes. They collectively enhance preparedness for emerging health crises, thus reinforcing the foundation for effective and resilient healthcare systems.

In this chapter, we demonstrated how the proposed digital twin approach was leveraged during the COVID-19 pandemic to understand infection spread dynamics for varying population, geographical factors, and environmental heterogeneities across different localities. We also discussed how it helped stakeholders, e.g., city administrators, devise targeted localized non-pharmaceutical interventions that effectively managed the spread of infection in diverse communities. Based on this experience, we are now exploring additional possibilities to address current healthcare challenges and further refining our approach to anticipate and mitigate future problems. By leveraging digital twins, we aim to understand emerging situations in healthcare ecosystem and develop adaptive solutions for rising health crises. Looking forward, healthcare digital twin requires interdisciplinary collaboration from fields, such as public health, epidemiology, AI, modelling, and simulation. Moreover, we need better support on data standards and ethical guidelines to use personal and population-level data responsibly and securely.

Our broad goal is to provide a forward-looking strategy and a digital-twin-based evaluation aid to anticipate and mitigate future risks for setting the stage for a responsive evidence-driven healthcare system that aligns with public health objectives and patient-centered care for the coming decades.

References

1. Ghosh, S. M. (2023). National Health Mission and the status of public healthcare in Indian states. *Social Change, 53*(4), 562–574.

2. Grieves, M., & Vickers, J. (2017). Digital twin: Mitigating unpredictable, undesirable emergent behavior in complex systems. In *Transdisciplinary perspectives on complex systems: New findings and approaches* (pp. 85–113).
3. Macal, C. M., & North, M. J. (2009, December). Agent-based modeling and simulation. In *Proceedings of the 2009 winter simulation conference (WSC)* (pp. 86–98). IEEE.
4. Bala, B. K., Arshad, F. M., & Noh, K. M. (2017). System dynamics. *Modelling and Simulation*, 274.
5. Riley, S., Fraser, C., Donnelly, C. A., Ghani, A. C., Abu-Raddad, L. J., Hedley, A. J., Leung, G. M., Ho, L.-M., Lam, T.-H., Thach, T. Q., Chau, P., Chan, K.-P., Lo, S.-V., Leung, P.-Y., Tsang, T., Ho, W., Lee, K.-H., Lau, E. M. C., Ferguson, N. M., & Anderson, R. M. (2003). Transmission dynamics of the etiological agent of SARS in Hong Kong: Impact of public health interventions. *Science, 300*(5627), 1961–1966.
6. Barat, S., Paranjape, A., Parchure, R., Darak, S., & Kulkarni, V. (2022). Agent based simulatable city digital twin to explore dynamics of COVID-19 pandemic. In *2022 winter simulation conference (WSC)* (pp. 557–568). IEEE.
7. Sargent, R. G. (2010, December). Verification and validation of simulation models. In *Proceedings of the 2010 winter simulation conference* (pp. 166–183). IEEE.
8. Barat, S., Parchure, R., Darak, S., Kulkarni, V., Paranjape, A., Gajrani, M., Yadav, A., & Kulkarni, V. (2021). An agent-based digital twin for exploring localized non-pharmaceutical interventions to control COVID-19 pandemic. *Transactions of the Indian National Academy of Engineering, 6*(2), 323–353.
9. Barat, S., Kulkarni, V., Paranjape, A., Parchure, R., Darak, S., & Kulkarni, V. (2022). Understanding emergent dynamism of COVID-19 pandemic in a City. *Transactions of the Indian National Academy of Engineering, 7*(4), 1347–1367.
10. He, S., Peng, Y., & Sun, K. (2020). SEIR modeling of the COVID-19 and its dynamics. *Nonlinear Dynamics, 101*, 1667–1680.
11. Clark, T., Kulkarni, V., Barat, S., & Barn, B. (2017). ESL: An actor-based platform for developing emergent behaviour organisation simulations. In *Advances in practical applications of cyber-physical multi-agent systems: The PAAMS collection: 15th international conference, PAAMS 2017, Porto, Portugal, June 21–23, 2017, proceedings 15* (pp. 311–315). Springer International Publishing.

Chapter 10
Knowledge-Orchestrated Digital Twin Suite for Smart Refinery Operations

Sandhya Seshagiri, Twinkle Khadka, Trilok Chand, Arpit Vishwakarma, Chetan Malhotra, Trinath Gaduparthi, and B. P. Gautham

Abstract Refinery operations involve hundreds of equipment and complex material flows through various processing units. Thousands of sensors monitor the process for any deviations from the set points leading to a flood of alarms that overload the operator in an emerging situation. Refinery processes are highly controlled where the deviations in controlled variables of a process are rare, but drifts are observed in manipulated variables as the control system automatically addresses the drifts. Digital twins of the processes offer additional insights, compared to the sensor data, into the processes in greater detail and can be used as predictive models and soft sensors to estimate impending deviations. However, to mitigate the deviations, a refinery operator or a process engineer uses knowledge from various sources in addition to the trends observed in monitored variables. Process knowledge scattered across diverse sources such as incident reports, root cause analysis documents, and standard operating procedures need to be reconciled to take a decision. In this chapter, we show how a formal representation of refinery process knowledge can be combined with digital twins and sensor data to derive more value from digital twins for process monitoring applications. We illustrate this in the case of fluid catalytic cracking and fractionation units of a refinery. We introduce a semantics-based platform called TCS PREMAP, where process ontology is used to express failure knowledge, orchestrate digital twins in the changing context of the refinery, and connect to real-time data to carry out root cause analysis.

S. Seshagiri · T. Khadka · T. Chand · A. Vishwakarma · C. Malhotra · T. Gaduparthi (✉) · B. P. Gautham
Tata Consultancy Services Research, Pune, Maharashtra, India
e-mail: seshagiri.sandhya89@gmail.com; twinkle.khadka@tcs.com; trilok.chand@tcs.com; arpit.vishwakarma@tcs.com; chetan.malhotra@tcs.com; trinath.gaduparthi@tcs.com; bp.gautham@tcs.com

V. Kulkarni et al. (eds.), *Digital Twins for Simulation-Based Decision-Making*,
https://doi.org/10.1007/978-3-031-89654-5_10

Introduction

In the era of Industry 4.0, digital twins are being used for process and asset management in almost all manufacturing and process industries such as oil and gas and chemical and automotive manufacturing [1, 2]. Asset or equipment digital twins are used to monitor asset health and estimate remaining useful life to aid maintenance planning [3], scheduling, and fault mitigation, while process digital twins are used for gaining insights into the process conditions for the purpose of performance management. As processes operate with assets and assets get impacted by processes, it leads to a complex interaction, especially as the number of assets and processes increase, resulting in a complex systems of systems scenario in a large manufacturing plant. During an emerging situation in a plant, operators and process engineers take decisions by combining insights from both process and asset digital twins with tacit process knowledge. In addition to the tacit expert knowledge they possess, they also leverage knowledge that is present in diverse and often siloed sources such as P&ID drawings, standard operating procedures, equipment manuals, maintenance logs, past incident reports, etc. and often consult other experts.

While process plants such as refineries tend to be highly controlled, still they need interventions from operators to mitigate or manage undesirable events. They often observe a large amount of sensor data and alarms displayed on control screens, use their knowledge to assess the situation, and make decisions/corrective actions if needed. Digital twins provide a lot more information to operators that are not easily obtainable from sensors directly. While this provides them with additional high-quality information, operators need to still apply their knowledge in an emerging situation, especially where multiple aspects of the complex plant are involved [4].

In this chapter, we present a knowledge-driven digital thread framework [5], where knowledge that is typically learnt/referenced by operators from various sources such as manuals, drawings, best practices, HAZOP documents, etc. is digitally captured in a way it can be reasoned upon contextually by considering the data coming from plant as well as digital twins. With this reasoning, operators are proactively alerted to impending events with potential remedies so that they can take better-informed decisions.

We demonstrate the above for monitoring a refinery with two core refining processes—fluid catalytic cracking (FCC) and fractionation. We emulate the plant processes by building a physics-based model for FCC and fractionator units [6]. We create data-driven process digital twins using neural networks that are trained on the data generated by the plant emulator. We induce a fault in the plant emulator and demonstrate how digital twins can be augmented with process and equipment knowledge to perform automated root cause analysis of process deviations.

Current State of Refinery Operations

A typical oil and gas refinery consists of multiple processing units that refine input crude feedstock into valuable products such as gasoline, diesel, aviation kerosene, light combustion oil, naphtha, etc. The length of the piping in a refinery runs into hundreds of kilometers indicating the complexity of process operations. Operators, schedulers, process engineers, maintenance engineers, and performance control engineers collaborate to enable smooth operations in a refinery. These different personnel view refinery operations from multiple angles. For example, an operator is concerned with improving the refinery productivity by adjusting the controls in the event of any deviations. On the other hand, a maintenance engineer is concerned with asset health to ensure adequate uptime of the refinery. A performance control engineer aims to adhere to the production schedule and assesses impact on plant economics.

Typically, refinery process operations are controlled via distributed control systems (DCS). The processes are controlled locally using PID (Proportional-Integral-Derivative) and other forms of controllers so that any deviation arising locally is addressed without central supervision. In addition to the DCS system, supervisory control and data acquisition (SCADA) systems are used to control processes in large plants. The operators in the control room monitor the operations by observing the data/alarms displayed and take control actions when needed.

Despite the advanced control systems being in place in a refinery, the operators are ever alert to emerging deviations or drifts in the process KPIs and product quality. In addition to process controls, an alarm system alerts the operator when a process variable breaches the control limits. By design, the alarm thresholds are set conservatively, and this leads to a profusion of alarms on a regular basis. This leads to a situation often referred to as "alarm flooding" where an operator is presented with hundreds of alarms. Many a times, these alarms disappear in a short time, and only a few of these alarms correspond to an issue needing attention. Identifying the root alarm corresponding to an issue amidst this situation leads to high cognitive load on the operator. Often operators ignore many alarms at an individual level based on their past observations. This may lead to missing out on critical alarms or a major event whose signature could be lying in a particular group of alarms active at a given time. Some of these situations may lead to immense damage.

Even if the root alarm is identified, the refinery process knowledge that the operator or process engineer uses to address the alarm is present in multiple sources. Sources such as Hazard and Operability (HAZOP) documents, Failure Mode and Effect Analysis (FMEA) documents, Root Cause Analysis (RCA) reports, Simulation (Digital Twin Execution) results, and past incident reports are used to address an emerging deviation. The refinery Operator reconciles the information across sources in different forms (text, images, tables) and also the dashboards of data flowing through the DCS system to decide a remedial action or plan for an impending deviation that may not be automatically handled by the control system. This leads to significant dependency on operators' expertise, workload, and other factors that may influence their cognitive ability, at times allowing for large uncontrolled and undesirable events to occur.

Hence, there is a need for a system where process knowledge along with its applicable context can be represented in a form understandable by computers and humans. Such a system can reason with this knowledge, as per the emerging context of the plant and deliver knowledge-based recommendations to the operator to aid decision-making, reducing uncertainties arising from the cognitive abilities of the operators.

Digital Twins in Refinery Operations

In refinery operations, process and asset simulators are used extensively for purposes of process optimization, what-if analysis, and failure scenario simulation [7]. Process simulators can be of varying fidelity, ranging from detailed physics-based models to data-based, statistical, or machine learning models. Using detailed process models in real time is prohibitive as plant dynamics change much faster than the detailed, physics-based models can capture. Data-driven models, or popularly called digital twins, have gained prominence in creating real-time digital counterparts of physical assets and processes [8]. Digital twins are designed to describe the process from a specific perspective and are in sync with the current state of an asset or a process.

With increasing usage of sensors in process industries, data-driven digital twins have gained prominence to estimate other parameters that cannot be directly sensed. These data-driven digital twins are created using statistical or machine learning models based on the past sensor data. This reliance on past data can bias the digital twin toward correctly identifying only the patterns that are present in past data. These digital twins may require constant retuning with human interventions once the plant scenario changes. The context of the plant in which these digital twins are created is lost once the digital twin is applied in isolation in a newer plant scenario. Recently, data-driven digital twins are combined with physics-based reduced-order models to take advantage of both the approaches. However, the process context for which the digital twin is created dictates its usability.

An oil and gas refinery consists of hundreds of pieces of equipment and sub-processes that are being monitored by operators for taking decisions. Digital twins are generally created for an equipment (e.g., a furnace) or a sub-process (e.g., atmospheric distillation process) level. These digital twins will be in sync with reality and continuously be sending out data to the control room dashboards. The operator looks at data coming from the physical sensors and digital twins and uses process knowledge to take an informed decision. If the processes run into hundreds, digital twins are also that many in number. The cognitive load on the operator will further increase as data coming from physical sensors and digital twins needs to be reconciled with the process knowledge.

To address this proliferation of data and digital twins in an industrial scenario, there is a need for using them along with the process operations knowledge in a more concerted manner. The proposed knowledge engineering framework addresses this by fusing real-time data sources, multiple digital twins, and process knowledge in a purposive manner to take better decisions [9].

Knowledge-Driven Digital Thread

A knowledge-driven digital thread (KDDT) proposed here combines process knowledge, real-time sensor data, and digital twins to enable better decision-making. The foundation of the KDDT is a semantic framework built using ontologies. The ontology acts as a vocabulary using which plant structure and knowledge are expressed in a machine-understandable form [10].

The KDDT framework as shown in Fig. 10.1 consists of domain ontology, knowledge base expressed in terms of domain ontology, orchestration layer, and application layer. The framework enables building applications for activities such as process monitoring or root cause analysis of failures in a process plant. Plant data, both historical and real-time data, is contextualized, and plant knowledge from various sources is curated in a formal knowledge base using a process ontology. A reasoning engine and orchestration engine power the application layer. The reasoning engine activates the knowledge curated in the knowledge base, and the orchestration

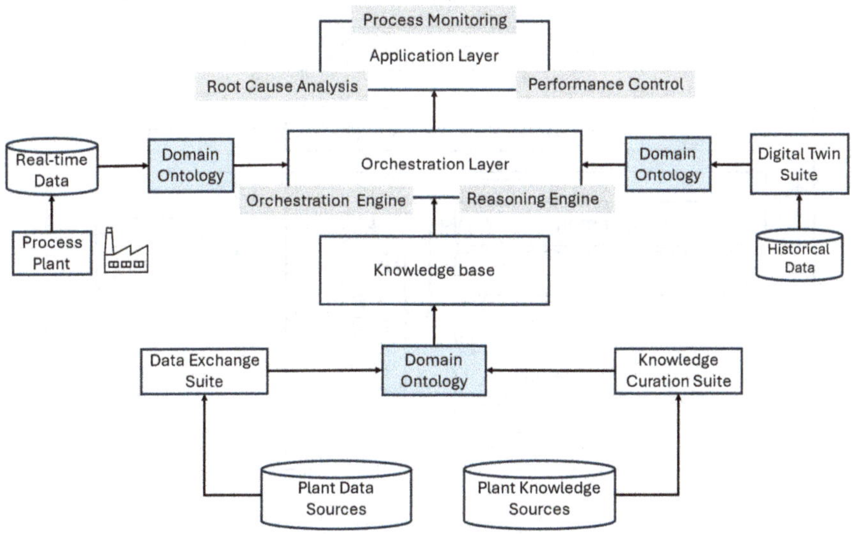

Fig. 10.1 Knowledge-driven digital thread with data and knowledge sources from plant system and digital twin suite

engine uses the current context of the plant expressed as a temporal instance of process ontology and coordinates digital twins, real-time data, and knowledge.

As can be seen in Fig. 10.1, domain ontology plays a central role in expressing knowledge in a formal manner in a knowledge base. The real-time data flowing through DCS systems is connected to reasoning engine via ontology. This helps in providing context for the incoming sensor data. Similarly, digital twins are orchestrated with context using process ontologies.

Process Plant

A manufacturing/process plant such as a refinery consists of a large number of interacting unit processes with underlying equipment such as distillation columns, reactors, regenerators, etc. These equipment form the part of a process circuit in the plant for refining feedstock through material and energy flows. Control systems, at multiple levels (Levels 0–2 as per the ISA-95/IEC 62264standard), are deployed on this equipment to control the process parameters so that a planned and optimum throughput or plant uptime is expected. These control systems operating at multiple levels are shown in Fig. 10.2.

Level 0 represents the field level (shop floor) of a process plant with elements such as manufacturing equipment, input and output materials, manufacturing process, human resource, sensors, and actuators.

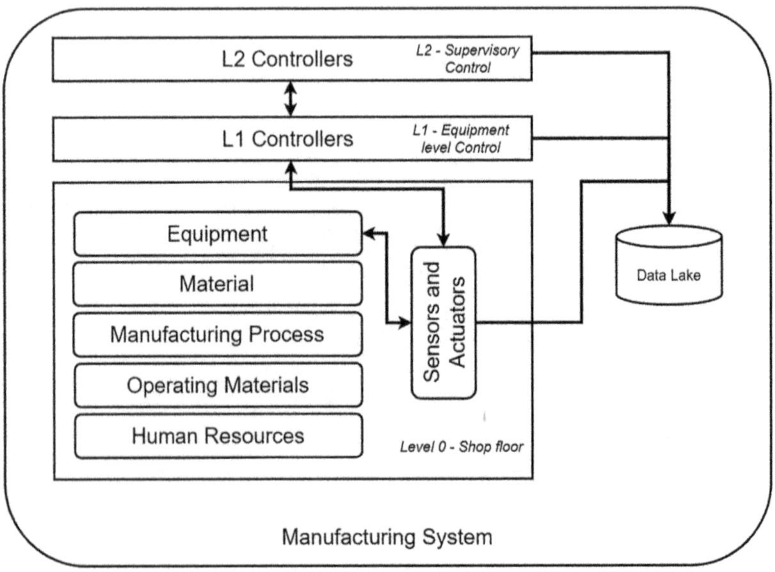

Fig. 10.2 Manufacturing System Hierarchy (Level 0–2)

Level 1 consists of equipment-level controllers such as PLCs (programmable logic controllers) or RTUs (remote terminal units) required for controlling the equipment. The L1 controllers are of hardware type whose inputs and outputs are connected to the equipment in field at Level 0. The role of L1 controllers is to perform desired control action to ensure that all the components in the unit process work within the set bound limits and drive the actuators based on the controller logic for automation of production process.

Level 2 consists of plant-level supervisory controllers such as SCADA/DCS/HMI systems that gather and analyze near-real-time data from equipment in field through L1 controllers to monitor and control plant operations. The Level 2 control system software computes, distributes, and displays the sensor data locally or to remote locations, helping control engineer monitor and take decisions.

Data Sources

Data sources include both historical and real-time sensor data from the plant. Real-time data can be continuously or intermittently available. For example, laboratory sample analysis of a feedstock in a refinery generates data once a day as opposed to minute-by-minute data coming from a pressure sensor of a reactor. The data of relevance here pertains to:

Materials flowing in and out of the equipment during manufacturing operations
Equipment state variables set by various levels of the control system (L1 and L2) such as operating set points, actuators' states, opening of the valves, or other process conditions

Information outputs such as manufacturing/process operating parameters (temperature, pressure, gas concentration, etc.) measured by the sensors or returned by actuators installed in the physical system and product quality parameters such as product composition, temperature, purity, etc., measured on the outgoing materials using sensors or from the laboratory, or equipment state data such as vibration levels

Knowledge Sources

Plant knowledge typically resides with operators, process engineers, and other plant personnel along with other documented knowledge sources. Details of process flow, equipment, and sensors are present in the Piping & Instrumentation diagrams (P&ID) in digital form. Failure mode and effect analysis exercise is carried out by process experts and documented in FMEA sheets. Additionally, safety experts carry out hazard and operability analysis and prepare the HAZOP document that contains deviations, their effects, and safe operating limits for a particular process. Incident reports are stored along with the RCA documents attached to each of the reports.

Long-term observations about the plant and processes are also documented to help plan for future capital investments (such as new equipment purchase, sensors, etc.). Further to this, tacit knowledge resides in the minds of plant engineer/operators/ subject matter experts and is expressed in the form of observations from inspections, rules of thumb, logbooks, safety audits, etc. Though formalized using structured templates, all these knowledge sources are siloed and in a semi-structured form. Plant personnel reconcile and reason with the knowledge before taking a decision in line with the current state of the plant. Digital twins can use this knowledge contextually if represented in a formal and machine-understandable manner.

Digital Twin Suite

A digital twin suite (DTS) is a collection of multiple digital twins (DTs) for a system or sub-system(s) for various views/purposes, e.g., DT for asset life prediction or predictive maintenance, DT for process performance, DT for soft-sensing, DT for predictive maintenance, DT for control, etc. The permutations of these across subsystems and purposes amount to a large number of digital twins. An illustration of a digital twin suite is shown in Fig. 10.3.

Digital twins can be a physics-based reduced-order model, data-based model, behavioral model, mathematical model, or a combination thereof. In the KDDT framework depending on the application context, one or more digital twins will be leveraged to serve the intended purpose of the application.

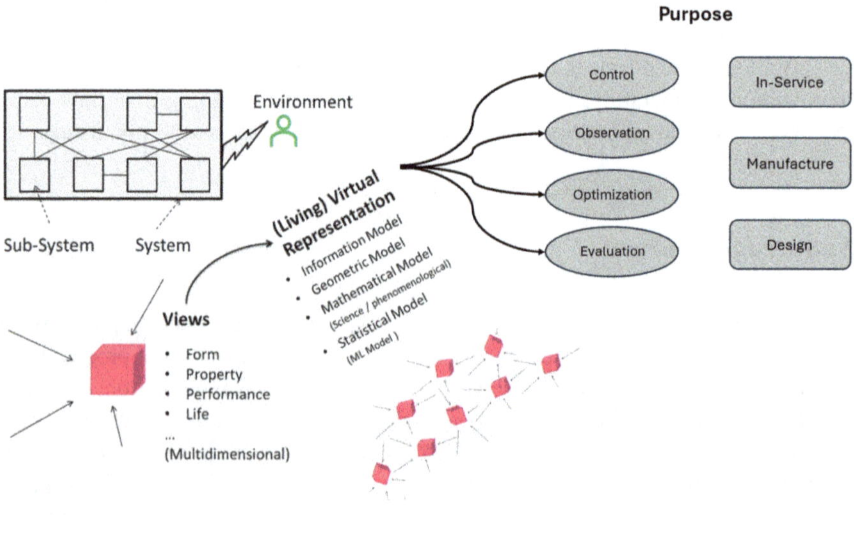

Fig. 10.3 Digital twin suite (DTS) with their purpose

Domain Ontology

A domain ontology provides the semantic foundation to:

Capture and organize domain-specific data and knowledge related to product, material, equipment, and manufacturing process
Represent knowledge in a digitized and machine-processible form in a knowledge base and enable contextual reasoning for decision-making
Orchestrate multiple digital twins in a context-aware manner

Within the domain of interest, ontologies provide a formal description of domain concepts and relationships among them. Besides the structural description of the plant, this framework also provides metamodels for representation of other artefacts such as digital twin or simulation tools. Figure 10.4 shows the three-level hierarchy of a manufacturing/process domain ontology used in the KDDT framework [10].

Meta level: The metamodel layer provides a higher-level abstraction of manufacturing/process plant. Relevant models for manufacturing/process domain can be classified into four subject areas—component/product, equipment, manufacturing process, and materials.

Subject level: Subject level provides flexibility to users to define their own domain at the specific subject level. Subject-level ontologies are created as instances of metamodel. For example, Fig. 10.4 shows subject-level instances of fluid catalytic cracking process in an oil and gas refinery. Refined crude products (gasoline) is created as an instance of product metamodel, reactor as an instance of equipment metamodel, fluid catalytic cracking process as an instance of process metamodel, and crude feedstock as an instance of material metamodel.

Instance level: At instance level, individual instances of component, equipment, process, and material are created and represented using specific values. Figure 10.4 shows instance-level definitions of subject-level elements, e.g., gasoline with throughput of 100 tons/day as an instance of an attribute of gasoline product, fluidized bed reactor as an instance of reactor, or reactor temperature of 1050 °C as an instance of reactor process parameter. Digital twin of the fluid catalytic cracking process can be represented as another instance of the subject model for purposes of monitoring and optimization. This digital twin consists of a reactor model/digital twin and associated parameters such as estimated throughput and reactor temperature.

Data Exchange Suite

The role of the data exchange suite is to transfer the data from data sources into KDDT framework. The data exchange suite contains one or more of the following sub-components as shown in Fig. 10.5:

Data extraction/query sub-component establishes connection with plant data sources to extract/query necessary data.

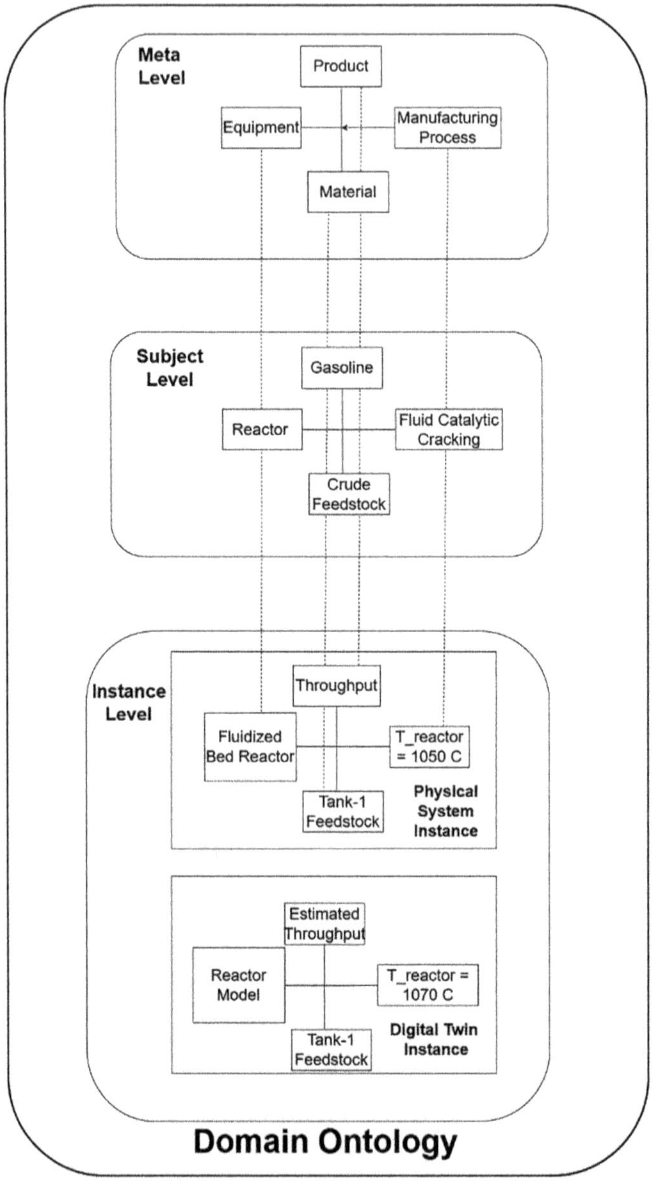

Fig. 10.4 Domain ontology: meta, subject, and instance layers with both physical instance and digital twin instance

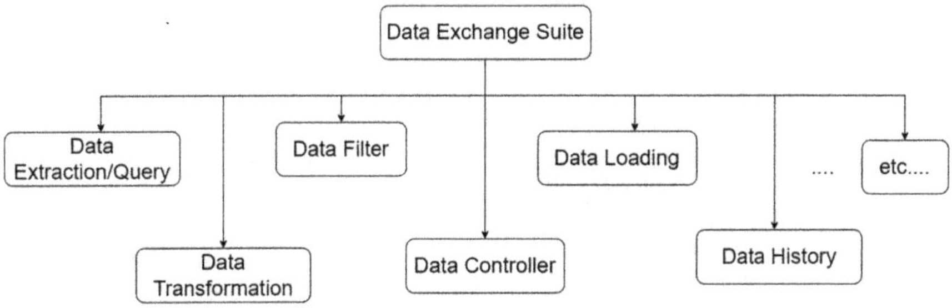

Fig. 10.5 Data exchange suite

Data transformation sub-component transforms the extracted data into a desired format for further usage.
Data filter sub-component filters out irrelevant information or noise in the transformed data and may impute missing data.
Data loading subcomponent delivers transformed and filtered data to other components of the system.
Data controller subcomponent takes care of time-based connectivity establishment with plant data sources for exchange of data.
Data history sub-component stores the history of past data for analysis.

Knowledge Curation Suite

The knowledge curation suite consists of a set of methods and tools to extract knowledge from various sources such as plant process diagrams, root cause analysis documents, equipment manuals, and incident reports. The curation suite can also contain modules that enable easier human feedback. The curation methods use various knowledge extraction techniques guided by the domain ontology of interest for a specific application. For example, for a root cause analysis application in a manufacturing process industry, relevant knowledge is curated using the FMEA ontology and process ontology.

Knowledge Base

The KDDT's knowledge base is curated using domain ontology and knowledge sources. This knowledge is in the form of rules, equations, expressions, procedures, tables, and logical workflows. Knowledge is represented in the form of individual atomic pieces of knowledge (a rule, expression, etc.) called knowledge elements [5]. A knowledge element consists of three main components: intent, context, and

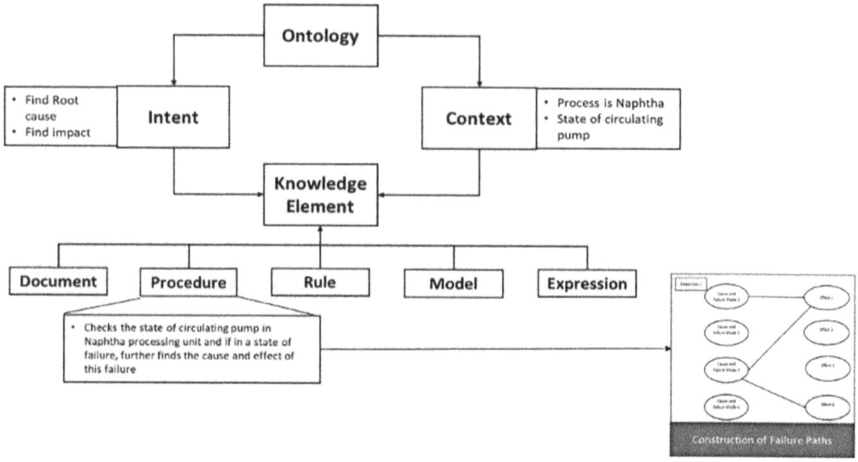

Fig. 10.6 Knowledge element for root cause analysis application with intent and context. The execution of knowledge element generates a causal chain

the knowledge body that is executable. This is shown in Fig. 10.6 for a specific application of root cause analysis.

The intent specifies the purpose of the knowledge element such as root cause analysis, assessment of asset health, etc. The context of a knowledge element specifies the system's context under which a particular knowledge element is relevant. For example, if a particular failure scenario is applicable for pumps that are used to pump slurry (a thick liquid byproduct of crude oil distillation) in a refinery, the context of applicability of knowledge is specific to pumps that are used in slurry processing and represented as such using the pump's equipment and the corresponding unit's process ontology.

The knowledge elements in the knowledge base get activated under a specific context of a system for a specific purpose during the execution of a monitoring/decision process. The reasoning engine enables the linking of multiple knowledge elements in a context dependent manner, forming a dynamic chain of knowledge. This dynamic chain of knowledge is traceable and provides explainability to decisions recommended by the KDDT workflow. For example, the dynamic linking of knowledge elements for root cause analysis is shown in Fig. 10.6.

Reasoning Engine

The role of reasoning engine in KDDT framework is to provide real-time guidance to the orchestration engine in the orchestration layer by performing reasoning over knowledge elements available in the knowledge base. The reasoning engine identifies relevant elements of knowledge in the knowledge base based on intent of the query and the set of active contexts such as:

Selecting contextual digital twins/models to represent the real-time manufacturing/process operations
Guiding the orchestration engine in diagnosis of process/equipment performance/health deviations by referring to knowledge base
Enabling a digital thread to formulate problems for optimization to make engineering/operations decisions that are optimal
Providing relevant information to the user based on the current context in a form that can be visualized and acted upon by the user or executed automatically by the orchestration engine, based on user's selection

Orchestration Engine

Orchestration engine coordinates with various components of the framework such as data exchange suite, digital twin suite, and physical system with the guidance of knowledge engine. Orchestration engine leverages specification of intents and identifies a step-by-step orchestration method and knowledge needed to solve the intended engineering/operations problem. A knowledge-driven digital thread orchestration system based on a generic process of decision making may be embodied for multiple purposes such as:

Enhancing real-time process and asset monitoring, diagnosing root causes for process/equipment deviations/failures, and providing remedial measures for deviated conditions
Performing what-if and if-what analysis for planning/forensic analysis of manufacturing operations
Enabling dynamic process optimization by taking online system/process level decision-making
Prescribing and implementing changes to the process under degradation of physical system
Performing prognosis of asset failure and recommendations of predictive maintenance

At Tata Consultancy Services, we have developed a foundational platform called TCS PREMAP that enables creation and execution of knowledge-driven digital threads [11]. This platform was developed using model-driven engineering concepts applied to the manufacturing/process domain. This platform possesses all the capabilities needed for a KDDT framework described earlier. The components of TCS PREMAP used for realization of KDDT are:

Ontology modelling framework to model domain at the right level of abstraction
A knowledge engineering framework for knowledge management

Simulation service framework for simulation/digital twin execution and tool integration
Machine-learning framework for analytics
Decision support systems, models, optimization techniques for decision-making and optimization

In the Section "Application of KDDT to a Refinery," we will discuss an application of the knowledge-driven digital thread framework along with digital twins in an oil and gas refinery for process monitoring and root cause analysis.

Application of KDDT to a Refinery

In this case study, KDDT framework is applied to two connected core units of a refinery—fluid catalytic cracking (FCC) unit and fractionation unit—to illustrate how process digital twins, real-time data, and failure scenario knowledge can be used to perform automated root cause analysis.

In a refinery, the crude oil feedstock is first processed by atmospheric/crude distillation unit (CDU) to separate out the light and heavy components. The bottom (heavy) products of the distillation unit are further processed in vacuum distillation unit (VDU). The atmospheric gas oil from CDU and light vacuum gas oil from VDU are fed to the FCC unit where these heavy components are further broken down into valuable intermediaries (such as Naphtha and FCC Gas Oil) under catalytic reactions.

Fractionator unit processes the output streams of FCC unit to obtain valuable products such as light naphtha, heavy naphtha, light combustion oil, and LPG. In terms of the working principle, fractionator unit is similar to distillation unit as it separates the mixture into individual components based on their boiling points. Figure 10.7 shows the FCC and fractionator units with various material streams.

Though the case study presented here was realized in an actual plant environment, it involves plant-specific proprietary information that cannot be made publicly available. Hence, for this case study, we use an open-source, physics-based simulation model proposed by Santander et al. [12] as an emulator along with relevant non-proprietary knowledge available in public domain. This physics-based model mimics actual plant using a reduced-order mathematical model based on the laws of conservation of mass, energy, and momentum [6]. The data generated by this physics-based simulator is used for building data-driven digital twins of both FCC and fractionation processes. A sketch of how a digital thread connects digital twins, the physical system, and process monitoring workflow for root cause analysis is shown in Fig. 10.8. While digital twins detect drift in controlled variables, the actual root cause is identified through the application of knowledge with context. The details of the process emulator, digital twins, and the process monitoring workflow are given in the sub-sections that follow.

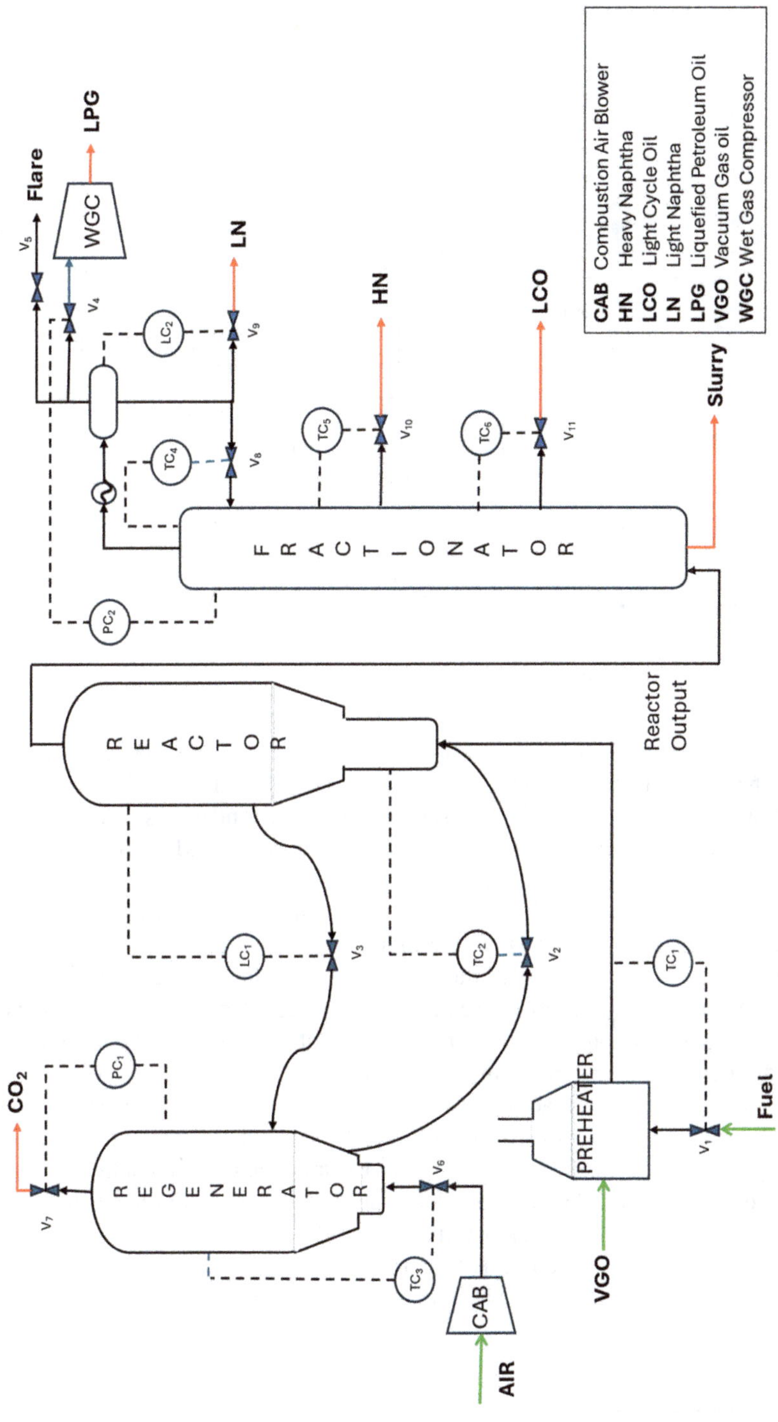

Fig. 10.7 FCC and fractionator unit. Yellow arrows indicate input material streams, red arrows indicate output material streams [12]

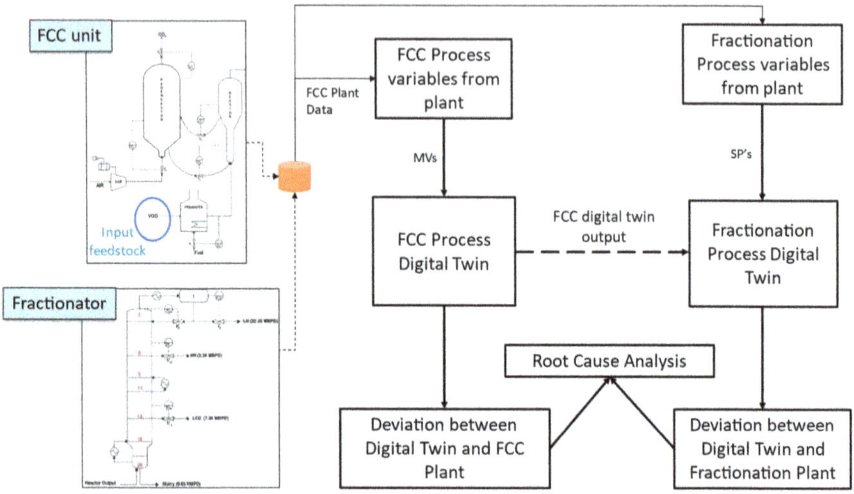

Fig. 10.8 Digital thread connecting process plant, digital twins, and causal knowledge

Process Emulator

FCC Process Emulator

FCC unit consists of three main sub-units: preheating furnace, reactor, and regenerator. The heavy oil material stream flowing from the bottom of distillation column is fed to a preheater furnace, which raises its temperature and enters a fluidized bed reactor through a riser. The reactions to convert heavy compounds into lighter compounds take place in the reactor using the catalyst flowing from regenerator. The reactor output then flows to the fractionator unit, where the separation of various fractions of the stream occurs as per the individual boiling point. The catalyst participating in the reactions is called the spent catalyst as the efficacy of the catalyst reduces due to deposition of coke on catalyst surface. The deposited coke is removed by coke-burning reactions occurring in the regenerator sub-unit, and the catalyst is restored for another round of use in the reactor.

The energy balance of reactor is assumed to follow the continuous stirred tank (CST) dynamics as in [6], where the enthalpy of the input and output streams, and cracking reactions, is considered [6]. The riser is modelled by the continuity equation in which the chemical kinetics model is incorporated. In addition, given the fast dynamics of the riser and the comparatively much longer dynamics of the reactor, a steady-state behavior is assumed for the riser. More details on the model can be found in Santander et al. [12] and McFarlane et al. [6].

Fractionation Process Emulator

A fractionation unit is a column of trays through which the vapor mixture consisting of multiple components rises up and cools into liquids of pure components as per their boiling point. These pure component liquids are collected in trays and pumped downstream for further processing. A 20-stage/tray fractionator is chosen for this study. The output of reactor in the FCC unit flows as an input material stream of the fractionator. More details of the fractionation emulator can be found in [12].

Control System

A set of PI controllers were modelled to simulate the regulatory control layer. The controlled variables, means of control (valves), and the manipulated variables are summarized in Table 10.1. A mapping exists between every manipulated variable (MV) and its valve position. The valve position spans values from 0 to 100% (from fully closed to fully open, respectively).

Table 10.1 List of controllers in FCC-Fractionator process along with their control and manipulated variables [12]

#	Controller	Controlled variable (CV)	Valve	Manipulated variable
1	TC1	T_{pre} (Preh. output stream)	V_1 (Preh. temperature)	F_f (Flow of fuel)
2	TC2	T_{rea} (Reactor temperature)	V_2 (Reactor temperature)	F_{rgc} (Flow of regen. cat.)
3	LC1	L_{rea} (Reactor inventory)	V_3 (Reactor inventory)	F_{sc} (Flow of spent. cat.)
4	TC3	T_{reg} (Regenerator temperature)	V_6 (Regenerator temperature)	F_a (Flow of air)
5	PC1	P_{reg} (Regenerator pressure)	V_7 (Regenerator pressure)	F_{fg} (Flow of flue gas)
6	PC2	P_{fra} (Overhead fractionator pressure)	V_4 (Frac. pressure)	F_{LPG} (Flow of LPG)
7	LC2	L_{fra} (Accumulator level)	V_9 (Accumulator level)	F_{LN} (Flow of LN)
8	TC4	T_{fra} (Overhead fractionator temperature)	V_8 (Fractionator temperature)	F_r (Flow of reflux)
9	TC5	T_{hnt} (HN 98% cut point (temperature))	V_{10} (HN flowrate)	F_{HN} (Flow of HN)
10	TC6	T_{lcot} (LCO 98% cut point (temperature))	V_{11} (LCO flowrate)	F_{LCO} (Flow of LCO)

Digital Twins of FCC and Fractionation Process

We built a data-driven model for prediction of the controlled variables. Two LSTM (long short-term memory) recurrent neural networks (RNNs) [13] are used as data models for FCC and Fractionation processes. A combination of open-loop and closed-loop simulation data was used to train these models. Inputs and outputs of the model are listed in Table 10.2.

It is assumed that feed vacuum gas oil (VGO), with an average molecular weight of 446.00 g/mol, is cracked into lighter molecules (pseudo-components, light gases) and coke. The pseudo-components (yfinal2 to yfinal6 in Table 10.2) mimic the actual components in a refinery in terms of thermodynamic and other properties of relevance. Here, pseudo-components 1 to 5 have average molecular weights (in g/mol) of 378.89, 292.18, 206.95, 120.94, and 85.13, respectively. The details of the neural network model used for FCC process digital twin are shown in Table 10.3. A schematic of the FCC process digital twin is shown in Fig. 10.9.

Table 10.2 Inputs and outputs for FCC process digital twin

Input	Output
Input feed quality (API)	Flowrate of VGO in reactor output ($yfinal_1$)
Preheater fuel supply flowrate (F_f)	Flowrate of reactor product pseudo component 1 ($yfinal_2$)
Feed temperature (T_{feed})	Flowrate of reactor product pseudo component 2 ($yfinal_3$)
Spent catalyst flowrate (F_{sc})	Flowrate of reactor product pseudo component 3 ($yfinal_4$)
Regenerated catalyst flowrate (F_{rgc})	Flowrate of reactor product pseudo component 4 ($yfinal_5$)
Combustion airflow in regenerator (F_a)	Flowrate of reactor product pseudo component 5 ($yfinal_6$)
Stack gas flowrate (F_{fg})	Flowrate of reactor product butane ($yfinal_7$)
	Flowrate of reactor product propane ($yfinal_8$)
	Flowrate of reactor product ethane ($yfinal_9$)
	Flowrate of reactor product methane ($yfinal_{10}$)
	Reactor total product flowrate (y_{total})
	Reactor pressure (P_{rea})
	Regenerator pressure (P_{reg})
	Preheater furnace temperature (T_{fur})
	Reactor riser temperature (T_{rea})
	Regenerator temperature (T_{reg})
	Weight of coke on spent catalyst (C_{sc})
	Weight of coke on regenerated catalyst (C_{rgc})
	Flowrate of reactor product coke (F_{coke})

Table 10.3 Details of the FCC process digital twin

Deep learning model used	LSTM
Total number of layers	3
Number of neurons in each layer	51,251,219
Optimizer	Adam
Number of data set used in training	380
Number of data set used in testing	1520
Number of epochs	100
Batch size	64

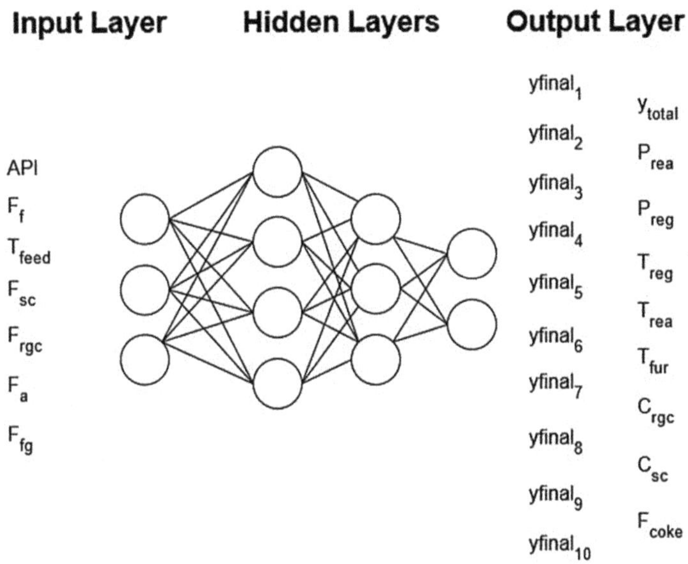

Fig. 10.9 A schematic of neural network used as FCC process digital twin

Fractionator data model is trained using the input and output data shown in Table 10.4. The output streams of FCC process digital twin form the input to fractionation process digital twin. The details of the neural network model used for fractionation process digital twin are shown in Table 10.5.

Process Ontology Creation and Failure Knowledge Representation

Using the three-level semantic framework detailed in the Section "Domain Ontology," process ontology is curated for the FCC and fractionator units for this case study. A part of the process ontology for FCC unit is shown in Fig. 10.10 along

Table 10.4 Input and output variable of fractionation process digital twin

Input	Output
Flowrate of VGO in reactor output ($yfinal_1$)	Flowrate of LPG (F_{LPG})
Flowrate of reactor product pseudo component 1 ($yfinal_2$)	Flowrate of LN (F_{LN})
Flowrate of reactor product pseudo component 2 ($yfinal_3$)	Flowrate of HN (F_{HN})
Flowrate of reactor product pseudo component 3 ($yfinal_4$)	Flowrate of LCO (F_{LCO})
Flowrate of reactor product pseudo component 4 ($yfinal_5$)	Flowrate of slurry (F_{slurry})
Flowrate of reactor product pseudo component 5 ($yfinal_6$)	
Flowrate of reactor product butane ($yfinal_7$)	
Flowrate of reactor product propane ($yfinal_8$)	
Flowrate of reactor product ethane ($yfinal_9$)	
Flowrate of reactor product methane ($yfinal_{10}$)	
Reactor total product flowrate (y_{total})	
Reactor riser temperature (T_{rea})	
Reactor pressure (P_{rea})	
Temperature of heavy tail cut point for HN product (T_{hnt})	
Temperature of heavy tail cut point for LCO product (T_{lcot})	
Overhead fractionator temperature (T_{fra})	
Accumulator level (L_{fra})	
Overhead fractionator pressure (P_{fra})	
Condenser temperature ($T_{condenser}$)	
Slurry temperature (T_{slurry})	

Table 10.5 Details of the Fractionation process digital twin

Deep learning model used	LSTM
Total number of layers	4
Number of neurons in each Layer	5,122,561,285
Optimizer	Adam
Number of data set used in training	380
Number of data set used in testing	1520
Number of epochs	100
Batch size	32

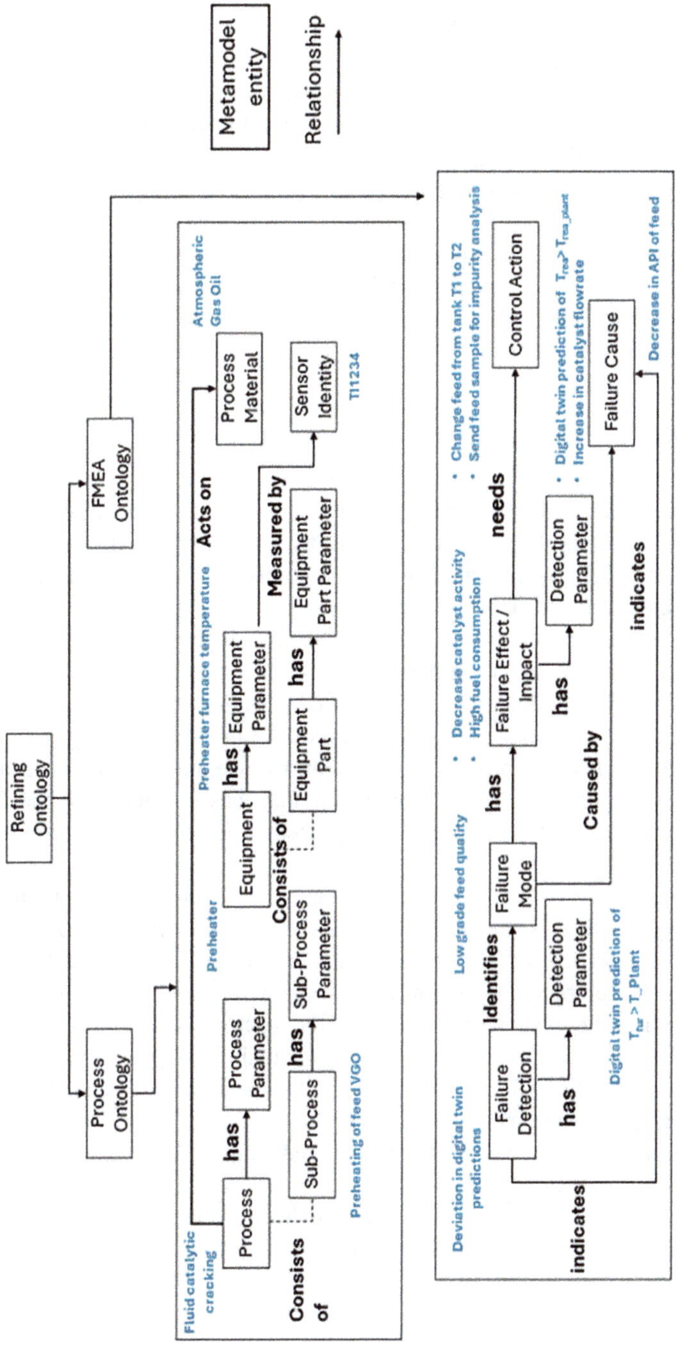

Fig. 10.10 FCC process ontology—with metamodel entities and instance entities

with metamodel entities and the subject/instance level entities for process, subprocess, equipment, etc.

The process failure knowledge present in various sources can be thought of as causal chains consisting of cause, failure mode, effect, and recommendations. Process failure knowledge in the form of causal chains for the FCC unit is shown in Fig. 10.11. Each entity in the causal chains shown in Fig. 10.11 is curated in the knowledge base as a knowledge element with intent and context. Both intent and context are expressed in terms of the process ontology shown in Fig. 10.10.

As can be seen from Fig. 10.11, the top-level deviation events have multiple root causes, and which root cause is relevant is decided by detections using digital twins, plant sensors, or both. The ontology and process failure knowledge are used along with the digital twins in a process monitoring workflow for root cause analysis.

Process Monitoring for Root Cause Analysis of Failures

Whenever any fault arises in a process plant, the control system automatically acts by changing the manipulated variables so that the controlled variable or the variable of interest is stabilized within the bounds of setpoints. Due to this, in an actual plant, the fault goes unnoticed. However, when a digital twin runs in parallel with the physical plant (with manipulated variables as inputs), it predicts the controlled variables. When there is a deviation between controlled variables of actual plant and digital twin, it indicates that the plant has deviated from the state represented by the digital twin and a potential fault has occurred. We use this guiding principle for utilizing digital twins in improving plant operations. We induce a failure scenario of feedstock quality drop in the plant emulator that was developed in the Section "Process Emulator," and the data that is generated is streamed as plant data for this case study.

Let's consider a scenario when there is a drop in input feed quality of FCC. Usually, the feed is heated to reach a set temperature. Because of the drop in feed quality, the preheater fuel consumption increases as it takes more fuel to keep the feed at a set temperature (due to impurities) before it enters the reactor. As a result, the catalyst flow rate increases to keep the reactor temperature at a desired set point, and the stack gas flow rate increases to maintain the regenerator pressure at a desired set limit. These decisions are taken by the control system to keep the throughput within some predefined bounds.

As the controlled variables of FCC (input feed temperature, reactor temperature, reactor inventory, regenerator temperature, regenerator pressure) are within a certain set limit, the plant operator may not notice the drift that is going on in the plant. However, the predicted controlled process variables such as reactor temperature,

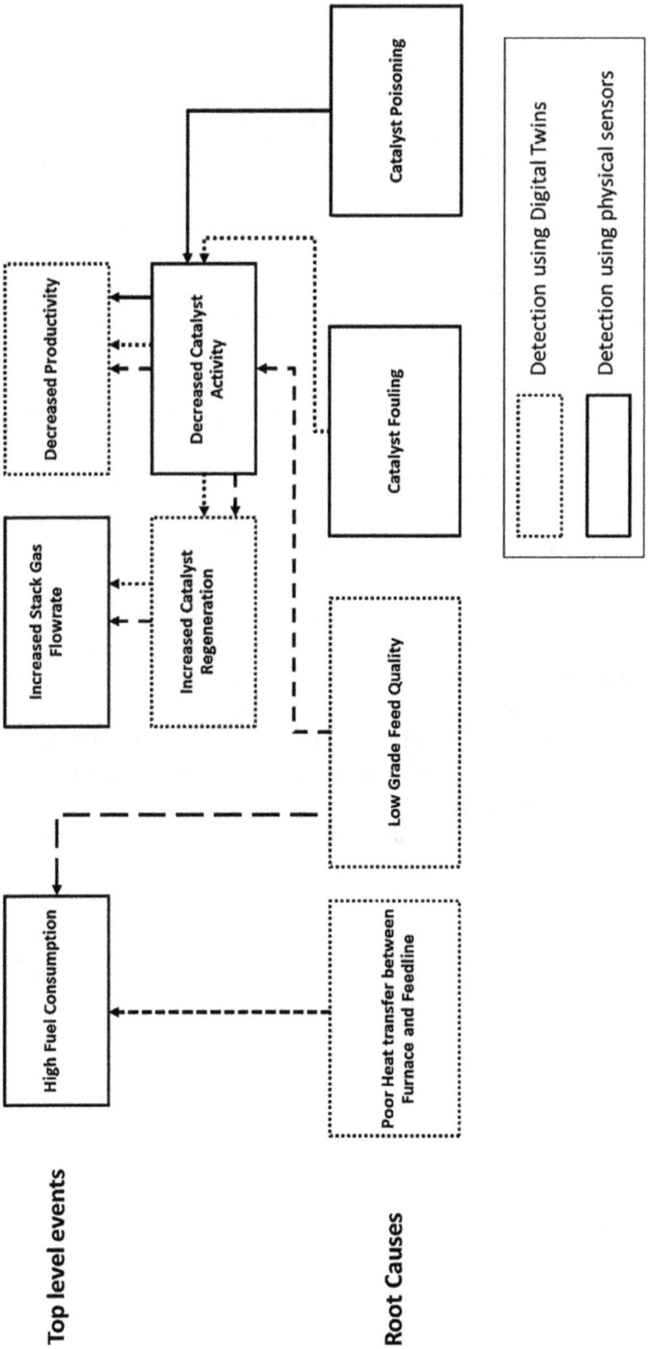

Fig. 10.11 Process failure knowledge in terms of causal chains and detection of failures/causes

regenerator temperature, and preheater furnace temperature using digital twins deviate from the current plant state, detecting an emerging drift in the plant behavior. Figure 10.12 shows how the predicted preheater and reactor temperature deviate from plant variables when input feed quality deteriorates.

If the difference between predicted process variables (by digital twin) and the plant variables exceeds a threshold, an underlying drift is detected in the processing unit. This is used as a detection condition in the failure knowledge element in the TCS PREMAP platform.

The individual entities of the causal paths shown in Fig. 10.11 are represented using the knowledge elements with relevant intent and context. The ability to represent failure scenarios and their effects in an atomic manner in terms of knowledge elements enables the process monitoring workflow to compose or assemble these events in a causal chain as per the system's context and suggest recommendations.

Typically, estimation of feed quality degradation requires one day of analysis in the wet lab. With the use of knowledge orchestrated digital twins, we can detect process deviations, estimate feed quality degradation during operations, and provide recommendation to switch to a crude supply from another source. This will help in improving the energy efficiency of the processing units in a refinery by replacing the impure crude with better feedstock.

The process monitoring workflow created in TCS PREMAP is shown in Fig. 10.13. This workflow uses digital twins of FCC and fractionation process and the streaming sensor data from the physics-based plant emulator to detect deviations or failure scenarios and trigger knowledge-driven root cause analysis. The root cause analysis identifies a causal chain starting from the top failure event/scenario and reaching the root cause. Recommendations to address the identified root cause are represented as knowledge elements in the TCS PREMAP knowledge base and shown to the operator for decision-making during an emerging situation. TCS PREMAP screen with causal chains and recommendations is shown in Fig. 10.14.

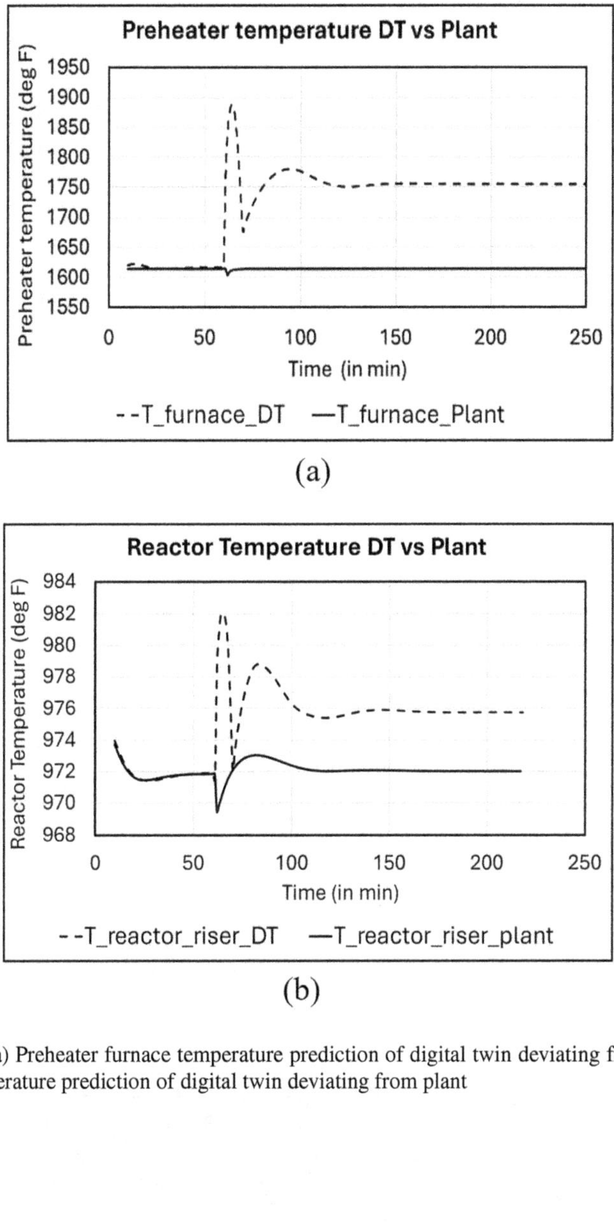

Fig. 10.12 (**a**) Preheater furnace temperature prediction of digital twin deviating from plant. (**b**) Reactor temperature prediction of digital twin deviating from plant

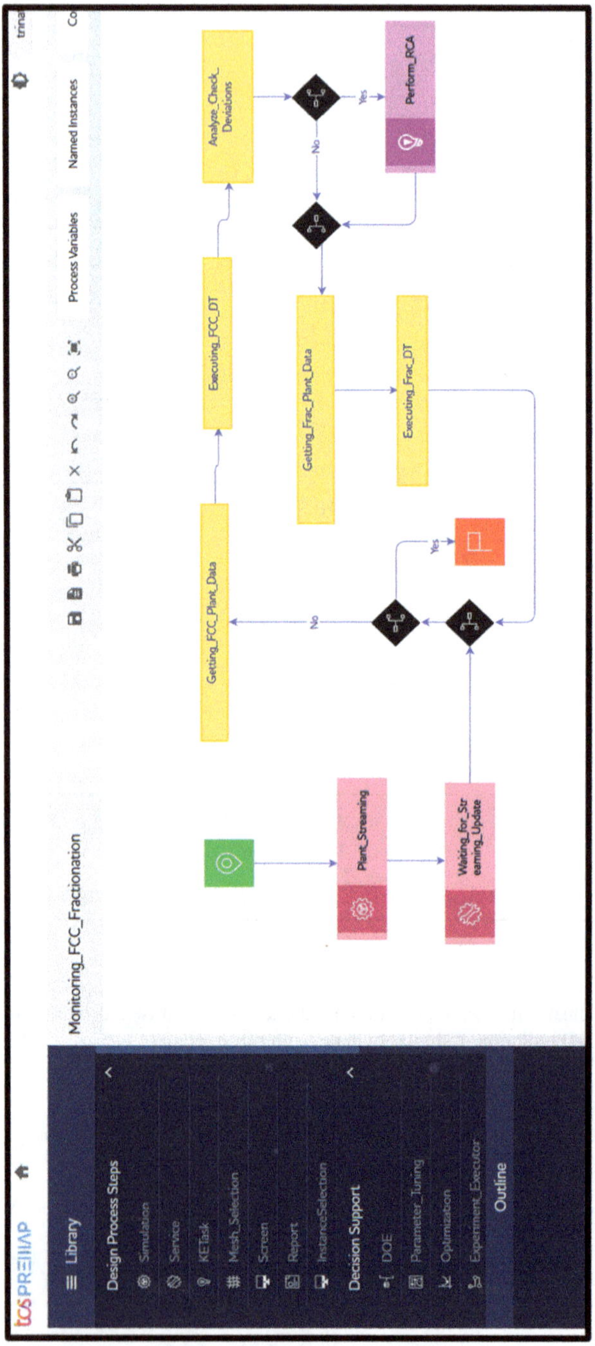

Fig. 10.13 Process monitoring workflow for root cause analysis

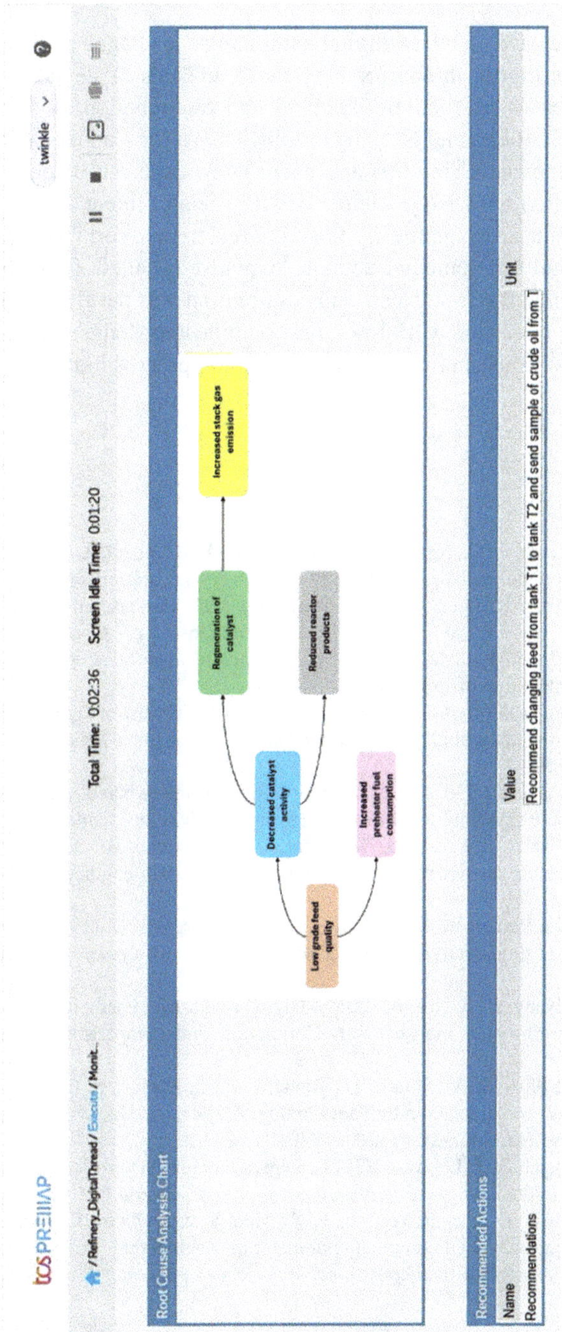

Fig. 10.14 TCS PREMAP screen showing a causal chain with recommended actions

Conclusion

In this chapter, we have seen how digital twins can be leveraged and orchestrated by knowledge-driven digital thread for root cause analysis of deviations in two oil refining processes—fluid catalytic cracking and fractionation. A framework was proposed to represent knowledge using ontologies in a form understandable by both humans and computers. Using this approach, knowledge can be decomposed into atomic pieces called knowledge elements with specific intent and context. These knowledge elements are dynamically linked in real time to form a causal chain providing explainability of remedial actions. A platform called TCS PREMAP was introduced on which the root cause analysis solution was developed. The platform enables creation of decision workflows that combine knowledge, real-time data, and digital twins for various applications in refinery and process industries [13].

References

1. Bongomin, O., Ocen, G. G., Nganyi, E. O., Musinguzi, A., & Omara, A. T. (2020). Exponential disruptive technologies and the required skills of industry 4.0. *Journal of Engineering, 2020*, 1.
2. Gregolinska, E., Khanam, R., Lefort, F., & Parthasarathy, A. P. (2022). *Capturing the true value of industry 4.0*. McKinsey & Company. Retrieved 06 December, 2022, from https://www.mckinsey.com/capabilities/operations/our-insights/capturing-the-true-value-of-industry-four-point-zero.
3. Aivaliotis, P., Chryssolouris, G., & Georgoulias, K. (2019). The use of digital twin for predictive maintenance in manufacturing. *International Journal of Computer Integrated Manufacturing, 32*(11), 1067–1080.
4. Grieves, M., & Vickers, J. (2017). Digital twin: Mitigating unpredictable, undesirable emergent behavior in complex systems. *Transdisciplinary perspectives on complex systems*, 85–113.
5. Yeddula, R. R., Vale, S., Reddy, S., Malhotra, C. P., Gautham, B., & Zagade, P. (2016). A knowledge modeling framework for computational materials engineering. In *SEKE, 2016* (pp. 197–202).
6. McFarlane, R. C., Reineman, R. C., Bartee, J. F., & Georgakis, C. (1993). Dynamic simulator for a model iv fluid catalytic cracking unit. *Computers & Chemical Engineering, 17*(3), 275–300.
7. Tao, F., Qi, Q., Wang, L., & Nee, A. (2019). Digital twins and cyber–physical systems toward smart manufacturing and industry 4.0: Correlation and comparison. *Engineering, 5*(4), 653–661.
8. Rathore, M. M., Shah, S. A., Shukla, D., Bentafat, E., & Bakiras, S. (2021). The role of AI, machine learning, and big data in digital twinning: A systematic literature review, challenges, and opportunities. *IEEE Access, 9*, 32030–32052.
9. David, J., Järvenpää, E., & Lobov, A. (2021). Digital threads via knowledge-based engineering systems. In *2021 30th conference of open innovations association FRUCT*.
10. Reddy, S., Gautham, B., Das, P., Yeddula, R. R., Vale, S., & Malhotra, C. (2017). An ontological framework for integrated computational materials engineering. In *Proceedings of the 4th world congress on integrated computational materials engineering (ICME 2017)* (pp. 69–77). Springer.

11. Gautham, B., Singh, A. K., Ghaisas, S. S., Reddy, S. S., & Mistree, F. (2013). PREMAP: A platform for the realization of engineered materials and products. In *ICoRD'13* (pp. 1301–1313). Springer.
12. Santander, O., Kuppuraj, V., Harrison, C. A., & Baldea, M. (2022). An open source fluid catalytic cracker—Fractionator model to support the development and benchmarking of process control, machine learning and operation strategies. *Computers and Chemical Engineering, 164*, 107900.
13. Sherstinsky, A. (2020). Fundamentals of recurrent neural network (RNN) and long short-term memory (LSTM) network. *Physica D: Nonlinear Phenomena, 404*, 132306.

Chapter 11
Digital Twin–Based Enterprise Ecosystems

Deepali Kholkar, Suman Roychaudhary, and Sreedhar Reddy

Abstract An enterprise ecosystem is a network of interacting business entities involved in the delivery of a set of complementary services, through both cooperation and competition. Each entity has a set of objectives and devises a set of strategies and capabilities to meet them. However, modern businesses operate in a highly dynamic and uncertain environment where each entity in the ecosystem affects and is affected by the others, creating a constantly evolving relationship in which they must continually adapt to meet their objectives. In this chapter, we present a digital twin-based architecture for driving these adaptation decisions in a value-integrator-based ecosystem. Digital twins enable risk-free business experimentation "in silico," helping stakeholders arrive at the right adaptive response through what-if and if-what simulation. We propose the notion of public and private digital twins to help business entities strike the right balance between cooperation and competition. We discuss a software systems architecture that helps operationalize the adaptation decisions in a human-in-control automated manner. We present a case study that illustrates some of these ideas.

Introduction

Modern businesses operate in a dynamic environment where there is continual unpredicted change in business domains, consumer needs, laws and regulations, and even technologies. Business enterprises need to be able to adapt to these changes to stay relevant, operate, and thrive despite the dynamism and uncertainty [1]. The interconnected nature of modern enterprises necessitates viewing them in the larger context of the business ecosystems they are part of to better understand the dynamism in their environment.

D. Kholkar (✉) · S. Roychaudhary · S. Reddy
TCS Research, Pune, Maharashtra, India
e-mail: deepali.kholkar@tcs.com; suman.roychaudhury@tcs.com; sreedhar.reddy@tcs.com

V. Kulkarni et al. (eds.), *Digital Twins for Simulation-Based Decision-Making*,
https://doi.org/10.1007/978-3-031-89654-5_11

An enterprise ecosystem is a network of interacting business enterprises including service providers, suppliers, distributors, consumers, regulators, etc., involved in the delivery of a set of complementary services through both cooperation and competition [2]. Each stakeholder has a set of objectives, devises a set of strategies to achieve these objectives, and brings to the table a set of capabilities to operationalize these strategies. Working collaboratively enables them to deliver greater value to the customer than they can individually, giving them greater market access and brand value.

However, a highly dynamic environment where each stakeholder in the ecosystem affects and is affected by the others creates a constantly evolving relationship in which each stakeholder must continually adapt to meet their objectives while maintaining an equilibrium state or pareto optimality. Stakeholder strategies and capabilities need to be suitably adapted on a continuous basis while considering complementary and conflicting objectives. This calls for sharing of the right information among relevant stakeholders while safeguarding individual interests. A flexible and need-based formation of stakeholder relationships along with integration of their services is essential to support information sharing. This is unlikely to scale if done individually where each stakeholder needs to interact directly with other stakeholders and can be addressed better if one of the ecosystem entities plays the role of a value integrator.

The value integrator is responsible for acquiring, integrating, and sharing the right information among stakeholders. Value integrator is also responsible for integrating and orchestrating services provided by the stakeholders. In a dynamic world where stakeholders as well as their objectives can change rapidly, the integration needs to be aware of these changes and adapt continuously to reestablish equilibrium.

Digital twins can greatly enhance this process by enabling risk-free business experimentation in silico to arrive at adaptation decisions faster, better, and cheaper. They enable stakeholders to devise right strategies through what-if and if-what simulation, significantly reducing the analysis and synthesis burden [3]. Digital twins can also help in effective operationalization of these strategies through the desired adaptation of enterprise processes and systems [4]. By supporting a digital twin-based architecture and providing the necessary digital twin services to stakeholders, a value integrator can significantly enhance the capabilities of the ecosystem, going beyond information sharing and service orchestration.

In the following sections, we discuss a digital twin-based architecture where each stakeholder has a pair of mutually consistent digital twins—a public digital twin that it shares with the rest of the ecosystem and a private digital twin that is local to itself. We discuss how this architecture can enable an enterprise to achieve the right balance between cooperation and competition and justify trade-offs among them.

We also discuss a software system architecture that helps operationalize adaptation decisions in an automated manner. We present a case study on wellness ecosystem to illustrate some of these ideas.

Value-Integrator-Based Ecosystems

In value-integrator-based ecosystems, one of the ecosystem stakeholders plays the role of a value integrator (VI) [5]. VI itself may or may not provide any end user services. Its primary responsibility is to serve as the central hub for (1) acquiring and integrating data from individual stakeholders and sharing it with the ecosystem and (2) integrating and orchestrating services provided by the individual stakeholders. Stakeholders register with the value integrator to participate in the ecosystem (see Fig. 11.1a).

Each stakeholder provides certain data to the value integrator that it deems fit to share with the rest of the ecosystem and in turn requires certain data from the value integrator that it deems necessary to enable it to collaborate with other ecosystem partners. What data to share with the ecosystem is a decision each individual stakeholder makes in a considered manner. While sharing more data encourages more cooperation, it might compromise a stakeholder's competitive edge. As discussed later, digital twins can be helpful in making the share-hide decision in an informed manner.

Each stakeholder brings a set of capabilities to the table and offers them to the ecosystem in the form of services. A stakeholder might in turn require services from other stakeholders in the ecosystem. As the ecosystem evolves, these provider-consumer relationships also evolve dynamically. Value integrator is responsible for integrating stakeholder services and orchestrating their interactions. Value integrator is also responsible for safeguarding the data exchanged during these interactions, as per pre-defined data contracts (based on share-hide decisions alluded to earlier).

Challenges

Dealing with dynamism and uncertainty: As described earlier, modern businesses are vulnerable to change along multiple dimensions that require suitable adaptive response in an ever-shrinking window of opportunity [1]. This effect gets multiplied in a connected ecosystem with each stakeholder's behavior affecting other stakeholders. How does a stakeholder efficiently identify the desired adaptation of its strategies and capabilities while preserving equilibrium of the ecosystem? How does it efficiently operationalize these adaptation decisions in its business processes and software systems?

Balancing cooperation with competition: An enterprise ecosystem comprises stakeholders that both cooperate and compete while maintaining an equilibrium. In this scenario, what strategies should be adopted by the stakeholders that maximize the beneficial effects of cooperation while minimizing the adverse effects of competition? For example, cooperative behavior requires sharing of information, while competitive behavior necessitates hiding of information that competitors might

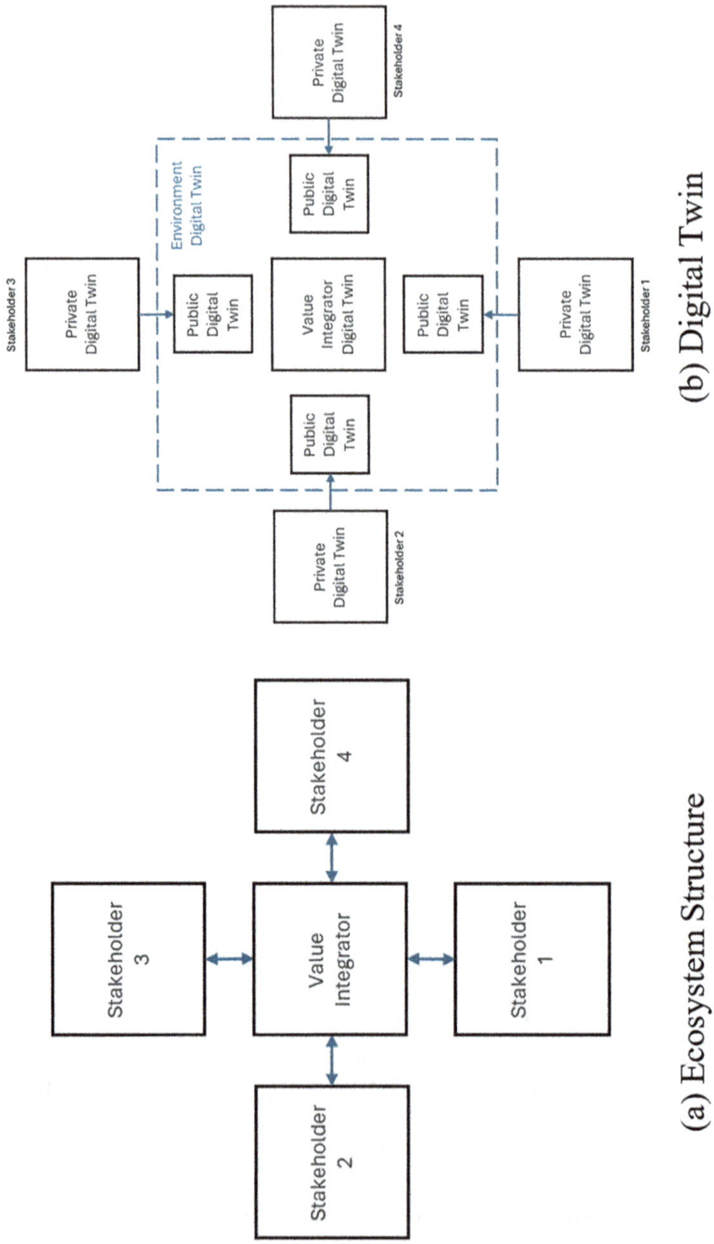

Fig. 11.1 Value integrator–based ecosystem

exploit. How do stakeholders strike the right balance, especially in a dynamic and uncertain environment?

Digital Twins for Making Adaptation Decisions

A Model for Decision-Making

A meta-model for decision-making is depicted in Fig. 11.2a. An enterprise as a system can be viewed as a transfer function from *Input* value space to *Output* value space. A system exists to meet a set of stated *Goals* while operating in a dynamic and uncertain *Environment* that may constrain inputs and/or system behavior. A system goal is an objective function over output value space and system execution *Trace* when the goal has temporal characteristics. Moreover, the goals can have a complex decomposition structure with interdependent and cross-cutting goals as shown in Fig. 11.2a. The former imposes an order on meeting the goals, and the latter usually leads to trade-offs. The *Levers* represent a set of candidate interventions that can be introduced to nudge the system. Applying a lever brings about a discernible change in system output or a derivation thereof of interest, i.e., a *Measure*. A goal is an objective function on measures and thus computable. The solution to a decision-making problem can be seen as an iterative process of *Analyze measures → Identify lever → Apply lever → Check satisfiability of goal.*

Enterprise Digital Twin

An enterprise digital twin (EDT) is a purposive virtual high-fidelity representation of an enterprise and its environment that is amenable to rigorous quantitative analysis through what-if and if-what scenario playing [6]. An EDT models the enterprise as a set of intentional autonomous interacting agents (see Fig. 11.2b). Each agent operates to achieve its own goals in a proactive manner wherein it may use other agents. An agent observes the environment, makes sense of the observations, and performs actions to achieve its objectives. The action could be changing the local state of agent or sending a message to other agents.

An EDT can serve as an in silico experimentation aid to support data-driven evidence-backed decision-making. Figure 11.2b describes a meta-model of a software system implementing the decision-making process described conceptually in Fig. 11.2a. A mapping exists between the decision-making model and the digital twin model, for example, *Goals* maps to *Goal*, *Measure* maps to *StateVariable*, and *Lever* maps to *Activity*. Thus, an EDT can be used for in silico realization of the iterative decision-making process, i.e., *Analyze measures → Identify lever → Apply lever → Check satisfiability of goal.*

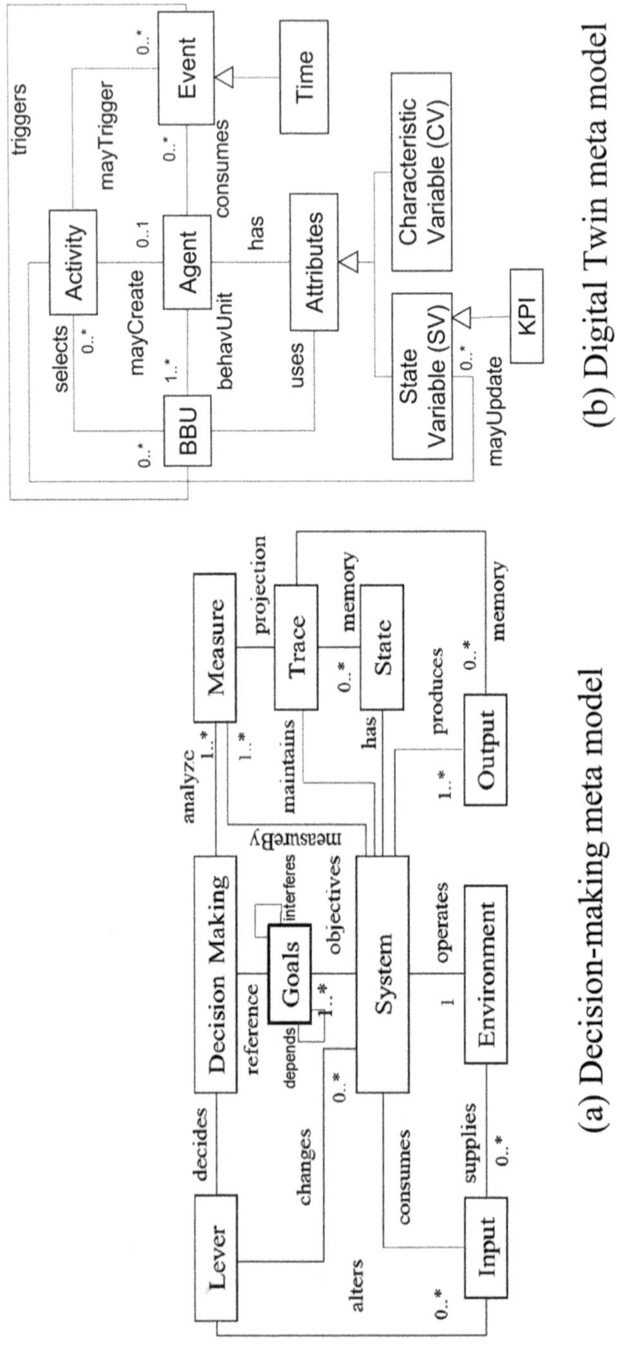

Fig. 11.2 Enterprise digital twin

Ecosystem Digital Twin

An ecosystem digital twin is essentially a composition of stakeholder digital twins. From the point of view of a specific stakeholder, the collection of digital twins of other stakeholders serves as its environment digital twin, as shown in Fig. 11.1b. However, a stakeholder might not want to expose the whole of its EDT to the ecosystem, as it risks exposing its internal goals, strategies, policies, and processes to the entire ecosystem. Instead, a stakeholder may only want to share those parts that it deems relevant to the ecosystem. At a minimum, this should include parts that interface with the ecosystem. A stakeholder might not be averse to exposing parts that reveal some of its goals and strategies if that helps collaborating partners make better decisions that are mutually beneficial. However, in a competitive environment, revealing some internal goals, strategies, and policies might be detrimental. To address this, we envisage two faces of an enterprise's digital twin—a public digital twin that it shares with the ecosystem and a private digital twin that is local to itself. A public digital twin is essentially an abstract projection of the private digital twin that selectively hides details.

At the interface level, the behaviors of both public and private digital twins are identical. However, the private digital twin contains a lot more detail that is internal to the enterprise, which the public digital twin hides while exposing only the relevant subset. For simulation, each stakeholder uses the collection of public digital twins of other stakeholders as its environment digital twin and its own private digital twin as the enterprise digital twin. Value integrator is the central hub that contains public digital twins of all stakeholders. Value integrator can check for behavioral consistency of public digital twins by validating them against past interaction traces (of real stakeholders). Value integrator may also provide the necessary infrastructure and services to stakeholders to manage and simulate their digital twins.

In a more nuanced architecture, a stakeholder may provide partner specific public digital twins where the extent of detail disclosed varies with the extent of cooperation it desires with each partner. Again, value integrator is responsible for ensuring that the right versions of public digital twins are made accessible to the right stakeholders.

Balancing Cooperation with Competition

To balance cooperation with competition, each stakeholder has to decide how much information it wants to share with the ecosystem vs how much it wants to hide. It needs to decide how much of its data as well as of its digital twin to share with the ecosystem (via public DT) and how much to hide. As with other decisions, this decision can also be helped by digital twin-based simulation. A stakeholder can play out various scenarios of sharing vs hiding, assess how they impact its objectives, and make an informed decision.

Adaptation Loop

From the point of view of adaptation, each stakeholder continually operates in an *Ascertain* → *Explore* → *Operationalize* loop, as shown in Fig. 11.3a.

In the "Ascertain" phase, a stakeholder analyzes data—both local and ecosystem level (provided by the value integrator)—to determine if its objectives are being met. If not, it enters the "Explore" phase.

In the "Explore" phase, a stakeholder experiments with its private digital twin and public digital twins of rest of the stakeholders of ecosystem to determine how it should adapt its strategies, capabilities, processes, and services to meet its objectives.

In the "Operationalize" phase, a stakeholder implements these adaptation decisions in its systems. Since modern enterprises are heavily software dependent, the realization of adaptation decision would typically mean adapting its software systems as discussed below.

Ensuring Equilibrium

Adaptive responses (and counter responses) of competing stakeholders can sometimes lead to instability in the ecosystem. Value integrator is responsible for detecting such instabilities, identifying the parties causing them, and coordinating with them to arrive at a compromise response that is pareto optimal. In an advanced setting, game theoretic concepts might be used along with digital twins to arrive at such pareto optimal responses.

Adaptive Software Systems

With increased pervasiveness of software systems within enterprises, new demands on enterprises translate to demands on their software systems. The need for systems to respond to dynamism and uncertainty in the environment is more critical since software systems now serve as a growth engine and decision-making aid for businesses and not just a means of automating operational processes. Current software engineering practices, however, result in systems designed to deliver a fixed set of goals assuming a static environment. In a dynamic environment, requirements are not completely known upfront, and what is known is likely to be uncertain. However, in the current practice, determinism is enforced in the specification using assumptions to achieve a tractable development process. This makes the resultant software brittle when subjected to changes in requirements, environment, or goals.

In order to overcome these challenges, Kholkar et al. [4] propose a novel architecture for continuous dynamic adaptation of software systems that brings in the notion of a system, environment, and goal model. We adapt that architecture as

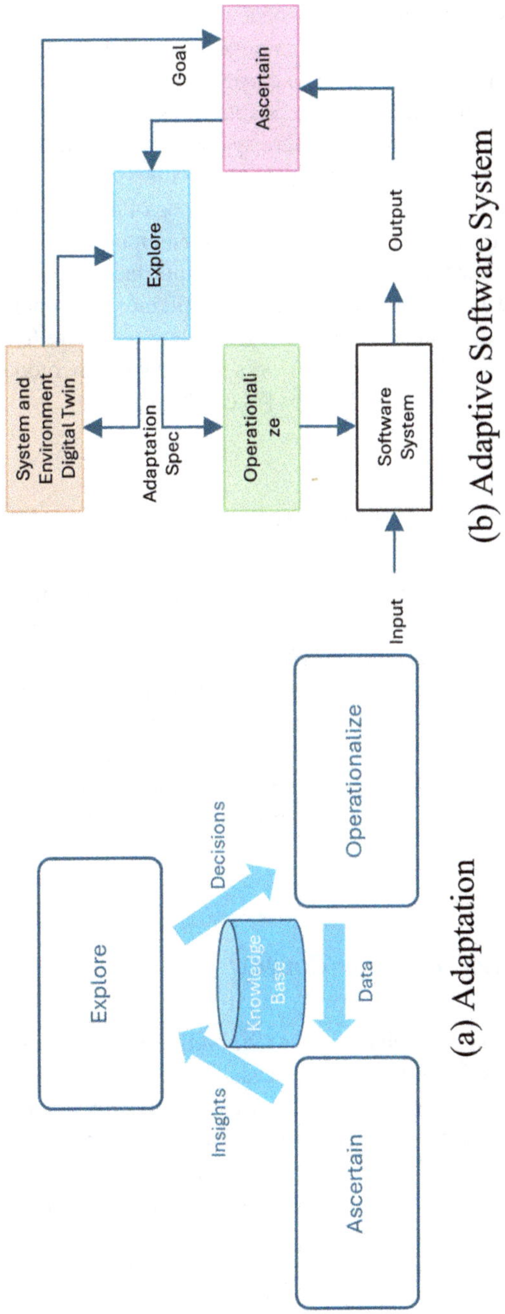

Fig. 11.3 Adaptive enterprise

shown in Fig. 11.3b with purposive digital twins constituting the core enablers of *Explore*, *Operationalize*, and *Ascertain* phases of the adaptation loop. The *Ascertain* component checks system goals against system output and, upon deviation, triggers the *Explore* component. The Explore component uses the system and environment digital twins to identify adaptations to be carried out to the system to meet the goals. The *Operationalize* component receives adaptation specifications from the Explore component and translates them to software system-specific implementation details. This component knows the relationship between the system digital twin and the software system and therefore can map the sequence of actions introduced into the system digital twin to its underlying system implementation. It is cognizant of the software system architecture (e.g., class model, interfaces, components) and programming language infrastructure in order to implement the changes into system code. For effecting adaptations in the software system, software feature models [7], reflective architectures [8], and frameworks for adaptation models like the one describing a language for feedback loops [9] can be used.

Case Study: Wellness Ecosystem

We illustrate these ideas using the wellness domain as an example of an adaptive ecosystem. Wellness needs of consumers encompass fitness, healthcare, nutrition, leisure, as well as health insurance. The wellness ecosystem consists of service providers for each of these requirements, manufacturers of wellness products as well as their networks of partner organizations, government and regulatory bodies, and the consumer population comprising individuals, families, corporates, and communities. A part of the wellness ecosystem including some of these stakeholders is depicted in Fig. 11.4. The next section outlines the wellness problem context in greater detail.

Wellness Ecosystem Problem Context

We list the specific goals and challenges of the wellness ecosystem and demonstrate utility of digital twins for addressing them as described in the preceding sections.

Collaboration and adaptation: A consumer aspiring for wellness typically interacts separately with fitness, nutrition, and healthcare providers for his needs in each of these areas. He needs to manage the interdependence and dynamism among these aspects himself while trying to achieve his wellness goals. For example, a switch from active to sedentary job necessitates commensurate changes to his fitness regime and nutrition intake to maintain wellness. The individual consumer might consult the appropriate nutrition and fitness experts for guidance; however, it is apparent that their advice would not work in isolation. Rather, healthcare, nutrition, and fitness experts need to collaborate to decide upon the course of action that

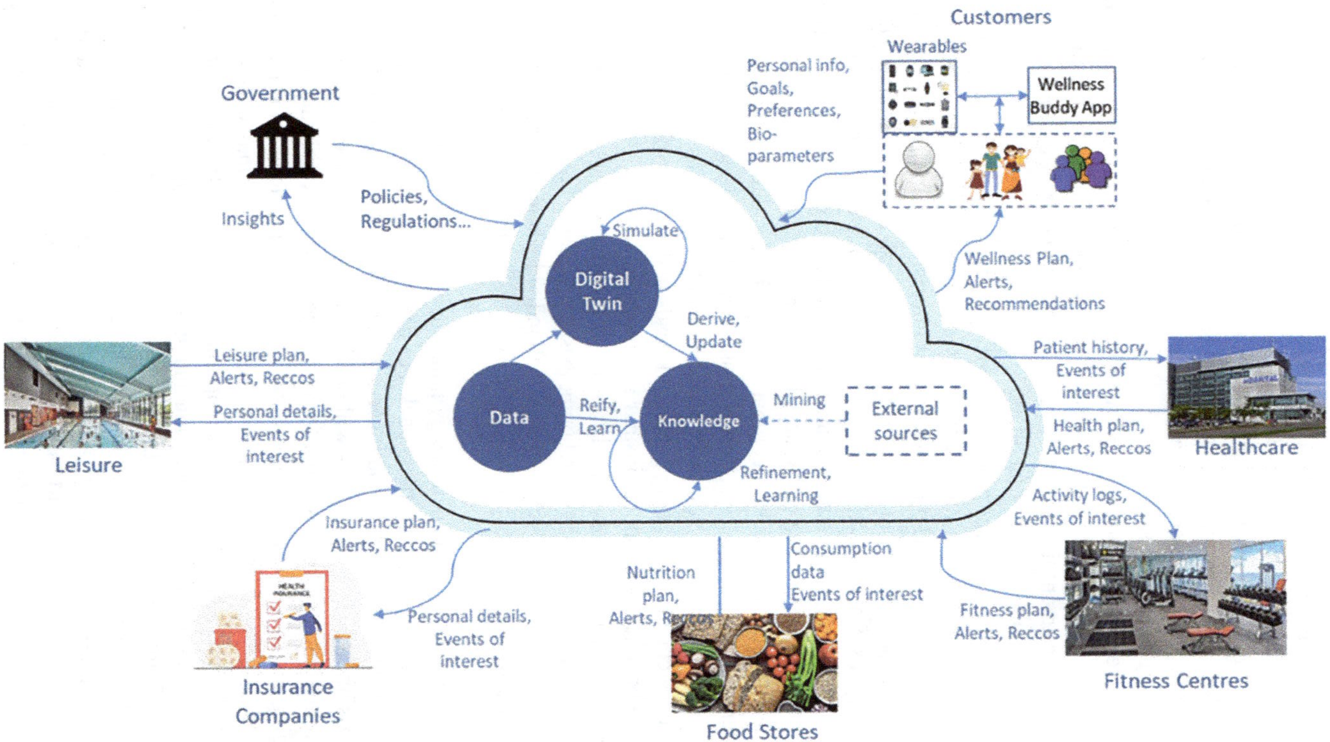

Fig. 11.4 The wellness ecosystem with central value integrator

would truly work to meet the customer's needs. Individual service providers may fulfil their goal of providing healthcare/nutrition/fitness services; however, their value proposition is complete only in conjunction.

Changes introduced in services by any of the collaborating participants are another potential source of dynamism in the ecosystem. Moreover, wellness needs of individuals change over time with age, changes in lifestyle, family commitments, etc. As a result, wellness plans as well as their implementation need to adapt suitably and continuously over time.

Balancing service provider goals: A service provider for any of the wellness needs aspires to provide fit-for-purpose services with the primary goal of maximizing return on investment that in turn depends upon sub-goals of customer satisfaction and maximum utilization of facilities.

Personalization: In current practice, service providers classify the target clientele into broad archetypes and define services catering to these archetypes. Archetypes are formed based on dimensions of interest, e.g., an insurance company would use age, occupation, medical history, and fitness level of the individual to define archetypes. Data is used if available; else, guestimates are used. In addition, they arrive at correlations among the dimensions in data, e.g., individuals in sedentary occupations tend to have low fitness levels, and low fitness level correlates to onset of health conditions such as coronary artery disease, diabetes, and hypertension in later years. An insurance company designs insurance products for this archetype, considering probability of onset of these health conditions at a certain age. Access to correct data minimizing guesswork leads to definition of insurance products that are beneficial to both the insurer and insured.

However, this strategy has some lacunae—it ignores the fact that correlations may change over time, and hence archetype-based product definition needs to adapt over time. Also, defined products may not fit all individuals in the archetype equally well. It is desirable to have product definition customized to individual profile and needs.

Similarly, a fitness center such as a gym may decide to invest in a set of exercise equipment and devise a set of fitness packages based on broad archetypes in target clientele such as youngsters, middle-aged officegoers, retired professionals, etc. Here, an assumption that youngsters will opt for vigorous exercises such as weight training, retired professionals will opt for yoga, and middle-aged clients will opt for light jogging may not hold for all individuals. It is quite probable that some youngsters will choose yoga, whereas some middle-aged customers may choose weight training. Such mismatches between assumptions and reality will lead to suboptimal fitness plans and suboptimal provisioning and utilization of exercise equipment.

Partial information and uncertainty: A fitness center also needs to consider the medical history and health conditions of an individual and the possible effects of a prescribed fitness regime. The gym may not have access to this information and secondly may not be equipped to assess health ramifications of the prescribed fitness regime. The gym by itself can at best cater to only one aspect of wellness and that too in a sub-optimal manner.

Finally, the gym also needs to be cognizant of other competing fitness facilities in the neighborhood. This too is fraught with uncertainty as only partial information about competitors is available. As wellness needs of individuals change over time, services offered by the gym need to adapt suitably and continuously.

In summary, all service providers need to address the issues of partial and uncertain information and changing landscape of customer needs and competition over time. It would be beneficial to all stakeholders to have a value integrator facilitating:

- Sharing of relevant information amongst service providers
- Integration of services offered by various service providers to meet wellness needs of customers
- Effective planning of capabilities and devising strategies for various service providers to maximize RoI

We envision a central entity called Wellness Provider that acts as a value integrator providing an integration platform for all wellness services and enabling a digital twin-based solution for effective planning and adaptation of all stakeholders in the wellness ecosystem.

To see the need for digital twin-based planning and adaptation, we elaborate below the objectives, capabilities, adaptation drivers, and possible adaptive responses of each stakeholder in the wellness ecosystem.

Wellness Stakeholders

Individual Consumer

Objectives: Maximize fitness and get access to good healthcare while minimizing medical expenses and achieving good work-life balance.

Capabilities of interest include overall health, ability to handle stress, capacity to exercise, and discipline.

Adaptation drivers include changes in age, health disorders, financial situation, fitness aspirations, and lifestyle changes.

Adaptive response: Individual may want the wellness plan to be refined, which includes choice of fitness regime, nutrition plan, health check-ups, health insurance, leisure activities, and their corresponding service providers.

Fitness Center

Objectives: Maximize customer footfall and satisfaction, maximize RoI in fitness equipment and facilities, and provide the right set of services to achieve these objectives.

Capabilities include fitness equipment and facilities, fitness packages, and training staff.

Adaptation drivers include changes in demographics, fitness needs, competitor actions, or black swan events like war, pandemics, etc.

Adaptive response: Gym may want to alter its size and layout, quantity and quality of fitness equipment, size and skill profile of training staff, fitness packages, etc.

Healthcare Provider

Objectives: Service as many patients as possible without compromising on quality of healthcare; maximize RoI in healthcare facility, diagnostic centers, medical equipment, and size as well as skill profile of staff; and provide the right set of services to achieve these objectives.

Capabilities include size and skill profile of staff, healthcare packages, medical equipment, diagnostic centers, and facilities.

Adaptation drivers include changes in demographics, competitor actions, or black swan events like war, pandemics, etc.

Adaptive response: Hospital may want to alter its size and profile in terms of diagnostics and equipment, quantity and quality of medical equipment, size and skill profile of healthcare staff, healthcare packages, etc.

Nutrition Providers/Food Stores

Objectives: Maximize customer satisfaction, sale, and profit, and minimize energy consumption and wastage toward environmental impact, sustainability goals, etc.

Capabilities include shelf space, number of brands and products, strategies for product placement, pricing and promotion, and size and quality of salesforce.

Adaptation drivers are changes in demographics, consumer needs, economic profile of the neighborhood, regulatory regime, competitor actions, etc.

Adaptive response of a food store comprises changing the mix of products and bands, product placement strategy, pricing and promotion strategy, increasing or decreasing shelf space, sales force, etc.

Insurance Company

Objectives: Maximization of sales, profit, customer lifetime value, average revenue per customer, and customer satisfaction while minimizing customer churn and rationalization of product portfolio.

Capabilities include insurance products covering various types of risks, services such as underwriting, claims processing, policy administration, and product creation, marketing, and servicing staff.

Adaptation drivers include changes in demographics, health conditions, fitness levels, and competitor insurance products.

Adaptive response includes changes to product portfolio, product pricing, product servicing, marketing, and sales strategies.

Leisure Provider

Objective: Maximization of measures such as sales, profit, customer satisfaction, and RoI in facilities.

Capabilities include leisure facilities such as resorts, theaters, cinema halls, restaurants, size and skill profile of staff, and the right set of services around these facilities.

Adaptation drivers include changes in demographics, state of economy, competitor actions, or black swan events like war, pandemics, etc.

Adaptive response: Leisure provider may want to alter the leisure packages and their price points, expand facilities, or resize and reskill the staff.

Services in each of these wellness aspects, viz., healthcare, fitness, nutrition, or leisure, complement one another and are also interdependent, requiring action to be taken on multiple fronts to satisfy an individual's wellness needs. For example, the health of an individual is impacted by his fitness and nutrition habits. Similarly, fitness regime needs to cater to individual's fitness needs while taking into consideration overall health and dietary habits. Dietary needs are a function of individual's overall health and fitness regime. A change in any one aspect impacts the other related aspects, requiring them to change appropriately so that overall wellness objectives continue to be met.

Need for Digital Twin–Based Planning and Adaptation

However, it is not easy to determine which adaptive response from which stakeholder, in what measure, will effectively meet a given adaptation need, given the complex interdependent nature of stakeholders. This is where digital twin–based what-if and if-what simulations will be of great help. One can quantitatively see the impact of different adaptive responses on various measures and assess how well they meet the objectives. One can also quantitatively see the possible ripple effects of an adaptive response of one stakeholder on other stakeholders and assess the impact on the ecosystem as a whole—all in silico, before implementing the response. Wellness Provider plays a key role in enabling this at the ecosystem level.

Wellness Provider–Driven Solution Approach

Wellness provider is a central entity that provides an integration platform for all stakeholders and services so that customers now need to interact with a single entity for their wellness needs. The wellness provider orchestrates services from individual service providers, taking care of interdependencies and ensuring necessary information is made available to each entity while safeguarding security and privacy policies. It tracks changes in the ecosystem and provides recommendations to affected stakeholders to optimize their objectives. It provides digital twin services to enable in silico experimentation to help stakeholders devise right strategies and arrive at right adaptive response.

To realize this vision, the wellness provider will need to:

- Onboard a wide range of service providers in each category to cater to needs and preferences
- Capture information about each service provider, their services, and interdependencies
- Acquire knowledge about customers' needs, preferences, and behaviors
- Provide appropriate choices to customers based on their preferences
- Schedule services optimally for meeting customer requirements while honoring ecosystem-wide constraints
- Monitor customer and service providers continuously to learn from their behavior and interactions
- Provide digital twin services for simulation-based exploration of decision space
- Make intelligent adaptation recommendations based on available information

As a result, the wellness provider helps each stakeholder benefit from collaboration as they gain access to the right information and insights and get advice to suitably adapt their capabilities, leading to improved services. The wellness provider also enables the ecosystem as a whole to deliver far greater value to all stakeholders through intelligent orchestration. Customers get a cohesive solution for all their wellness needs customized to their individual goals and preferences that will adapt with changing situations. Being part of the ecosystem, all service providers have the added advantage of enhancing their customer base. Uncertainty in the environment may cause disruption, affecting various stakeholders in the ecosystem. Wellness provider facilitates a coordinated adaptive response to this disruption, thus ensuring a smooth and speedy transition to a stable state.

Collaboration and Competition

Stakeholders engage in a competitive as well as collaborative relationship. For example, collaboration with healthcare providers will help fitness centers propose custom fitness plans that are mindful of individual health conditions such as hypertension, diabetes, etc. Collaboration with nutrition experts will help supplement fitness plan with appropriate diet charts. On the other hand, a fitness center competes with other fitness centers, and a healthcare provider competes with other healthcare providers. When a fitness center changes its fitness packages, other fitness centers may be forced to customize their packages to stay competitive.

As these stakeholders operate in a highly dynamic environment, these customizations need to be effected on a regular basis. Access to purposive digital twins can enable business experimentation in silico, leading to informed decisions regarding these customizations in collaborative as well as competitive scenarios. Use of public and private digital twins for each stakeholder helps them strike the right balance between cooperation and competition.

Information that is beneficial to share with the ecosystem from a collaboration perspective goes into the public digital twin, and information that is detrimental to share with the ecosystem from a competition perspective is kept strictly in the private digital twin. A stakeholder may share different levels of information with different stakeholders, depending on whether they are collaborators or competitors. Thus, there can be stakeholder specific versions of public digital twins. Table 11.1 lists what a fitness center might share with some of the stakeholders. Wellness Provider is responsible for ensuring that the right public digital twin version is shared with the right stakeholder.

In addition to sharing information on its services and capabilities, a stakeholder may also selectively share information on some of its goals, measures, and levers with its partners if that helps them cooperate better. Table 11.2 lists, for some of the stakeholders, what goals, measures, and levers they might be willing to share with the ecosystem and what they might want to keep strictly private (not even to be shared with the value integrator). On similar lines, private and public digital twins can be defined for other stakeholders of wellness ecosystem. While Table 11.2 only lists goals, measures, and levers, there exists a corresponding agent model that is not shown due to space limitation.

Table 11.1 Information shared by a fitness center with competitors and collaborators

Stakeholder	Competition	Collaboration	
Fitness center	Other fitness centers	Healthcare provider	Nutrition experts
	Restricted public data: Fitness services (gym, Zumba, Pilates, yoga), fitness equipment types, condition, trainers, customized and varied fitness plans, pricing of services. Public data: hours of operation, location	Customized regimen as per health condition, injury treatment, and rehab	Dietary advice as per health condition and fitness regimen

Table 11.2 Digital twins of wellness ecosystem

Stakeholder	Public digital twin	Private digital twin
Individual	Goals: Maximize fitness, minimize healthcare expenses, good work-life balance Measures: BMI, key health parameters, hospital bills Levers: Exercise regimen, food intake, leisure activities, stress management	Additional goals: Career progression, financial health, social health, etc. Additional measures: Salary, promotions, investments, expenditure, social network, vacations, etc. Additional levers: Work hours, social interactions, expenditure control, etc.
Gym	Goals: Maximize customer footfall and satisfaction Measures: Customer count, CapEx Levers: Fitness plans portfolio, pricing	Additional goals: Maximize RoI in fitness equipment and facilities Additional measures: Customer rating, customer churn, OpEx Additional levers: Marketing campaigns, staff training, staff incentives, facility renovation, equipment upgrade
Hospital	Goals: Service as many patients as possible without compromising on quality of the healthcare Measures: Patient count, occupancy, CapEx Levers: Healthcare plans portfolio, pricing	Additional goals: Maximize RoI in healthcare facility, diagnostic centers, and medical equipment Additional measures: Patient feedback, adverse event count, OpEx Additional levers: Marketing campaigns, staff hiring, staff training, staff incentives, facility renovation, equipment upgrade

Making Adaptation Decisions

In an ecosystem, change might originate from multiple sources. For instance, an individual's fitness aspirations may change, a healthcare provider may upgrade its service packages, a new fitness center may join, etc. When wellness provider detects such a change, it identifies the stakeholders impacted by the change and initiates an adaptive response. This can happen in two stages. In the first stage, value integrator uses public digital twins available to it to identify a set of recommendations for affected stakeholders. In the second stage, a stakeholder takes these recommendations and refines them by using its private digital twin along with the public digital twins of other stakeholders shared with it.

As discussed earlier, adaptive responses (and counter responses) of competing stakeholders can sometimes lead to instability in the ecosystem. Wellness provider is responsible for detecting such instabilities, identifying the parties causing them, and coordinating with them to arrive at a compromise response that is pareto optimal. In an advanced setting, game theoretic concepts might be used along with digital twins to arrive at such pareto optimal responses.

Technology Readiness

Much of the core technology infrastructure to support enterprise ecosystems already exists, for example, sharing data while honoring privacy and security contracts, orchestrating and integrating services, and software architectures to support runtime adaptation. Enterprise digital twin is an emerging technology to support decision-making in the face of uncertainty. However, construction, use, and upkeep of purposive digital twins is a knowledge-intensive endeavor, demanding deep domain and technical expertise, which typically is in short supply. Moreover, this people-centric approach does not scale effectively. To address this concern, there is a need for knowledge-enabled automation aids that help one operate at an elevated level of expertise. Can large language models be exploited? Can the necessary copilots be developed to ease construction, use, and upkeep of purposive digital twins? Can these copilots be engineered to continuously improve over time with usage? We believe results of these investigations will significantly accelerate adoption of digital twins as a core enabler of adaptive enterprise ecosystems.

References

1. Hoogervorst, J. A. P. (2009). *Enterprise governance and enterprise engineering*. Springer Science & Business Media.
2. Peltoniemi, M., & Vuori, E. (2004). Business ecosystem as the new approach to complex adaptive business environments. *Proceedings of eBusiness Research Forum, 2*(22), 267–281.
3. Kulkarni, V., Barat, S., Clark, T., & Barn, B. S. (2022). Digital twin as an aid for decision-making in the face of uncertainty. In *2022 winter simulation conference (WSC)* (pp. 1371–1385). IEEE.
4. Kholkar, D., Roychoudhury, S., Kulkarni, V., & Reddy, S. (2022). Learning to Adapt–Software Engineering for Uncertainty. In *15th innovations in software engineering conference* (pp. 1–5).
5. Hein, A., Weking, J., Schreieck, M., Wiesche, M., Böhm, M., & Krcmar, H. (2019). Value co-creation practices in business-to-business platform ecosystems. *Electronic Markets, 29*, 503–518.
6. Barat, S., Kulkarni, V., & Bhattacharya, K. (2022). Enterprise digital twins for risk free business experimentations. In *2022 winter simulation conference (WSC)* (pp. 2864–2875). IEEE.
7. Batory, D. (2005). Feature models, grammars, and propositional formulas. In *International conference on software product lines* (pp. 7–20). Springer Berlin Heidelberg.
8. Ferber, J. (1989). Computational reflection in class based object-oriented languages. *ACM SIGPLAN Notices, 24*(10), 317–326.
9. Vogel, T., & Giese, H. (2012). A language for feedback loops in self-adaptive systems: Executable runtime megamodels. In *2012 7th international symposium on software engineering for adaptive and self-managing systems (SEAMS)* (pp. 129–138). IEEE.

www.ingramcontent.com/pod-product-compliance
Lightning Source LLC
Chambersburg PA
CBHW050438140725
29540CB00005B/30
9783031896538